Drama und Theater in Südasien

Herausgegeben von
Heidrun Brückner

Band 9

2011
Harrassowitz Verlag · Wiesbaden

Between Fame and Shame

Performing Women – Women Performers in India

Edited by Heidrun Brückner,
Hanne M. de Bruin and Heike Moser

2011
Harrassowitz Verlag · Wiesbaden

The book has been printed with financial support from the women's representative of the University of Würzburg.

The picture on the cover shows 9-year old M. Poongavanam in a female role of Kattaikkuttu (courtesy: P. V. Jayan).

In order to view the audio-visual resources supporting the written contributions in this book, please access the following URL online:
http://www.indologie.uni-wuerzburg.de/women_performers/welcome/.

Bibliografische Information der Deutschen Nationalbibliothek
Die Deutsche Nationalbibliothek verzeichnet diese Publikation in der Deutschen Nationalbibliografie; detaillierte bibliografische Daten sind im Internet über http://dnb.d-nb.de abrufbar.

Bibliographic information published by the Deutsche Nationalbibliothek
The Deutsche Nationalbibliothek lists this publication in the Deutsche Nationalbibliografie; detailed bibliographic data are available in the internet at http://dnb.d-nb.de.

For further information about our publishing program consult our website http://www.harrassowitz-verlag.de

Typesetting in Sabon/Linotype, special characters by Rainer Kimmig, Tübingen.
Printed on permanent/durable paper.
Printing and binding: Hubert & Co., Göttingen
Printed in Germany

ISSN 1431-4975
ISBN 978-3-447-06281-7

Contents

Technical Notes

Note on the audio-visual resources accompanying the contributions in this book

In order to view the audio-visual resources supporting the written contributions in this book, please access the following URL online: *http://www.indologie.uni-wuerzburg.de/women_performers/welcome/*.

Note on transliteration

The contributers to this book have followed the generally accepted English spelling of words from Indian languages or the standard transliteration with diacritical marks.

Foreword

This book highlights the involvement of women – real or through representation – in a range of performances found in different geographical areas and among different social groups in India. It is the outcome of the 3rd International Würzburg Colloquium on Indian Studies entitled *Changing Roles and Perceptions of Women Performers in Indian Culture* held at the University of Würzburg, Germany, in 2005, and aims to help us understand better the troubled relationship between women and public performances.

The format and the (limited) funding of the colloquium did not permit us to invite many participants from India. As the convener of the colloquium Heidrun Brückner decided to publish the papers together with Hanne M. de Bruin of Kanchipuram in India, and Heike Moser of Tübingen. The editors invited additional contributions to widen the scope of the publication.

Even though each essay focuses on a particular kind of ›performance‹ this book will not attempt to theorize the concept of ›performance‹. ›Performance‹ here is used loosely to refer to a number of cultural events, which are – in varying degrees – set apart from day-to-day life because they involve or create a ›special place‹, a ›special time (frame) and / or occasion‹ and use ›special people‹, for instance trained or initiated performers and ritual specialists. The cultural performances described in the following essays range from possession performed by women as a religious service to a deity or as medium of access to ›divine discourse‹ to on-stage performances by professional actresses representing different performance genres.

There is a regional focus on South India, especially Kerala and Karnataka. The authors of the essays are anthropologists (Claus, Schömbucher, Guillebaud), folklorists (Rai), Indologists (Brückner, de Bruin, Moser, Johan, Griebl / Sommer), sociologists (Schulze) and theatre scholars (Daugherty, Pitkow) from India, Europe and the USA. The analytical style and subject matter of the contributions differ considerably. In Schulze's essay the subjective, emotional voice of the author will be heard clearly, while Claus and Schömbucher take more distant, analytical views offering theoretical frameworks for understanding the changing status of performance genres and the role of women performers therein. Two essays focus on the position of women performers in India's single surviving Sanskrit theatre, the Kutiyattam of Kerala, tracing their history and contributions (Moser and Daugherty). Others focus on the social context within which performances operate and the ways society looks upon these forms and their female practitioners (Rai, Brückner, Griebl / Sommer, and Guillebaud). The last two essays analyse in detail the representation of women in Kutiyattam and Kathakali through the interpretations of female roles by male performers (JOHAN, PITKOW). The essays have been arranged under three different headings on the basis of their subject matter and principal emphasis: Theory, Historical and Social Context, and Interpretation.

I and my co-editors hope that this volume will fill in a few fragments of our understanding of and appreciation for women performers in India – their fame and infamy, and the pleasures and perils of being visible – as a woman – in the public (performance) space. We also hope that the juxtaposition in the following essays about cultural performances, which differ widely in form, (geographical) location, performance conditions, social status of the performers and perceived efficacy (ritual, emotional and economic), will offer new leads for analyzing and understanding the relationships between performance, gender and the world.

The Colloquium received financial support from the Women's Office of the University of Würzburg. The main credit for conceptualizing and articulating the themes of the book goes to Hanne M. de Bruin who contributed the introductory essay. Heike Moser took charge of the technical production of the manuscript and the audio-visual materials published along with it on a website (*http://www.indologie.uni-wuerzburg.de/women_performers/welcome/*). Some of the recordings of oral literature provided on the website are first-time publications of the respective genres. Creating the website was a major challenge that Heike Moser met with the support of Sina Sommer of Würzburg. The editors thank Ms. Sommer for her sustained and creative technical assistance. The publication of the book was, again, made possible by the University of Würzburg Women's Office whose funding we most gratefully acknowledge. We also thank our publisher, Otto Harrassowitz, Wiesbaden, and especially Dr. Krauss, who did not hesitate to embark with us on a new, experimental mode of publication combining a printed book with an open-ended website.

Heidrun Brückner, Würzburg
1st November 2010

Contextualising Women and Performance in India

An Introductory Essay

Hanne M. de Bruin

For A. Sathya (13 years) – talented girl whose desire to become a professional Kattaikkuttu actress was aborted when her parents took her out of the Kattaikkuttu Gurukulam / Theatre school at the time of writing this essay.[1]

Performances and their validation

The field of performance in India is so rich and disparate that it is impossible to generalize and, for instance, speak of ›Indian theatre‹ or ›Indian dance‹. In many instances the boundaries between forms / genres of performance – where one practice ends and another one begins – and their distinguishing characteristics have not been clearly established and cannot be easily grasped by outsiders to these forms. The problems involved in assessing – by whom and for whose benefit? – the ›viability‹ and ›validity‹ of performance aesthetics and contents of individual forms are mind-boggling; the outcome(s) often are subjective and at times disparaging, in particular for subaltern performers and audiences who own and practice marginalized forms.

The tricky issue of the endorsement or rejection of performance genres and practices, and the participation of women therein, as fulfilling or not fulfilling the ›norm‹, pervades many of the contributions to this book. It is proof of the complex negotiation processes through which ›modernity‹ – and what it represents for different groups – has been and continues to be contested by all stakeholders in the Indian field of performing arts.[2]

1 See for a photograph of Satya in the role of a Kuratti (Lady of the nomadic Kuravar clan), the online power point presentation »Contextualizing Women and Performers« accompanying this essay, ILLUSTRATION 20. For the sake of readability, I have not used diacritics in the representation of personal names, performance genres and other non-English words. Different transliterations are current in the popular media; for instance, *kuttu* may be spelled as *koothu*, Kattaikkuttu as Kattaikoothu, Terukkuttu as Therukoothu and Kutiyattam as Koodiyattam.

2 Adapting Bourdieu's »field of cultural production« to the world of performance, I have used the term »field of performing arts« to refer to the arena of diffuse forces representing the various agents involved in the performing arts during their attempts to maximize their

The validation of performances and their inclusion into the dominant cultural fold are part of a much wider discourse, which emerged among the growing Indian middle classes at the end of the 19th century. According to Partha Chatterjee, these new Indian middle classes took over and adapted, as part of the nationalist project, the »civilizing mission«, which the colonial power had embarked upon earlier. Nationalism's ideological response to the denunciation of Indian tradition by the colonial power was to invent a new ›classical‹ tradition primarily based on textual sources – reformed and restructured in such a way as to fortify it against the colonial charges of barbarism and irrationality. This ›classical‹ tradition became the yardstick with which cultural expressions (and social values and norms) were measured (CHATTERJEE 1993: 118–127). The reinvention of India's ›classical tradition‹ resulted in a rupture between performances considered respectable and ›high‹ and others labelled ›low‹, ›folk‹ or whatever other term the elite found fit to denote the different aesthetics, practices, contents and purpose of these forms.[3] It also resulted in an adaptation of the 19th century missionary, moralistic and pedagogical, colonial discourse, which sought to reform expressions of ›low culture‹. The following example concerns a theatre performance (the genre is not identified by the author) in what is now Tamil Nadu:

> »[...] In the eighties and nineties of the last century, a drama in the Tamil country was something to be looked down upon not only for its lack of any intrinsic value but for the lack of character, respectability and purity in those who were connected with it. For a multitude of reasons no parent in any decent family would willingly allow a member of his family of any age or sex to see a play.« (GOPALRATNAM 1981 [1956]: 119–120)

And a little further in the same publication we read that:

> »[...] As for the quality of the performance, it is difficult to conceive of anything more crude and primitive [...].« (*ibid.*: 120)

A book on Tamil theatre, published as recently as 1981, captures the agency of the middle classes in their drive for civilization and reform of the degenerate culture of the lower classes and castes as follows:

> »[...] The selfless services of the erudite scholars have resurrected the Tamil drama from the pits of negligence and withering. In the hands of street dancers drama became worse and worse losing its artistic values. Throughout the night they shouted and hooted in the name of singing and hopped and leaped instead of acting. In the

share in the limited material and symbolic power (prestige, authority, legitimacy) generated by the field, and the complex and constantly changing relationships between these agents (BRUIN 1999: 7).

3 This is not to say that no division existed between ›high‹ and ›low‹ cultural expressions in pre-colonial India; see also the discussion on pp. 25–27 of this essay.

morning they went from door to door with stretched arms to get something to fill their belly. Their action on stage and their behaviour in the streets were nothing but a great disgrace to the noble art. Respectable people looked down at them with utter contempt. Something substantial had to be done to restore the stage from the ugly hands of these street dancers.« (A. N. Perumal as quoted in BRUIN 1999: 94–95)

Please note that the attributes used to describe these ›folk‹ performances – ›crude‹ and ›primitive‹ – single out the aesthetics of these forms and the respectability and morality of the performers so as to make the disqualification of their art forms and personae sound ›reasonable‹.[4] The practitioners are described as totally unable to produce true ›art‹, while the above descriptions call up such an appalling picture of performance that nobody in his right mind would ever think of attending such a show.

The sorry state of affairs with regard to the ›quality‹ of the folk performing arts is usually blamed on the lack of education of its practitioners and audiences (aesthetic sense apparently being the result of formal education). Scholars and the media have repeatedly drawn our attention to the poor state of many of these ›folk traditions‹.[5] Notwithstanding the fact that most contemporary ›folk‹ performers have a hard time making a living, this does not necessarily mean that their performances are no longer popular and in demand. I sometimes feel that the description of ›folk‹ forms as being on the verge of extinction serves a self-fulfilling prophecy of the elite.[6] It assists them in eliminating forms not fitting into the label of ›(proper) Indian cultural identity‹ or rescuing traditions from a certain death and reforming them so as to fit the norm. It is unfortunate that the 19th century moralistic jargon and pedantic attitude remain intact among a section of the middle class elite, also today, apparently with the aim to distinguish ›low‹, ›poor‹ art forms from their own ›high‹, elite culture.

In an attempt to claim equal representation of its citizens' cultural expressions, the State has created a special niche for ›folk arts‹, which nowadays find a place in cultural festivals and are entitled to awards and financial assistance.[7]

4 This reminds one, of course, of Pierre Bourdieu's groundbreaking work on the judgement of taste (BOURDIEU 1984). Further investigation is required into (the construction of) Indian »taste« and aesthetics vis-à-vis social values and status.

5 For doubts expressed in the English press with regard to the vitality of the Terukkuttu / Kattaikkuttu theatre, see »The Colours are Fading« by Laksmy Venkiteswaran, *New Indian Express* of 28 September 2008 and »Reviving Therukoothu« by S. S. Kavitha in *The Hindu* of 23 December 2006 and compare these statements with the figures of the Kattaikkuttu Sangam, an association of rural, professional Kattaikkuttu / Terukkuttu performers, which show that professional Kattaikkuttu / Terukkuttu companies perform between 100 and 150 all-night shows per year, all of which are patronized and paid for by village audiences.

6 On the theme of »vanishing« cultures and ethnographers' agency in »salvaging« and representing cultural phenomena threatened with extinction, see CLIFFORD 1986: 112–113.

7 See for instance *http://indiaculture.nic.in/indiaculture/youngwrks.htm*, the website of the Ministry of Culture, Government of India where the following performance categories are

Yet, this pursuit of equality does not seem to have effectively changed the cultural hegemony established by the Indian middle classes – which is not to say that this hegemony has not been challenged in post-Independence India. Marginalised groups have claimed – with greater or lesser success – recognition and respectability for their cultural expressions and practices as is apparent, for instance, from recent scholarly attention for Dalit literature and Dalit theatre. The contestation of control over sites of cultural production, and the ›unlikely‹ collaborations to which this may give rise, can be gauged from the fact that the political establishment repeatedly has sought the help of non-elite performance forms to address a politically aware but ›non-reading‹ audience (*e.g.* NAREGAL 2001: 269–270, with regard to Maharashtra). For dominance to make itself felt, and contained, a dialectic relationship with those who challenge its powers is a prerequisite.

Nationalism and the new woman

As part of the nationalist project women's emancipation came under scrutiny. The position of Indian women in ›modern‹ society was revalidated and reinscribed with norms of conduct and female decorum that fitted the dichotomy between the home / inner and the world / outer. As Partha Chatterjee has argued, the nationalists, in their attempt to subvert colonial hegemony, projected the East as superior over the West in its spiritual power. They located spiritual power in the inner domain (home / mind) of Indian culture and projected spiritual freedom as an inalienable good, which colonial power could never appropriate. The ›new‹ modern woman was to be the safekeeper of the home, which, in addition to her family, also came to represent the site of the nation's spiritual values.[8] Her spirituality and natural modesty provided an ›inner, natural protection‹, which enabled her, unlike the female performer who supposedly lacked these qualities and was firmly situated in the public space, to leave the domestic sphere and participate in the dealings of the external world (*e.g.* access to formal education) without having to sacrifice her femininity.[9]

identified as entitled to financial assistance: 1. Indian Classical Music, 2. Indian Classical Dance, 3. Theatre, 4. Visual Arts, 5. Folk, Traditional and Indigenous Arts, 6. Light Music: a) Thumri, Dadra, Tappa, Qawali, Ghazal; b) Light Classical Music based on Carnatic style etc.; c) Rabindra Sangeet, Nazrul Geeti, Atulprasad.

8 For the idea of the new woman in pre-Independence India see, for instance, CHATTERJEE 1993: 126–157, SINGH 2009: 270–272 and *passim* and, for a comparison of the same idea in a Western context, GARDNER 2003 [1998]: 74–79. For the representation of women in her »de-sexualized« form of the mother / goddess in relation to Tamil culture and language politics, see RAMASWAMY 1998 [1997]: 114–134.

9 Chatterjee's inner-outer argument is more complex according to Nivedita Menon. The abolition of the *devasasi* system(s) and Kerala's experience of matriliny suggest different trajectories through which male nationalist elites in different situations negotiated colonial

The ideal of the ›new‹ woman contrasted starkly with the social and cultural conditions in which the majority of the people lived. This led to the strengthening of yet another dichotomy between the ›new‹ woman – naturally modest, civilized and middle or upper class – and the ›common‹ woman defined as a lower class / caste female believed to be coarse, loud, vulgar, quarrelsome, devoid of superior moral sense, sexually promiscuous and subjected to brutal oppressing males. It was the degenerate position of these women that the nationalist project intended to reform. In concreto, this resulted in a new colonial relationship between the hegemonic dominant elite of the middle classes and those groups who were excluded (on the basis of their culture, caste or religion) from, or not wholeheartedly included into, the making of the nation and, subsequently, from full Indian citizenship.

We can begin to discern the role and contribution of women performers to the Indian stage and public space only when viewed against the unresolved tensions that inhibit the cultural hegemony of the middle classes and the enormous multiplicity and diversity of the Indian field of performance. In actual practice, the many different sectors of performance, be it theatre, dance or ritual practices covered by those problematic terms of ›classical‹ and ›folk‹, often remain aloof and ignorant of each other's existence (Deshpande *et al* 2009: 14). Therefore, whatever direction our analysis takes, we should remain astutely aware of this diversity and multiplicity, the cultural role models and identity which different groups in India have set themselves and the subsequent conflicts these have been able to generate, as well as our incapacity to really ›know‹ the field in its entirety.

Representing women on stage: Absence and invisibility of women performers

One of the themes that crops up again and again in the histories about gender and performance is the perceived undesirability of women to perform on the public stage. In many cultures the involvement of girls and women in public performances was, and sometimes still is, seen as highly problematic. Europe did not permit women to act or even to sit in audiences in the theatre until the late 17th century. Acting only began to be seen as a ›respectable profession‹ towards the end of the 19th century (Gay 2003: 25–28).

When women are present on the stage, their respectability is often judged on different terms from that of actors. Actresses' defiance of socioeconomic prescriptions about genderized social roles and working spheres stigmatizes their

modernity. While in both these cases an important aim was to bring women's (sexual) autonomy and sexuality under patriarchical control (so as to conform to the norm of the ›new modern Indian woman‹), they also contested the (perceived) image of emasculated (Hindu) men and sought to retrieve or reconstitute normative masculine figures (Menon 2007: xxii-xxv).

personae – both on and off the stage. The social stigma on female performers is perpetuated by the context and conditions in which they are presented on stage and the circumstances of their work: this may be the location / neighbourhood where they perform, their life-styles and modes of travel (including a (semi) nomadic existence), the physical set-up of the performance area, ways of costuming and conventional gesture and body language used on the stage.[10] For Drama actresses in Tamil Nadu,[11] for instance, the presence of a makeshift, raised stage represents ›respectability‹ (as against the ground-level performances of Kattaikkuttu / Terukkuttu, which is the local competitor of the Drama genre). However, the stage – as a separation / barrier between performer and spectator – seems to also provide the Drama actresses with a form of ›privacy‹ within the public space, in addition to providing personal safety from the physical vicinity and touch of all-too-eager (and often drunk) male spectators. Ironically, the concept of an elevated stage with backdrops and wings was copied from the Victorian stage and introduced in India as a ›modern‹ novelty during the colonial times. Susan Seizer has analyzed in detail how actresses of the Special Drama popular in South Tamil Nadu (a genre akin to the Drama of North Tamil Nadu) cope with their stigmatized identities as women and performers through what she calls »the roadwork of actresses«. Because these travelling actresses do not have access to the unproblematic and secure domestic identity that defines (internalized) femininity, they try to assert their ›respectability‹ and femininity through outwardly adopting all the features and mannerisms of a ›good woman‹ while inventing strategies that allow them to bend the parameters of the norm so as to include themselves. They create private spaces within the public sphere in an attempt to garner some respect that insideness affords respectable women, use kinship terms to address their co-performers (pre-empting suspicions with regard to [sexual] relationships), and enact during performances the moral stance of good women to counteract the transgressive double entendre dialogues – attempts which tend to be foiled by the very men with whom they share the stage (SEIZER 2005: *passim*).

Tracy Davis analyzes how the eroticization of the female form / body in live theatre of the Victorian age served the interests of particular social groups to the disadvantage of the women performers themselves (DAVIS 1991: xvi and 137–163). Hereto she uses the theatrical *mis en scenes* and pornographic pictures of actresses, books and periodicals in Victorian Britain, as indicative of society's deep lying ideology with regard to women on stage. Ballet's petticoats and skirts became fetishised as erotic signs of what they seemed to fail to conceal. Pornographically literate men wrote (and read) about the »fleshings« the ballet girls

10 For images of the life-style, mode of travel of ›low‹ performance genres, such as traditional Circus (Kazhaikkuttu) and Record Dance, see the on-line power point presentation »Contextualizing Women and Performance«, in particular ILLUSTRATIONS 1 to 7.

11 »Drama« here refers to a genre also known as Natakam or Company Drama. See on the Drama in Tamil Nadu, for instance, BRUIN 2001: 56–74.

were wearing making these pink-coloured tights into signifiers of skin, eroticism, and sexual stimulation (DAVIS 1991: 133–134). A pivotal emblem and point of reference in the discussion of female performers in India is the Devadasi, whose complex artistic and political history has left a lasting impression on the entire profession of female performer. The Devadasi's professional skills and performance rights, transmitted along the female line, and her personal life as the concubine / partner of one or more different males, challenged colonial and post-Independence morality and patriarchy. As the anti-Devadasi Acts which are in force in different parts of India until this day, show, the Devadasi's position in society became untenable. Her economic independence and the public visibility of her female sexual identity and inter-caste descent did not fit the project of ›modernity‹ and the invention of the ›new‹ Indian woman. Consequently, the Devadasi and her art form were legally banned from the public *and* the domestic sphere.

The Devadasi embodied society's fear for the female performer as a siren, whose ›attraction‹ (genuine or cultivated through her mastery over theatrical skills) trapped ›decent‹ boys into falling (and paying) for her charms and who lured away ›good girls‹ into a ›bad profession‹. Yet, not unlike the female ballet-dancer referred to above, the Devadasi was an object of erotic fetishisation in the male imagination of both the East and the West apparently right from the onset of the colonial encounter (BRUIN 2009: 254–255). The Devadasi's, and other women performers' sexual identity, visible through her physical presence on the stage and available to the (male) fantasy through her stage performance, printed images and (erotic) books, distinguished actresses from ›normal‹ women.[12] Whereas sexuality as an (analytical) theme pervades the writing on women and performance in Western scholarship, this theme is largely lacking from the critical discussions about women in / on the Indian stage, including the present contributions.[13] Sexuality concerns not only the representation of women performers as sex objects sexually ›available‹ as commodities in different times and cultures revealing a double standard of moral conduct for men and women, but also the performance of sexuality. The latter involves the »active agency of women and men performing and writing with a self-consciousness about placing their bodies [...] in particular ›spaces‹ (in terms of sexual orientation, theatrical modes of representation, public spaces).« (GOODMAN, GAY 2003 [1998]: 7).[14]

12 In this respect Partha Chatterjee remarks that in contrast to the construct of woman as sex object in Western patriarchy, the nationalist Indian male thinks of his own wife, sister and daughter as ›normal‹, *exactly because* she is not a ›sex object‹, while those who could be ›sex objects‹ are not ›normal‹ (CHATTERJEE 1993: 132).

13 Hansen and Seizer have done ground-breaking work in analyzing female sexuality and identity with regard to cross-dressing and female representation on the Parsi stage (HANSEN 1998 and 1999) and with regard to comedy and women performers in the Special Drama genre in Tamil Nadu (SEIZER 2005).

14 The agency of voyeurism, mentioned below, has much do with the ways in which women and their sexuality are perceived by those viewing the performances: the intention and

Feeling uncomfortable with the presence of women on the public stage because of the potentially voyeuristic nature of theatre and women performers' potential instrumentality in influencing others' minds, in addition to changing the (re)presentation of women on the stage and in actual life, patriarchal societies have confined women to the domestic sphere and have made public performances out of bounds for most of them.[15] The sanctions against women on the stage have resulted in the underrepresentation of women in the public (performance) space and in untold misery for those women who earn(ed) their living in the performing arts.[16]

In India the absence of women from the stage is both real and imagined depending on the performance genre or practice concerned, and is intricately linked up with society's perception of women performers. Even when it was obvious that women did and do perform, Indian society, too, has had trouble in recognizing their presence and acknowledging their contributions.[17] So how are women / the female represented in performances?

direction of the spectator's gaze determines the respect of the actress on stage. For some modern Western actresses, who have opted for a career in the theatre and for whom performing defines their identity and agency, the voyeuristic nature of theatre does have a positive, though not much talked about, aspect. Being a woman performer yields power on stage – power that is feared and nourished depending on one's own position and point of view. A few of the leading actresses in the UK, who were interviewed by Alison Oddey, spoke of their attraction to performance, because of the satisfaction (»kick«) they derived from embodying a character and presenting it to critical, live audiences (ODDEY 2005: xiv and *passim*). Jill Dolan, who in her introduction to her book *Presence & Desire: Essays on Gender, Sexuality, Performance*, writes that she is not ready to give up the intense pleasure she finds in a powerful female performer. »I still find radical her power to know, intellectually and psychophysically, how to yield the authority of stage presence, how to control the seductions inherent in the frame, how to speak the language so that authority, seduction, and language mean something different about the status of women in culture« (DOLAN 1993: 1). These kinds of in-depth analysis of the emotions generated by (seeing and performing) women on the stage are not yet available for theatre / performance in India. An analysis of the inner motivating forces of why women have opted for a professional career in the performing arts in spite of its social stigma would be welcomed by research students and young Indian women considering such a career.

15 The voyeuristic nature of theatre has, of course, to do with the fact that live performances require the physical presence on stage of the performers. The display of the female body on stage to audiences comprising unknown male spectator was / is in many societies perceived as transgressing the norms of female propriety resulting in the exclusion of women from the public view.

16 For the life history of one such famous actress, Binodini, who lived and worked in Calcutta from 1863 to 1941 see, for instance, BHATTACHARYA 1998: 3–17 and CHATTERJEE 1993: 151–155.

17 See, for instance, Sajiha Madathil's book *Malayalanatakashtricharithram* (in press) on the forgotten or ignored role of women in the Malayalam theatre and a write up about the book, announcing its release, by Reema Narendran in The New Indian Express (NARENDRAN 2010).

Female impersonators

Some performance genres reacted to social sanctions against women performers by employing male performers to act female roles, thus making these genres the sole prerogative of men (Kathakali, Kattaikkuttu / Terukkuttu, Kuchipudi), or by having cross-dressed female impersonators compete with actresses in the successful embodiment of codified feminine appearance and conduct (Parsi theatre, [Company and Special] Drama in Tamil Nadu).[18] As suggested by JOHAN in this book, women performers may have responded to their virtual exclusion from or their minimal presence on the Kutiyattam temple stage (though currently not from the secular stage) by creating their own women's performance genre, the Nangyar Kuttu. Their successful claim to a separate niche in the performance arena speaks for the agency of these high caste women performers.

In India and Europe, the public stage appears to have been most accessible to women at either the highest or the lowest levels of the social hierarchy. Women got involved in performances through their own choice and agency, because their families were involved in a particular performance tradition, and sometimes through coercion. However, the stigma attached to acting / performance was greatest for women performers whose social position was low. While women of high(er) status performed at private occasions and courts, thus enjoying royal / high status patronage, women performers at the other side of the social continuum performed, and in India continue to perform, in public, often at makeshift performance venues and / or as part of unregulated travelling troupes. Operating outside the formal sector the access of these women performers to social prestige, respect, financial security and, nowadays, social security in the form of medical insurances and / or pension schemes was and is very restricted.[19]

In India the existence of these low status women performers operating within the unrecognised, informal performing arts scene has largely remained hidden, because dominant scholarship has failed to recognize and value their personae and performances sufficiently to record them.[20] As we have seen above

18 For visual examples of female impersonators – men acting female roles – see also the online power point presentation »Contextualizing Women and Performance«, in particular ILLUSTRATIONS 8 to 13.

19 According to Katherine Cockin with reference to theatre in Europe »[...] women have had a longer history as performers in theatres of low status and informal organization and as travelling players performing often without a script on makeshift stages in the open street, than in the high status theatres equipped with permanent buildings and royal patronage. Women therefore performed in a number of spaces and in a number of ways which have been invisible to theatre historians and literary critics.« (COCKIN 2003 [1998]: 19–20). The same holds true for women performers in India – in the past and today.

20 See also Ananda Lal in his introduction to the *Oxford Companion on Indian Theatre*, who writes that in contemporary discourse among conservative city-based Indian theatre workers, »folk and traditional forms do not even qualify as ›theatre‹« (LAL 2004: ix).

with regard to the Tamil theatre, the ›illegitimate‹ stage, if at all commented upon by academics or the press, often invited criticism directed against the lack of education and ›morality‹ of its low caste / low status practitioners, which were believed to result in ›below standard‹ performances. The participation of women in these performances tended to confirm the lowness of these public presentations.

Irrespective of the performances they were involved in, and irrespective of their actual behaviour, performing women the world over have been equated with prostitutes. Stigmatising women performers as whores, strumpets and nautch girls – terms that symbolize the counter-image of the ›good woman‹ – has been the cruel sanction implemented by male dominated societies against women who dared to defy the rules of ›appropriate‹ female behaviour. Like the stigma attached to the illegitimate, ›folk‹ stage, the stigma attached to women performers criticizes the social and educational background and the moral integrity of the artist and her performance *praxis* shaped by the historical context and social conditions under which it had emerged, instead of evaluating her skills and the quality of her performance. Women performers were often regarded with suspicion and judged, not on their acting skills, but on their (real or assumed) off-stage sexual relationships (HANSEN 1999: 143; GAY 2003: 25–6; ODDEY 2005; BRUIN 2009: 252–253). Therefore, women performers involved in ›folk‹ performances, face a double stigma: firstly, on account of being a woman performer defying the accepted rules of female propriety, and, secondly, on account of the low status attributed by society to the ›folk‹ performances in which she acts. In spite of, or thanks to, ›modernity‹ this double stigma continues with undiminished power until this day, effectively controlling the entry of Indian women into public performances.[21]

Men and women alike have denied or neglected the presence and contribution of women performers to the Indian stage on the grounds that their participation in the performing arts would be ›unnecessary‹ (there are female impersonators who do a better job) or ›uncalled for‹ (being on the stage is

21 The Kattaikkuttu Gurukulam in Tamil Nadu tries to alleviate this double stigma by providing professional training in Kattaikkuttu (a theatre genre labelled ›folk‹ and / or ›low‹) in combination with quality education to underprivileged, rural girls and boys. The fact that the future performers have completed their elementary and secondary education heightens their status and that of the theatre and equips the young performers with knowledge and skills needed to embark upon a professional career in the performing arts. The Kattaikkuttu Gurukulam runs a special All Girls Programme supporting girls in their training as actresses and the complex negotiation processes with their (extended) families, which perceive »being an actress« as a threat to their family honour. The Kattaikkuttu Gurukulam supports also the Kattaikkuttu Young Professionals Company, which is the first-ever mixed gender professional Kattaikkuttu theatre company. For visual imagery of the Kattaikkuttu Girls, see the online power point presentation »Contextualizing Women and Performance«, in particular ILLUSTRATIONS 16–34, and the video clip »Snippets« about the daily life of the students of the Gurukulam made by Sue Rees.

›not done‹ for a girl from a decent family). Large sections across all layers of Indian society do not allow girls / women to opt for a career in the performing arts, to represent women and the feminine on the stage and be instrumental in creating their own meaning and artistic productions, because their presence on the public stage and in the public space is perceived as counterproductive and threatening to the male construct(s) of the ›good Indian woman‹. In a patriarchical hierarchy the exclusion of women from ›bad professions‹, such as acting or dance, is instrumental to guarding her chastity and preserving her family's honour. Her seclusion, good manners and subservience confer prestige on the men in her family (»my wife does not work«). As Pitkow and Johan show in their descriptions of the interpretation of female roles by male Kathakali and Kutiyattam performers, theatre provides a powerful instrument to reflect on the patriarchal constructs of the ideal Indian woman. Kathakali's division of female roles into three different types – *minukku*, *lalita* and *kari* – offers, through its prescriptive stereotyping of the embodiment of female behaviour, sensibility and decorum (or the lack thereof), a psychological insight into how Kerala upper-caste male society views and fears ›woman‹.

Minimizing embodiment and mobility

In addition to having male performers act the roles of female characters, other strategies have been employed to minimize the physical presence of women on the stage. Women performers have been assigned those aspects of the performance, which require the least physical mobility and embodiment: rather than being a character moving on the stage and displaying her body to a critical audience, in Kutiyattam there are sequences where the Nangyar is seated, more or less immobile, on the stage, lending only her voice to the female character embodied by a male performer. In other instances, female presence on stage might be substituted through material objects or a flame (see Johan in this volume). A substitution of a different kind, but probably also aimed at minimizing the ›uncontrolled‹ display of female bodies in public, appears to have occurred in the Siri cult in Tulunadu, Karnataka. Griebl / Sommer describe how the possession of Siri women is considered an expression of ›abnormal‹ and ›undesirable‹ female behaviour. The changed perception of the middle classes of what is in essence a devotional practice involving the physical bodies and minds of the female devotees has led to a decline in the number of women getting possessed. It appears to have motivated Siri women and their families to substitute possession as a way of service to the Goddess with the (disembodied, individualist) service of gift giving or *kanike*. Rai points out that low caste, skilled singers of the *paddana* genre in Tulunadu have found recognition for their broadcasted performances, because they sing the *paddanas* in an unpossessed state outside a ritual context for an invisible (radio) audience (Rai in this volume). Limiting a woman's performance to the (recorded) sound scape, which eliminates the physical presence of her body, confers greater prestige onto the performance and the performer. The outcome of modernity here seems to have resulted in women becoming increasingly invisible and ›dissociated‹ from their own bodies as instruments of performative expression. Their physical bodies are substituted – by symbolic artefacts indicating female presence or by opting for different, disembodied performance practices, such as gift giving, recordings limiting her performance to the sound scape only, and minimizing her mobility, both on and off the stage.[22] This process calls to mind the phenomenon of Sanskritization / Brahminization formulated for the first time by M.N. Srinivas, and further elaborated by eminent scholars, such as J. Heesterman, in which lower and middle castes and classes emulate Brahmanic / Sanskrit values and culture in their attempt for upward mobility. The ›disembodiment‹, or exclusion of the human body from performance, can be seen as an effort to gain in respectability and authority by eliminating the impure, sexualized human body from the act of performance, thus severing and elevating the latter from the problematic, strife-ridden, mundane world of human relationships (HEESTERMAN 1985: 81–94).

Prior to 1850 music, dance and dramatic performances in India appear to have been restricted in circulation and subject to feudal forms of patronage – at the high end of society by the aristocracy and at the middle and lower ends by local systems of interdependent relationships regulating the division of labour, ritual and performance tasks and determining the relative status of a performer and her genre in the local society. Historically, being a *professional* performer in India appears to have been linked almost always to membership of a particular caste or family lineage, even though within our contemporary commercialised context it is somewhat unclear how exactly this early ›professionalism‹ should be defined. Within such feudal contexts participation in theatre, dance and music was as much a right as an obligation.[23] In the case of women, their participation in live performances was bound to bring with it the visual, and, at times, physical access of male spectators to their bodies, in particular when their (low) caste status and / or poverty made these women performers subservient to their male patrons. As a result, being a woman performer determined not only one's caste identity, but often also the sexual identity of a woman as being ›available‹ as a mistress or being ›owned‹ as low(er) caste commodities obliged to ›perform‹ (*e.g.* REGE 2002: 1038–1047).

The emergence of a commercial entertainment economy during the second half of the 19th century resulted in the birth of new forms of drama and enter-

22 With regard to the undesirability of too much movement on the (Tamil) stage, in particular, see SEIZER 2005.

23 See with reference to the rural stage in Tamil Nadu and the *mamul* system, which divided occupational, ritual and performance rights-cum-obligations among different non-Brahmin service castes, BRUIN 1999: 62–63 and 82–84.

tainment combining Indian and European stage practices and technologies (BRUIN 1999: 143–158 and BRUIN 2001: Introduction). It also led to a commodification of these new, hybrid forms of theatre and the more traditional performance forms, competing with these new forms for a share in the newly emerging performance market. The commercialisation of the stage challenged older representational practices, including the performances of feminine identity, unlocking a new arena in which gender norms and images could be articulated and debated (HANSEN 1999: 128). Whether these new representational practices were favourable to the access of women to cultural performances and to their status as women performers in terms of social prestige and agency and how the representation of the ›modern‹ affected their performances, for instance, by a transition from a ritual to a secular stage, is an issue of debate in the following essays.

Negotiating tradition and modernity: Between Shame and Fame

A second theme that pervades the contributions to this book is the complex negotiation process through which both ›tradition‹ and ›modernity‹ are being construed by different actors in the field of the performing arts. This process should be seen against the complex history involving India's colonial experience, the project of nationalism and nationalism's contribution to the shaping of India's post-Independence cultural identity and its complex field of performing arts. After Independence the State took over the role of principal patron and arbiter assessing whether or not cultural performances fulfilled the accepted cultural norms and fitted within the boundaries of its self-constructed cultural identity.

As illustrated above, rather than contrasting polarities, ›tradition‹ seems to be enveloped by ›modernity‹ and *vice versa*. In their aspiration for ›modernity‹ the new Indian middle classes differentiated themselves from the many ›little and low traditions‹ and their ›common exponents‹ by juxtaposing them to a ›high‹, ›classical‹ ideal, which they helped conceptualize and instil with meaning themselves. Performance practices and behaviour deviating (too much) from the construed ideal, such as possession, cross-dressing, and women performing in public, were seen, and if one reads the following contributions, still are seen by some, as superstitions, mental or moral aberrations of the lower classes / castes or simply ›not done‹ by decent women. Visibly different displays of the body, be it the wearing of matted locks or the wearing of no clothes at all (but *neem* leaves instead, see BRÜCKNER in this volume), have invited condemnations of the sanitary and moral state of the wearers. In all cases the ›backward‹ and / or illiterate backgrounds of the practitioners are blamed for their ›faulty‹ behaviour and ›ignorance‹. This denigratory discourse under the flag of ›modernity‹ aimed to convert the low ›other‹ – marginalized, displaced or disadvantaged individuals and groups – into decent Indian citizens. Its effects, but perhaps not its efficacy, are aggravated and amplified by the attention these ›deviating performances‹ receive in the media (see the »Crime Story« sequence on-line accompanying the article of GRIEBL / SOMMER). Though nowhere openly expressed the discourse is definitely politicized, involving legal issues (such as the various anti-Devadasi acts still in force and attempts by State governments to ban possession and animal sacrifice at religious festivals) and does receive the support of particular NGOs, which might or might not work in tandem with the government or political parties (BRÜCKNER in this volume). How much of the negative attitudes that persist today towards practices, behaviours, visual images and language that do not fit the norm was influenced by the colonial experience and its after-effects, and how much of the division between ›high‹ culture and ›low‹ culture dates back to pre-colonial Indian society is unclear, but should be part of our questioning. With reference to pre-colonial Maharashtra, Veena Naregal writes that the elite intellectual discourse on the one hand, and ›ordinary‹ textual and cultural forms and ›popular‹ religious practice on the other, were characterized already then by a low degree of integration. According to Naregal »this lack of cultural cohesion surely stemmed from a severely segmented social structure« (NAREGAL 2001: 42).

As far as women and women performers are concerned, norms of female modesty and conduct appear to have been in force for a long time. In the case of Tamil language and culture, the concept of women's *karpu* or »chastity«, here interpreted as a woman's devotion to a single husband, is an old and important one (also BRUIN 2009: 248). *Cilappatikaram*, one of Tamil's classical texts (200–300 AD), in which *karpu* is a central theme, describes Parvati during a dance contest with Shiva, as:

> The Celestial One (Imaiyan / Shiva) rose to the performance
> of the Kotticcetam in total unison with Umai (Parvati)[24] –
> Her garments remaining undisturbed, her bracelets motionless
> Her waistband serene, the swing of her soft breasts suspended
> Her earrings perfectly still, her jewel-like bun unruffled
> (*Cilappatikaram* 28, lines 71–75)

This description of Parvati as a »still picture«, does not even provide a clue of the Goddess being engaged in a physical and fierce dance contest with Shiva (which she cannot win as she would have to sacrifice her ›modesty‹ by lifting her leg as high as or higher than Shiva does). The visual image of immobility in performance, which is constructed here, is suggestive of Parvati's total respectability and virtue (*karpu*), in particular because it is contrasted with the image

24 According to the *Tamil Lexicon* (University of Madras) one of the 11 kinds of *kuttus* (dances) performed by Shiva.

of a passionate Shiva, whose entire body and mind are involved in exhibiting his famous *tandava* dance.

At a time when old practices were rejected, new ›traditions‹ appropriate to India's new cultural identity combining secular and spiritual aspirations, were imagined and invented. The birth of the classical South Indian dance Bharatanatyam is the example *par excellence* of such an invented tradition. Its emergence from the older Sadir, the disinheritage of the traditional performance community (the Devadasis) from its art form, and Bharatanatyam's subsequent rise to fame – in its own homeland Tamil Nadu, in India and abroad – have been extensively documented and analysed in a number of publications (*e.g.* ALLEN 1997; O'SHEA 1998; MEDURI 2009 [2008]).

Women's deviations from or adjustments to the constructed ideals of the ›good woman‹ and ›good art‹, have resulted in a discourse of shame and fame in which female respect, personal integrity, and family honour are at stake. The starkly visible and deviating / defiant persona of the female professional performer appears to have been pivotal, and perhaps a catalyst, in foregrounding what Lata Singh has called the »actresses' question« (SINGH 2009: 270–294): To be or not to be a ›good woman‹ and, I would add, to be or not to be a ›good performer‹. The actresses' question not only looks at how society sees a woman performer, but also includes the question of the agency of women performers themselves in negotiating their reputation within the family and society at large vis-à-vis pursuing their artistic calling or economic need to be a performer.

Women's agency: to perform or not to perform

When women opt for a career in the performing arts, such a choice often results from their own agency and their ability to negotiate and validate such a choice – for themselves, at home and in society. Going against the grain and becoming a woman performer throws up mental dilemmas and agony, which women have addressed in different ways. The satisfaction derived from performance is one way of coping with the social stigma attached to women performers (and to ›low‹ status performance genres).[25]

On my way back from Europe to India in June 2010 I happened to watch on a Jet Airlines flight the Hindi movie, *Teesri Kasam* (1966) directed by Basu Bhattacharya. The film addresses several different issues, among them the double standard of a man fascinated by a woman on the stage but imagining this woman to be ›good‹ (and therefore a ›non-performer‹), the almost casual acceptance of the woman performer, of her stigmatized persona, but also her active

25 Other ›coping strategies‹ to alleviate the stigma of being a woman performer in a genre, which commands little social standing, have been described by, for instance, Susan Seizer (SEIZER 2005: *passim*).

agency in opting for a life on stage when she has the choice of becoming a ›good woman‹ by marrying the hero.

Teesri Kasam has Raj Kapoor and Waheeda Rehman in the lead roles of Hiraman, a poor, rather simple man driving a bullock cart for a living, and Hirabai, a famous (probably urban) Nautanki dancer on her way to join a theatre company performing at a village fair. While the film romanticises the *naïve* love between these two unlikely people, it also pictures the dancer as a strumpet showing quite realistically the goings-on in the Nautanki company and the conventional reactions of an all-male, rural audience towards the female Nautanki dancers. As Hiraman attends the Nautanki performances secretly – his family back home should not find out that he indulges in such an unsuitable pastime – he becomes aware of the fact that other people see Hirabai as a prostitute and it disturbs him. He tries to shield her and protect her from the negative views of society. The bond between the two grows stronger as the days pass. Hiraman gets involved in fights with local people who speak against Hirabai and her profession. Hirabai tries to make him understand the harsh reality of her life and the fact that she is not the virgin beauty he holds her for. Hiraman asks her to leave her profession and start living a ›respectable life‹. Somewhat surprisingly, Hirabai refuses to give up her acting / dancing career as she cannot live without the art of performance; the two separate and return to their own environments.

A totally different portrait of the agency of a woman in the performing arts is that of the famous Rukmini Devi. In a recent publication Avanthi Meduri has highlighted the role of Rukmini Devi, to whom she refers as a »dancer-historian«, in the shaping of Bharatanatyam.[26] Meduri analyses the hybridity of the newly invented tradition describing how Devi simultaneously grounded the dance in a glorified and romanticized artistic past as described in the *Natyasastra* and used novel techniques and symbolism (proscenium stage, backdrops, stage lights, oil lamp and statue of Nataraja on the stage) to address middle class, urban aspirations and establish a modern nationalist Indian aesthetics. Devi's instrumentality in accomplishing the validation of the dance tradition, be it in a different form and by a different group of exponents, cannot be underestimated. She had to act against severe opposition of sections among the urban elite society, which saw the custom of dedicating girls to temple deities (as a prerequisite for their involvement in the ritual temple dance) and the real and perceived excesses to which this custom gave rise, as detrimental to the progress of Indian women. Her agency and artistic vision were facilitated by her Brahmin background, her exposure to scholarly knowledge of Tamil and Sanskrit (through her father Nilakantha Sastri), theosophy (through her marriage to Theosophist G.S. Arundale), and other dance forms (through her travels abroad with Annie

26 Balasaraswati, a contemporary of Rukmini Devi but born in a traditional community of dancers, played an equally important, but different, role in historicizing and defining the shape of Bharatanatyam.

Besant and Arundale), and in general through the urban-cosmopolitan setting in which she came to live. As the founder of Kalakshetra, the institution of classical dance and music in Chennai, she became world famous and she received numerous awards for her contribution to the reinvention and revalidation of South Indian dance as Bharatanatyam. What Rukmini Devi achieved through her high social status and cosmopolitan exposure, would probably have been unthinkable for Tamil / Indian women of a lower standing who were less well connected (MEDURI 2009 [2008]).[27]

Kutiyattam, the oldest surviving Sanskrit theatre, has gone through a similar process of ›revival‹. In contrast to the Sadir, which, in its new *avatar* as Bharatanatyam came to be owned by a new, and in terms of caste and social status, totally different group of female (and male) performers, the revalidation of Kutiyattam did not lead to the total rejection of its traditional female exponents. A possible explanation may lie in the fact that Kerala society has always openly acknowledged the mixed caste descent of its female Kutiyattam performers or Nangyars, whereas in Tamil society the mixed cast background of the Devadasis and their off-spring is perceived as highly problematic (BRUIN 2007: 55–56). As MOSER and DAUGHERTY argue in this volume, the traditional Nangyars continued to perform on the ritual temple stage simultaneously with the emergence onto the public stage of new female exponents who had learned the tradition, still under the tutelage of traditional gurus, in newly established performing arts institutions, such as Kerala Kalamandalam and Natana Kairali / Ammanur Chakyar Modham. While the ritual performances by the old Nangyars, who held the right to perform on the temple stage, differed widely in artistic content and elaborateness from that of the ›new‹ Nangyars, the old Nangyars were never formally or legally expelled from the temple stage. Yet, they appear to have been unhappy about the growing lack of approval of their services by the temple-authorities and the quality of their own performances, which they blamed on their lack of training.[28] As a consequence they appear to have no longer been able to derive pride and artistic satisfaction from their stage appearances.[29]

The institutionalisation of the performing arts – often as part of a wider effort to reinvent Indian performance traditions and protect them from ›extinction‹ – and the emergence of secular performance venues and opportunities,

27 For yet another recent publication on Rukmini Devi's life, artistic career and agency in shaping Bharatanatyam and Kalakshetra, see SAMSON 2010.

28 A similar argument was employed by rural Devadasi performers in Tamil Nadu (BRUIN, RAJAGOPAL 2001) interview with M. Dhanammal, a Devadasi in rural Tamil Nadu.

29 While some of the old Nangyars envy the newer generation of performers for their artistic skills, Kapila Nagavallikkunnel, who is one of today's outstanding young female Kutiyattam exponents admitted that she felt sad that she has been denied entry to the ritual stage on the grounds that she does not belong to the traditional Nangyar community (personal interview, December 2009).

appears to have greatly facilitated the opening up of these forms to newcomers. Among these newcomers were not only male students, who belonged to castes different from those of the traditional performers; for the first time in the history of most of these forms, the newcomers included also a few women some of whom now have emerged as well-known performers in their own right. The contributions of DAUGHERTY, MOSER, PITKOW and GUILLEBAUD speak of the new agency of these women performers in Kutiyattam, Kathakali and Kaikkottukali. The entry of women performers appears to have been made possible by the fact that the transmission of these performance genres has been lifted out of the traditional contexts and now takes place within an institutionalised environment. Within Kutiyattam a new generation of women performers has seized the possibility to create (their own) meaning on stage through the development of fresh artistic work, which places the representation of women on the Kutiyattam stage in an entirely new light. GUILLEBAUD, with reference to the song and dance tradition of Kaikkottukali, explores how Brahmin women in Kerala appropriated the »musical authority« of the form in order to distinguish it from Kaikkottukali's ›uncivilized‹ renderings by low caste performers and establish themselves as the foremost and authentic exponents of Kaikkottukali. In addition to highlighting the contestation of a domestic / folk tradition by its high caste and low caste exponents, GUILLEBAUD'S contribution provides an insight in how Kaikkottukali, through the agency of its female Brahmin exponents, came to represent Kerala's national culture and how, in its new *avatar*, ironically it had to become accessible to non-Brahmin practitioners, too.

On the lower side of the social spectrum, the need to be as close as possible to what society has ordained to be a ›good woman‹, has led to women giving up established performance practices and practices of worship and / or to substitute them with practices that are felt to fit modernity and the picture of the good Indian woman better. The negative connotations that came to be attached to the performance of possession by Siri women in Tulunadu has resulted in a decline in the number of women participating in these possession rituals (GRIEBL / SOMMER). Similarly, BRÜCKNER signals a decline in (publicly) visible sessions with mediums, both male and female, and cases of devotees falling into a trance, and to a decline in the number of Jogappas (cross-dressed male devotees) at the full-moon festivals for the Goddess Renuka-Ellamma in North Karnataka. It is unclear whether the decision of (women) performers to forsake ritual performance practices, which until quite recently were taken for granted as an aspect of their local culture, is self-consciously motivated, possibly under influence of Western education promoting ›rational values‹, or whether it is the result of persuasion. For most of these women performers appear to be under pressure from their close family members, who feel ashamed about the participation of their wife, mother, daughter, sister or aunt in possession practices dubbed ›unwomanly‹, ›unfit for women‹, to let go of these ›undesirable‹ performance practices. Here, as well as in the case of other performance practices and genres that fall outside the view and ways of life of the urban middle classes, the tension between modernity and localized personal and emotional, devotional practices and ›folk‹ performances – what they stands for (or once stood for) for insiders and what they communicate to uninitiated outsiders – is very palpable. In situations of unequal economic and symbolic power, the agency of women performers is limited. Their safest option appears to be to internalise the perception, in part or totally, that devalues their established practices as backward, undignified, irrational and inappropriate and to back out or substitute their customary performance practice with a less embodied one so as to protect their reputation and prestige.

SCHÖMBUCHER's essay highlights a modern-day possession event, which contrasts in many respects to the (as recent) possession events described by GRIEBL / SOMMER and BRÜCKNER. SCHÖMBUCHER's chief informant, Bhulekamma, acts as the medium of the goddess Nukalamma in southern Orissa. She is able to handle and accommodate the request to interpret the problems of a high caste client effortlessly without her low caste status being an apparent obstacle to her professional reputation and social respect. Her greater agency appears to lie in the fact that she is a professional performer of possession séances who works on her own, knows the ins and outs of her trade and is fully in charge of the medium and its flexibility. This enables her to accommodate what SCHÖMBUCHER calls an »unusual demand«. On the other hand, the possessed Siri women are ›lay‹ performers forming part of a collective of women. They appear to have far less agency in steering the performance, which is ›managed‹ increasingly through the services of a male Kumara.

Inside and outside perspectives

This brings us to a last, more theoretical theme touched upon in some of the contributions to this book: the perspectives of insiders to a performative genre or practice, in particular with regard to the praxis of performance, its intention and (perceived) meaning and efficacy, and the view of outsiders. As CLAUS shows, inside and outside perceptions are not necessarily the same. Even if outsiders, in particular scholars, try to get as close as possible to an insider's perspective, through participation in a performing arts form or through long time association with informants and / or getting involved in practical work, it remains often hard to elicit a ›critical‹ opinion from inside participants. Many professional performers consider criticizing colleagues with whom they stand in a competitive relationship not as ›good practice‹. In the case of forms that are transmitted orally and organically – a process that differs considerably from teaching Western performing art forms – it often takes time, consistent prodding and reading between the lines to get an idea of what might be meant and why.

Elaborating upon Dundes' concept of »folk (or oral) literary criticism«, CLAUS feels that the critical voice of the academic, which is presumably more objective and authoritative because based on broader data, might silence the interpretations of informants. He recommends that we listen better to the subjective voices of our informants: What do they have to say about variations in performance? How can their critique of performance inform and sensitize our own interpretations?

SCHÖMBUCHER, in her essay about the divine discourse of Bhulekamma when possessed by the Goddess Nukalamma, extends the principal of listening to the consumers of the performance: What did the listener hear or what did she want to hear? She describes the expertise of the female medium of finetuning the words of the Goddess towards the needs of the client. The open, dialectic procedure adopted during a séance enables the listener to select the ›right‹ statements and neglect other ones, thus exercising her own ›critical‹ ability of judging the effectiveness of the performance. Referring to Austin's important work *How to do things with words?*, SCHÖMBUCHER proposes that possession here should be analyzed in terms of language: Language not only represents or refers to reality; it also creates it. Listening – whether by a trained researcher or a medium's client – is a cultural practice informed by cultural concepts and driven by a set of culturally and personally defined expectations with regard to the desired outcome of these performance events. While the strategies highlighted by CLAUS and SCHÖMBUCHER differ in the centrality they attribute to the researcher and the informant, they appear to be equally ›critical‹ as far as it concerns the selection of statements that fit our (emotional, social or academic) purposes best.

I would like to conclude by returning to the constructions of ›tradition‹ and ›modernity‹. Both these concepts have been invoked, recreated and refined to defy, firstly, colonial dominance, and secondly, to cope with the far-reaching changes that have taken place in pre- and post-Independence India. Recent scholarship has made it clear that ›tradition‹ and ›modernity‹ are not static, nor are they necessarily contrasting ideas. Here a word of caution is in place with regard to the manner in which local informants perceived tradition (*sampradaya*) – in this case the ›folk‹ tradition of Kattaikkuttu (theatre) and its principal performance repertory revolving around the retelling in Tamil and theatrical embodiment of selected episodes of the *Mahabharata* epic. The informants were male performers and male and female spectators. It was not unusual to hear them claim that Kattaikkuttu ›never changes‹. The *Mahabharata* epic on which most Kattaikkuttu plays are based, was repeatedly described as ›imperishable‹ (*azhiyata*) – a qualification which suggests the epic's eternal nature in the form of a kind of abstract ›static-ness‹ implying the exact opposite of a dying tradition. However, when questioned about differences between Kattaikkuttu performances thirty years ago and nowadays, informants would be quick to point out the many changes that have occurred (changes, which were often judged negatively and attributed to the influences of *kali yuga*). Similarly, they were ready to talk about the differences in performance styles of different companies as well as analyze actors' different interpretations of the same character in a play. If local informants acknowledge such subtle variation and change of the tradition, but define it simultaneously as unchangeable, the question is: What does their idea of tradition entail and refer to? Are we, as outsiders to the tradition, talking about the same thing as our informants, who, as repositories and first-hand recipients have more inside, though not necessarily analytical, knowledge of the tradition than we have? The local perception of ›tradition‹ seems to refer, not to its actualised, tangible expressions, but to an omnipresent (eternal) abstract, a kind of blueprint that is able to accommodate and reproduce all change without affecting or altering its core ›meaning‹ – perhaps a kind of ›life insurance‹ against change, in particular change that takes place at today's rapid speed?[30] Rather than focusing on the (un)changeability of tradition, we could begin to look at what the core of a tradition represents for its insiders, in addition to trying to define its boundaries – and its flexibility: how far does the capacity of a tradition stretch to accommodate change without being annihilated or transformed into something else? When is a proposed or actual change so extreme that local consensus no longer recognizes and / or agrees to accept it as (being part of) ›tradition‹? How is such a consensus with regard to what is acceptable in / as performance brokered? Challenging these boundaries and stretching them are, of course, matters with which modern theatre and dance have been experimenting; none of such performances is represented in this volume.[31] The information our questioning, including an investigation of experimental performances, will generate, will provide us with new insights as to how and why performances change and find validation.

Ending on an optimistic note, it seems that many, if not all traditions, possess the inherent flexibility to accommodate women as performers. If tradition is perceived as an abstract blueprint adaptable to change that does not affect the core, such a perception will enable traditional gurus to transmit their knowledge and skills to students, irrespective of gender and caste. However, it will be at the discretion of society at large, in particular the ›modern‹ middle classes, whether it will allow girls and women to avail themselves of this opportunity in order to embark on a career as a professional performer with social dignity and economic viability.

30 In my earlier work on the Kattaikkuttu theatre tradition I have proposed the idea of an ›oral reservoir‹ as a cognitive construct that serves as a repository of a number of interlinked regional performance traditions and prompts their actual, contextualized expressions in the form of live performances (Bruin 1999: 164; Bruin 1991: 98). A similar idea could be used to define ›tradition‹ as a broader concept, not confined to performances alone.

31 See for two examples of modern theatre the online power point presentation »Contextualizing Women and Performance«, Illustrations 14 and 15.

Conclusions

In anticipation of the following essays, a first tentative conclusion that may be drawn here is, that modern Indian society, notwithstanding the fact that it needs female performers in order to assert its cultural identity through public theatre and dance, has still not been able to fit these working women comfortably into the new model of the ›good women‹. The threat women on the public stage (be it a theatrical platform or a circumscribed ritual arena in the public space) pose to male patriarchy and national hegemony, in combination with the ability of performance to bring out and subvert hidden agendas and emotions, explains to some extent why there has not been sufficient, critical attention – in performance studies as well as feminism and women's studies – for the issue of women performers in India. Those authors, who have written on women in performance, have primarily focused on the historical and social contexts which were detrimental to women performers and women's agency in general. Issues of women's sexuality, as an inherent part of performance, and the construction and interpretation of woman and femininity on the stage deserve further investigation in order to heighten our understanding of women performers and their contribution to public performances.

The double stigma attached to their profession *and* their professional and personal lives pre-empts the ascription of ›respectability‹ to a woman performer. The lower the social and economic status of the woman performer, the deeper is the stigma. Therefore, a second conclusion that could be drawn is that ›modernity‹ appears to have disenfranchised non-elite women most from two important freedoms: that of *choice* and *self-expression* through public performances. In many instances modernity and its ›norms‹ appear to have complicated the participation of women in ritual and folk performances that do not fulfil society's established cultural norms of seclusion and female modesty. In the case of forms which require embodiment, such as theatre, dance and possession rituals, much of the cultural and social critique has focused on the (sexual) bodies of the performers and their visibility in the public space as incompatible with the feminine ideal and as ›violating‹ the decency, honour and authority of their male relatives in particular. In spite of actresses' smart attempts to subvert and flex the boundaries of the acceptable, it remains a huge and difficult task to break new grounds in making the performance of those parts of culture, which are pivotal to the local cultural identities of the underprivileged, socially acceptable and truly recognized. Women performers operating in the popular, non-elite performances genres, which are patronized by the low(er) class and caste strata of society, without exception express the wish that none of their daughters shall succeed them in the performance profession subjecting them to the shame which they experienced as women performers: »Let the (female) profession die when I die on the stage«.[32]

The flip-side of the coin is that women, who are mostly of higher class / caste status and who are involved in cultural performances that do fulfil the accepted norms, have become more vocal and have contributed actively to the revitalization and re-actualization of traditional performances and the creation of new (visual and textual) meaning through the production of new plays. The contributions of these women performers have found a wide recognition. It has brought them fame, though not always professional / emotional satisfaction.[33]

Hanne M. de Bruin
Würzburg / Kanchipuram, 14 July 2010

Literature

ALLEN, MATTHEW HARP. 1997. »Rewriting the Script for South Indian Dance«. *The Drama Review* 41, 3 (155): 63–100.
BHATTACHARYA, RIMLI (TRANS. AND ED.). 1998. *Binodini Dasi: My Story and My Life as an Actress*. Delhi: Kali for Women, 3–17.
BOURDIEU, PIERRE. 1984. *Distinction: A Social Critique of the Judgement of Taste*. London: Routledge.
BRÜCKNER, HEIDRUN; ELISABETH SCHÖMBUCHER; PHILLIP B. ZARRILLI (EDS.). 2007. *The Power of Performance: Actors, Audiences and Observers of Cultural Performances in India*. New Delhi: Manohar.
BRUIN, HANNE M. DE. 1991. »Analysis of an oral theatre text: Preliminary findings«. *Journal of the Institute of Asian Studies* (Madras) 8, 2 (March 1991): 98–130.
----. 1999. *Kattaikkuttu: The Flexibility of a South Indian Theatre Tradition*. Gonda Indological Studies Volume VII. Groningen: Egbert Forsten.
---- (ED.). 2001. *Seagull Theatre Quarterly* 31 (September 2001). Calcutta: The Seagull Foundation for the Arts.
----. 2007. »Devadasis and Village Goddesses of North Tamil Nadu«. In: *The Power of Performance: Actors, Audiences and Observers of Cultural Performances in India*. Ed. by Heidrun Brückner, Elisabeth Schömbucher and Phillip B. Zarrilli. New Delhi: Manohar, 53–83.
----. 2009. »Kattaikkuttu Girls«. In: *Theatre in Colonial India: Play-House of Power*. Ed. by Lata Singh. New Delhi: Oxford University Press, 241–269.
----; P. RAJAGOPAL. 2001. *In Their Own Words: The Unheard History of the Rural Tamil Stage as Told by Four of its Professional Exponents*. Interviews on video. Leiden: International Institute for Asian Studies [ISBN 90-74917-25-9; NUGI 086].
CHATTERJEE, PARTHA. 1993. *The Nation and its Fragments: Colonial and Postcolonial Histories*. Princeton, New Jersey: Princeton University Press.
CILAPPATIKARA MULAMUM. ARUMPATAVURAIYUM ATIYARKKUNALLARURAIYUM. 1978. Chennai: Dr. U. V. Saminatiyar Library.

32 Interview with M. Shanmugavalli, contemporary Drama Actress, in BRUIN, RAJAGOPAL 2001; also SEIZER 2005: 330.
33 See also footnote 29 above.

CLIFFORD, JAMES. 1986. »On Ethnographic Allegory«. In: *Writing Culture: The Poetics and Politics of Ethnography.* Ed. by James Clifford and George E. Marcus. Berkeley, Los Angeles: University of California Press, 98–121.

COCKIN, KATHERINE. 2003 [1998]. »Introduction to Part One« [›The History of Women in Theatre‹]. In: *The Routledge Reader in Gender and Performance.* Ed. by Lizbeth Goodman with Jane de Gay. London, New York: Routledge, 19–24.

DAVIS, TRACY C. 1991. *Actresses as Working Women: Their Social Identity in Victorian Culture.* London, New York: Routledge.

DEHSPANDE, SUDHANVA; AKSHARA K.V.; SAMEERA IYENGAR (EDS.). 2009. *Our Stage: Pleasures and Perils of Theatre Practice in India.* New Delhi: Tulika Books.

DOLAN, JILL. 1993. *Presence and Desire: Essays on Gender, Sexuality, and Performances.* Ann Arbor: The University of Michigan Press.

GARDNER, VIV. 2003 [1998]. »The New Woman in the New Theatre«. In: *The Routledge Reader in Gender and Performance.* Ed. by Lizbeth Goodman with Jane de Gay. London, New York: Routledge, 74–79.

GAY, JANE DE. 2003 [1998]. »Naming Names: An Overview of Women in the Theatre, 1500–1900«. In: *The Routledge Reader in Gender and Performance.* Ed. by Lizbeth Goodman with Jane de Gay. London, New York: Routledge, 25–28.

GOODMAN, LIZBETH; JANE DE GAY (EDS.). 1998 (reprint 2003). *The Routledge Reader in Gender and Performance.* London, New York: Routledge.

GOPALRATNAM, V.C. 1981 [1956]. »Tamil Drama«. In: *Indian Drama.* New Delhi: Ministry of Information and Broadcasting, Government of India, 119–126.

HANSEN, KATHRYN. 1998. »Stri Bhumika: Female Impersonators and Actresses on the Parsi Stage«. In: *Economic and Political Weekly* (29 August 1998): 2291–2301.

––––. 1999. »Making Women Visible: Gender and Race Cross-Dressing in the Parsi Theatre«. *Theatre Journal* (The John Hopkins University) 51: 127–147.

HEESTERMAN, J.C. 1985. *The Inner Conflict of Tradition: Essays in Indian Ritual, Kingship, and Society.* Chicago, London: University of Chicago Press.

LAL, ANANDA (ED.). 2004. *The Oxford Companion to Indian Theatre.* New Delhi: Oxford University Press.

MEDURI, AVANTHI. 2009 [2008]. »Temple Stage as Historical Allegory in Bharatanatyam: Rukmini Devi as Dancer-historian«. In: *Performing Pasts: Reinventing the Arts in Modern South India.* Ed. by Indira Viswanathan Peterson, Davesh Soneji. New Delhi: Oxford University Press, 133–164.

MENON, NIVEDITA (ED.). 2007. *Sexualities. Issues in Contemporary Indian Feminism.* New Delhi: Women Unlimited.

NAREGAL, VEENA. 2001. *Language Politics, Elites and the Public Sphere.* New Delhi: Permanent Black.

NARENDRAN, REEMA. 2010. »Breaking the silence on women artists«. *The New Indian Express* (21 July 2010): Express Buzz section.

O'SHEA, JEANET. 1998. »›Traditional‹ Indian Dance and the Making of Interpretive Communities«. In: *Asian Theatre Journal* 15, 1: 45–63.

ODDEY, ALISON (ED.). [2]2005. *Performing Women: Stand-Ups, Strumpets and Itinerants.* New York: Palgrave MacMillan.

PETERSON, INDIRA VISWANATHAN; DAVESH SONEJI (EDS.). 2009 [2008]. *Performing Pasts: Reinventing the Arts in Modern South India.* New Delhi: Oxford University Press.

RAMASWAMY, SUMATHI. 1998 [1997]. *Passions of the Tongue: Language Devotion in Tamil Nadu, 1891–1970.* New Delhi: Munshiram Manoharlal Publishers.

REGE, SHARMILA. 2002. »Conceptualizing Popular Culture: ›Lavani‹ and ›Powda‹ in Maharashtra«. *Economic and Political Weekly* (March), 1038–1047. [An extract of

this essay is reprinted in SINGH 2009: 132–154 under the title »Some Issues in Conceptualizing Popular Culture: The Case of the Lavani and Powada in Maharashtra«].
SAMSON, LEELA. 2010. *Rukmini Devi: A Life*. New Delhi: Viking / Penguin Group.
SEIZER, SUSAN. 2005. *Stigmas of the Tamil Stage: Ethnography of Special Drama Artists in South India*. Durham, London: Duke University Press.
SINGH, LATA (ED.). 2009. *Theatre in Colonial India: Play-House of Power*. New Delhi: Oxford University Press.

MULTIMEDIA

A FILM CLIP by Sue Rees (2006) and 34 ILLUSTRATIONS show extracts from the daily routine of students at the Kattaikkuttu Youth Theatre School and can be accessed online: *http://www.indologie.uni-wuerzburg.de/women_performers/contributors/de_bruin/*.

Part I

Theory

Reflections on Folk Literary Criticism

Peter J. Claus

»As a terminological aid for the collection of meaning, I have proposed ›oral literary criticism‹. The term is obviously derived from ›literary criticism‹ which refers to a host of methods of analyzing and interpreting works of written literature. Even a beginner in literary criticism soon discovers that there are alternate and rival interpretations of the same work of art. The identical phenomenon occurs in the case of folklore which for the sake of discussion we may call ›oral literature‹ [...] For each item of oral literature, there is a variety of oral literary criticism, This is an important point inasmuch as folklorists, despite the fact that they are accustomed to thinking of variation in the texts of folklore, often wrongly assume that there is only one correct meaning or interpretation.« (DUNDES 1978 [1966] [»Metafolklore and Folk Literary Criticism«] 40–41)

This paper is dedicated to the memory of the late Professor Alan Dundes, friend and colleague, whose ideas have inspired not only this paper, but all of my ventures into India's folklore.

Introduction

Since Dundes introduced the term in 1966 many scholars have utilized the concept of »oral (or folk) literary criticism«, but few have explicitly incorporated a discussion of folk literary criticism into their analyses of specific traditions. At best, most involve the folk only in exegesis, or »folk exegesis«, the interpretation of symbolism from an emic perspective.[1] Ethnographers still tend to obscure the relationship between the researcher and the traditions researched and coopt the folk role in the literary criticism and interpretation of that tradition. Admit-

1 Anthropologists, too, began to take folk exegesis seriously during the 1960s. Many writers recognized a distinction between their own analytic models and the native folk models of society. The terms etic and emic began to represent the difference between supposedly objective, scientific categories and the unique perceptions from within a culture. Explanation of cultural institutions and activities, while exploring the latter, normally rested on the former. Victor Turner, for example, in his tripartate scheme for analysing ritual, acknowledged folk exegesis as a first step in understanding ritual, but ultimately offered explanation at the level of pre-cognative psychology, accessible only to the anthropologist.

tedly, for the researcher steeped in the aesthetic traditions of another culture, it is often difficult to separate one's own analytic and critical insights from those one acquires in the process of gathering research materials. Researching a tradition, the scholar assimilates evaluative criteria from informants, merging these with his / her sensibilities acquired since birth, in school and through reading. In the end, in writing up the analysis and publishing it, the scholar is expected to assume a stance of mastery over a broad and representative collection of data and to expound on it with authority and originality. This makes it difficult to acknowledge or incorporate folk literary criticism or even to distinguish his / her own insights and interpretations from the folk who contributed to it. Although many folklorists and anthropologists do acknowledge by name those informants who shaped their interpretations of cultural phenomena, rarely do they explicitly distinguish their own insights from those of their informants, or explore the fundamental differences between them, or recognize that those differences will endure.

Pāḍdana As a Genre

The *Tulu Pāḍdanas* are a complex genre of oral tradition involving a fairly broad spectrum of Tuluva society occupying the area along the southwestern coast of India where Tulu, a Dravidian language, is spoken. There are at least two distinct major traditions, or sub-genres: »planting songs« (*nēji nāṭina pāḍdana*), normally sung by women, and bardic caste ritual songs. In some regions, by some singers, these two sub-genres are distinguished by the terms *pāḍdana* and *sandi*, but often a terminological distinction is not made, or the terms are used somewhat indiscriminately. As an analyst, the latter tradition set (what is sometimes called *sandi*, ritual songs) I would divide further into at least three sub-sub-genres: each sung by one of the different castes of professional performers, the Pambadas, the Paravas and the Nalkes.[2]

Many professional folklorists, both Western and Indian, have preferred male over female performers in their collections and research. Abstractly – outside of a specified context – native informants, too, usually associate *pāḍdana*-singing with men of the Nalke, Parava and Pambada caste. Nevertheless, village women are usually more likely to be knowledgeable about the songs and singing competence, and most women of any of the non-Brahman castes are capable of singing a few to many songs, or at least participate in the singing. In the fields women of many different castes sing (or listen) together. In ritual contexts the whole village is an audience, but it is generally only the women who listen

2 For an example of women singing a *pāḍdana* in the fields while planting paddy seedlings see the video clip associated with this article [see FILM CLIP 1]. For singing in the context of a *bhūta kōla*, see ILLUSTRATIONS 4–6 online.

intently to the song. And even in that context, men are given prominence, but women are important in the maintenance of the tradition. The male singer is usually accompanied in his singing by a female relative [see ILLUSTRATIONS 4 and 5], and, especially in the Parava community, but also in the Nalke community (although far less so amongst the Pambada), women are important links in the chain of *pāḍdana* transmission within the families. Finally, a purview of a large representative distributional collection of *pāḍdana*s, I suspect, would reveal that many of the narratives, even those falling in the ritual sub-genres, have a common ›origin‹ in the women's fieldsong tradition.

Although most Tuluvas think of the *pāḍdana* »fieldsong« tradition as being sung in the context of the work in a paddy field, this is not truly the only context in which it occurs.[3] Some singers informed me that they learned the songs from their mothers or other older kinswomen by having them recited, partly in prose, partly in song, while performing household tasks. Thus, *pāḍdanas* sometimes occupy a niche similar to folktales.[4] I have heard women sing when they are feeling lonely, in the evening, alone in the house. I have also heard women discussing – relating and reciting, singing – *pāḍdanas* in the evening, at times of leisure. On several occasions I have heard a woman exemplify the story of a *pāḍdana* by alternating between singing and narrating in prose. Several women said they sing *pāḍdanas* »in their mind« at times when they are feeling reflective.[5]

In a ritual context the presentation is dominated by the professional dancer and the village is an audience. But that does not mean it is necessarily an attentive audience. In any case, *pāḍdana*-singing does not expect an audience. Even in the fields, two women working side by side sing together.[6] Other women working near them in the field may listen, but they may also ignore them and

3 The *pāḍdanas* are one of two types of songs women sing in the field. The other is called *kabita*. *Kabitas* are sung in large groups, with one woman singing a lead verse and the others responding with a chorus. *Pāḍdanas* are generally sung between two women, with the lead singer singing a stanza and the other repeating that stanza. The two singers link their recitation by singing the final phrase in unison, a feature called by them, *voipunu*, ›pulling‹, ›lifting‹, ›dragging‹ or ›stretching‹. In contrast to the *kabita*, the manner of singing a *pāḍdana* is intimate and serious. Not all regions of Tulunad make this distinction, however, and in regions where the distinction is not made, the style of *kabita* singing is not found. Udupi, the region where Kargi lives, does not make the distinction. In areas where the *kabita* style is unknown, there are some songs which might otherwise be sung as *kabita* are sung as *pāḍdana*.

4 While collecting folktales I have found that women frequently tell *pāḍdana*-stories in this prose narrative style. Other researchers report similar findings (Bilimale, personal communication).

5 From what women have told me, it seems this ›mental performance‹ as well as prose narrative forms, often predicate a fully articulated oral performance, although I would hesitate to use the word ›rehearsed‹ to describe the relationship.

6 In this regard, *pāḍdanas* are unlike some other fieldsong traditions (see FOOTNOTE 7) which women sing that are sung with a large group chorus. For those, one could argue that the ›audience‹ is necessarily enfolded into the tradition.

strike up a conversation among themselves. For the sake of clarity in the recording, when I collected songs for my study, I collected from women singing in pairs, but not in the context of transplanting. The location was usually their own home, during the day and during the months January through June, when agricultural work is at a lull. Although this is not a traditional context, women rarely felt uncomfortable with the situation and readily understood its advantages. In their minds, this was not merely an acceptable alternative, but in most ways one which is preferable to the ›normal‹ context.[7]

The Project and the Situation Briefly Described:

Over a two decade period from 1967 to 1989 I had collected a number of versions of five *Tulu Pāḍdanas*. The collection includes variation roughly representative of the length and breadth of Tulunad. The versions included both those sung in a ritual context and those in a women's fieldsong traditions. Throughout this period I had also been scrutinizing the collection, identifying the nature of the variation, and trying to determine the causes for the various types of differences. By 1990 I had written a number of papers describing the results of this collection, research and analysis.

Then, during the fall of 1990 I spent three days with a skilled singer, Kargi Mundaldi, going over all of the taped versions and asking her to critique and comment upon the variations. In a paper (CLAUS 1995) presented earlier (but I think never published) I described our discussion as a contribution to the understanding of »folk literary criticism«. In it, I juxtaposed some of my own analyses and speculations about the dynamics of *pāḍdana* singing and transmission against Kargi's opinions of the same data. Here, I want to expand on some

7 In my mind, the unconventional setting affects the performance in two significant ways: (1) In the recording context the songs tend to be longer and more complete in some respects. In the field, singing is frequently discontinued if there is objection by the working team of women. Non-singers may begin carrying on disruptive conversations. Sometimes there are objections to singing particular songs. Sometimes the women get bored with their singing. Sometimes there is objection to the way a lead singer is singing (*e.g.* if she leaves out an important detail or her version is seen as being unacceptably deviant). Sometimes only part of a song is known, but the women enjoy singing only the portion they know. (2) In the recording context there are frequent discrepancies between the verses sung by the lead singer and the following singer. Most of these discrepancies appear to be »allo-semantic« and insignificant. The women, themselves, did not seem aware of them, but there could have been a conscious effort to conform. In the field and while singing in a group, such individual discrepancies would probably not be noticed. Only in the case of two women who sang many songs for me, could I detect discrepancies which approached the character of a dialogue, with the second singer clarifying, interpreting, correcting, elaborating or otherwise intentionally altering the lead singer's verse. There were a number of occasions when the women later discussed details which differed between the version they had just sung and other version they knew.

of those thoughts now that the tradition itself has changed radically due to various kinds of media treatment and scholarly study of it and other oral traditions around India.

Voices

I had, in the course of collection, talked with many of the singers about the particular songs as well as the tradition [see ILLUSTRATIONS 7–9]. During these conversations – usually just after they had sung – I would make inquiries concerning whatever I might have thought to represent omission or significant variation from what I would have expected. These conversations provided many revelations about the tradition and interesting insights about the particular songs, and I incorporated much of what I learned into my own understanding of the tradition. But my own interests and perspective differed from that of any particular singer. I was aware of variation they could not have known about. In the beginning, I used to ask them to comment on differences between their rendition and others I had heard. The usual response was a noncommittal: »They sing it that way, we sing it this way.« Or, in a more critical vein: »That isn't correct (*sari attü*), I have sung it the way the elders sang it. One shouldn't change the *pāḍdanas*.« I often encountered a disdain for the Tulu spoken in other regions, »theirs isn't pure (*sudda*) Tulu, the traditions there have gone down«, implying that mixture with other languages (mostly Kannada) contaminates the Tulu traditions, or perhaps that modern education (in Kannada at the government schools) has meant that traditional Tulu customs are being forgotten.[8] Sometimes mention of variation seemed to be regarded as threatening and offensive. It is inappropriate that there should be variation in the *pāḍdanas*, especially those which were regarded as most sacred. To point out differences between versions is to suggest that either the singer or the tradition had allowed faulty transmission. There should be no differences in truth (*satya*).[9] While I

8 Which is indeed true: families who send their children to school often do so that they may engage in modern economic and social pursuits. In the schools, Tulu is usually prohibited and often Tulu traditions – regarded as backward and filled with useless superstition – are ridiculed by the teachers. In the course of my investigations I encountered two school teachers who seemed to take it as their duty to point out the deficiencies of the singers (»They have forgotten the songs and add to them new ideas.«) and the songs. I was sometimes questioned as to the appropriateness of studying the *pāḍdanas* and the ritual traditions that accompany them, in as much as giving attention to them was a form of accrediting them.

9 Although there is no belief that the *pāḍdanas* are the recorded word of God, like the Bible, there is certainly the belief that they represent an ancient wisdom more profound than modern thought. It is felt that the *pāḍdanas* preserve this and should not be changed by any singer. – Even in the discussions recorded here, there were times when theology rather than literature came close to the surface. Salya began to repeat that Jumādi, the main

was collecting versions from around the district I tried to straddle the dilemma of avoiding confrontation and eliciting critical comment on variations by making only brief remarks on differences and allowing the singer to express her opinion, but not pursuing any inconsistencies. My interest was in »folk literary criticism« not in the ›correct‹ version or whether there was any kind of ›truth‹ contained in the tradition.

My contact with most of the singers was too brief to try to provoke elaborate criticism. My position as a foreigner, a scholar and a researcher with resources far beyond those of the singers put them in a disadvantage that discouraged much comment. While many singers were pleased that I had taken up an interest in the *pāḍdanas*, which they agreed were worthy of the attention, and proud enough of their own abilities to think they could ably represent the tradition with their songs, there was a reluctance to criticize the tradition in front of an outsider. Although many singers feel the *pāḍdanas* are their tradition and they are confident of its tenets, they are apt to show great diffidence to the scholar's position in society and feel it is not their place to contradict him. The situation was reinforced by my travels and recording: I seemed to them to have the weight of numbers and concrete evidence on my side. Only a few singers were bold enough to express themselves elaborately in my presence, and then, perhaps, only because I knew them through colleagues, younger men of their village with whom they themselves were very familiar.

My relationship with Kargi was different than with other singers.[10] I had worked with her for many years. I had in the past presented her with some of the results of my research. Initially, she reacted much the same as other singers. But over the years we worked together Kargi thought much about the *pāḍdana* tradition and her own versions of the songs. She had apparently reflected on some of the same issues I had, although no doubt from a different perspective. In 1988 there were several occasions I had presented some of my material to her and asked for comment. The samples were short and my questions had to do with identification of style, not interpretation of variation. By the intensity with which she listened to the pieces, she seemed obviously fascinated by the material, but, in the particular instances, could not help me. But Kargi had a good ear and a much better auditory memory channel than I had and two years

deity of the *pāḍdana*, was the same. Even Kargi occasionally became a bit uneasy with some of the variation. Often the uneasiness was relieved by laughter and the explanation that the stories do change as they move from place to place away from where they originated. – There was one point, however, in the discussion of the *Parnderu Pāḍdana* where Kargi made a strong objection to the version just heard, insisting it was not only wrong, but ›sinful‹, *pāpa*. I have heard her make similar theological objections to versions of the *Siri Pāḍdana* which differ from her own. As a participant of the Siri cult, during which the *pāḍdana* is sung (in part, at least) her objection in this case may have to do with authenticating her possession by a the Siri spirit as opposed to some other (impostor) spirit.

10 For photographs of Kargi depicting several dimensions of her as a person, see Illustrations 1–3 online.

later made comments to me which indicated she had been mulling the material over in her mind in the intervening period. Her comments lacked an attitude of threat and instead assumed a curiosity rather like my own in the range of variation present in the songs.

The years of our working together and the strength of Kargi's personality, along with the familiarity of the setting, minimized the foreignness of my means of obtaining the kind of folk literary criticism I had hoped to. Nevertheless, the reader should keep in mind that the whole agenda was of my making and that Kargi was being paid for the three days of our conversations. This dialogue between scholar and singer is at least one step removed from true and spontaneous folk literary criticism, which, I suspect, would not be in a form readily useable for Western academic interests in any case.

Kargi

Kargi was of the Mundala caste, traditionally regarded by others as »lowly« (*dikkenakalu, hārijana*). Even in 1968 when I first worked in the villages around Hiriyadka members of this caste lived in the cattle sheds of agriculturalists in a relationship that was indentured. For a monetary advance they contracted their entire labor for a period of time. Because they were unable to freely work in the labor market for that period of time, at the end of it they were no better off than when they started and were forced by circumstance to borrow again and extend their indenture indefinitely. Locally, the Mundaldakalu were called Bākaderu, a term which refers to their form of servitude. Indenture of this kind is illegal and in coastal Karnataka is now more strictly enforced, but I still encounter it in my work in the rural areas of other parts of Karnataka and Andhra Pradesh.

As indentured servants, the Mundaldakalu spent their lives on the farms of their masters, at their beck and call most of the day and night. The form of paddy cultivation practiced in Tulunad is labor intensive, especially for women, and especially intensive during transplanting season shortly after the onset of the monsoons. Land is measured in the number of women required to plant it. Having indentured servants relieved the women of a family from this work and at the same time ensured that a minimum amount of labor was available. The indentured duties of Mundalda men similarly substituted for the labor that men in a family would otherwise do. In return, they were given housing with the animals, which they fed, cleaned up after, cared for and guarded. In many ways, though, they were regarded as junior members of the family: they were fed and clothed, given an allowance for petty spending (coffee, tea, alcohol and snacks) and free time after all work was over to go to town (Hiriyadka) and carry out their own caste and family duties.

The Mundalda women worked in the fields along with women of the family and wage-laboring women of other castes. Mundalda men did the work of other men, often along side the men of the family, and they were often consulted for their expertise, but never given decision-making powers. In many ways their cultural knowledge was little different from other Tuluvas, except in matters which proportionately served to distinguish the land-owner and his family. By relieving the land-owner from performing their own labor the very presence of the Bākaderu afforded the land-owner the opportunity to take up more modern pursuits. Thus, for example, while the women of land-owning families usually did not know fieldsong *pāḍdanas*, women of the Bākaderu caste often excelled in them.

In 1975–76 when I began working with Kargi and the Mundalda community in Hiriyadka they had recently been given land by the government to build their own houses on the hillside. A dozen or so houses had already come up. Kargi, though, had inherited a house and a small plot of land leased to her uncle (mother's brother) by a landlord. In the uncle's time a portion of the land had been converted to rain-fed paddy field, yielding a dozen mudi of rice in good years. This and the small vegetable garden and a few coconut and arecanut palms were not enough to feed the family, but when the land reform act of the early 1970s gave rental properties to the tenants, they became landowners, one of the very few members of their caste in the region to have done so. Their status was different from others in their caste, and perhaps they were overly proud of it. They also lived apart from the growing community of Mundala living on government-given land on the other side and down the road.

Kargi spent her youth in the village, working as a wage laborer. She clearly remembers singing *pāḍdanas* with the women of the village. She claims her aunt (mother's brother's wife) was very knowledgeable in *pāḍdanas* and that she learned particularly from her. She was 11 years old when she married Salya. Her uncle had chosen this boy from another village ten miles away and across the river for her because he needed someone around to help with his property. At some point, probably before she was thirty, she started working in the coffee plantations in the Ghats around Koppa. Working on the plantations was not unlike the practice of indentured servitude practiced in the village. But she maintains that women sang *pāḍdanas* when they worked there, too. And they would sing in the evenings and nights to pass the time. Since women came to the plantations from many different villages and different castes, she got to know a number of different forms and variations she might not have heard had she remained in the village.

In her late 50s when I met her in 1975, Kargi worked along with other women in the fields or on the hillsides gathering »green manure« almost every day. She was well known for her knowledge of *pāḍdanas* and for her singing voice. She was respected by women of other castes but her relationship with members of her own caste was rather more tenuous. Her husband, Salya, who had stayed in the village, was still closely associated with his castemates even though he was not himself a »local boy«. Over the decade and a half I worked with Kargi on *pāḍdanas*, things gradually changed both in their relationships with other households in their caste and within the Mundala caste itself. Some of their »problems« had to do with their relationship with me, but most had to do with particular family matters.[11] The upshot of it was that they became increasingly alienated from other local members of their caste.

The Questions Asked

To review some of the issues raised by this Colloquium and in the literature written over the past decade and a half since 1990, I returned to my earlier interview with Kargi. The questions I asked her at the time had to do with the nature of variation in the *pāḍdanas* I had encountered, whether they were introduced by individual singers or whether they reflected the voice of tradition, how much context (the exigencies of ritual, the nature of the audience), region (spacial distance, societal and communication discontinuities), caste, or stylistic changes, (etc.) which, over time, lead to the specific changes I had noticed in my corpus. I asked her to comment on selections of the recorded versions, on instances where the songs differed from hers or where singers themselves ran into problems due (I supposed) to difference between the singers. I was open to her input even when it differed from my own guesses: indeed, that was the whole point of the exercise. On the whole she responded admirably to what I supposed was for her a new situation. Some of my questions and her responses are presented below to exemplify the different nature of our perspectives at the time.

My first questions to Kargi had to do with the relationships between the Parava versions of a particular *pāḍdana* and the song in her own fieldsong tradition.[12] After we listened to a portion of it on the tape, I began with a question concerned with the direction of transmission. Are there reasons to suppose that the *pāḍdana* might be transmitted in one direction or the other?

11 Their only child, a son, died leaving his wife and child, who continued living with them after his death. The wife took on a lover who did not get along well with Kargi and Salya and the house was plagued with quarrels. The man was a member of their caste, but lived in the now greatly expanded Mundala settlement on the hillside and these quarrels spread there in the usual tangle of local intra-caste politics and factions. At one point, over the matter of pre-inheritance division of the property a fight broke out within the community and the police were called in. By the early 1990s, Kargi and Salya were living alone and socially ostracized by their caste. When Kargi died Salya was left alone and spent most of his time with his Bant neighbor with whom he and Kargi had always a close relationship.

12 The *pāḍdana* is *Pangala Bannare* (also identified as *Baggula Bannare, Māni Bāle, Mayandala, Marlü Jumādi, Kōlata Bāri Jumādi,* etc.) as sung by Darnamma Paravedi (lead singer) and Appi Pujarti at Darnamma's house on October 26, 1990. The tape is available at the Regional Resource Centre for Folk Performing Arts, Udupi. A short extract of the singing is included online with this article [see AUDIO]. For a photograph of Appi Paravedi in the context of a *kōla* see ILLUSTRATION 5.

Question: The Paravas there told me that this *pāḍdana* is not sung in the fields, but she knows it because the Paravas sing it at the Mayindala *kōla.*[13] Why don't the Paravas sing the *Mayindala Pāḍdana* in the fields?

Salya: They won't give it. They won't give it to people of other *jātis*. Just like with the *Kordabbu Sandi*: we men won't give it to women. You shouldn't tell it to them (*panyere balli*). One will have fright (*uggrama*) unless one has experience (*anubāva*) in these matters.

Kargi wants to hear more of the *pāḍdana*. So we listen to another ten or fifteen minutes of the tape. The second singer is clearly having trouble repeating the follow up role, causing both singers to stumble at times. I ask Kargi what she is thinking.

Kargi: They don't sing it like that here. Here they begin with Pangala Bannara's matters. In the fields and others, too. The Paravas sing it at the *garoi*, but I don't go there so I don't know how they sing it. This is not the kind to sing in the fields.

Question: It doesn't fit the work?

Kargi: That's right. This is the way the Paravas sing while doing a *kōla*. How is that? Like this. You play a *tembere*. They, the man, sings in front, the woman follows.

Question: So that is why Appi Pujarti is having difficulty?

Kargi: That's right, Appi is singing like a field song.

After many more questions I suggested (my hypothesis, based on my analysis of the variance) that maybe singing in the fields is where this *pāḍdana* originated. Kargi, however, sees the origin of the *pāḍdana* emerging directly from the sacred event taking place at a specific location, the manor house of Pangala Bannara. The *garodi* she refers to is a shrine to Jumādi at that place. What she appears to have in mind is that it originates as a commemorative legend sung of the deity at the shrine.[14]

13 Bebi Paravedi, a Parava women whose house is not far from Darnamma's, had told me that only the Paravas in that region sang the *Mayindala Pāḍdan*a and that they did not sing it in the fields. The reason she gave me that they didn't sing it in the fields was that it was sacred, »pertaining to the spirits« (*deyyagati*, *būtadati*) and so, »we won't give it to others in the paddy fields (seed beds)«. We collected her version of the *Mayindala Pāḍdana*, which included a much more elaborate version of the Prologue and confirmed for me that this was the *Rajapujari Pāḍdana*.

14 Kargi has not been to that shrine, however, and is not certain where it might be, although I remember in the past I had discussed with her my visit to one of the manor houses in the village of Pangala, 6 miles south of Udupi, and told her of a shrine I saw there which

In another exchange of observed differences, Kargi again remarks about singing styles and incompatibility that can arise from this. But her main criticism is toward younger singers who don't learn properly from their elders.

Kargi: Older people should lead if they know the *pāḍdana*. But if they don't know the song, [The name of a a younger person] can sing.

Question: Does it make you feel bad to sing support? There is no question of one greater than the other, one higher, the other lower?

Kargi: No, not like that. I wouldn't feel bad (*bejar*). But those who know the songs will lead.

Question: What if you have two people who are equally good singers (*sari kaṭṭü gottunḍü*). Is there a question of who leads?

Kargi: No. They may speak about it, but they don't question it. »I'll sing first, otherwise you sing and I'll follow«, they'll say. And, see, if I'm not there, another will lead. [In the sense that for a given *pāḍdana*, if Kargi knows it better than others, she will sing it, but if she is not there, then some one else who knows it can sing it.]

Question: There is no competition to see who is better?

Kargi: Yes there are such people.

Question: What do they do?

Kargi: Let's say I'm singing the lead. They will drop a line (*aksara*) and go ahead a bit. They don't say [that they want to go ahead], but seeing this, I'll say, [using a tone of sarcastic annoyance]: »Ok, you sing ahead (*īya dumbu panla*), I'll follow (*yān piravu panpe*).« [After a pause Kargi continues with an example:] Like last year, singing with Payyu, [referring to a recording session the previous year when she had gotten annoyed with her friend Payyu, a younger woman of the Mundala caste, for not following properly. At the time, she scolded Payyu with sarcasm similar to the statement above] she several times would go ahead.

Question: [Remembering the situation I asked] She went ahead in the story or added some words? Gave extra information?

contained the images of Jumādi and Mani Bale. This may not in fact be the original shrine, though. There are other shrines to Mayindala in that region and some of them stand alone, not a part of the *garodi* complex, and it is a Pambada who performs the *kōla*. Interestingly, Kargi made at least one other reference to this fact: when I asked for comment about the name Kantu, the person who performs the *kōla* in the song and whose caste is given as Parava. Salya thinks they simply made a mistake, but Kargi cuts him off, saying that the singers are associated with the *garodi* where Paravas do the *kōla*. But in the song, the shrine is at Pangala Bannara's *chavadi*. Pambadas do the *kōla*.

Kargi: She was giving extra words (*jāsti kortini*). What I would sing, she would sing more and I'd get confused (*yāne pannaḍa, ālü raḍḍü panu uppunu, enkü kaṭṭunu*). If the follow singer sings a bit (*aksara*) from ahead, when going forward, I get lost (*eṅkü kaṭṭunu*).

Kargi's example probably speaks more to the lack of respect she felt was due to her from Payyu than to a competition of skill. She regards Payyu as her »protegee«, someone to whom she is rather self-consciously teaching *pāḍdanas.* I think Kargi felt Payyu being impatient and uppity in not singing the support line exactly as it has been sung by herself. Earlier in that session, I remember, Kargi had ridiculed Payyu for not using the correct meter (*dai*), which also caused Kargi to trip over the lines and make mistakes. Kargi was probably also conscious of one of her songs being documented and preserved by the recording and did not like the discordance in the way the song was coming out.

In another example, I question whether variation comes through continuous expansion and contraction of the *pāḍdanas* while singing in different contexts and different size tasks.

Question: What portion would you leave out if the field were a short one?

Kargi: If it were small? You would sing a short one from the beginning! [laughs] But, if I had to make it short I would stop wherever we were.

Singers do both of these things, I know. Kargi then gave the example of a field in which it is mandatory that a certain *pāḍdana* (the *Manjetti Gone Pāḍdana*) be sung. The *pāḍdana* is a long one, however, and other women working in the field may not want to sing, preferring to talk and gossip instead. Nevertheless, a small portion must be sung and once that portion is over, they simply stop singing.

I, on the other hand, give examples where the singer might be apt to lengthen or shorten the *pāḍdana* by adding or leaving out a few lines of description. Kargi insists though, that that sort of shortening is useless. »What's the point if you don't sing it correctly? If something is left out, it's not like it is left out on purpose, it is just what happens when you sing. You don't leave out anything [...] that would be useless.« She and Salya agree that those who are listening would not be able to piece together the events of the story if things were left out.

To exemplify her point, Kargi tells a long story derived from a *pāḍdana* about the beginning of the world as we know it in which Narayana Devaru first gave the names of many plants, animals, fish, etc. Each is described in a particular context and having a particular use, from which the name is derived. The piece is a rich example of what a folklorist would call »folk etymological exegesis« and is indeed an item deserving preservation, but for Kargi, it is more than just that. The whole piece consists of the very sort of ›optional‹ description I had been suggesting could be left out if one wanted to shorten the *pāḍdana*. »What of interest would be left?«, she seems to be saying.

Kargi: Singing *pāḍdanas* is the same as anything else: if you don't do it completely it isn't right. You see, we have these *pāḍdanas*, right? They have come down to us just as they were. If people had cut them and shortened them, would we have them now? It is the same with us. If we don't sing them properly the younger generation won't learn properly. That's why they should be taped [speaking of the work she and I have been doing over the years, and perhaps chiding me for not recording all of the ones she has wanted me to record].

While there was no variability in the versions of the *Mayindala Pāḍdana* in the fieldsong tradition which Kargi found unacceptable – would not follow as a support singer – there were versions of the *Parndērü Pāḍdana* which she found completely unacceptable. These were rather complex matters and ones which I have puzzled over during my collection and analysis. (See the APPENDIX at the end of my paper for a synopsis of the complete narrative and an analysis of two versions.) Kargi, too, was puzzled and had difficulty making sense of the versions. At first she viewed the differences as problems in story construction. She acknowledges that there is the possibility that motifs within an episode might get jumbled or that motifs might be included from a different *pāḍdana* which would have repercussions for the further development of the story (or episodic) line. None of the versions of the *Mayindala Pāḍdana* had instances of these kinds of variation. But in the *Parndērü Pāḍdana* the differences go deeper than this (see APPENDIX). The versions I have collected could be separated into two distinct forms.[15] The greatest difference exists between those most widely separated geographically. Those, it might well be argued, are different *pāḍdanas* which happen only to share a resemblance in the names of the heroes and heroines.

Kargi said she had not heard any version of this *pāḍdana* in which Parndēdi had only one child. This prompted me to ask her the hypothetical question: »If you were singing with another woman, with the other person leading the song, and that person sang a version in which Parndēdi had only one daughter, would you also sing it that way?«

Kargi: That I couldn't sing. I would have to say, ›it's not like that. In our place we sing it this way‹. I would *have* to say that. [laughs] There is no other way to sing it. I would challenge [the person] on that: there were two children. Even if the lead singer sang it that way, there is no way I would say there was only one child. When they sang it that way I'd say: ›You said there was only one child born? It wasn't one child; Parndēdi bore two children.‹

Question: Could it be this is a different *pāḍdana*?

15 Or three partially overlapping versions.

Kargi: No it's just that they learned it that way. A different story? I have just never heard where she had just one child.

As we listen to more southern versions of this *pāḍdana* more confusion creeps in as the names change further: Parndērü becomes Mālāra Baḷḷāl and his wife is called Kāpura. Kargi attributes some of these differences to differences in regional language, but laughs nervously, becomes increasingly scornful, and begins to doubt whether this is indeed the same *pāḍdana*. It is only the persistence of the name Karnige which continues to link the versions, but that is enough for her to regard them as versions of the same *pāḍdana*. She increasingly sees the southern versions as being filled with mistakes and speaks of these derisively. She describes the incident at the garden – found in the southern version, but not in hers – as »a big surprise«, not found in any version she had ever heard before. When she hears that Parndērü beats his niece, her tone became serious: »She's his niece, isn't she? He won't touch her. An uncle won't touch his niece.« She refuses to accept that it is Jumādi who causes the rice to be contaminated and tells, in her version, how all of this happened. There is, in their version, in her words, »no sense to it«. She can understand the story, but can't interpret it. It offends her that Parnderu eats his niece's flesh. »In no *pāḍdana* does an uncle eat the flesh of a niece. That never comes. It doesn't look very nice. This is not the way to sing the *pāḍdana*. In some places they add things. This is sinful (*pāpa*). This is the *Parnderu Pāḍdana*, but Jumādi putting the flesh for him to eat? I haven't heard this. I have never heard this in any place. I can't even guess how this came to be. It is possible that there are changes in names and other things, but Jumādi bringing the flesh and giving it to the uncle can't happen. That's impossible. It's hard to even listen to this. I shiver.«

Academic Questions and Singers' Voices

What I gained from this conversation was:
(a) Confirmation of some of my hypotheses.
(b) Insights into the importance of operational attitudes which govern change and variance.
(c) Ideas from a singer about the nature of the genre itself.

These gains all stem from the different perspectives Kargi and I had in relation to the *pāḍdanas*. We both moved closer to a common perspective. And as we did, I worried that my role would become superfluous. She was at the helm of the tradition, I was just an observer, a reporter.

But what has happened in the meantime is that the conversations in the fields has changed to an extent that perhaps both Kargi and my perspectives are rendered history. *Pāḍdana* singing has almost disappeared.

Kargi (and her voice) was a traditional and a conservative one. She insisted on a *guru-siśya* relationship toward the younger generation. She held the *pāḍdana* tradition as sacred, morally based, a documentary historical oral textual tradition. Although certain styles and portions of certain *pāḍdana* are ›owned‹ by certain castes or characteristic of certain regions, the *pāḍdana* stories themselves are the shared understanding of the Tuluva people. She acknowledged – but rather fatalistically – that change happens: this is Kali Yuga. In fact, she viewed change rather like we do.

She and most of the other singers in my collection are particularly critical of young people and their attitude toward the *pāḍdana* and what they stand for: the immanent loss of the tradition. Maybe it has always been that way. But some popularly held oral traditions have disappeared. There had been a lively and interesting song tradition which people of a household sang while pounding off the husk of the parboiled and dried paddy, ready for storage in mudis. When the husking machines in small, local rice mills became ubiquitous in the villages and cheaper than doing the labor-intensive work at home the song tradition disappeared along with the paraphenalia and location in the house where husking was done. Perhaps because this tradition was decidedly secular and mildly (at least at the literal level) risque I have never heard anyone lament its loss to the culture or to folkloristic collection.

I have encountered in other parts of Karnataka and Andhra Pradesh other marvelous and even sacred historical narrative traditions which have disappeared in recent memory. The Piccakoṇḍḷu (or Hēḷava) narrative performances, along with their intricately painted scrolls and extensive genealogical records have now largely disappeared. In this case, they were maintained by one caste (the Piccakoṇḍḷu) for another, higher caste, who regarded the Piccadoṇḍḷu as lowly probably precisely for the service they performed. Even attempting to collect and archivally preserve the historically valuable information contained in the tradition is resented, particularly by the young people of the caste who do not wish to live with the burden of evidence that their ancestors' were held in low esteem. The traditions once again gain value only when art dealers come to the villages to purchase the scrolls for sale in the antique art market, a context where they are often misidentified and misrepresented and utterly lacking in knowledge of the past performance tradition for which they were brought into existence. But as one Piccakoṇḍḷu put it: »Our fathers sold the scrolls and gave us pigs«, meaning that with the money they got they bought food, but, given their mentality, the food they bought, pigs, when eaten, served only to perpetuate their lowly status. »Nothing gained, everything (tradition?) lost.«

In the paddy fields older singers complain that brash young women tell them to »stop that mournful singing«. They interrupt the *pāḍdana* singing with loud conversation about Hindi films and sing instead the latest Hindi and Kannada cinema songs. The *kabitas* continue to be sung because they are more lively, more playful. They often speak to unfairness, class issues, gender issues, complaints about work, in particular the work of young women such as themselves. Although I have not collected an adequate corpus of these songs, it seems to me they are more capable of creative expansion, the addition of impromptu verses speaking to very contemporary themes, if not identifying particular individuals. In other words, they are much closer to the kinds of women's songs collected by RAHEJA and GOLD in their now well-known study, *Listen to the Heron's Words* (1994) and heard in the film *Dadi's Family.*

What is needed, perhaps, is a new Tulu fieldsong study, one which has to be recorded in the fields themselves. It is there that the significant conversation (discourse) is taking place. There was justification in moving the *pāḍdana* singing to the courtyard of the singers' house because *pāḍdana* singing was traditional and sacred, a ›serious‹ tradition. But it was conservative and represented a form of conservative cultural tradition. Whether they represented agreement and compliance within the community overall is a matter of speculation, but to the extent that Kargi was representative of her gender and ›low caste‹ perspective, it was a perspective shared broadly by the community. The community today is more fragmented, more divided on moral issues and political ideologies, and beset by the influence of a number of new technologies.

Folklorists have recently turned their attention to folklore as discourse. In a recent conference of Indian folklorists held in Chennai (organized by the National Folklore Support Centre and sponsored the Central Institute of Indian Language and Indira Gandhi National Centre for the Arts) papers were addressed to the ways performance traditions of many sorts could usefully be seen as the voice of the people. Most of the papers seen to be significant were those which focused on the contestations between the people (although it was often unclear who »the people« were) and the government. Listening to these papers, it occurred to me that traditional folklore genres are less representative than the silence and the disruption one actually experiences in the world. The voices of the young women disrupting *pāḍdana* singing of their elders, or replacing it with film songs are loud and clear. Folklorists may not like it themselves, but the world is rapidly changing in ways they have yet to address. Not one of the papers spoke of the spread and influence of the global political economy and culture; not one pointed out the displacement of local tradition by pan-Indian, urban middle class ›classical‹ ones, or the influence of the Indian TV and cinema industries on local tradition; not one of the papers reflectively discussed the hegemonic influence of the academia itself as arbitrators of tradition. While I am certainly an advocate of studying folklore as discourse, it seems to me that such selectivity will narrow our contribution to meaninglessness. To study folklore as discourse, one needs first to place oneself in the midst of a broad range of societal conversations, and that, it seems, we are either unable or unwilling to do.

Appendix

I have collected eight versions of the *Parndērü Pāḍdana* from various regions of Tulunad. Some of the versions are identified as the *Karnaga Pāḍdana* and consist of what may be regarded as a short form, covering only the death of Parndērü's niece, Kannyage, or, as she is called in some of these versions, Karnaga. All of these versions as well as all of the other five *pāḍdanas* which I collected during my 1986–89 research project are available on tape and digital disk from the Regional Resource Centre for Folk Performing Arts in Udupi.

The version presented below in prose narrative summary was collected from Kargi Mundaldi of Anjar village near Hiriyadka in 1975. S.A.Krishnaiah collected her version again in 1986 and found it to be very similar to this earlier recitation.

There is a published version of a *pāḍdana* which begins with the same line (*mitt-onji Mallar-guttu, tirt-onji Mallar-guttu*) and concerns characters named Parndērü and Karnaga translated into Kannada by K. Vadiraja Bhatta (1974: 156–61) in brief prose form, under the title Jumādi. Heidrun Brückner has collected four additional versions from two Pambada men, a Pambada woman and a Parava woman (personal communication). All of these are of the short, Karnaga type.

I have described the kinship relations and discussed their social and moral implications in an earlier paper, entitled *Kinsongs* (Claus 1991). There, I compare the narrative consequences of kinship relations in three *Tulu Pāḍdanas*. The synopsis of the story which follows comes from that publication (pages 151–156).

The Story of Parndērü

Parndērü and his sister, Bāre Parndēdi, lived at Mallara Guttu.[16] Their father had died and their mother died giving birth to Parndēdi. Parndērü, himself, raised his younger sister with great care and affection.

Mattara Mayinda Heggade lived at Mattara Guttu. He was thinking: »My mother's brother's (*tammale*) children are at Mallara Guttu. I should make a marriage alliance (*poddu barpene yanü*) with that place.« So he sets off from Mattara Guttu to speak to Parndērü.

»You are the children of my mother's brother. Uncle has died and Auntie has passed away. What will you do with that motherless child? I am having to cook myself and eat alone in my manor. Your sister is my rightful bride (*maitidi*). By birth she is the daughter of my mother's brother: by right, one I might marry.

16 A *guttu* is a Bant manor house.

You must give her to me in marriage (*dharma dare*). You have to have her sent to Mattara Guttu to do the cooking there.«

Thus they were married and Heggade brought her home to Mattara Guttu. One day he told her he was going out to adjust the water in the fields. Meanwhile, Bāre Parndēdi prepares to cook. She cleans the house and bathes. The hearth fire had gone out, so she took a coconut shell and fibre and went to the neighbor's to get coals for starting the fire.

The neighbor women see her coming at a distance, and she calls to them. But Bāre Parndēdi was not the mother of a child, yet. She had not attained maturity (*madümal ayinijji*), not yet begun her menstrual cycles. It was now a year and she hadn't given birth. The neighbor women insulted her. »Hide your children! Close the door!«, they said.

Hearing this, Bāre Parndēdi threw away the coconut shell and fiber which she was carrying and came back to Mattara Guttu. She entered the bedroom, put down a mat, and lay face down on it.

When Heggade returns from his work he looked for her. When he finally finds her hiding in a dark room, he asks her what the trouble is. She tells him that the neighbor women insulted her by calling her a barren woman.

Mattara Mayinda Heggade thought about this. »Fix your hair and put on a sari«, he says. »Let us go to Mallara Guttu.« There, Parndērü says they must go to their *mulastana* and make an offering.[17] So the three of them go and make the required offering and return. Parndēdi takes holy water of the family deity, Jumādi, from the tank at Mallara Guttu. As she climbs the stairs of the tank, when she reaches the 16th step, she attains maturity (*madümal atalü*). Then she went to the courtyard of Mallara Guttu and wrapped her arms around the pillar of the pavilion (*dampada kamba*) and bowed her head.

When her brother, Parndērü, invites her in to eat she tells him that she is menstruating. So Parndērü's wife, Duwu, brings out food: rice leftover three days, a water mango which a widow had touched and a chili pepper in which two stones had been put (all very defiling and inauspicious – Duwu is attempting to bring ruin on Parndēdi's descendants).

But Parndēdi doesn't touch her food. Her brother comes and asks: »Why are you just sitting and staring? Eat!«

»I'm not hungry«, she replies. »I have a terrible pain in my stomach. Take the food and put it in the trough for the buffalo. Husband, get up! Let us go to Mattara Guttu.« Heggade takes leave of his brother-in-law and they return home.

They are coming back to Mattara Guttu. On the 30th day of the month Parndēdi has her period and goes to the river to bathe. That month she became pregnant. On the sixth month she tells her husband her stomach is heavy with

17 »Place of origin«, meaning a temple (or its tank or a sacred grove there) at the place where the family originated. This place and the deities there are felt to be the source of generation and continued regeneration.

child. On the eighth month Heggade tells her he will perform the pregnancy ceremony (*bayake*) and that she must then return to Mallara Guttu.

Parndēdi says: »I won't go to Mallara Guttu. Even if I died, I would stay at Mattara Guttu.« Heggade performs the *bayake* ceremony, buying Parndēdi a silk sari and a gold chain. The neighboring women are called to serve Parndēdi special foods and to bless her with offerings.

On the ninth day of the tenth month, on the ninth minute of the ninth hour, she calls out to her husband that she is in labor. The midwife comes. From her one stomach she bore two children. As the babies are born, Parndēdi died.

Heggade weeps and mourns her death. He sends a letter to inform Mallara Guttu. Duwu receives the letter. She tears it up and throws it away. When the messenger returns back to Mattara Guttu Heggade wonders why there is no reply to the letter he sent. He sends another letter, but again Duwu gets it and tears it up. At the time, Parndērü was out adjusting the water level in the paddy fields. When he returns he sees a bit of the torn up letter. He is able to read a few words of it and learns of the news. He cries out in grief and races to Mattara Guttu. »*Ayyo* brother-in-law! What's news? What's the story? You have to cut the babies' umbilical cords and clean them up. You have to give them names. If they are to come and live at Mallara Guttu the first born has responsibility for watching after matters inside the house and should be called Kannyage. The second born will have responsibility for matters outside and should be called Kāpora.«[18] Parndērü had a funeral pyre and Parndēdi was cremated.

Heggade then tells Parndērü: »I will not give the children, I will raise them and care for them.« Parndērü then said that he would return when the children were grown.

The children matured quickly. When they were seven years old Heggade called his brother-in-law. »I have raised and cared for the children whose mother died. These are the descendants of your shrine (or ›germinating seed‹, ›sprout‹, *ādikoi*). For the past seven years I have raised them in Mattara Guttu. Take them to Mallara Guttu, brother-in-law. Go and be in peace.« But Parndērü tells him: »You should bring the children to Mallara Guttu.« When they reach Mallara Guttu Parndērü calls out to Duwu: »I have returned and brought along our nieces.« Duwu does not get up and look. Parndērü asks his brother-in-law to sit down. »Let us eat what ever there is ready.« He gives him a glass of water. »I don't want it«, replies Heggade, »I will be going now«. At this Parndērü takes offense and insists that he sit and stay. Heggade stays for the meal. Duwu brings and serves the food she has prepared. Heggade and Parndērü ate, and when they were finished they chewed betel. Heggade again says he will be going, and tells Parndērü to watch after the children carefully. Before he leaves Heggade

18 I have not encountered this custom of assigning responsibilities and corresponding names to children by the order of birth in other *pāḍdanas*. Nor do I understand the relationship between the names and the responsibilities. His concern is clearly for the children, his descendants, not the loss of his sister.

embraces the girls. They cry, but he tells them to stay and he will return, that their uncle, his brother-in-law is there to watch after them. After reassuring them, he leaves.

After some time, there was a gathering of the important people of the region and Heggade had to attend. He called to his wife, Duwu, and told her: »Listen, a messenger has come with a letter for me I have to go to a meeting. You have to prepare food for me immediately.«

But Duwu replies: »Husband, I am old. I can't see. I can't walk. I can't move my arms. There are your nieces. the first born, Kannyage, has responsibility for watching after matters inside the house and the second born, Kāpora, takes responsibility for matters outside. Tell them.«

So Parndērü calls Kannyage and tells her to prepare a meal before his journey. Kannyage chooses the finest rice from the store room and goes to the garden to choose the best vegetables for the curries. When Kannyage went out, Duwu leapt up and got a handful of unhusked paddy and a handful of pebbles and put them in the plate of rice which Kannyage had prepared and set aside. Kannyage returns and cuts up the vegetables and rinses them and brings them to the hearth to cook. When everything is finished she brings the food out and serves her uncle. Parndērü takes up a handful of rice, but all he gets is a handful of paddy. »Kannyage! Come here. What kind of rice is this?«, he asks. »There is unhusked paddy in the rice«, she replies, »so that you may become famous as an arbitrator at the council«.[19]

Parndērü takes up another handful of rice, and he gets hair. »What is this in the rice, Kannyage!«, he asks again. »There is hair (*tare*) in the rice so that you will get a reputation for being a leader with a good head (*tare*)«, she replies.

He takes a third handful of rice and he gets pebbles (*kallü*). Again he asks Kannyage: »What is this in the rice?« This time she replies: »There are stones in the rice, Mamaji, so when you go to the meeting you will be changed to stone (*i.e.* adamant in decisions).«

Hearing this, Parndērü is furious. His anger fills the seven worlds. »Listen, child, may that which was made for me, be the rice for Jumādi, who sits in the shrine of our house.«[20] He left the meal and leapt up, saying: »Give it to Jumādi!« He dressed and went to the council meeting.

Meanwhile, Kannyage calls for her sister, Kāpora, to come and bathe, and together they go off to Mallara tank. Kannyage and Kāpora go down the steps. They let their hair down loose and lower their head into the water. As the girls bend their head the goddess of the house, Jumādi, comes and pushes them into

19 She apparently does not realize the truth of her uncle's claim, and responds to it as if it were a joke, or possibly jokes, herself, to cover her embarrassment. The replies all contain puns.

20 This statement is a curse (*wak*). It is not that he wishes ill toward the household deity, but that he offers this feast prepared for him to the deity. If there is fault in it, let Jumādi take action. See CLAUS 1979.

the tank. Then in the form of a red hawk Jumādi flies to the council meeting. There, in a vision, she tells Parndērü: »I have finished the work you were thinking of.«

In a flash, Parndērü realizes what has happened. »But I didn't mean what I said in anger!«, says Parndērü. »Because of a curse uttered in anger, your lamp, too, will go out.« He races home.

There he calls out to Kannyage and Kāpora. They are not there. He calls to Duwu. He is afraid for Kannyage and Kāpora. Duwu says to him: »Husband, there is a saying, ›When a frog becomes too large it searches for a bigger pond. When a girl becomes proud she won't stay in the house.‹ As soon as you went off to the council meeting they said ›let's go to the Mallara tank and bathe‹.«

So Parndērü went to the tank. There he sees the pair of flower pods of the arecanut palm, dancing and playing on the water of Mallara tank. »Rama! Rama!«, he cries. »The children whose mother died when they were born, the children my brother-in-law raised for seven years and I took in for eight – you took them today, Jumādi? A bud so carefully cared for; can it be so quickly snatched away? Who is to keep your lamp lit from now on?« He takes the silk shawl from his shoulders and goes down to the tank holding it in front of him. »If you children are innocent, you must come ashore, you must come to my silk shawl.« The two corpses, in the form of two arecanut flower pods, dancing and playing on the water, come to the edge of the tank and into his shawl.

He sends a letter to Mattara Guttu. »The children whom you raised with such love and beauty fell into the tank at Mallara guttu and died today.« As Heggade reads it he thinks: »Did you take the life from these innocent children, brother-in-law? The children whose mother died when they were born, the children whom I raised with such care?« He leaves Mattara Guttu and rushes to Mallara tank. »It appears your Jumādi doesn't want a lamp lit. Your family line has ended, the bud removed. What is the use of just standing here looking?«

The two corpses of Kannyage and Kāpora are taken and placed on the pyre and are cremated.

Heggade then says: »I will go to Sāmdērü (*swāmi dēvaru?*) and ask to have my daughters back.« Going to the place of Samderü (*Swāmidēvaru?*), he asks: »Hear me Sāmdērü. Your nieces, two Siris, you must give to me.« Sāmdērü replies that there are two Siris, the highest, in Medima Loka, his nieces and that he will give them for a price. »For each step you must give a fine of one sovereign.« Heggade agrees to give the amount. Thus Sāmdērü created from two Siris of Medima Loka two girls of the lower Siri Loka (the earth), saying to them: »Go to the lower Siri Loka, to the *būḍu* (manor house) of Mayinda Heggade. They will give a fine for each step and a sovereign for each *ajje* (footprint).«[21]

21 This is clearly reference to ritual of some kind. Neither the singer nor I could recall anything exactly like it in existence today. However, the scene bears some resemblance to what goes on at a Siri jatre, where women who are afflicted with various illnesses and unwanted spirit possession become possessed by Siri spirits and are able to air their prob-

So Heggade returns to the cremation grounds along with the two Siris. The Siris gathered the ashes of the pyre into a heap. Then they created water in a vessel. They created a stick of *nāgara darba* (a reference to a Sanskritic ritual item). Then they put the water on the ashes. The two girls, Kannyage and Kāpora rose up and sat. »May you return to live«, said the Siris. Then they touched the *nāgara darba* to the top of their heads and Kannyage and Kāpora stood up. »*Ayyo*«, cried the girls, »where did you come from? Our Aunt removed us. She put paddy and stones and coconut in the rice we made. Then our Uncle got angry, sisters. ›This is not food made for me, but for Jumādi‹, our uncle said. Then our Jumādi took us«, replied Kannyage.

Heggade heard these words. He gave the Siris the price he had agreed: a fine for each step and a sovereign for each *ajje*. Then he brought the girls back to Mallara Guttu where they tell Parndērü the story. Parndērü calls Duwu to come out. He takes her by the neck and pushes her. She falls onto the courtyard floor. »You can go wandering the villages begging. Never enter my house again«, Parndērü tells her.

NORTHERN VERSION	SOUTHERN VERSION
Parndērü and his sister, Parndēdi, are orphaned at a young age. He raises her. She marries Mayinda Heggade. She leaves her matrilineal house to go live at her husband's house.	Parndērü and his sister, Parndēdi, are orphaned at a young age. He raises her and she marries Mayinda Heggade. She leaves her matrilineal house to go live at her husband's house.
After some time she fears she is infertile and they along with Parndēdi's brother, Parndērü, go to their family shrine (*mulastana*) and make an offering to have descendants.	After some time she fears she is infertile and they along with Parndēdi's brother, Parndērü, go to their family shrine (*mulastana*) and make an offering to have descendants.
Returning to Parndērü's house (Parndēdi's own matrilineal house), Parndēdi has her first menstrual period. Parndērü's wife, Duwu, insults her by treating her in disrespectable ways.	Returning to Parndērü's house (Parndēdi's own matrilineal house), Parndēdi has her first menstrual period. Parndērü's wife, Duwu, insults her by treating her in disrespectable ways.

lems so that others may hear. Furthermore, in the some of the myths associated with that cult, there is reference to Siris being granted to devotees as children (descendants) and, after they die a tragic death, return to Medima Loka to take their original forms. The presiding deity in these myths is, however, called Bermerü. See CLAUS 1978.

Northern Version	Southern Version
Parndēdi and Mayinda Heggade return to his (husband's) house, where she conceives, but dies giving birth to *twin girls, whom Parndērü names Karniga and Kapura.*	Parndēdi and Mayinda Heggade return to his (husband's) house, where she conceives, but dies giving birth to *a single baby child, a daughter, whom Parndērü names Karniga.*
The girls are raised at Heggade's house, but later, at maturity, they are brought to Parndērü's house, their matrilineal home.	The girl is raised at Parndērü's house, her matrilineal home.
	Parndērü asks Jumādi to protect his garden against thieves.
Parndērü is called to a meeting of the local chieftains.	Parndērü is called to a meeting of the local chieftains.
Karniga prepares a meal for him.	Karniga prepares a meal for him by *picking vegetables in the garden.* She is confronted by Jumādi (in human form) who warns her not to take the vegetables from this garden. Karniga disregards the warning.
Duwu puts stones and other objects in the food served to Parndērü.	*Jumādi causes stones and other objects to appear in the food* served to Parndērü.
When Parndērü goes to eat, he discovers the objects in his food and becomes angry with Karniga.	When Parndērü goes to eat, he discovers the objects in his food and becomes angry with Karniga.
He curses her in the name of Jumādi.	*He beats her* (in some versions he attempts to rape her), *she escapes by climbing a tree. He follows her. She jumps into a well.*
	Karniga's corpse is cremated.

Northern Version	Southern Version
Parndērü goes off to the meeting of local chiefs.	Parndērü goes off to the meeting of local chiefs.
When the girls go to the tank to bath, Jumādi pushes the girls into the tank and they drown.	
At the meeting Jumādi takes the form of a hawk and shows Parndērü a vision of the girls' death.	Parndērü encounters Jumādi in human form.
Parndērü leaves the meeting fearful of the consequences of Jumādi's powers.	Parndērü is sent away from the meeting.
Parndērü finds the corpses of the girls in the tank and has them cremated. He calls Heggade (the girls' father) to the funeral. Heggade goes to the realm of the god Sāmdēru and asks that the girls be returned. Sāmdēru sends two Siris to earth in their form, giving life to their ashes. The girls accuse Duwu of her misdeeds. Parndērü banishes Duwu.	*Jumādi comes in the form of a hawk and takes a piece of the partly cremated flesh of Karniga and places it in a curry so that Parndērü eats it. Jumādi then takes the form of a hunter and reveals to Parndērü the true cause of his niece's death. Duwu is killed and cremated.*

References

CLAUS, PETER J. 1978. »Heroes and Heroines in the Conceptual Framework of Tulu Culture«. *Journal of Indian Folkloristics* 1, 2: 28–42.

----. 1979. »Mayndala: A Myth and Cult of Tulunad«. *Asian Folklore Studies* 38, 2: 95–129.

----. 1991. »Kinsongs«. In: *Gender, Genre, and Power in South Asian Expressive Traditions.* Ed. by Arjun Appadurai, Frank J. Korom and Margaret Mills. Philadelphia: University of Pennsylvania Press, 136–177.

----. 1995. »A Folk View of Variation in the Tulu Paddana Tradition«. Unpubl. paper presented at the XIth International Society for Folk Narrative Research Conference, Mysore, India.

----. 2001. »Variability in the Tulu Paddanas«. *Cahiers de Littérature Orale* 50: 129–158.

DUNDES, ALAN. 1966. »Metafolklore and Oral Literary criticism«. *The Monist* 60: 505–516.

DWYER, KEVIN. 1982. *Moroccan Dialogues: Anthropology in Question.* Baltimore: Johns Hopkins University Press.
GOODWIN, CHARLES; JOHN HERITAGE. 1990. »Conversation Analysis«. *Annual Review of Anthropology* 19: 283–307.
RAHEJA, GLORIA GOODWIN; ANN GRODZINS GOLD. 1994. *Listen to the Heron's Words: Re-imagining Gender and Kinship in North India.* Berkeley: University of California Press.
VADIRAJA BHATTA, KANARADI. 1974. *Paddanagalu (adhyayanatmaka samgraha).* Kinnigoli: Yugapurusa Prakatanalaya.

MULTIMEDIA

The multimedia files can be accessed online: *http://www.indologie.uni-wuerzburg.de/women_performers/contributors/claus/*

AUDIO FILE:
Paramale Ballal (also known as Jevu Maniga), a *Jumādi Pāḍdana*, in two different styles of singing (field song style and *bhūta kōla* style).
Singers: Appi Pujarti (field song style) and Dhanamma Paravedi (*bhūta kōla* style).
Content: 1. *Paramala / Jevu Maniga Pāḍdana* in a field song style with Appi Purjarti leading. 2. Short break / Krishnaiah and Claus talk with the women. 3. *Jumādi Pāḍdana* in a *bhūta kōla* style with Dharnamma leading.

FILM CLIP: *oṇṭyamma dēvi pāḍḍaṇa*
yānu ōlū gobbūnu appēre yānu ōlu sōrpūnu Ayreāpati dēvigēnā (ī)
mundilēde tippī mucci gobbū māga gobbula andē paṇuvōlu ālu appe kuntyamma dēvigē
Ahā birē ṇērē māṇilu battāḍa yanna gobbu keṭṭavu panuvōlu Ayrapāti dēvigē
bireeṇērē māṇilu battāḍa yanna gobbu keṭṭavu māmi paṇuvōlu ālu Ayrapati dēvigēnā
bireeṇēre māṇilu battāḍa yanna gobbu keṭṭavu māmi paṇuvōlu ālu Ayrapati dēvigēnā
yānu ōlu gobbūnu apperē yānu ōlu sōrpūnu appēre paṇuvōlu Ayrpāti (ī)
kudurēda nindiligē tulasikaṭṭē mande madya dārigu tippi mucci gobbula paṇuvēru rappe kontyamma dēvigēana
Kudurēdā manṭapōḍu tippi mucci gobbu māga paṇuvērā lapperāru appe kuntyamma dēvigēanā
birēeṇērē māṇilu battāḍa yanna gobbu seṭṭavu apperē enna tippī ella bandu paṇuvōlu dēviālu Ayrapati dēvigēnā
birēeṇērē māṇilu battāḍa yanna gobbū seṭṭāvu apperē enna tippī chellāḍu Ayrapati dēvigēna
yānu ōlu gobbūnu apperē yānu ōlu sōrpūnu anvōlu Ayreapatī dēvigē (ī)
yānu ōlu gobbūnu appērē yānu ōlu sōrpūnu anvōlu Ayreapatī dēvigēnā (ī)
Kudurekaṭṭō lāyōḍānda tippī mucci gobbulā paṇuvēru appe kuntyamma dēvigē
Kudurekaṭṭā lāyōḍānḍa tippi mucci gobbulā maga appe kuntyamma dēvigē
Kuduredā mag(v)utē appēre enna gobbu seṭṭave appēre enna tippī chelladuve panuvōlu Ayrapati dēvigēnā
Kudurēdā mag(v)utē patyaḍā enna tippi cellāḍu appēre
ennā gobbū seṭṭave enuvōḷu Ayrapati dēvigēnā
yānu ōlū gobbūnu appēre yānu ōlu sōrpūnu envōlu Ayreāpati dēvigēnā
yānu ōlū gobbūnu appēre yānu ōlu ...

PHOTOGRAPHIES

The photographs for this article were taken by S.A. Krishnaiah, Senior Folklorist, Regional Resource Centre for Folk Performing Arts, Udupi and reproduced here with his permission. Krishnaiah and I often worked together on fieldwork projects. Not only are the photographs his, much of the collected knowledge and information was gathered by he and I together in such a way that it would be impossible to credit one or another of us as the collector.

ILLUSTRATION 1: Kargi Mundaldi
Kargi received a State Government, Karnataka Janapada and Yakshagana Academy award, 1989, the first such award given for the singing of *pāḍdanas*. The award is regarded as the most prestigious achievement award for folk performers in the state. She also received awards from Tulu honorary and academic academies. Kargi passed away on April 25th, 1994, a full moon night, and the night of the Siri Jatra at Hiriyadka, where she had Siri »darśana« (possession by a siri spirit) all her life. Local Tulu and Kannada newspapers carried articles about her death under the headline, »The Queen of Pāḍdana Singers Is No More«.

ILLUSTRATION 2:
Kargi and Payyu. Although not taken during a recording session, this is a familiar setting to the author as he had recorded hundreds of hours of *pāḍdanas*, stories, and conversations about Tulu oral literature and religious practice. Often the recordings took place in the courtyard of Kargi and Salya's house at the edge of Anjar village and lasted far into the night. At other times we recorded on the veranda of my house.

ILLUSTRATION 3:
Kargi, Salya, and their daughter-in-law and grandson receive blessings from their caste and household deity, Kordabbu. All through Tulunad, Kordabbu is the hero and patron of the Mundala community. Salya was a patri of Kordabbu and performed daily *pūja* at the Anjar village Kordabbu shrine near Hiriyadka. Besides being a devotee of Siri, Kargi herself was deeply devoted to Kordabbu.

Pāḍdanas in the Bhūta Kōla Context:
ILLUSTRATION 4:
Domba Nalike and Duje are from Arava Village, Ninibaakilu House, Aladangadi, Beltangady Taluk, Karnataka. At the time, Domba was about 35 years old and his wife around 30. They are of the Nalike community. The Kalkuda *kōla* is performed during the Siri Jātra, as are the *kōlas* of Kshemakalla Panjurli and Maysandaya (see below), but by different communities of performers. Although today the activities of the Siri Jātra dominate, it is likely that earlier (say before 1950) the several *kōlas* had been the main, if not the only, ritual performances.

Illustration 5:
This is Appi Paravedi singing a *pāḍdana* during a *kōla* at the Urmbitota Siri Jātra (see photo above) Whether it is the Kshemakalla Panjurli or Maysandaya is unclear in the photo. In either case, she later told me that her younger male relative who performed the dance during the *kōla* was not very familiar with the pāḍdana and would not have been able to sing it alone.

ILLUSTRATION 6:
Kordabbu sings his own song to the villagers during the *kōla* in a form called »*madu panpini*«. This form is sung in the first person, and the bhūta describes the greatness of his deeds and the recognition of his powers.

Pāḍdanas in Other Contexts:
ILLUSTRATION 7:
Kōṭi and Chennaya are remembered by their song during the preliminary preparations of a wedding ceremony among the families of the Billava community. Here, the author and S.A. Krishnaiah had come to the village of Nandolige to record *pāḍdanas* as sung by Sitakka Pujarti and Paddakka Pujarti. They were then invited to attend this ceremony during which men and women of the Billava community adorn their hands with henna (*mehendi*) designs. Women of the community sing the portion of the long *Kōṭi Chennaya Pāḍdana* where the twin heroes receive their first haircut, a sort of initiation / puberty ritual, removing the taint of birth and childhood to become »radiant«. Being good singers, Sitakka and Paddakka took turns leading the singing during this activity is amongst the women.

ILLUSTRATION 8:
Here Sitakka and Paddakka relax and we talk about *pāḍdanas* after singing. This session was probably in the courtyard of Sundaram Shedty, a landlord of Nandalige village whose family and properties are mentioned in most versions of the *Siri Pāḍdana*.

ILLUSTRATION 9:
Here, the author is talking with Kargi Pujarti of Urikitota after recording her singing the *Siri Pāḍdana*. Kargi Pujarti becomes possessed by Siri during the annual Siri Jātra at Urikitotta. Her daughter (front row, left), also named Kargi, has now taken her place at the Siri Jātra. The *Siri Pāḍdana* is one of Tulunad's longest and most famous *pāḍdanas*, but it is not sung during a *kōla*, nor even sung in its entirety as a fieldsong. It is primarily transmitted by women, but some men – especially those who serve as Kurmar during the Siri Jātra – also know the *pāḍdana*. However, only very small portions of it are sung by Siri women and male Kumars during a Siri Jātra. At the Urikitota annual Siri Jātra only two women and a Kumar become possessed regularly. Urikitotta is said by some to be where Siri's granddaughters, Abbaga and Daraga, drowned in the well, as described in the *Siri Pāḍdana*.

Divine Words, Human Voices

Listening to the Female Voice in Performances of Possession

Elisabeth Schömbucher

> I am convinced that India will be a very different country five years from now: an average Indian will be more than twice as rich and will probably live in the fastest growing economy in the world. [...] Racy, fast and unstoppable: that is how change is taking place in India. Redefining standards, aspirations, values and visions is the very spirit of one of the world's most ancient civilisations. (GHOSH 2005: 125)

Different forms of possession have been widely observed and described by anthropologists for many decades. Anthropological literature covers various interpretations of spirit possession as a form of mental illness or psychic stress, and spirit mediumship as a form of folk religion or medical therapy on the village level.[1] In the years 1992 and 1993, I carried out field research on possession mediumship among the Vāḍabalija, a Telugu speaking South Indian fishing caste. In the course of a previous stay in the years 1979–81, I came across regular séances of possession during which various goddesses spoke through their female media to the village people. To find out what exactly the goddess says and how she says it, I taped, transcribed, and translated various possession séances of four media. What made the words divine words? What made them effective? What did the listeners hear? These were among the questions I wanted to answer. Time passed over this research and when everything was about to be published, other questions came up. Will recent developments make possession obsolete? Will possession as a mode of communication with deities vanish? Will it be perceived more and more as a superstitious, rural, backward cultural practice, the way some high-caste urban Indians have described it to me occasionally during my fieldwork? Will secularisation go along with economic development and global influence? Is it one of the things that get ›redefined‹, as Ghosh predicts?

When I visited the Vāḍabalija again in 2003/04, modernity had reached the fishing village. Quite a few things had changed. A new lane through the village had been constructed with electricity for the houses adjacent to it. Motor boats

1 See for example CLAUS 1984, KAKAR 1981, KAPFERER 1991, LEWIS 1989, OBEYESEKERE 1981, STANLEY 1988. For a detailed account of the anthropological literature on possession see SCHÖMBUCHER 1993 and 2006.

had replaced sail boats. I was eager to find out about the changes in possession mediumship. One medium had died, another had moved to another place. The two remaining media still became possessed by their respective deities. I was invited to attend several possession séances. The audience consisted of men and women, as had been the case ten years ago. One medium had developed a more ironic style. In her divine speech, there had been various ironic or even cynical fits of laughter which I had not heard before. The men who had gathered in front of the deity were wearing wristwatches, sun glasses and sparkling white shirts. Everybody listened as concentratedly as ten years ago and everybody was engaged in a dialogue with the deities as intensely as before. When I asked: »What did you ask the goddess and what did she say?«, the answer was just as laconic as ten years ago: »We have no fish. The goddess said: ›You have neglected me. Therefore you do not catch any fish. You have to worship me. Then I will look after you.‹« This led to other questions: What is it that makes divine words so indispensable? Why do the fishermen still listen to the divine words spoken by a possessed medium? Why is modernity not characterized by secularization?

Nūkālamma – goddess of all castes

To answer these questions I will present the case of a high caste woman who went »to the feet of the goddess« speaking through a low caste medium. G.P. Lakshmi, a fifty-year-old Brahmin woman, wanted to know if she could also ask the goddess after having heard that I was interested in possession and therefore visited several media.[2] When we asked Bhūlēkamma, medium of the goddess Nūkālamma, whether G.P. Lakshmi could attend a séance, she not only agreed immediately but added that, since Nūkālamma is such a powerful goddess, she would not only speak to the Vāḍabalija, but to people of all the different castes. G.P. Lakshmi and Bhūlēkamma, who had not met before, had a short conversation in my presence. The medium did not know the client's background as she did for Vāḍabalija clients who came to listen to the goddess. The medium could not refer to well-known events in the client's past which would then be interpreted and reinterpreted in the dialogue between medium and client. Her statements could only be based on the hints she got from the very short conversation with this unknown clients in the morning. After speaking to another client and a break of about 25 seconds, the goddess spoke again, this time to G.P. Lakshmi.

2 This possession séance took place on March 24, 1991. G.P. Lakshmi was »modern« in the sense that she belonged to the urban middle class and had access to modern medicine to cope with her problems.

Translation of the divine words[3]

1 *ammo*, what, on me, *annā*
2 my mother, with the name Nūkamma
3 whether she considers our troubles or not
4 which are before us, in this world
5 what kind of troubles we will get, *ammō*
6 *amma*, this woman was made to come to the feet of the goddess
7 for this entire world, she is the creator, *ammā*
8 she is the goddess for everybody, *ammō*
9 she suffers from all sorts of troubles, *annā*
10 this [goddess of] Anakāpalli, seventy times
11 Nūkāmma's name resounds
12 *ammō*, you have to talk, *ammo*
13 *olē*, this is your caste, *annō*
14 but we children do not, do not belong [to this caste], *anna*
15 we are the children of another caste, my mother
16 *olē*, with us there is sin, my mother
17 *olē*, with you, there is virtue, my mother
18 if you talk to our children
19 if you hit us and abuse us, my mother
20 to me, to whatever place I will go, my mother
21 to us, these fears, *ammō*
22 to us, there is no opportunity for them to come, *anō*
23 you [polite], thinking about this in your thoughts, *ammā*
24 you, camphor on the fire, *ma tallō*
25 you have put, *māyammā*
26 to us, in our future, *annagāni, ammō*
27 whatever the wishes are, which we are thinking, *gāni ammō*
28 whether they will be fulfilled for us or not, *māyamma*
29 you are thinking in your thoughts, *amma*[4]
30 all that we need, will it come
31 whether that letter will come to our hand or not
32 *amma*, for that, you on earth have put camphor into the fire, daughter
33 the word in your navel, *ammō*
34 the word in your thoughts, when it will be considered
35 it is Nūkamma of Anakāpalli
36 then, the name of this powerful fort will go to Nūkamma[5]
37 then, she will be praised

3 For the transcript of the original text see the APPENDIX at the end of this article and also the audio version of the recorded text online [AUDIO 1].

4 *parugeṭṭu*, lit. »to run, to hurry«; translated here as »to think«.

5 The temple of the goddess Nūkālamma (or Nūkamma) in Anakāpalle is called »fort«.

38 on this black paper, *cimmā*
39 on this white paper
40 this black letter, *cimmā*
41 whether it will be there for us or not, *anō*
42 whether it will go or come for us, or not, *ani*
43 within this month, *cimmā*
44 whether it will be taken away or not
45 not even in the business, we have done
46 in the way we moved, *anna*
47 who is taking it away from us, *cimmā*
48 if it is not the god of our house
49 then small and big people are taking it away
50 or my milky white deity is taking it away
51 this is in your thoughts, *ammā*
52 because it is in your thoughts, *ammā*
53 you have to tell all these words, *ammā*
54 until the two hours this morning, you didn't know anything
55 one day, after two months will have passed
56 *olē*, in the Lord's [Jagannāth's] kingdom, *cimmā*
57 the work you have considered
58 the thoughts you have thought
59 for you, it will happen exactly like this, *ammā*

G.P. LAKSHMI: If everything turns out well for me, I will give you a sari. How will my body [health] be? How will it be in my house? Tell me!

60 *ammō*, if you ask me to explain your desperation[6]
61 for the past 15 days, until this day, *anna*
62 *olē*, your body to you [*hm*][7]
63 will become heavy, daughter [*hm*]
64 your body will become water to you [*i.e.* weak], daughter [*hm*]
65 your legs will become weight to you [*hm*]
66 your head will become weak to you
67 early mornings, after dawn, *ammā*
68 your desperation
69 in your eyes, it will be pitch-dark
70 when you are full of that
71 your head is going round and round like a wheel, *cimmā*
72 by putting your head down
73 you are remaining like that, *amma*

6 *āgamu*, lit. »offence, misbehaviour«, is translated here as »desperation«.
7 G.P. Lakshmi's approval at the end of each line.

74 in these sixteen bones
75 as if somebody has put a magic spell on the heart
76 as if the fire came to you
77 to destroy you, *ammā*
78 your four veins
79 are being dragged and pulled
80 in your desperate situation
81 your twelve bones are in such a bad condition, daughter
82 in your memory, *cimmā*
83 the burning sensation is coming from outside
84 it occurred to you
85 as if somebody squeezes your throat
86 you sink down, daughter
87 you think that those words are wrong, *ammā*
88 you think that I commit sins, daughter
89 you want to see my power, you
90 whether this goddess can tell the illness in my body or not
91 which life I live, whether she can tell or not [*hm*]
92 wherever I go, whether I succeed or not
93 with such thoughts in your heart, daughter
94 you put camphor on the fire for me, daughter [the medium slaps her thigh]

This is followed by a short interval of 15 seconds. The medium breathes heavily pressing the air through her teeth. This shows that the goddess is still present in her body and in an aroused state. Nobody in the audience speaks.

95 *ammō*, I will tell you, *ammō*
96 on which day you, *annagāni*
97 on the *ranga purnima*[8], *ammō*
98 when that day was gone, daughter
99 if there is no satisfaction for you, I will bring satisfaction, daughter
100 from that day onwards, *ammō*
101 you go outside, but you don't go inside the house, *amma*
102 the words which you speak, *cimmā*
103 the money in your hands
104 it is going outside, it is not coming into the house, *ammā*
105 to you and to your husband, *cimmā*
106 among the letters, in one word, *cimmā*
107 it went outside [beyond your control]
108 from the day, it went outside, *ammō*
109 there is no income anymore in your house, *ammā*

8 *ranga*, »color«; *purnima*, »full moon«, refers to the Holi festival on March 1, 1991.

110 such an income, *cimmā*
111 has this man taken it away or has it been seized by somebody's quarrelsomeness, *ani*?
112 or is there somebody who has done you an injustice? Like this, it is in your thoughts, *ammā*
113 I shall answer such questions
114 to which place you went, you don't know, *ammā*
115 you, in this public place
116 you have become the letter, *ammō*
117 my troubles
118 in this public place
119 whether it is my milky white deity, whether it is my father or my mother
120 whether you should leave the kingdom of the Lord [Jagannāth]
121 and visit my hilly place or not, *anō*
122 this exists in your thoughts on that day
123 on that day, *ammā*
124 this one matter
125 since this *ranga purnima* day
126 in your thoughts
127 on the day when it happened
128 in your hand
129 on your sleep-bed
130 you made a fist
131 while you were making a fist
132 a man came, *ammā*
133 on white paper
134 a black letter, *ammā*
135 was added, *ammā*
136 in western direction, *ammā*
137 he walked away, *ammā*
138 in the moment of walking away
139 while you were dreaming
140 when you suddenly woke up
141 what happened, oh God?
142 my father, is he not here?
143 my parents, are they not here?
144 *abbā*, who took it away? that's what you think, *ammā*
145 you think in your thoughts, *ammō*
146 since this day, for you
147 whatever you are planning to do,
148 it is not going right for you, *ammā*
149 only water
150 it doesn't become milk, *ammā* [a short interval of 15 seconds]

G. P. LAKSHMI: »Whatever she says, everything is right.« [After this comment, the medium breathes heavily and continues with the recitation.]

151 *ammō*, you have one wish, *ammō*
152 when my father was here, when my mother was here, he didn't appear, the man
153 I travel in so many countries [kingdoms], but my country wasn't shown to me
154 throughout the year, for weeks and months, I showed support to the Lord
155 I climbed the Lord's hill
156 I climbed the twelve hills and offered *namaskār* to the Lord
157 we stopped our pilgrimages
158 in the kingdom of this Oriya God, we
159 became Oriya people and travelled [only here], that's what you thought, daughter
160 for how long did we live like this, why did we get these troubles for such a long time?
161 the incoming money was just enough for them
162 not a single paisa was left for us
163 until today, for one month
164 tears have flowed from the left eye and from the right eye
165 you go to your sleep-bed
166 with this day, our food will be finished, Lord
167 you don't provide us with food [any more], indeed
168 you, on your sleep-bed, *ammā*
169 in the last six months, until this day, how you went to so many places, you don't know
170 on that day, the shaking and lameness came to you, *ammā*
171 loss came into your house, *ammā*
172 since that loss
173 five weeks have passed, *ammā*
174 don't you know that it happened five weeks ago?
175 on that day, your heart, *ammā*
176 was broken into pieces
177 in the kingdom of this Lord [Jagannāth]
178 even if I beg for alms
179 there will be no food available for me, that's what you think, *amma*
180 you thought that this goddess, Nūkamma, couldn't tell, *amma*
181 do not be afraid, *ammā*
182 for some moments you feel better, in some moments your head is reeling, *ammā*
183 your, which man, on that day
184 on the Holi-day, you

185 he was thin and weak, *ammā*
186 he came from the Western direction
187 what's the matter, *ammā*, are you feeling well or not, he said
188 that he asked you, *ammā*
189 where did your husband go to, *ammā*, he asked
190 he asked you, *ammā*
191 from that day onwards, *ammā*
192 if white paper comes
193 [with] black letters, *ammā*
194 it will be torn into pieces
195 for you, the letters, *anna*
196 are visible, *ammā*
197 from that day onwards
198 up to your house
199 there is no happiness
200 if you speak one word
201 it will become two words[9]
202 your back [the medium slaps her thigh]
203 will be touched by them, *ammā*[10]
204 not on this morning, *ammā*
205 at the end of this month
206 in the coming month
207 such, *ammō*
208 what has been said
209 if it gets well
210 then call [me] mother
211 if it doesn't get well
212 if you recover what you have lost
213 then it is Anakāpalle Nūkamma, my mother, then that name goes to the powerful fort
214 among the leatherworkers, the washermen, the shepherds, the peasants,[11]
215 among the eight *varṇas*
216 from Calcutta
217 up to Madras
218 my name is Gaṅga
219 if I am such a goddess
220 I will make you recover what you have lost
221 if not, I will remain a sandal under your foot
222 fold your hands [for *namaskār*] and go, daughter

9 In the sense of »ambiguous, causing misunderstanding«.

10 In the sense of »the words strike back«.

11 Māla (leatherworkers, Untouchables), Nīlavallu (lit. »waterpeople«, *i.e.* washermen), Golla (shepherds), Kāpu (peasants).

A short interval follows. Actually, with the last line, the medium has signalled the end of her recitation. After the following short conversation between Ramana Murthy and G.P. Lakshmi, the medium begins again to speak.

G.P. LAKSHMI [to R. Murthy]: Are you asking now?
R. MURTHY: You ask (for me), please!
G.P. LAKSHMI [to the goddess]: *Amma*, this man, whose name is the name of the Tirumala-god, he came with me. Will you speak to him about something, *ammā*?

223 *amma*, on Tuesday, I, *anna* [G.P. LAKSHMI: *yes*]
224 if you need it, *ōyammō* [*yes*]
225 at 7 o'clock in the morning for you, *amma*
226 at this time, in the old net [*yes*]
227 I, in this net made of virtue
228 whatever the sin you committed against the father
229 I will tell, my mother [*yes*]
230 tonight, to your children
231 I will show my name, *ammo* [*yes*]
232 but on Tuesday, *ammo* [*yes*]
233 I will give that answer
234 *ōlē*, those remaining questions, *ammo*
235 on the day, when they wear the *boṭṭu* [*yes*]
236 in how many calamities they are, *māyammo*
237 in their house there is loss, *anna* [*yes*]
238 how many people's throats they have cut[12]
239 *ōlē*, in the child's interest, I will be going
240 *ōlē*, I will push him into the ditch, *ōri*, *anna*
241 in whatever direction he is, *māyammo*
242 I put my hand into his pocket, *anna*
243 the one who has pushed him into the ditch, *anna*
244 I will tell you, daughter, *anna*
245 tonight, I will walk over to your house
246 in your sleep I will give [answers]
247 if I do this to your body, *ammā*
248 if I give such answers
249 such a goddess, if I bring her to this place
250 I will tell / give you such a sign, *ammā*
251 such a son and his thoughts I take
252 such a son I will throw into the ditch
253 and crush him in the ditch

12 In the sense of »how many people they have cheated«.

254 I will make his house suffer from loss
255 if I get praised
256 if I am Nūkamma, with so many names
257 if I take him away from your family
258 you can call me such a goddess, *ammā*
259 my town is not your town, not your village, *anakamma*
260 I am the goddess of the sixty-six castes (*jātulu*), *ammā*
261 I am not the goddess, *ammā*, of only one caste
262 I am speaking to Golla, I am speaking to Gavara, I am speaking to Brahmins
263 I am speaking to Kōmati, *ammā*
264 for all eight *varṇas*
265 I am the mother
266 I am not the mother for [only] one man
267 my father Śiva, my miracles, he is unable to tell my miracles
268 you are not greater than my father
269 fold your hands and go, *ammā*
270 do not be afraid
271 I am going

G. P. LAKSHMI: »She says, she will be speaking on Tuesday. She says everything correctly.«
SOME MEN IN THE AUDIENCE [laughingly]: »You are not used to that, are you?«
G. P. LAKSHMI: »Everything is correct. Everything right.« [to me, in English]: »Everything truth. Six months not feeling well.« [to R. Murthy]: »Isn't it, since June my health is not good. But next month I will be feeling well. That's what she said, isn't it.« [to me, in English]: »Next month everything cured.« [...] »Five Rupies, *kurkuma*, *kumkum*, I have given [...].« [During this conversation the medium belches repeatedly. This shows that the goddess is now leaving her body.]

Textual analysis

In this relatively long recitation, lasting for 17 minutes, the medium has a threefold task: First, she has to talk to a client who is not known to her. The two have met only once for a very short time in the morning. Bhūlēkamma belongs to a low-status group of fishermen, G. P. Lakshmi hails from an urban Brahman family. One is illiterate; the other is fairly highly educated. However, inequality of status is reversed here. As the medium of a powerful goddess, Bhūlēkamma is of crucial importance in her village context. Compared with G. P. Lakshmi, in ordinary life she would just be an uneducated, poor, low-caste village woman, but in this context, she incorporates a powerful goddess, and a high caste woman is listening to her words. Second, the goddess is supposed to make a meaningful statement regarding G.P. Lakshmi's personal problems and name the causes. However, Bhūlēkamma has only a vague and stereotyped idea about G.P. Lakshmi's living-conditions and her way of looking at things. Third, the medium has to maintain a discourse in which the divine words gain authority for persons who are not used to communicating with deities in such a way. The medium manages this threefold task easily and in an impressive manner. The recitation is fluent, the tone determined. There is neither insecurity nor hesitation. Regarding its content, this recitation is amazingly consistent, although it differs from recitations which refer to the Vāḍabalija.

Right at the beginning, in lines 1–22, G.P. Lakshmi is quoted. The lines refer to the thoughts she had in mind while putting camphor on the burning coals (23–25). She had asked herself whether this goddess with the name »Nūkamma« would also take care of her difficulties (1–5). The goddess is presented as Nūkamma from Anakāpalli, goddess for all, who is considered to have created the world (7–8), and who is from a different caste than G.P. Lakshmi (13–15). Nevertheless, G.P. Lakshmi worships her, and this fact is expressed poetically with the parallelism »with us there is sin, my mother; with you, there is virtue, my mother« (16–17). Assurance is also given that, if the goddess speaks to the children, even if she beats or scolds them, she will eventually take away their fears (18–22). These are supposed to be G.P. Lakshmi's thoughts, but they are also the central preoccupations of the medium. G.P. Lakshmi is referred to in the polite second person plural (*mīru*).[13] The most important points are mentioned right in the beginning, such as the fact of belonging to different castes (*jāti*) and the unlimited power of the goddess, who doesn't differentiate among her devotees.

After identifying the initial thoughts G.P. Lakshmi had in mind while putting camphor on the coals, Nūkālamma continues to quote more thoughts of G.P. Lakshmi (32). She is said to ask herself whether all her wishes would be fulfilled (27–28) and, more specifically, whether a »letter« (*akṣaramu*) would come into her hand (31). If these pleas were to be fulfilled Nūkālamma would be praised and her temple in Anakāpalli would become a powerful fort (35–36). After G.P. Lakshmi's promise is quoted, the »letter« is again taken as a topos and is even specified as a black letter on white paper (39–40). The inconsistency »on this black paper« (38) is immediately corrected to »on this white paper« (39). Thus, in a very general way, witchcraft as a probable cause for the problems is introduced. Black letters on white paper are spells (*mantras*), with which G.P. Lakshmi's family could have been bewitched. With the questions »who is taking it away from us?« (47) and »my milky white deity is taking it away« (50), the thoughts and worries of G.P. Lakshmi are quoted again (51). In line 54,

13 When the goddess speaks to Vāḍabalija devotees, she uses *nuvvu* (2nd person singular).

the goddess (or rather the medium) refers to the situation earlier that morning, when G.P. Lakshmi talked for »two hours« with Bhūlēkamma about possession, not knowing anything about the power of the goddess (54). This is followed quite suddenly by the first specific announcement: that the crisis will be over in two months (55–59).

Up to this point, the divine explanations have been rather general. The cause for the problems could be witchcraft. The difficulties will be solved in two months. A short interval follows in which the medium and the client have an opportunity to react to the recitation and alter the course of the divine interpretation. With the promise to give a sari to the goddess, G.P. Lakshmi asks whether her personal health (»my body«) and her family situation (»my house«) will improve. With an exclamatory »*ammō*!« the goddess announces an explanation of G.P. Lakshmi's »desperation« (60). She begins with a statement regarding time (»for the past fifteen days«, 61) which is picked up and altered several times in the course of the recitation. With G.P. Lakshmi's approval of every line, the goddess continues to narrate her state of health in drastic words. Not only does she describe the state of G.P. Lakshmi's body as »heavy, full of water, weak, destroyed by fire«, but she lists individual parts of the body, describing the changes in them in drastic terms: legs, head, eyes, the sixteen bones, the heart in the chest, the four veins, the twelve bones, the throat (65–85). The sensation and pain in these parts of the body are so dramatic that witchcraft seems the only plausible explanation: »as if somebody has put a magic spell on the heart« (75); »as if somebody is squeezing your throat« (85).

Immediately after this impressive description, the goddess refers to G.P. Lakshmi's possible doubts concerning the divine explanations (»you think, those words are wrong«, 87). G.P. Lakshmi gets reproached for thinking, »what can this goddess tell me about my health and my life?« – and G.P. Lakshmi agrees (91). For the third time, a passage ends with the accusation that G.P. Lakshmi had put camphor on the embers with such scepticism in her mind. This time, the accusation gets enforced by the determined voice and the fact that the medium slaps her thigh vigorously (94). This is followed by another short interval, of 15 seconds. The goddess is still in the body of her medium. Her aroused state is manifested by the medium's heavily pressing the air through her teeth. This short interval is an occasion for both the medium and the listener to enter into a dialogue and to evaluate what has been said so far. The medium's argument either gets approved and can be further elaborated on, or it is criticized and has to be readjusted accordingly. However, in this case, nobody from the audience speaks, and Nūkālamma continues with her interpretation. The time references now become more precise. Instead of »fifteen days ago« (61) now the »colour *purnima*« (97) is mentioned, a festival which had in fact been celebrated three weeks earlier. On this day, the suffering began. The effects on the »body« having already been described, the medium now refers to the »house« (and the second part of G.P. Lakshmi's question). Words, money, she herself, everything goes »outside«, nothing »comes back«, and her wealth slips through her fingers (101–105). Again, the medium mentions witchcraft (letters, words) and asks carefully and in a general way, who, or rather whose quarrelsomeness, could have been the cause for this, or, if it was perhaps »this man« (111–112).

With the announcement »I will answer such questions« (113) and after quoting four times G.P. Lakshmi's thoughts (119–122), the goddess describes the sorcerer's attack with the help of a rather stereotyped action. At Holi, while G.P. Lakshmi was sleeping during the day, an unknown man put white paper with black letters in her hand and went away toward the west (128–137). The moment he left, G.P. Lakshmi woke up and felt that something strange had happened (138–145). Since that day everything has failed. Whatever she touches becomes »water, not milk« (149–150). All these incidents indicate witchcraft. Typically, the accusations are not expressed specifically but rather hinted at metaphorically (»a man«, »during your sleep«, »black letters«, »Western direction«).

The goddess stops for a moment and an amazed G.P. Lakshmi comments that »everything she says is right«. The goddess is encouraged and continues in the same direction. With the opening line »you have got a wish« (151), the manner of argumentation changes. Until now, the past has been mentioned and specific events in the past have been depicted. Now the goddess argues prospectively and talks about solutions in the future. At first, she again quotes G.P. Lakshmi's wishes, or rather thoughts. She mentions especially the longing for Andhra Pradesh that G.P. Lakshmi shares with the Vāḍabalija, since both are *vidēśi* (foreigners) in Puri. She also mentions that worshiping the deities had not brought the expected results. Despite several pilgrimages »to the twelve mountains« during which the deities had been worshiped and asked for support, the reward failed to materialize. Instead, the income got smaller and smaller and soon »the food will be finished« (166). The tragic situation is reinforced by the poetic expression »the tears flow from the right eye and from the left eye« (164). It is repeated again how the suffering began six months ago on the »sleep-bed« and how the »heart was broken into pieces« (168–177). The description shows an increase in duration: The suffering is said to have existed for the past fifteen days (61), since the colour-*purnima* (97, 125), for one month (163), for five weeks (173), for six months (169). Such a variety of time references enables the audience to identify with the divine explanations. The goddess offers several alternatives and cannot be made responsible for incorrect information.

After inserting again G.P. Lakshmi's scepticism regarding Nūkālamma's power (178–180), the goddess continues to describe the suffering. She refers to a man, thin and weak, coming from the Western direction, who started to talk to G.P. Lakshmi (183–190) and tore up white paper with black letters on it. At the end of this description the medium slaps her thighs forcefully in order to give emphasis to her words. The description contains attributes of witchcraft which are repeated in different ways. From line 205 onward, the goddess promises that in the coming month things will improve and that G.P.Lakshmi will recover the »things lost«. The improvement will be only gradual. No fixed date is mentioned. All this is due to Nūkālamma's favour, because she is the goddess of all castes and of the »eight *varṇas*«, and she is worshiped from Calcutta to Madras (213–218). The range of Nūkālamma's power is referred to in social as well as geographical terms; however, only low-status-groups are mentioned (leather workers, washermen, shepherds and peasants). In case Nūkālamma cannot grant this favour and restore the things lost, the devotees can kick her with their feet (219–221). With the phrase »fold your hands and go, daughter« (222), Nūkālamma announces the end of her detailed statement.

G.P.Lakshmi seems to be satisfied by the divine explanation. She asks her companion whether he wants to ask something now. He proposes that she should ask for him, since he isn't as well versed in or convinced about the whole situation. G.P.Lakshmi's question »Will you speak as well to him who has got the name of the Tirumala-God?« is rather general and doesn't pose a specific problem. In fact, both of them assume that the goddess knows his problems.

The goddess postpones her statements concerning Ramana Murthy until Tuesday at 7 o'clock in the morning. Then she will talk about »whatever sin was committed against the ruling father« (223–229). With G.P.Lakshmi's approval at the end of each line, the divine recitation could come to an end, but the goddess again addresses her problems. Before answering the »remaining questions« on Tuesday (234) she will come »tonight« to G.P.Lakshmi's house (230, 245) to improve her situation and to punish the sorcerer. She will throw the sorcerer into a ditch, trample him underfoot and damage his house (252–254). If she succeeds, people should praise her as a goddess (255–258). Beginning with line 259, Nūkālamma again refers in great detail to the fact that she is a goddess not only for the Vāḍabalija but for all the 66 castes (260), and that she will speak to everybody (262), even if they are from a different town. Golla (shepherds), Gavara (Adivasi), Brahmans and Komaṭi (merchants) are the castes named here (262–263), in contrast to line 214, where Golla, Mālā (leather workers), Washermen and Kāpu (peasants) are mentioned. This line seems to refer specially to Ramana Murthy and G.P.Lakshmi, since they belong to the Komaṭi and Brahman castes, respectively. The goddess continues by saying that not even Śiva could perform her miracles (267), since she is the most powerful goddess, not only the mother of one person, but goddess for all. With the standard lines »fold your hands and go«, »do not be afraid«, »I am going« (269–271) Nūkālamma ends her recitation.

G.P.Lakshmi's reaction »everything she said is right« shows amazement but also respect for the goddess. According to the goddess, G.P.Lakshmi has not been feeling well for the last six months. G.P.Lakshmi confirms this, saying that she has not been feeling well since June. This is a period of nine months, but such inconsistencies don't seem to bother G.P.Lakshmi. More important is the statement that »next month« she will feel better and that »everything will be cured«. In this moment, G.P. Lakshmi doesn't perceive Nūkālamma as a mere local goddess worshiped by members of a low caste, but as a powerful goddess who has described past events correctly and whose forecasts can certainly be trusted.

The divine discourse lasts for 17 minutes and is characterized by long, continuous narrative passages which are repeated several times with slight variations. The narrative sequences are interrupted several times by statements about the power of the goddess and her ability to help human beings, such as the lines »if there is no satisfaction for you, I will bring satisfaction« (99), »I will make you recover what you have lost« (220), »I am not the mother for only one person« (266). With these statements the formal structure of this recitation differs from other recitations, which are meant exclusively for a Vāḍabalija-audience. In this recitation, G.P. Lakshmi's supposed and unjustified doubts about the power of the goddess are mentioned repeatedly. In this way, the medium tries to establish divine authority beyond the caste of the Vāḍabalija. G.P. Lakshmi's consent shows that the medium is in total command of the situation and able to adapt to the altered circumstances.

The medium's speech is fluent and self-confident. Her self-confidence is manifested even further when she speaks in an energetic tone or slaps her thighs. The use of metaphors and poetic expressions indicates that this is not everyday conversation but ritual discourse. For example, the term »sleep-bed« (*nidra mancamu*) is used instead of the ordinary term »bed« (*mancamu*) (129, 165). Other poetic devices are parallelisms such as »with us there is sin, my mother, with you there is virtue, my mother« (16–17) or metaphors, such as »black letters on white paper« or »[everything] becomes water, it doesn't become milk« (149–150).

G.P. Lakshmi's crisis is presented vividly and in great detail. The medium has to adjust to a new situation and carefully feels her way forward. Since there are no objections, she gets more and more self-assured and continues with her interpretation. Why does she describe repeatedly and extensively G.P. Lakshmi's personal crisis? Why are the elements body, house, economic situation, and witchcraft repeated several times? The divine discourse is an open, dialogic procedure and not an apodictic causal statement or presentation of ultimate solutions. The direction of the interpretation can be altered again and again. Thus, the statements regarding time are varied several times and the audience has the opportunity to find the »right« timing and neglect the other ones. G.P. Lakshmi selects one statement regarding time as correct without saying that the other ones are incorrect. Similarly, various references to the body, the house, the economic situation and witchcraft enable the audience to »select« what sounds convincing to them. In the course of such an »open« proceeding the audience is given a chance to interpret the divine interpretation. To listen to a divine discourse means emphasizing some phrases and neglecting others.

A comparison of this divine discourse with Nūkālamma's utterances to her Vāḍabalija devotees, which I have done elsewhere,[14] shows that the language of the goddess is more polite with more poetic phrases when she talks to a stranger. Her argumentation is different as well. No wrath, no threats, no accusations (as in the case of Vāḍabalija devotees), but rather unlimited benevolence on the side of the goddess, who emphasizes her divine power time and again. After sounding out carefully possible interpretations, the medium offers witchcraft as a diagnosis. An unknown third person is made responsible for G.P. Lakshmi's suffering. This interpretation is plausible but also stereotyped. In contrast to other cases, where, according to the goddess, the suffering is caused by the devotee him- or herself through lack of worship, in this case G.P. Lakshmi is not accused. G.P. Lakshmi's precise question about her health is answered with a narrative passage in which the condition of her body is described in drastic terms. However, the phrases and metaphors used for this are also universally applicable.

The medium emphasizes repeatedly how the stranger is sceptical and doubtful about the power of the goddess. This reflects both the social inequality between the medium and her client, and the supposed inequality between a local goddess and the more universalized Hindu deities. The medium refers to the morning when G.P. Lakshmi, who until then »didn't know anything«, heard for the first time about the goddess and her medium. These allusions show that the topics had been discussed already during everyday conversations and are now reformulated as divine discourse.

Conclusion

The divine words of the goddess Nūkālamma, spoken with the human voice of her medium Bhūlēkamma have also convinced an audience outside her immediate vicinity. What makes these words divine words? What makes them effective? What do the listeners hear? Whenever, after a possession séance, I asked, with these questions in mind, »What did the goddess say?«, a long recitation would be summarized in just one or two sentences, as for instance »She said, you didn't worship me. Therefore, I have made your child sick. You have to worship me and make offerings«. Although such a summary turned out to be always correct, the question then remained, »what else did the goddess say?« As Nuckolls rightly states, possession is expressed verbally and therefore has to be analyzed in terms of language (NUCKOLLS 1991, 1992).

As a speech event, the possession séance has to be seen as a cultural praxis in which human lives and their contexts are constructed and performed with linguistic means. According to speech-act theory, language not only represents or

14 For a comparison see SCHÖMBUCHER 2006.

refers to reality; it also creates it (AUSTIN 1962). Divine presence is created verbally, based on the assumption that gods or demons exist as persons (not merely as symbols).[15] Not only are words in performances referential, but they also construct meaning.[16] According to Foley, the power of words is derived from the performance as an enabling event and a certain tradition as an enabling referent (FOLEY 1995: 208). Foley has created the term »performance arena« as »the locus where an event of performance takes place, where words are invested with their special power« (FOLEY 1995: 209). Words spoken through a possessed medium do not convey meaning on their own. One important factor of the »performance arena« is the audience, which gives words their illocutionary power. What is spoken during states of possession is interpreted through listening. Besides speaking, listening is a cultural practice influenced by cultural concepts (BURGHART 1996).

What do listeners hear when deities speak to them? As a performative event, a possession séance among Vāḍabalija consists of three sections, which I call the evocative, narrative, and directive parts of the séance.[17] Divinities are not simply present in humans, but the divine presence has to be actively created. Among the Vāḍabalija, it is created in the evocative section of a séance through panegyric elements in which the goddess praises her own power and proclaims that she and all the other deities have always protected the devotees. The language is highly formulaic and repetitive. In the case of G.P. Lakshmi, however, the medium had to cope with the specific situation of a woman who does not normally belong to the audience. Therefore, Nūkālamma is portrayed as »goddess for all castes«. In the narrative sections, the goddess recounts the reasons for individual misfortune, illness, etc. This has to be specific. It has to fit individual experience as well as cultural models of misfortune. In G.P. Lakshmi's case, the discourse is successful, despite the fact that the medium doesn't know much about G.P. Lakshmi's personal situation. Witchcraft is selected as the explanation for health problems. Another explanation would have been the neglect of the goddess and her subsequent wrath. With witchcraft as cause, the devotee doesn't get accused, but an unknown third person is made responsible for the misfortune. In the directive passages the goddess gives instructions for future actions. Very often, she demands that people should increase the worship of the goddess or give specific offerings. In G.P. Lakshmi's case, no such demands are made. Instead, she announces the time when the situation will improve.

While the evocative passages bestow the power of the divine utterances, it is the narrative passages that make the divine words true. In the narrative passages the goddess proves that she knows everything and that everything she says is correct. This is also confirmed by G.P. Lakshmi. The third section, in which

15 See for example DAVIS 1979; KJAERHOLM 1982.

16 See also FREEMAN 1993, 1999.

17 For a detailed account see SCHÖMBUCHER 2006.

the goddess gives directives to her devotees, is developed in a dialogue with the audience. The audience may protest in the beginning against the demand of a sacrifice and it is negotiated between audience and goddess to what extent her demands are justified and acceptable. Only mutual agreement makes the divine demands obligatory. In G.P. Lakshmi's case, no negotiations take place: G.P. Lakshmi approves of what the goddess says. There are no demands on the side of the goddess; this is probably due to the fact that the medium is not very familiar with G.P. Lakshmi's situation.

It is the audience who gives authority and efficacy to the divine words. When the Vāḍabalija summarized divine words for me, they would mention the directives, the demands of the goddess. If I insisted long enough, they would give an account of the narrative passages in which the causes of misfortune had been explained. Interestingly, in these passages the audience frequently heard more and different things than what I could find in the translations of the texts. Often, the audience members' own versions were mixed with the divine version. They never mentioned the evocative and panegyric elements with which divine presence was created. There was no need for that, because divine presence and power is accepted beyond doubt.

Words spoken in a state of possession cannot be efficacious on their own. Despite the ritual setting in which they are spoken and the communicative competence of the possessed person, they need an addressee who makes them efficacious. Merely being spoken does not provide words with illocutionary power, but it does act as a presupposition for listeners to provide them with that power. G.P. Lakshmi, as a stranger, listening to the divine words, made them efficacious by acknowledging them as »right« or »true«.

From the perspective of an indigenous listener, possession mediumship is an occasion where human beings (medium and audience) can create a divine presence for a short while. From the perspective of an external listener-cum-observer who acknowledges speech-act theory, the possessed media are extraordinarily gifted persons who are able to create a divine presence and interpret the world by their specific communicative competence and poetic talent. Their interpretations are only efficacious if acknowledged by the audience. For both kinds of listeners, possession is not primarily a healing ritual, although illness is a frequent topic, nor is possession primarily divination, although questions concerning the future are answered. Possession is also an occasion to worship the gods, to be near them and talk with them. Viewed this way, possession is not a »premodern« way of explaining things, but one of several possible discourses to explain personal misfortune, illness that is hard to diagnose, bad luck, etc. It is easily accessible and comparatively inexpensive. In terms of efficacy, divine words are comparable to other forms of discourse and are not easily replaced by modernity.

One final question remains to be answered. How does modernity act upon the status of female media? At least in 2004, the two remaining media did not seem to have lost authority. They were still very much needed as a medium for communication with the deities. There was no notion of indecency around possession. On the contrary, the media were held in high esteem – at least by the persons who attended possession séances. However, there have probably always been those persons among the Vāḍabalija who are sceptical about certain media and might not attend their possession séances. From the very beginning of my research, I came across sceptical voices regarding possession. Some (men) would tell me, that I shouldn't take it too seriously, since these women were just faking to be possessed by a goddess. Others would tell me, that what I see now is but a poor imitation of the »real« possession as it had been practiced a generation ago, when the female media were »really« powerful and feared by normal persons. One reason for the impression that the status of the media had not deteriorated might be the fact that the audience is a »closed one«. The Vāḍabalija have always been careful about strangers attending the séances. G.P. Lakshmi, although a stranger, could attend a séance because she »believed« in the fact that a goddess can speak through a human being. At the beginning of my fieldwork, there was a lot of apprehensiveness about my participation as an outsider. It took me a long time to gain the confidence of the Vāḍabalija and to destroy their fear of me as an outsider taking pictures or even filming their séances and selling it to the Bombay film industry where people would either laugh at them or frown upon them. We agreed that I would not film them and that I would take photographs only after the goddess had left their body. From today's perspective, the prudence of the Vāḍabalija-women seems to be far sighted and more than justified.

Appendix

The words of the goddess Nūkālamma: Transcript of Audio 1 *(online: http://www.indologie.uni-wuerzburg.de/women_performers/contributors/schoembucher/audio_files/)*

1 ammo ēmo mā mēda annā
2 māyamma Nūkamma nāmanē
3 mā āpadalō encutārā lēdā
4 māki venanna ī lōkamu mēda
5 māku ēmi naṣṭamu vastādi ammō
6 amma ī amma pādālu kāḍiki pilupincu konnadi gaṅgā
7 lōkāni kella lōka karta ayinadi ammā
8 idi kaliyāniki kaliya gaṅga ayinadi ammō
9 idi vaḍḍādi māḍugulu ammā
10 ī anakāpalli ḍabbai vēḷālu

11 idi pērēllutunnadi nūkammā
12 ammō lāḍi tīrutāvu ammo
13 olē mīyā mī yokka jāti annō
14 mēmu biḍḍalamu mari kāda mari kādanna
15 mēmu parajāti biḍḍalamu māyammo
16 olē mā kāḍā pāpambu māyammo
17 olē mī kāḍā puṇyambu māyammā
18 mā biḍḍalaki inabarci tīritē
19 nuvvu koṭṭi tiṭṭinaṭṭē māyammō
20 nāku ē cōṭakellite māyammō
21 māku ī yokka edalu gāni ammō
22 māku vaccēṭitāya lēdu anō
23 mīru yādamulō anukōyi ammā
24 mīru aggi mēda guggilamu mā tallō
25 mīru vēsi tīrināru māyammā
26 mā mundaṭiki mākannagāni ammō
27 māmu anukonnikā kauvulu gāni ammō
28 māku celli tāda lēdani māyammā
29 nī yādamulō parugeṭṭitunnadamma
30 māvanni ī varsa rālanna
31 ā akṣaramu mā cētiki vastādi lēdani
32 amma ilalōni mīru aggi mēda guggilam vēsēru kūturā
33 mī nābilōni paluku ammō
34 nī yādamulōni paluku encitīrite
35 idi anakāpalli nūkammē
36 idi kāṇḍra kōṭa pērellutādi nūkammā
37 idi śēbhāsu anipincukuṇṭādī
38 ī nallaṭi kāgitamu mēda cimmā
39 ī tellaṭi kāgitamu mēda
40 ī nallaṭi akśaramu cimmā
41 māku avutādi avvadani anō
42 māku pōyindi vastādi rādu ani
43 ī nela rōjula baṭṭi cimmā
44 mādi eṭṭirītigā pāḍu ayipōtondō
45 mēmu cēsina vyāpāramulō gādu
46 mēmu ellina naḍakalōnanna
47 idi evaru tannuka pōtunnarō cimmā
48 lēdu māyinṭi dēvuḍutannestunnaḍā
49 lēdu cinnalu peddalu tannuka pōtunnarā
50 lēdu mā pāla daivamu tannēstunna dani
51 nī yādamulō unnadammā
52 nī yādamulō unnandu kammā
53 aṭu paluku vēla ammā

54 ī reṇḍu gaḍiyalu poddu aṇṭu teliya lēdā
55 reṇḍu nellu poddu pōte
56 olē bābu rājyam mēda cimmā
57 nuvvu anukonna pani
58 nuvvu talancina tanupu
59 nīku kaccitamu avutādi ammā

G. P. LAKSHMI: nāku kanuka anni panulu ayite nīku cēra istānu. ēmi nā vallu elā vuṇṭundi iṇṭilō elā vuṇṭndi. adi ceppu.

60 ammō nī yokka āgambu nēnu vippamaṇṭe
61 ī rōjuki 15 gaḍiyala poddununci anna [*hā*][18]
62 olē nī vallu nīkē [*hā*]
63 tolibuḍakalauvutundi kūturā [*hā*]
64 nī vallu nīku nīru avutundi kūturā [*hā*]
65 nī kāllu nīkē baruvu avutunnayā [*hā*]
66 nī tala nīkē isurutunnadā
67 udayamu tellavāri pōyinappaṭi kammā
68 nīyokka āgamē
69 nī kallu ciṭṭacīkaṭi kammutunnayā
70 nī mayi aṇṭē
71 parabhūlu antaṭi tiriginaṭṭu cimmā
72 nuvvu bur̥r̥a kindaki peṭṭesi
73 nuvvu uṇḍi tīru pōtunnavu ammā
74 ī padahāru emmukalu
75 guṇḍu mantarincinaṭṭu ammō
76 nīku aggi vaccinaṭṭe
77 nīku maṇṭalēllutādi ammā
78 nī nālugu narālē
79 gunjukuṇṭāvi ammā
80 nī yokka agamē
81 nī panneṇḍu emukalu aṭṭi tīrigā lāgutunnayi kūturā
82 nī yokka yādamulōna cimmā
83 aggitīsi bayaṭiki paḍi pōyinaṭṭē
84 nīku ayya pōyē
85 nīku pēka ūpiri salapakaṇṭā
86 nuvvu cērabaḍi pōtāvu kūturā
87 ā yokka paluku abhaddamā aṇṭāvā ammā
88 nēnu pāpāniki elli pōyānā kūturā
89 nā yokka śakti cūḍa nāki nuvvu
90 ī amma nā vaṇṭilōna rōgamu ceppụtādā lēdani

18 G. P. Lakshmi's approval at the end of each line.

91 nēnu batikē batuku cepputādā lēdani [*hā*]
92 nēnu velle cōṭa jayamu avutāda lēdu ani
93 nī yādamulō peṭṭu kōyi kūturā
94 nāku aggi mēda guggilam vēsēvā kūturā [the medium slaps her thighs]

This is followed by a short interval of 15 seconds. The medium breathes heavily pressing the air through her teeth. This shows that the goddess is still present in her body and that she is in an aroused state. Nobody in the audience speaks.

95 ammō nēnu vipputānu ammō
96 ē rōjuna nuvvu annagāni
97 raṅgula punnambu ammō
98 ē rōjuna vellindi kūturā
99 nīku tanupu lēkapōte tanupu cēstūnnanu kūturā
100 ā rōju kāḍi nunci ammō
101 bayaṭiki pōvaḍamu gāni iṇṭilōki rāvaḍamu lēdammā
102 nuvvu āḍina paluku cimmā
103 nī cētilō paisā
104 adi paiki vellutundigāni inṭilōki rā lēdu ammā
105 nīku nīyokka bhartaki cimmā
106 akśarāla kinda okka māṭalōna cimmā
107 adi paiki pāri pōyindammā
108 ā pāri pōyina kāḍi nunce ammō
109 nī yinṭiki rābaḍulu lēdu ammā
110 ī yokka rābaḍi cimmā
111 eṭṭiritigā ī naruḍu paṭṭuka pōyāḍā evarainā kāccāramu tīsiko pōyindi ani
112 lēdu evvaḍu ayinā anyāyamu kaṭṭu kunnaḍani nī yādamulō kalugutunnadi ammā
113 nēnu antaṭi kauvulu vippi tīrutānu
114 nuvvu ē cōṭaku vellevu teliya lēdu ammā
115 nuvvu racca rēku lōnā
116 nuvvu akṣaramu ayi ammō
117 nā yokka kaṣṭamu
118 ī racca rēku mēda
119 nā pāla daivamu ayitēnēmi nā tanḍri ayitēnēmi nā talli ayitenēmi
120 ī bābu rājyānā viḍici peḍatādō
121 nā unna sthalamu cūputādi lēdu anō
122 nī yādamulō kaligi tīrindammo ā rōjuni
123 ā rōjunēnammā
124 ādō yokka pannu
125 ā raṇgula punnami nāḍē
126 nī yokka yādamulōnē
127 kaligina rōjunē

128 cētilōkammā
129 nī nidra mancamu mīda
130 nuvvu piḍukullu baṭṭināvammā
131 piḍukullu baṭṭindē
132 naruḍocci ammā
133 tellaṭi kāgitamu mīda
134 nallaṭi akṣaramammā
135 cēripēsi ammā
136 paḍamaṭi bhāgamammā
137 naḍici pōyāḍa ammā
138 naḍici pōyi kṣanānnē
139 nuvvu kalagāsē
140 digguna lēci pōye
141 ēmi rā dēmuḍā
142 nā bāla taṇḍri lēḍu gāsi ēmo
143 nā talli taṇḍrulu lēru gāsēmo ani
144 abbā evaḍu tannika pōyāḍu ani nuvvu ammā
145 nī yādamulō anukunnavammō
146 ā rōju kāḍinunci nīkē
147 nuvvu anukonna pani
148 nīku raiṭu avva lēdu ammā
149 nīlēgāni
150 pālu avva lēdu ammā [a short interval of 15 seconds]

G. P. Lakshmi: inkēmi ivi ceppinavanni raiṭē. [After this comment, the medium breathes heavily and continues with the recitation.]

151 ammō nīku okka kōrika unnadi ammō
152 nā taṇḍrivunnappuḍu nā tallivunnappuḍu cūpincāḍu kāḍu bābu
153 nēnu rājyālu tirugutunnanu gāni nā rājyamu nāku cūpinca lēdani
154 nēnu ēṭi mēda vāri nellu bābu ādharuvu cūsēdānanu
155 nēnu bābu koṇḍa ekkedānamu
156 nēnu pannenḍu parvatālu ekki bābu haṣṭamu peṭṭukoṇḍidānanu
157 māyokkā yātralu mānukunnamu
158 ī bābu oḍḍi rājyamulōna mēmu
159 oḍḍi vāramu ayi tirugutunnamu ani anukunnavu kūturā
160 enta gālamu mēmu unṭe enduku ī yokka aṭṭu yēpaṭlu gāni mabbu māku lēgāni
161 vaccina paisā dānikē saripōtandi gānō
162 māku tirigi māku malli māku paisa lēdu ani
163 ī rōjuki nela okka rōju baṭṭikummā
164 ī kannīru ī kuḍikannīru eḍama kanṭiki vestūnnavu
165 nuvvu nidra mancamu mēdiki veltūnnavu

166 ī rōju tōṭi sarē gāsamu bābu
167 nannu cūḍavu gāsamu sumī
168 nuvvu nidra mancamu mēda ammā
169 ī rōjuki āru nellu eṭṭirītigā ē cōṭaku vellevu teliya lēdā
170 ā rōju nīku kudupu kuṇṭu vaccindi ammā
171 nī iṇṭilōna naṣṭam vaccindi ammā
172 ā naṣṭānikammā
173 aidu vārālu ayināvi ammā
174 aidu vārālu aṇṭē teliya lēdā
175 ā rōju guṇḍe nīkammā
176 baddalai pōyinaṭṭe
177 ī bābu rājyana
178 muṣṭi daṇḍukunna
179 nāku dorakadu gāsam anukunnavu amma
180 īyamma nūkamma ceppadanukunnavu ammā
181 nīku vaccina bhayamu lēdammā
182 ā gaḍiyalōna nuvvu bāguṇṭunnavu ā gaḍiyalōna nīku tala isurutunna
        dammā
183 nī ē naruḍu ā rōjunē
184 punnamināḍu nuvvu
185 bakka palacagā unnaḍu ammā
186 paḍamaṭi bāgāmu nunci vacci
187 ēmamma bāgunnarā lēdu ani
188 ninnu aḍigāḍu ammā
189 bābu ekkaḍakellēḍu ammā ani
190 ninnu aḍigāḍu ammā
191 ā rōju kānunci ammā
192 tellaṭi kāgitamu vastē
193 nallaṭi akṣaramu ammā
194 cirigi pōyinaṭṭē
195 nīku akṣarālu anna
196 kāpaḍutundi ammā
197 ā rōjukānunci
198 nī iṇṭivarkē
199 sukhamu lēdammā
200 okka māṭaṇṭē
201 reṇḍokka māṭayi
202 nī vāpukammo [the medium slaps her thighs]
203 muṭṭu kuṇṭundammā
204 poddu allā vaddu ammā
205 ī nela ākharuvulō
206 vacci nelalōnē
207 antaṭi ammō

208 ī yokka anina
209 mēlu avitē
210 ammā ani pilu
211 mēlu gāpōtēvammo
212 pōyindi nīku vacci cūpitē
213 ānakāpalli nūkamma unnadi māyamma kāṇḍra kota pērellutundō
214 mālōḍiki nīlavāḍiki gollavāḍiki kāpuvāḍiki
215 aṣṭādi varṇamukindē
216 kalkattākāḍinuncē
217 meḍrāsu vellina dāka
218 pērēllutunna gaṅganē
219 aṭṭi gaṅganu avitē
220 pōyindi nīku rappistānu
221 lēkapōtē nī kālu kinda jōḍu ayi uṇṭānē
222 hastamu peṭṭu kōyi vellu kūturā

A short interval follows. Actually, with the last line, the medium has signalled the end of her recitation. After the following short conversation between Ramana Murthy and G.P. Lakshmi, the medium begins again to speak.

G. P. Lakshmi [to R. Murthy]: nuvvu aḍugutunnavā?
R. Murthy: mīru aḍugutunnarē.
G. P. Lakshmi [to the goddess]: amma nātō bāṭu tirumala bābu vaccēḍu. ataniki ēdainā cepputāvu ammā?

223 amma maṅgala vāramu nāḍu nēnu anna [*hā*][19]
224 nīku kāvālaṇṭenē ōyammō [*hā*]
225 nī ēḍu gaṇṭala poddukamma
226 ālakālanē vāpātavalalōnā [*hā*]
227 nēnu valakāḍa punnempu valalōna
228 ole pālagā taṇḍri kaḍa pāpambu
229 nēnu inabarcitāni māyammā [*hā*]
230 ī rātri mīyokka biḍḍalaki
231 nāyokka pēru cūpincitinammo [*hā*]
232 maṅgalavāramunāḍugāni ammo [*hā*]
233 nēnu istānu ā yokka vidānā
234 ōlē ā yokka śēṣamuddalammo
235 āḍi boṭṭu vēsukunna rōjuna [*hā*]
236 ālu enta āpadalō unnarō māyammo
237 ālu illu naṣṭambu gāni anna [*hā*]
238 ālu entamandi gontuka kōsināru

19 [*hā*] are G. P. Lakshmi's agreements.

ōlē biḍḍaḍu vaḍḍi mēda vellinōḍini
ōlē gōtilō ki dincinī ōri anna
āḍu ē mukhāna unnaḍō māyammo
vāḍu jōbilō cēyya vesigāni anna
āḍuni gōyyalōni dincina vāḍinanna
nēnu cepputānē kūturinē anna
ī rātri nī iṇṭiki naḍustānu
nī niddaṭlōni nēnu tīsi ceptānu
adi kāyamu cēsukōyi ammā
antaṭa kauvulu nēnu icci tīritē
antaṭi gaṅganu ikkaḍaki rappincu konna dānini ayite
nīku antaṭi ānavālu cepputānu ammā
antaṭa koḍuku eṭlu ēparlu tīsi
antaṭa koḍukunu goyyi tīsērē
ā gōtilō tokkina vāḍinē
āḍi illu nēnu naṣṭamu peḍatānu
nēnu śēbhāsu anipincukōyi
nēnu pērlu teccukunna nūkammanu ayitē
nī kulamulōni vāḍini paṭṭikellina dānini avitē
antaṭa gaṅganu ani pilucuduvu gāni ammā
nā ūru nī ūru gādu nī palle gādu anakamma
aravai āru jātulaku nēnu gaṅganu ammā
vaṇṭi jātikē kādu amma nēnu gaṅganu
golla aṇṭunnanu gavara aṇṭunnanu bāpana aṇṭunnanu
kōmaṭi aṇṭunnanā ammā
aṣṭādi varṇamulaki
nēnu ammanammo
ō yokka naruḍikē kādu ammanu
mā bābu īśvaruḍu nāyokka māyalu māyokka māyakāna lēkapōyāḍu
mā bābukanna peddavāru kādu mīru
hastamu peṭṭukōyi vellaṇḍi ammā
mīku vaccina bhayamu lēdu
nēnu velli pōtunnanu

G. P. Lakshmi: ī maṅgalvāram ceptunnandi. ani raitu ceppindi.
Some men [laughingly]: alavāṭu lēdu.
G. P. Lakshmi: ani right, everything right. [To me]: everthing truth. Six months time not feeling well. [To R. Murthy]: kādā. Jūne ninci nāku oṇṭlō bāgā lēda. Kanni, vacci nella bāgā untadi. Ceptundi, kādā. [To me]: next month everything cured. [...] ayidu rupaylu, pasupu, kunkum iccanu [...]. [During this conversation the medium belches repeatedly. This shows that the goddess is now leaving her body.]

References

AUSTIN, JOHN L. 1962. *How to do Things with Words*. Oxford: Oxford University Press.

BURGHART, RICHARD. 1996. *The Conditions of Listening. Essays on Religion, History and Politics in South Asia*. Ed. by C. J. Fuller and J. Spencer. Delhi: Oxford Univ. Press.

CLAUS, PETER J. 1984. »Medical Anthropology and the Ethnography of Spirit Possession«. *Contributions to Asian Studies* 18: 60–72.

DAVIS, RICHARD H. 1997. *Lives of Indian Images*. Princeton: Princeton University Press.

FOLEY, JOHN MILES. 1995. *The Singer of Tales in Performance*. Bloomington, Indianapolis: Indiana University Press.

FREEMAN, RICHARD. 1993. »Performing Possession: Ritual and Consciousness in the Teyyam Complex of Northern Kerala«. In: *Flags of Fame. Studies in South Asian Culture*. Ed. by H. Brückner, L. Lutze and A. Malik. Delhi: Manohar.

----. 1998. »Formalised possession among the Tantris and Teyyams of Malabar«. *South Asia Research* 18, 1: 73–98.

----. 1999. »Dynamics of the Person in the Worship and Sorcery of Malabar«. *Purusartha* 21 (Special Issue: *Possession in South Asia. Speech, Body, Territory*. Ed. by J. Assayag and G. Tarabout): 149–182.

GHOSH, NAYANTARA. 2005. »India Inc. Global Marketing Strategies and Cultural Identity«. In: *Import Export. Cultural Transfer. India, Germany, Austria*. Ed. by Angelika Fitz, Merle Kröger, Alexandra Schneider and Dorothee Wenner. Halle (Saale): Werkleitz Gesellschaft e. V.

KAKAR, SUDHIR. 1983. *Shamans, Mystics and Doctors. A psychological enquiry into India and its healing traditions*. Oxford: Oxford University Press.

KAPADIA, K. 1995. *Siva and Her Sisters: Gender, Caste, and Class in Rural South India*. Oxford: Westview.

----. 1996. »Dancing the goddess: possession and class in Tamil South India«. *Modern Asian Studies* 30, 2: 423–445.

KAPFERER, BRUCE. 1991 [1983]. *A Celebration of Demons. Exorcism and the Aesthetics of Healing in Sri Lanka*. Bloomington: Indiana University Press.

KJAERHOLM, LARS. 1982. »Possession and Substance in Indian Civilization. Thoughts emanating from field-work in South India«. *Folk* 24: 179–196.

LEWIS, I. M. 1989 [1978]. *Ecstatic Religion. A Study of Shamanism and Spirit Possession*. New York and London: Routledge.

NUCKOLLS, CHARLES W. 1991. »Deciding how to decide: Possession Mediumship in Jalari Divination«. *Medical Anthropology* 13: 57–82.

----. 1992. »Divergent Ontologies of Suffering in South Asia«. *Ethnology* 31: 57–74.

OBEYESEKERE, GANANATH. 1981. *Medusa's Hair. An Essay on Personal Symbols and Religious Experience*. Chicago, London: University of Chicago Press.

SCHÖMBUCHER, ELISABETH. 1993. »Gods, Ghosts and Demons: Possession in South Asia«. In: *Flags of Fame. Studies in South Asian Culture*. Ed. by H. Brückner, L. Lutze and A. Malik. Delhi: Manohar.

----. 1994a. »When the Deity speaks: Performative Aspects of Possession Mediumship in South India«. In: *Jahrbuch für musikalische Volks- und Völkerkunde*. Vol. 15. Ed. by J. Kuckertz. Eisenach: Karl Dietrich Wagner.

----. 1994b. »The consequences of not keeping a promise: Possession Mediumship among a South Indian Fishing Caste«. *Cahiers de Littérature Orale* 35: 41–64.

----. 1994c. »Die Göttin und ihr Medium: Über Autorenschaft bei medialer Besessenheit«. *Jahrbuch für transkulturelle Medizin und Psychotherapie* 6: 241–255.

----. 1998. »Death as the Beginning of a New Life. Hero Worship among a South Indian Fishing Caste«. In: *Ways of Dying. Death and its Meanings in South Asia.* Ed. by E. Schömbucher and C.P. Zoller. Delhi: Manohar.
----. 1999. »A Daughter for Seven Minutes: The Therapeutic and Divine Discourses of Possession Mediumship in South India«. *Purusartha* 21 (Special Issue: *Possession in South Asia. Speech, Body, Territory.* Ed. by J. Assayag and G. Tarabout): 33–60.
----. 2001. »Inviting Deities into Lord Jagannāth's Town: The Religious Practice of the Vāḍabalija Fishermen of Puri«. In: *Jagannāth Revisited: Studying Society, Religion and the State in Orissa.* Ed. by H. Kulke and B. Schnepel. Delhi: Manohar.
----. 2004a. »Exorcism«. In: *South Asian Folklore: An Encyclopedia.* Ed. by Peter J. Claus and Margaret A. Mills. New York: Garland Publishing Inc.
----. 2004b. »Possession«. In: *South Asian Folklore: An Encyclopedia.* Ed. by Peter J. Claus and Margaret A. Mills. New York: Garland Publishing Inc.
----. 2006. *Wo Götter durch Menschen sprechen. Besessenheit in Indien.* Berlin: Dietrich Reimer Verlag.
----; HEIDRUN BRÜCKNER. 2003. »Performances«. In: *The Oxford India Companion to Sociology and Social Anthropology.* Ed. by Veena Das. New Delhi: Oxford University Press, 598–624.
STANLEY, JOHN M. 1988. »Gods, Ghosts, and Possession«. In: *The Experience of Hinduism: Essays on Religion in Maharashtra.* Ed. by Maxine Berntsen and Eleanor Zelliot. Albany: State University of New York.

PHOTOGRAPHIES

The photographies are taken by the author and published online: *http://www.indologie.uni-wuerzburg.de/women_performers/contributors/schoembucher/illustrations/.*

ILLUSTRATION 1: Bhulekamma, medium of the goddess Nukalamma, in her house shrine, just after the possession.
ILLUSTRATION 2: Priest (*dasusu*), invoking the deity into the body of the medium.
ILLUSTRATION 3: Medium of the goddess Kotta Rajulu, listening to the divine words spoken through her and taped by the author.
ILLUSTRATION 4: Rajamma (left), a ›professional listener‹, who is able to explain and interpret the divine words to the audience, listening to the divine words together with the medium of the goddess Kotta Rajulu (right).

Part II

History and Social Context

Folk Culture and Modernity

The Case of Goddess Reṇukā-Ellamma and her Special Devotees

Heidrun Brückner

Introductory

This article deals with the impact of modernization on a popular religious cult of the Deccan and especially on the perception of certain groups of devotees and the service they render to the deity. The paper is based mainly on observations and visual documentations made in 2007 and 2009 at the large temple centre of the goddess Reṇukā-Ellamma in Saundatti, Belgaum District, North Karnataka. My focus is on the text, analysis and interpretation of a pamphlet or leaflet distributed at the site as part of a campaign by government agencies and NGOs against certain assumed or actual religious practices [ILLUSTRATIONS 1–3, 28].[1,2]

I shall first provide some basic information about the myth, the cult and the temple of the goddess. Next I will discuss the situation at the site in 2007 and provide a brief sketch of developments since the early 1980s. Finally, I will identify some of the strategies certain groups of devotees seem to adopt in response to the threats against their devotional practices.

Reṇukā-Ellamma is one of the most popular goddesses of Northern Karnataka and the adjoining regions of Maharashtra and Andhra Pradesh. Her most important temple centres at Saundatti and Chandragutti attract large crowds of pilgrims every year on the main festival days. In neighbouring Maharashtra, too, this goddess has major temple centres, besides being an important household and family deity, as in Northern Karnataka.[3] Her mythology partly overlaps with that of the village goddesses Māriamma / Mariamman and others

1 In the present paper I use the Sanskrit- and Kannaḍa-spelling of names according to context. Thus, Sanskrit *devadāsī*, but Kannaḍa *dēvadāsi*.

2 My thanks are due to Hanne de Bruin, Kanchipuram, Vera Perrone, Stuttgart / Rio de Janeiro, and Janaki Nair, New Delhi, for helpful comments and discussions of earlier drafts of this paper. The credit for checking the English style goes to Anne Feldhaus, Tempe, Arizona.

3 Concerning the cult and its centres in Maharashtra see STARK-WILD 1997; for domestic worship see MALLEBREIN 1993.

in Karnataka, Andhra Pradesh and Tamilnadu. The goddess is also worshiped under her name Reṇukā-Ellamma in small village temples as a village goddess.

The Myths

A special feature of the mythology of this goddess is the blend of Sanskritic and popular traditions conveyed by her names, Reṇukā and Ellamma. The Sanskrit story is found in epics and Purāṇas in the context of the mythology of Paraśurāma, one of the *avatāras* of god Viṣṇu. His parents, the sage Jamadagni and the princess Reṇukā, provide him with a double identity as Brahmin and Kṣatriya.[4]

Reṇukā is depicted as the ideal *pativratā* (chaste wife), single-mindedly serving her husband and assisting him in performing his religious observances. This service provides her with special powers such as being able to fetch water from the river without carrying a pot. But one day, when she sees – in the water – the reflection of a Gandharva couple sporting in the sky, her attention is diverted for a brief moment and she loses her special powers. Her husband curses her and orders his sons to punish and behead their mother. Only the youngest one, Paraśurāma, obeys his father's command and is rewarded with a boon. He uses it to bring his mother back to life – without her remembering what has happened. The Sanskrit narrative then turns to events mainly concerning Jamadagni and Paraśurāma. Among other things, king Kārtavīryārjuna kills Jamadagni in order to steal the wish-granting cow Kāmadhenu. In revenge, Paraśurāma not only slaughters his father's murderer, but vows to clear the earth of all Kṣatriya clans.

The numerous vernacular folk versions of the story correspond with the Sanskritic narrative upto the point when Reṇukā is decapitated by her son. But then, in all these versions, bringing his mother back to life poses a problem for Paraśurāma, because she has run away and sought refuge with an Untouchable women, hugging her tightly. Paraśurāma beheads both of the women with one stroke. Later, by mistake, he transposes the heads and puts his mother's head on the Untouchable woman's body. Reṇukā's husband, Jamadagni, does not accept this composite figure back as his wife, curses her to suffer from a skin disease, and sends her away into the forest. There, she encounters two Nātha Yogins who help her. She is cured of her skin disease by bathing in a particular pond. Later, the Yogins, Reṇukā-Ellamma, and the Untouchable woman of the Māḍiga community, Mātaṅgi, who had helped Reṇukā, all get established in their own temples. Many versions and retellings of the story have been summa-

4 See GAIL 1977 for a study of Paraśurāma in the epic-puranic tradition.

rized or studied by SUNKAPURA (1977), BRUBAKER (1978), SHULMAN (1984), ASSAYAG (1992), STARK-WILD (1997) and others.[5]

The Site at Saundatti: Localisation of the myth, annual cycle of rituals and major pilgrimages

The protagonists and many of the central events of the narrative are locally associated with the temple of the goddess at Saundatti in North Karnataka [ILLUSTRATIONS 4–8].[6] Half-way up the hill (and the seven valleys) among which her temple is situated, we find the tank, called Jōgula Bhāvi [ILLUSTRATIONS 9, 10, 14], in which Reṇukā-Ellamma bathed and was cured of her skin disease. Pilgrims take a bath there first [ILLUSTRATION 11], dress in fresh Neem leaves [ILLUSTRATIONS 45–47], worship goddess Satyavva by circumambulating her adjoining temple [ILLUSTRATIONS 12, 13; FILM CLIP 1] and rush uphill to the main temple, in which Reṇukā-Ellamma's head is the image worshiped in the sanctum (*garbhaguḍi* / *garbhagṛha*) [ILLUSTRATIONS 6–8, 59, 60]. In the narrow lanes in front, *i.e.* east, of the temple there is a shrine for Kālabhairava, right on the passage leading to the temple, and for the two Yogins who rescued Reṇukā in the forest [ILLUSTRATIONS 15, 16; FILM CLIP 1 and 2]. Their names are Ekkayya and Jōgayya. The passage leads to a lane where Mātaṅgi, with whom the goddess sought refuge and who was killed along with her, has a small underground rock temple [ILLUSTRATIONS 17–20; FILM CLIP 2]. This temple faces east, as does that of the goddess herself. People are supposed to offer worship first at Mātaṅgi's temple. Mātaṅgi is the special goddess of the Māḍiga caste. Girls and women dedicated to her are also refered to as Mātaṅgis. Her image consists of an aniconic stone covered with kumkuma and turmeric powder [ILLUSTRATIONS 19, 20; FILM CLIP 2]. A short distance to the northeast, on top of one of the seven hills that form Ellamma's »Seven Valleys«, her husband Jamadagni's small, octagonal temple stands as a kind of landmark [ILLUSTRATION 21; FILM CLIP 1]. Next to it is a small shrine, renovated a few years ago, that houses some aniconic stones that are identified as parts of Reṇukā's dead body [ILLUSTRATIONS 22, 57, 58]. People say that this is the place where Reṇukā was beheaded by her son Paraśurāma.

To the north, south and west of the main temple of the goddess, there is more open space, as compared to the eastern area with its lanes, shops, shrines and

5 The story of the transposed heads became known in Europe as early as the 18th century through the travelogue of P. Sonnerat. It was first published in French in 1782 and one year later, in 1783, in German translation. Goethe made use of it for his *Paria*-trilogy, published in 1823 and consisting of the three poems *The Paria's Prayer*, *Legend* and *Thanks of the Paria*. See BRÜCKNER 1999 for further references.

6 The temple complex has been studied most comprehensively by ASSAYAG (1992), who also provides elaborate information about the Lingayat priestly families who run the temple.

residential quarters. Behind the temple, a short distance to the southwest, her son Paraśurāma has a small sanctuary, with a cradle suspended at the entrance [ILLUSTRATIONS 23, 24; FILM CLIP 2]. Further southwest, three springs in a rock enclosed in stone basins provide special water that gets sprinkled on the pilgrims. In front of the basins, there are provisions for bathing. Finally, a largish temple of Śiva as Mallikārjuna is found on the western side of the goddess's temple [ILLUSTRATION 25; FILM CLIP 2].

In the annual ritual cycle, pilgrims and devotees are attracted to the temple on all full-moon days (Ka. *huṇṇime*; Skt. *pūrṇimā*), but some full moons stand out as of special significance and attract hundreds of thousands of pilgrims from Northern Karnataka and Maharashtra [ILLUSTRATIONS 48–56].

What are probably the largest crowds assemble for Bhārata Huṇṇime [ILLUSTRATIONS 15, 16, 24, 30–60; FILM CLIP 1] in the month of Māgha (January-February) and for Navarātrī-Vijayadaśamī in the autumn. Three more full moons are of importance as marking the wedding of the goddess and the beginning and end of her temporary widowhood. The first of them, called Davanada Huṇṇime or Muttaide Huṇṇime (»full moon of the auspicious married women«), is celebrated in the month of Caitra (April-May).[7] The second is named Hostilina Huṇṇime (Ka. *hostilu*, threshold) – or, colloquially, Raṇḍe Huṇṇime (widow's full moon) – and falls in the month of Mārgaśīrśa (November-December).

On this occasion, as witnessed by the author on 24th and 25th December 2007, the image of the goddess is taken in procession in a palanquin to the temple of Jamadagni [ILLUSTRATIONS 21, 26]. Jamadagni is supposed to have been killed on this day by Kārtavīryārjuna, and the bangles worn by the image are broken as a mark of widowhood. The same is done with all her images in the portable shrines carried by devotees. The image itself, in each case, is covered with a cloth. After the palanquin has returned to the temple, the functioning of the temple is almost completely suspended until the next full-moon day, called Banada Huṇṇime (in Puṣya, December-January).[8] The pilgrimage on this third important full moon day was witnessed on 31st December 2009 [ILLUSTRATIONS 2, 3, 6, 9–13, 17–21]. Early in the morning of this full moon night, a Mahāpūjā (»great pūjā«) is conducted in the temple of the goddess.

Pilgrims come to Saundatti in groups consisting of families, castemates and village neighbourhoods from various places in Maharashtra and Karnataka. They travel mainly by bus, jeep or car and they camp at the site for several nights. Bullock carts, which formerly dominated the scene, have become fewer in recent years. Boards, leaflets and brochures at the temple are mostly bilingual

7 This is the usual date for the wedding of South Indian goddesses, irrespective of mythological references. Compare the wedding of goddess Mīnākṣi of Madurai and others (HARMAN 1992 [1989]).

8 This day is, according to ASSAYAG (1992: 132–33), also considered an important day for domestic worship of Ellamma.

in Marāṭhī and Kannaḍa. The groups often bring images of the goddess from their homes, and purify the images and conduct *pūjā* for them at the site. This includes the preparation of special food items kept in small baskets in front of the larger basket with the decorated image of the goddess, and the singing of devotional songs [ILLUSTRATION 27; FILM CLIP 1]. Pilgrims come in continuation of family traditions, to fulfill or renew vows, or to make new vows. They may also avail themselves of the services of special groups of devotees of the goddess who have (for the most part) been dedicated to her in childhood [FILM CLIP 1].

Special Devotees of the Goddess and their Changing Perception

A special feature of many popular cults of the Deccan is the practice, on the part of certain communities, of dedicating children to the service of deities like Khaṇḍobā-Mailāra, Mādeśvara or Reṇukā-Ellamma. Besides family traditions of dedicating, for example, the youngest son, promises to offer a child are also made in times of affliction or in cases of childlessness. As in the brahmanic rite of *upanayana (*investment with the sacred thread) or the *dīkṣā,* initiation, into Vīraśaivism and other religious orders, the dedicated persons undergo an initiation refered to by various vernacular terms. The devotional practices of these people vary according to the deity and according to the particular service for which they are dedicated. SRINIVAS (1976: 308) speaks of »priest-cum-mendicant orders among the non Brahmin castes«. Many people who have been dedicated to a god as children become professional singers, musicians, and dancer-performers of the oral epic traditions of the deities [ILLUSTRATION 29].[9]

Goddess Reṇukā-Ellamma's special devotees are the Jōgappas and Jōgammas. These devotees still play an important role as religious specialists, both in domestic worship and at the temple [ILLUSTRATIONS 30–45; FILM CLIPS 1 and 2].[10] Both Jōgappas and Jōgammas undergo particular initiation rituals to become servants or children or spouses of the goddess.[11] The initiates undergo the initiation in accordance with a family tradition, or in fulfilment of vows made by their parents, or of their own accord after experiencing a personal call from the goddess in a dream, or as a way of seeking refuge with her in order to solve personal problems. Thus, several Jōgappas told me that the goddess appeared to them in a dream during puberty and requested them to serve her by becoming Jōgappas and not entering into manhood. In accordance with these different reasons for becoming a Jōgappa, we can also understand better that some of them are transgender people, others appear to be transvestites with hyper-

9 See BRÜCKNER 2009b: 213–215.

10 See MALLEBREIN 1993.

11 The initiation is also perceived in terms of a wedding to the goddess, or, as others say, to her husband Jamadagni.

feminine behavior and some seem to be just men dressed in saris.[12] Jōgappas normally live in communities and move about in groups of three or four, singing, dancing and performing in praise of the goddess. One of them carries on his / her head the goddess's image, fixed on a brass pot and used for worship [ILLUSTRATIONS 40, 42, 43]. This person also acts as a dancer, balancing the pot on his / her head and sometimes performing almost acrobatic feats with it. Some members of the audience fix currency notes on the pot in appreciation of the performance. The other troupe members accompany the dancer with songs. For musical accompaniment a one-stringed instrument and a *caudike* are used. A *caudike* looks like a small wooden drum, open at one end, with a cluster of brass bells affixed to it. It produces a characteristic, intense sound [ILLUSTRATIONS 30, 33, 34, 54; FILM CLIP 1]. Some Jōgappas (and Jōgammas) also act as mediums of the goddess whom devotees consult through them. The Jōgappas identify themselves with the elder brothers of Paraśurāma who refused to kill their mother; they were cursed, in the folk version, by their enraged father to become eunuchs.

Many of the dedicated females, the Jōgammas, used to make a living by visiting a certain number of houses assigned to them on Tuesdays and Fridays, and on special occasions when they conducted domestic rituals there. In return, they received alms in kind. Girls dedicated to the goddess at a young age normally cannot get married, as they are married to the goddess, or, as some say, to Jamadagni. One section among them, especially those who wear matted hair, live as renouncers or female ascetics. The appearance of matted hair is also considered an indication of the call of the goddess [ILLUSTRATIONS 31, 32]. Many of the Jōgammas come to the temple of the goddess on full-moon days carrying basket-shrines (*jaga*) or pot-shrines (*koḍa*) on their heads and collecting alms in return for blessing the devotees and giving them *kuṃkuma* etc. as *prasāda* [ILLUSTRATIONS 35, 44].

Formerly, some groups of Jōgammas performed *dēvadāsī*-like functions in the temple of the goddess, such as fanning the deity with Yak-whisks or simply sweeping the temple. Another group, refered to as Basavis, used to be initiated in order to provide a substitute son for their parents.[13] The Basavis did not get married, but lived with a man in the village. They themselves or their male offspring could obtain the legal and ritual rights of a son in relation to their parents.[14] Yet others were at the service of different male partners and come closest to what is today labeled as »Devadasis«. It is important to note that all these differentiations are ignored in the modern public discourse about these groups.

12 Jōgappas should not be equated with Hijras. They do not undergo castration rituals and they are buried as males (Vera Perrone, oral communication).

13 The term alludes to the *basava*, the village bull, who is left to roam freely in the village.

14 See ASSAYAG 1992: 163 and NAIR [2011]: chapter 6.

The Impact of Modernity: Scandalising Devotional Practices

In the 1980s, public outrage was provoked by media reports about young female initiates of the goddess Reṇukā-Ellamma ending up in urban, commercialised prostitution in the red-light areas of Mumbai and other big cities.[15] These reports drew public attention to the large regional temples of the goddess at Saundatti and Chandragutti in North Karnataka. Besides the initiation ceremonies conducted by temple priests, what especially attracted media persons and various kinds of activists was the practice of wearing hardly any clothes, just a dress of twigs with fresh green Neem (Margosa) leaves, while covering the distance between the bathing tank and the temple. Activists tried to restrain devotees from performing this religious service (*sēve*). Agitation and public attention reached a first peak in 1986, known as the so-called »Chandragutti Case«, when devotees turned against journalists, activists and the police who were supposed to protect them. This, again, triggered further debates in which a wider public became involved.[16]

In 1984, the government of the State of Karnataka published the »Karnataka Devadasi (Prohibition of Dedication) Act, 1982«[17] with the objective of preventing the dedication of females as »Devadasis« in the State. The Act assumes that »such practice leads women so dedicated to a life of prostitution«. »Dedication« is defined as »the performance of any act or ceremony, by whatever name called, by which a woman is dedicated to the service of any deity, idol, object of worship, temple, other religious institutions or places of worship«. The Act specifies that »devadasi« »means a woman so dedicated« and »woman« »means a

15 I do not discuss the issue of prostitution that dominates the public discourse in any detail in the present paper. I therefore do not refer to the literature focussing on it, often in the context of AIDS. For a recent article in this vein see the chapter on »Daughters of Yellamma« in Dalrymple 2009 and the references given there. For a thorough study of the concept of Devadasi and important issues of purity and auspiciousness connected with it see Marglin 1985, especially the introductory and final chapters.

16 There was a large feminist group involvement in preventing dedication. Opposition came from very different quarters: feminists, old style social workers, right wing Hindus, Dalits, and government agencies. See the article by Anantha Murthy, a leading writer and intellectual of Karnataka, whose differentiated stance brought him criticism from all these quarters (Anantha Murthy 2002 [1986]). He gives a vivid account of the debates. For a discussion of notions of modernity and the role of the media, see Appadurai 2005, especially the first chapter.

17 The text is reproduced as an appendix in Assayag 1992: 494–96. The Act replaces the earlier Bombay Devadasi Protection Act of 1934 and the Madras Devadasi (Prevention of Dedication) Act of 1947 (Madras Act 31 of 1937). The 1947 Act is quoted in full in Marglin 1985, 305–6 (note 7), who notes that the princely states of Mysore and Travancore had passed similar legislation much earlier, namely in 1910 and 1930. On the history of the Mysore legislation concerning the abolition of the institution of Devadasi and its impact on the economic situation of numerous women, see Nair [2011]: chapter 6, »The Illicit in the Modern: Banning the Devadasi«. According to Nair, the government order for complete abolition was passed in 1909.

female of any age«. The Act declares »dedication as devadasi to be unlawful«, stressing that »any woman so dedicated shall not thereby be deemed to have become incapable of entering into a valid marriage«. The fourth paragraph is entitled »Marriage of devadasi« and states that becoming a ›devadasi‹ does not make a woman's marriage invalid or her issue illegitimate. The fifth paragraph is concerned with penalties, the sixth with »Protection of action taken in good faith«, the seventh with »Power to make rules« and the last with repeal of earlier Acts (see footnote 17).

The definitions given in the Act provide comprehensive legal grounds to sanction any religious practice involving the dedication of females by criminalising it wholesale. The legal discourse ignores the religious dimension of cults comprising such practices. It reconfirms and continues colonial notions of Hindu religious practice, more than thirty years after independence.

Nicholas Dirks has argued »that colonial rule took on an anthropological cast of mind in the late 19th century.« In this context, Hinduism was redefined as a religion and its practices distinguished from mere »customs«. Whereas religion proper was protected, »any form of custom that seemed either dangerous to the colonial state or offensive to the various agencies – from missionaries to social reformist groups – [...]« was excluded from these provisions (DIRKS 2004: 150–151). Dirks mainly bases his argument on the 19th century »Hookswinging Controversy« and the previous one about *sati*, which both led to the denunciation of popular religion (2004: 159), having first generated the categories of low, popular and high, classical religion (2004: 176). The Devadasi Act quoted here still reflects a similar approach to »custom«, with a special emphasis on female practice.

One of its major concerns is the protection of »valid marriage« and, by implication, the confinement of females to the domestic sphere, in contradistinction – one may assume – to an itinerant lifestyle, moving alone and independently in public space. It should also be noted that a Sanskrit term, »Devadasi«, is introduced here that is not in use among the local population. In this way, a comprehensive category is created that ignores the distinctions between different modes of dedication on the local level. Remembering M.N. Srinivas' analysis of »Sanskritization« and »Westernization« going hand in hand, the use of this Sanskrit word in a legal text inspired by British colonial law can be considered a case in point (SRINIVAS 1952).

Against the background of the Karnataka Devadasi Act, the pamphlet collected at the Saundatti temple more than twenty years after the Act's publication, in 2007 [see ILLUSTRATION 1],[18] can be read as an attempt to implement and update the Act, applying its very general statements to individual, localised devotional practices and extending its applicability to groups and practices not

18 The full text in roman transliteration and with a complete English translation is reproduced in the appendix. ILLUSTRATION 1 is a scan of the original.

mentioned in the Act, such as the dedication of males or transgender persons to the goddess.

The pamphlet starts in the style of a public political speech, appealing to people's solidarity in abolishing social evils and in striving for peace and social harmony. In a social reform rhetoric, illiteracy and »superstition« or »blind belief« (*mūḍha nambike*) are held responsible for exploitation and harassment, especially of women and children. The »blind ritual practices« (*andha ācaraṇegaḷu*) of the »devadasi custom« (*dēvadāsi paddhati*) are given as an example. The appeal seems to be addressed mainly to ›educated‹ people of the middle classes who can read and write and who are requested to instruct those who cannot. The use of terms such as »blind belief«, »blind ritual practices« and »custom« recalls the rhetoric typical of 19th-century Christian missionaries and British administrators that was just refered to in connection with the argument of Dirks (2004).

In addition to the textual dimension, the pamphlet, in each of the eight sections that follow, illustrates its points by small drawings, probably to make the points comprehensible for people who cannot read. In the first of these eight sections, the tone changes from persuasion and appeal, which dominates the introductory paragraph, to the threatening legal discourse of the Karnataka Devadasi Act quoted above. The English term »dedication« is specified in Kannaḍa by saying it is an offence to make any woman a *dēvadāsi* »by tying beads on her« (*muttu kaṭṭu,* ›tying beads‹, stands for the act of initiation). The illustration shows four women involved in an initiation ceremony (*muttu kaṭṭuvudu*) and a policeman with handcuffs approaching in the background. The figure of the initiate is crossed out with a large »X« in order to represent the prohibition.

The second section requests people to stop giving alms to persons (Jōgammas and Jōgappas) who approach them carrying the basket shrine (*jaga*) of the goddess on their head, and to discourage them from following this practice. The illustration shows a Jōgamma standing at the door of a house and receiving grain as alms from the lady of the house, who is assisted by another woman. The figure of the Jōgamma is crossed out. In the second sentence, the term »Dēvadāsi-women« (*dēvadāsi-mahiḷeyaru*) is introduced and used twice, whereas at the beginning and end of the section the reference is to Jōgammas and Jōgappas. In this way, Jōgammas are equated with Devadasis and Jōgappas are also included under the Karnataka Devadasi Act.

Interestingly, this section also specifies some of the disapproved practices by censuring them. We learn that Jōgammas are invited for marriages, house-warming ceremonies (*gṛhapraveśa*), fairs and harvest festivals, and that they are given grain, jowar, cloth, money and gifts on these occasions.

The third section refers to possession mediumship, the illustration showing a woman consulting a Jōgamma medium. The figure of the Jōgamma is crossed out. The text mentions only two ways of accounting for this phenomenon, which is a widespread religious practice: either the possessed medium is suffering from a mental disorder or he / she is pretending and cheating in order to get recognition and / or to make money. Again, the »Dēvadāsi custom« is blamed. People who become possessed by the goddess and serve as mediums are asked to see a doctor to get cured. The practice of acting as a medium of the goddess (and, by implication, consulting such a medium) is contrasted to »true devotion« (*nijavāda bhakti*).

The fourth topic taken up in the pamphlet is matted hair. Devotees believe that it is a sign of the appearance of the goddess if a person's hair gets matted. Especially in the case of young girls, portions of their hair getting matted is considered an indication of the call of the goddess, and it is thought that such a girl should be initiated into the goddess's service. The authors of the pamphlet, on the contrary, explain the appearance of knots and so on in the hair as a sign of a particular infection, called Plaika Phalanika, caused by lack of hygiene and cleanliness. At the end of the paragraph, the authors assure people that the goddess consents to cleaning such hair and removing the knotted portions. The topic is taken up again at the very end of the pamphlet, when people are invited to have their hair cleaned at the office of the Devadasi Rehabilitation Project.

It should be noted here that matted hair, in the Hindu tradition, is a distinctive mark of ascetics, especially Śaiva ascetics, and of god Śiva himself, who is viewed as an ascetic in a part of his mythology and iconography. In the temple complex of the goddess at Saundatti, Śiva, Reṇukā's husband Jamadagni and her son Paraśurāma, as well as the two Yogins (depicted in the paintings and statues in the Kālabhairava temple) who rescued Reṇukā in the forest, are all shown with a topknot of matted hair. The same applies to Pārvatī in the myth in which she serves Śiva as a meditating ascetic and competes with him in the vigour of her asceticism in order to obtain him as a husband.

The negative view of matted hair as expressed in the pamphlet is primarily directed against a sub-group of Jōgamma devotees of the goddess who live as itinerant female ascetics. There is no reference to the matted hair of male ascetics being objectionable in any way. Accordingly, the illustration shows a woman cleansing the long matted tresses of a Jōgamma.

The next point concerns the practice of wearing a dress of Margosa (Neem) leaves to worship the goddess in fulfilment of a vow. After taking a bath in the Jogula Bhavi tank, most devotees, especially males and children, used to wear only a loincloth underneath their leaf dress. In the pamphlet, it is assumed that devotees are »naked« except for the Margosa leaves. This is described in strong terms as an »uncivilised custom« (*anāgarika paddhati*). People are appealed to »to save civilisation« by wearing clothes underneath the leaves. They are assured that wearing clothes in addition to leaves will secure them the grace of the goddess. The illustration, again, reveals that the appeal is primarily addressed to women. It shows a young woman wearing only a leaf dress with her picture crossed out and another woman wearing a sari and some leaves on top of it as an example of the proper way to dress. The focus on female devotees is also stressed by refering to the goddess as a great Pativratā, or chaste woman serving her husband – another Sanskritic-brahmanic concept.

Section six hits out against the Jōgappas, considered here as men pretending to be women by wearing a sari and asking for alms in the name of the goddess. The explanation given for this behaviour is that such persons suffer either from mental weakness or disturbance or from physical defects. If neither of these alternatives applies, it is assumed that the men just want to make a living the easy way. In brackets, the text tells us that, as a rule of nature, there are only two genders, male and female, and that god would not ask men to behave like women. People are requested to take or direct such persons to a doctor to cure them so that they can lead a decent life. The illustration shows a Jōgappa dancing in front of a group of (mainly male) spectators wearing a sari and carrying a pot shrine (*koḍa*) on his head. His figure is crossed out.

The topic of section seven is initially somewhat surprising in the present context. It concerns the practice of people playing Ōkaḷi (Holi) by splashing coloured water on other people. The illustration shows a group of men splashing water on a lone woman, whose sari gets dishevelled in the process. The group of men, whose clothing and hairstyles mark them as belonging to different communities, is crossed out. Again, the text uses very strong terms and sees civilisation itself as at stake, refering to the practice as an »inhuman custom«. The text appeals to people to lead a pure, civilised life.

The last section of the pamphlet is directed against child marriage. In the drawing, we see a child couple during a wedding ceremony, surrounded by priests and elders. In the background, a policeman is approaching with handcuffs. The child couple is crossed out. This short, final section of the pamphlet refers to the Child Marriage Prohibition Act 1929, according to which it is a punishable offence to arrange a marriage for a boy below 21 or a girl below 18 years of age. There is no explicit reference to a religious context here, but one should keep in mind that marriage is the major *saṃskāra* or life-cycle rite for women and that the initiation as a Jōgamma is equated with a wedding.

As already mentioned above, at the end of the pamphlet, the authors invite persons with matted hair to come to the office of the Devadasi Rehabilitation Project and have their hair cleaned. The names and addresses of the organisations involved, which were already given at the beginning of the pamphlet, are repeated here in more detail, with postal codes and telephone numbers.

Reviewing the text of the pamphlet as a whole one can make out a clear structure:

The general introductory paragraph sets the stage and introduces negatively charged terms in speaking about the practices to be censured. The terminology can be traced back to the 19th-century Christian missionary and British colonial administration divide between true religion and mere »custom« characterised by »blind belief« and »superstition«.

Of the eight points made in the pamphlet, the first and the last ones provide a kind of legal frame, both refering to particular »Acts«. The most important point is the first one, intended to stop the initiation of females into the cult of the goddess by applying the Karnataka Devadasi Act. Since young girls are the group the Act and the activists are most eager to protect, there is a certain logic in concluding the list with a reference to the Child Marriage Prohibition Act concerned with the marriage of young girls – a ceremony that can be compared to an initiation. Thus, the Child Marriage Act reinforces the Prohibition of Dedication Act.[19]

Almost all remaining points can be brought under two interrelated heads: female mobility and female decency. What is called »begging« involves the movement of a woman with her portable shrine in public space and her visit to different houses. This practice is refered to as a »disaster« or »calamity«, probably because women are not supposed to move freely on their own and interact with people from different communities not related to them. The portable shrines themselves can almost be viewed as symbols of mobility.

All points made in the text show a strong concern with the female body and its exposure or concealment, and a preoccupation with advocating controlled and reserved female behaviour and appearance in public, including a neat and clean sari and conservative hairstyle (with the hair oiled, parted, combed and tied). Proper dress and proper hairstyle are equated with wifely decency, propagating the role model of the married woman serving her husband.

»Improper« dress and hairstyle may also be one of the reasons for censuring possession mediumship by considering the mediums as either mentally disturbed people or cheats. Generally, during possession trance, the medium's hair is kept loose and gets disheveled. To reinforce possession, particular body movements are made that appear involuntary and uncontrolled and, in the case of a woman, may involve the disarrangement of her sari, possibly exposing parts of her body to public view. The sessions take place in open spaces at the temple site.[20] Some of the possession mediums also have matted hair. Female initiates with matted hair often follow an itinerant lifestyle and live on their own.

In the pamphlet, matted hair is viewed, in medical terms, as an indication of an »infection« caused by lack of hygiene and cleanliness. Matted hair worn by women is one of the main targets of the activists, and its removal is one of their main concerns. The topic is therefore taken up again at the end of the text, when the pamphlet invites women to have their matted hair cleansed in the office of the rehabilitaion project.

19 There is no reference to the Child Marriage Acts of 1978 and 2006, mentioned *e.g.* by NAIR [2011].

20 See GRIEBL / SOMMER's analysis of the Siri tradition in the present volume and their similar observations with respect to the exposure of the female body during possession trance.

It is noteworthy that the term »Plaika Phalanika« for the infection supposed to cause matted hair is a Kannaḍa adaptation of the Latin term »Plica Polonica«, »Polish Plait«, refering to the phenomenon of matted hair; the term was used in Europe from about the 17th to the end of the 19th century.[21] The »Polish Plait« was rather widespread in Europe, too. Its perception underwent changes between the 17th and the 19th century similar to the changes in 20th-century India reflected in the pamphlet. In Europe, too, matted hair was associated with a religious meaning, or, in the Christian context, with »superstitious beliefs« that stopped people from removing it. In the 19th century, it came to be perceived as a disease caused by lack of hygiene and became part of the growing concern for »public health«. People, especially doctors, were advised to cut off the matted hair in order to treat the infected skin of the head. By the beginning of the 20th century, the phenomenon seems to have largely disappeared and there are no more references to it in the literature.

The point the text makes about wearing Neem dresses is aimed exclusively at having women cover their bodies in public. Being »naked« underneath the leaf dress is considered an »uncivilised custom«. Proper dress, *i.e.* a sari underneath the leaves, is associated with the concept of the goddess as a Pativratā, a chaste woman.[22]

On the same lines, splashing coloured water on women during the Holi festival is treated as a separate issue, again focussing on the possible exposure of the female body. The Kannaḍa term refered to here by the word »Holi« is »Ōkaḷi«, explained in Kittel's dictionary as »a red liquid of various ingredients which is sprinkled or squirted upon persons at the hōḷi feast, at the close of a temple festival, or at marriages«. As Vera Perrone tells me, the actual reference may be against a former practice at the near-by Hanumān temple, where higher caste men would hire a low-caste woman to allow coloured water to be splashed on her. At the same time, the wives of these higher caste men would beat their husbands with sticks. In the small drawing on the pamphlet it seems to be the female »victim« of the splashing herself who holds a kind of rod in her hand with some leaves on it, may be trying to hit the men. Again, the wording of the pamphlet does not make this possible background explicit.

The sixth section of the pamphlet, censuring the practice of the Jōgappas, complements the points made in the other sections. Like the Jōgammas, Jōgappas are condemned for »begging«, but especially for wearing a sari and

21 I am grateful to Vera Perrone, who pointed this out to me and refered me to the Wikipedia entries.

22 There was a practice of »naked worship« *(battale sēve)* at the temple of the goddess at Chandragutti. It used to take place at night in the dark. Devotees who performed it either wore Neem leaves or covered their bodies with turmeric (*ariśīna*) or ashes (*vibhūti*). This practice may be the actual target of the point made in the pamphlet, although there is no explicit reference to it (Vera Perrone graciously provided this information given to her in interviews with devotees).

thereby »pretending« to be women. It is assumed either that they are sick and need medical treatment or that they are cheating – the same alternatives already encountered with respect to possession mediumship. The possibility of a third gender or transgender persons seems to be unthinkable; the text refers to the »rule of nature« that there are only two genders, male and female. »Men« in saris encroaching upon femaleness as postulated in the pamphlet blur these clearcut categories. Jōgappas who do not get married and have families the normal way run counter to the notions of the text and the values it propounds.

One more target of the activists not mentioned in the pamphlet has to do with the temporary widowhood of the goddess starting on the full moon night of Hostilina Huṇṇime. On this night, the palanquin of the goddess is carried to Jamadagni's temple where the bangles of her idol are broken, marking the beginning of a period of widowhood.[23] Her Jōgamma devotees used to join the procession, break their own bangles and those of her images in the portable shrines, and bemourn the death of her / their husband Jamadagni. In 2007, the event, falling on the night of December 24th, was witnessed by the present author. The whole day and night, activists of the Devadasi Rehabilitation Project kept on declaring over megaphones that breaking one's bangles is unlawful and against the goddess's wishes. After nightfall they continued their agitation and megaphone speeches right next to the Jamadagni temple. The procession took place under heavy police protection. The atmosphere was highly charged. Nobody except the priests accompanying the palanquin were permitted to enter the Jamadagni temple or even get near the entrance. Some women told us that they were scared of being fined and taken into police custody if they broke their bangles at that time. Most of them abstained from doing so – at least at this crucial moment and locale.

Why would the act of breaking one's bangles along with the goddess and putting on new ones the very next day be such an offence as to require aggressive agitatation and intervention to stop it? I would assume that going through wedding (initiation) and widowhood on a divine or religious plane would, again, question the human institution of marriage so highly valued by the activists, government agencies, the law, and middle class society at large.

23 The motif of widowhood of the goddess and certain of her devotees and its being cyclically re-enacted requires further study that would go beyond the scope of the present paper. Widowhood stands in stark contrast to the notion of permanent auspiciousness associated with the Devadasi as a Nityasumangali, an ever-auspicious woman. The motif of widowhood and mourning, mainly by male and transgender devotees, is found in an entirely different mythological context in the Tamil cult of Aravan. See HILTEBEITEL 1995.

Developments between the 1982 and the 2007 Bhārata Huṇṇime Jātres: Some observations

In order to form a rough idea of the possible impact of the agitation on the practice of the devotees – reliable data not being available – I will give a brief comparative account of my personal impressions and visual documentation of the Bhārata Huṇṇime Jātre in 1982 and 2007. What struck me most in 2007 was the observation that the number of Jōgappa groups and individual Jōgappas seen at the Jātre had decreased.

So had the number of sessions with possession mediums, both male and female, going on openly at the site, and the cases of devotees falling into a trance while moving in procession or circumambulating the temple (but see FILM CLIP 1 for instances of both in 2007).

Concerning the Neem-leaf dresses, I wonder whether, in the past, there were really fewer people wearing clothes underneath the leaves. As far as I remember, and as can be seen on some of the visuals, even back in 1982 adult women wore clothing underneath the Neem leaves; only some boys, men, and little girls were wearing just a loincloth or underpants. In 2007, I saw only one little girl who was wearing Neem leaves with just underwear beneath. A few of the men were even wearing pants and shirts or vests underneath the leaves [see FILM CLIP 1].

It is impossible to determine whether this is due to the work of the activists or just the expression of a general change in habits of dress. There seems to be a tendency to use fewer Neem sprigs, often just one in the mouth and one on the head or near the waist. It may have become more difficult to procure the sprigs in large quantities. Many people may also be content with fulfilling their vow with a minimum effort in this respect.

The number of Jōgammas with matted hair had markedly decreased. At least, I did not catch sight of any women with matted hair in 2007. This decrease may in fact be a result of threats by the law and the activists. Jōgammas say that women with matted hair are scared that their hair will be completely cut off if they show up at the Jātre. They no longer go to the temple on major festival days, when the activists and the police are around, but come a few days earlier or later, or they visit smaller village temples instead.[24]

The same seems to apply to initiation ceremonies. Here, in addition, a distinction has to be made between the initiation of young girls, which is at the centre of the entire »Devadasi« issue, and the initiation of adult women, who may also be married. Initiation ceremonies of young girls are supposed to go on in secret and at increased fees because of the danger of being arrested.

24 One woman said she saw no problem in having the matted hair removed. If the goddess so desired, she would make it appear anew (HAHN 2010).

Other initiations seem to be possible even without a male priest, purely as a women's affair. Thus, a few days prior to 2007 Bhārata Huṇṇime, we[25] chanced upon an elderly Jōgamma who was first acting as a possession medium for a group of villagers, mainly men, and who then proceeded to conduct an initiation-cum-consultation ceremony for a middle-aged married woman. The woman had suffered from health and other problems, and then had had a dream that to get relief she should enter into the service of the goddess.

The ceremony took about 45 minutes and consisted of a *pūja* for the goddess in the *jaga* shrine, a *pūja* of the woman by the senior Jōgamma and vice versa, and a sequence during which the woman could pose questions to the goddess. One additional requirement was the presence of three more female devotees of the goddess, who also participated in the rituals.[26] The senior Jōgamma did not have matted hair and kept her hair loosely tied even during the seance, in which she served as a possession medium. The entire ceremony was conducted in a matter-of-fact way in the open space between the temple of the goddess and the Mallikārjuna temple.

It was evident that none of these women had anything to do with prostitution, but all were normal villagers engaged in practicing their devotion to the goddess in order to obtain her blessings and protection and lead a fulfilled and peaceful life.

Conclusion

Analysing the Karnataka Devadasi Act and the activities and pamphlets of organisations trying to implement it at the temple of goddess Reṇukā-Ellamma at Saundatti in North Karnataka, we can observe that the legal discourse of the Devadasi Act is complemented by a medical and sanitational (or public health) discourse in the pamphlet, which also includes a moral discourse. All these discourses are interwoven to mark the practitioners of popular religion as backward, uncivilised, superstitious, immoral and indecent. Their practices are ›criminalised‹ and ›pathologised‹ because they deviate from the cultural mainstream of the middle classes, which is also supported by the media. The main thrust is directed against women who do not follow the lifestyle of middle-class wives. Legally »valid marriage« to a single husband and the exclusive serving of this husband according to the Pativratā ideal is propagated as the highest value. Such a lifestyle would not permit women to render religious service by

25 My thanks are due to Prof. Shalini Raghunath, Dr. S. Shireshi and Prashant Naregal, all of the Karnatak University, Dharwad, who accompanied me to the site on 30th January 2007 and helped me communicate with the devotees and document the ceremony in question.

26 See FILM CLIP 2, a 3.5 minute edited and sub-titled version of the video documentation of the ceremony.

performing domestic rituals in other houses and collecting alms on certain days. A marital tie to a deity is denounced.

In actual fact, rural Jōgammas appear to be very capable of combining a married life in the civil sense with their devotional practices.[27] In response to the agitation and police control going on at the large temple centres of the goddess, they make certain adjustments, but continue to serve the goddess in ways they feel are beneficial for them.

Appendix

Transcription and translation of the pamphlet distributed at the Ellamma Temple, Saundatti, in 2007

[For a photograph of the pamphlet see Illustration 1 online]

»Karmaṇi« – Karnāṭaka Rājya Mahiḷā Abhivṛddhi Nigama mattu MĀS – Ghaṭaprabhā (Dēvadāsi Punarvasati Yōjane – Beḷagāvi)
Karnāṭaka State Women's Development Organisation and MAS – Ghataprabha. (Devadasi Rehabilitation Project – Belgaum)

> *Mānyarē,*
> *banniri, anēka śatamānagaḷindalū anakṣarate, mūḍha nambike, paraspara śōṣaṇe, daurjanyagaḷinda baḷalida samājavu 21nēya śatamānadalliyādarū śānti, nemmadi paraspara sauhārdateyinda bāḷuvantāgali endu prayatnisōṇa. halavu mūḍha nambike, svārthadinda mahiḷeyaru mattu makkaḷa mēlāguttiruva śōṣaṇe daurjanyagaḷannu taḍegaṭṭalu sāmājika jāgṛtiya kahaḷeyannu moḷagisōṇa. samājadalli nāgarikarū saha tamage tiḷiyadē māḍuttiruva kelavu ācaraṇegaḷinda dēvara hesarinalli mahiḷe[ya]ru mattu makkaḷannu bali tegedukoḷḷuva dēvadāsi paddhatiyantaha andha ācaraṇegaḷu janajīvanada mēle bīruttiruva duṣpariṇāmagaḷa bagge tiḷiyōṇa mattu tiḷisōṇa.*

Respected People,[28]
Come on! For many centuries society has been suffering from illiteracy, superstition, mutual exploitation and harassment; let us try at least in the 21st cen-

27 Benjamin Hahn (Hahn 2010) has interviewed several women in a village near Dharwad who all were married and handed on their status of a Jōgamma »inherited« from their mother-in-law within the family to their own daughter-in-law.

28 My thanks are due to Dr. S. Shireshi, Dharwad, and Profs. Chinnappa Gowda and Viveka Rai, Mangalore, who helped me at different stages to prepare the English translation of the pamphlet.

tury to live in peace, comfort and mutual harmony. Let us blow the trumpet of social awareness in order to prevent exploitation and harassment of women and children through superstition and selfishness. In society, even civilised people, without being aware of it, by practicing some rituals in the name of god, use women and children as sacrificial victims as in the Devadasi custom; let us realise and instruct others about the evil consequences of [such] blind ritual practices affecting the lives of people.

1 [ILLUSTRATION 1a: Sketch of dedication ceremony]

Karṇāṭaka Dēvadāsi samarpaṇā niṣēdha kāyde 1982 ra prakāra yāvudē heṇṇige muttu kaṭṭi Dēvadāsiyannāgi māḍuvudu aparādha intaha kṛtyakke prōtsahisidavarige mattu bhāgiyādavarige 5 varṣa kaṭhina śikṣe hāgū rū. 5.000,- gaḷa varege daṇḍa vidhisalāguttade.

According to the Karnataka Devadasi Dedication Prohibition Act 1982 it is an offence to make any woman a Devadasi by tying the beads to her; those who encourage such an act and those who take part in it are liable to five years of severe punishment and a fine of up to 5000 Rupees.

2 [ILLUSTRATION 1b: A Jogamma standing at the door of a house and receiving grain as alms]

Dēviya jaga hottubaruva Jōgamma / Jōgappagaḷige bhikṣe / jōga nīḍuvudannu nilisi. Dēvadāsimahiḷiyarannē maduve, gṛhapravēśa, jātre, suggigaḷalli nīvu kareyisi, ādarisi nīḍuva, kāḷu, jōḷa, baṭṭe rokka, uḍugoregaḷa āsegāgi baḍa Dēvadāsimahiḷeyara hāgū itarara makkaḷū saha jōga bēḍuva kasubannē avalambisi, Jōgamma athavā Jōgappagaḷāguvante āguttide. tamage tiḷiyadē āguttiruva ī anāhutavannu tappisi jōga / bhīkṣe [sic] bēḍuvavarige adannu biṭṭuduḍidu badukalu tiḷuvaḷike nīḍi. āga Dēvi nimmannu meccuttāḷe, harasuttāḷe.

Stop giving alms (*bhikṣe / jōga*) to Jogammas / Jogappas who come carrying the basket(-shrine) of the goddess! If you invite Devadasi women on the occasions of wedding, house-warming, fairs and harvest festivals and, with respect, give them grain, jowar, cloth, money and gifts, you encourage the children of poor Devadasi-women and of others, too, to depend only on the profession of begging alms and to become Jogammas or Jogappas. Save them from this disaster of which they are not aware themselves, and instruct those who beg alms to give it up. Then the goddess will be pleased with you and bless you.

3 [ILLUSTRATION 1c: Women consulting a Jogamma medium]

Dēvaru bandante āḍuvudu kelavarige mānasika sanni athavā khāyileyādare innu kelavarige samājadalli mannaṇegaḷisuva mattu jīvana sāgisuva sulabhada dāriyāgide. intahavaru janarannu vañcisutta Dēvadāsi paddhatiyannu prōtsāhisuttirabahudu. antahavarige sariyāgi tiḷuvaḷike nīḍi, mānasika daurbalyavannu saripaḍisikoḷḷalu nurita vaidyara sahāya paḍeyalu tiḷisi. nimma nijavāda bhaktiyinda dēvara śaktiyannu gauravisi.

Acting as if possessed by god (»as if god has come [upon them]«) for some is a mental disorder (»hysteria«) or disease, for some others it is an easy way to get recognition in society and to make a living. Such persons, by cheating people, may be encouraging the Devadasi custom. Giving proper knowledge to such people, tell them to take the help of expert doctors to rectify their mental disorder. Respect the power of god with your true devotion!

4 [ILLUSTRATION 1d: Women cleansing a Jogamma's matted hair]

Tale kūdalannu hikkadē (bācadē), eṇṇe hākadē, svaccha māḍadē iruvudarinda adu gaṇṭāgi jiḍḍugaṭṭuttade. idarinda kūdalige ›plaikāphalānikā‹ emba sōṅku taguli, holasāgi, jiḍḍugaṭṭida sattakūdalāguttade. idannu Dēviyadendu kelavaru nambisi pūjisuttāre mattu halavāru khāyilegaḷige tuttāguttāre. intaha janarige tiḷuvaḷike nīḍi, jiḍḍugaṭṭida jaḍeyannu svacchagoḷisikoṇḍu ārōgyapūrṇa jīvana naḍesalu sahāya māḍi, Dēvi idannu opputtāḷe.

Not combing, not putting oil on, and not cleansing the hair of the head causes it to get knots and become sticky. Because of this, the hair is infected by the »Plaikaphalanika« infection; becoming dirty, the knotted hair becomes dead hair. Some believe and worship this as the goddess (Devi) and they will be subjected to various diseases. Give knowledge (instruction) to such people, help them to clean the knotted hair and to lead a healthy life. The goddess consents to this.

5 [ILLUSTRATION 1e: A woman wearing only Margosa (Neem) leaves directly on her body and another woman wearing the leaves on top of her saree.]

Mahā pativrateyāda Dēviya hesarinalli bettalāgi bēvina toppalu dharisi sēve sallisuvudu anāgarika paddhati. āddarinda mai mēle baṭṭe dharisikoṇḍu bēvina toppalu dharisi sēve sallisi nāgarikateyannu uḷisi, Dēviya kṛpege pātrarāgi.

It is an uncivilised custom to render service naked or wearing [only] fresh Margosa (Neem) leaves in the name of the goddess who is a great Pativratā, a chaste woman. Therefore, save civilization and be subjected to the grace of the goddess by rendering service to her wearing clothes on the body [first] and [then] putting on fresh Margosa (Neem) leaves [on top].

6 [ILLUSTRATION 1f: A Jogappa dancing in front of a crowd]

Gaṇḍasaru heṅgasarante naṭisuttā sīre dharisi koḍa hottu tiruguvudu, mānasika daurbalyadinda athavā dōṣayukta aṅgāṅgagaḷannu hondiruvudarinda athavā iveraḍū illadiddalli jīvana nirvahaṇegāgi sulabhada dāri hiḍiyalu naṭisuttalū irabahudu. (dēvarē sṛṣṭisida prakṛti niyamadante ›heṇṇu‹ mattu ›gaṇḍu‹ emba eraḍu niyamagaḷiruvāga dēvarē ī niyamada viruddhavāgi gaṇḍasarannu heṅgasarante vartisalu kēḷuttārennavudu sariyē? nīvē yōcisi) antahavarige agatyaviddalli vaidyara sahāyadinda sariyāda oḷḷeya jīvana naḍesalu tiḷuvaḷike nīḍi.

There are men who act like women wearing a saree and going around carrying a pot [on their head]. This [behavior] may be due either to mental weakness or to physical defects (»having defective body parts«). Or, if these two [reasons] do not apply, they may also be pretending in order to make a living the easy way (»to have an easy way for livelihood«). (As a rule of nature created by god there are only two genders, »female« and »male«. Is it correct that the same god, against this rule, asks men to behave like women? Think for yourselves!). To such people, if necessary, give knowledge to lead a good life with the help of doctors.

7 [ILLUSTRATION 1g: Men playing Holi and splashing a woman with coloured water]

›ōkaḷi‹yalli heṅgasarige rāḍi nīru eracuva amānuṣa paddhatiyannu nilisi. brahmacāri Hanumanta dēvara hesarinalli mahiḷeyarige ī rīti apamāna māḍuvudu sariyalla. buddhivanta janarē 21neya śatamānadalliyādarū pariśuddha nāgarika jīvanavannu hondalu paraspara tiḷuvaḷike nīḍi prayatnisi.

Stop the inhuman custom of throwing dirty water on women at the Okali (Holi) festival! It is not right to disgrace women in this way in the name of god Hanumanta, the chaste one (Brahmacari). Oh you intelligent people, make an effort to give knowledge to each other at least in the 21st century to lead a pure, civilised life!

8 [Illustration 1h: A wedding ceremony with children getting married. In the background, a policeman is approaching with handcuffs]

> *Bālyavivāha nigraha kāyde 1929 ra prakāra huḍaganige 21 mattu huḍugige 18 varṣa vayassāguvudaroḷage maduve māḍuvudu śikṣārha aparādha. ī aparādhadalli toḍaguvavarige daṇḍa hāgū śikṣeyannu vidhisalāguttade.*

As per the Child Marriage Prohibition Act 1929, arranging marriage for a boy below 21 and a girl below 18 years of age is a punishable offence. Those who take part in this offence will be fined and punished.

> *(Yāvudē divasa ī keḷagina viḷāsadalli gaṇṭāda jaḍeyannu biḍisi svaccha-goḷisalāguvudu. nimmalli antahavariddare jaḍe svaccha māḍisikoḷḷalu kaḷuhisi koḍalu kōralāgide.)*

(On any day, at the address given below, knotted, matted hair will be disentangled and cleansed. If you have such persons you are hereby requested to send them for cleansing their matted hair.)

> *Dēvadāsi punarvasati yōjane, mahiḷā abhivṛddhi mattu saṃrakṣaṇā saṃsthe (māsa), Ghaṭaprabhā – 591 306, tā: Gōkāka, ji.: Beḷagāvi. Tel. 0831 386724*

Devadasi Rehabilitation Project,Women Development and Protection Institute (MAS), Ghataprabha 591 306, Gokak Taluk, Belgaum District. Phone (0831) 386724.

List of Visuals

All visuals have been taken at the Sri Renuka Devi temple in Saundatti, North Karnataka. They are published online: *http://www.indologie.uni-wuerzburg.de/women_performers/contributors/brueckner/.*

Film clip 1 – video recording on Bharata Hunnime day 2007 (2 February 2007) edited by S. Shireshi and the author

Content: The recording, which starts at the Jogula Bhavi tank and Satyamma (Satyavva) temple, shows pious activities of the devotees such as bathing, putting on fresh Neem leaves, and circumambulating the temple. A group is performing puja and singing devotional songs in front of the image of the goddess that they have brought from their home. Glimpses of the temple of goddess Reṇukā-Ellamma and the surrounding sanctuaries are also given.

Film clip 2 – video recording, 30 Jan. 2007, edited by S. Shireshi and the author

Content: The recording at the temple premises focuses on a session during which an older Jogamma initiates a middle-aged woman into the service of the goddess. The woman had suffered various afflictions and was being initiated in order to overcome her problems. In the beginning, the same elderly woman is seen acting as a possession medium consulted by a group of devotees.

ILLUSTRATIONS AND ACKNOWLEDGEMENTS

Of the 60 pictures (59 photographs and one scan) four were taken on 30 Jan. 2007 by Prashant Naregal (no. 15, 16, 24, 28). Eleven were taken by the author on 24 and 25 December 2007, another four on 30 and 31 December 2009. Numbers 30–60 are digitized slides taken by the author in the first days of February, 1982. Nine photographs (no. 2, 3, 10–13, 18–20) were taken by S. Shireshi on 30 and 31 December 2009.

1 Scan of a pamphlet distributed in 2007 at the Sri Renuka Devi temple, Saundatti, requesting people to stop their religious practices
2 Stall of »Karmani« rehabilitation project, near Satyamma temple and Jogula Bhavi tank, 2009
3 Banner at the »Karmani« stall, requesting women to wear a saree underneath the Neem-leaf dress, 2009
4 The fort at Saundatti, 2007
5 Malaprabha river, along the road from Saundatti town to the temple of the goddess, 2007

(6–8) The temple of the goddess

6 View of Sri Renuka Devi's temple from the west, 2009
7 Close-up of the temple tower, 2007
8 The temple illuminated on the eve of Hostilina Hunnime, 2007

(9–14) At Jogula Bhavi tank

9 View from the road to the river and the Jogula Bhavi tank
10 Pilgrims camping and eating meals at the Jogula Bhavi tank, 2009
11 Devotees bathing in the Jogula Bhavi tank, 2009
12 Steps leading to the Satyamma temple and Jogula Bhavi tank area, 2009
13 The temple of Satyamma / Satyavva viewed from above, 2009 (compare FILM CLIP 1)

14 A group of pilgrims with a Jogappa performing puja near the tank, 2007

(15–25) Sanctuaries near the main temple of Goddess Renuka-Ellamma

15 Inside the newly renovated Kalabhairava temple, 2007 (the painting shows Renuka being blessed by Siva and the Yogins Ekanath and Joganath)
16 Kalabhairava temple: Statues of the two Yogins, a figure of Renuka and a Sivalinga, 2007
17 The temple of the goddess Matangi, from the outside, 2009
18 The temple of goddess Matangi: Entrance, 2009
19 The interior of the temple of goddess Matangi, 2009
20 The aniconic representation of goddess Matangi in her underground temple, 2009
21 Jamadagni temple and a shrine said to house the body parts of Renuka, 2009
22 Interior of shrine housing the body parts of Renuka, 2007 (cp. 57, 58)
23 Pilgrims in the open space between the main temple of goddess Renuka and the temple of Parasurama, 2007
24 The interior of the Parasurama temple, 2007
25 The Mallikarjuna (Siva) temple, south of Renuka's main temple, 2007

(26–29) Devotees

26 Jogammas waiting at night to join the procession of the goddess' palanquin, 2007
27 Pilgrims from Maharashtra who have set up a temporary shrine for the goddess north of her temple, 2007
28 Rock painting: »Stop begging and giving alms«, 2007
29 A Gorappa devotee of god Mailara asking for alms near the temple of the goddess, 2007

(30–56) Pilgrims and special devotees (1982)

30 A young Jogamma with a stringed instrument
31 A young girl with slightly matted hair
32 A child Jogamma with matted hair
33 An old woman with a stringed instrument
34 A group of musicians
35 Women and a portable shrine (jaga)
36 An old Jogappa wearing a Sari
37 A Jogappa
38 Women with koda-pot-shrines in the temple courtyard
39 Women with koda-pot-shrines in the temple courtyard

40 A Jogappa and a Jogamma with koda-pot-shrines in the temple courtyard
41 A Jogappa in the temple courtyard
42 Two Jogappas with koda pot-shrines on their heads
43 Three Jogappas posing with their pot-shrines in the bazaar street near the temple
44 A jaga basket shrine
45 A group of women and a young girl after their bath, preparing to put on Neem leaves
46 A group of men and women wearing Neem leaves
47 A man with Neem leaves on his head and in his mouth
48 Pilgrims on their way to the temple with their bullocks
49 A decorated bullock
50 Pilgrims camping near a bus
51 Pilgrims camping
52 Pilgrims camping on a hill, with a temple (Jamadagni's?) in the background
53 Camp with the paraphernalia / portable shrine of the goddess
54 Camp with the paraphernalia / portable shrine of the goddess and musical instruments
55 A young mendicant boy
56 A fortune-telling parrot

(57–60) Sanctuaries of the goddess (1982)

57 An open air sanctuary next to the Jamadagni temple with aniconic stones and a linga (cf. 22)
58 An open air sanctuary next to the Jamadagni temple with aniconic stones and a linga (cf. 22)
59 Shrine on the roof of the goddess's temple
60 Shrine on the roof of the goddess's temple, close-up of 59

REFERENCES

ANANTHA MURTHY, U. R. 2002 [1986, 1988]. »Why Not Worship in the Nude? Reflections of a Novelist in His Time«. In: Id., *Literature and Culture*. Compiled and edited by A. J. Thomas. Calcutta: Papyrus, 45–64.

APPADURAI, ARJUN. 2005 [1996]. *Modernity at Large. Cultural Dimensions of Globalization*. Minneapolis, London: University of Minnesota Press.

ASSAYAG, JACKIE. 1992. *La Colère de la Déesse Décapitée. Traditions, Cultes et Pouvoir dans le Sud de l'Inde*. Paris: CNRS.

BRADFORD, NICHOLAS J. 1983. »Transgenderism and the Cult of Yellamma: Heat, Sex and Sickness in South Indian Ritual«. In: *Journal of Anthropological Research* 39: 307–322.

BRUBAKER, RICHARD L. 1978. *The Ambivalent Mistress. A Study of South Indian Village Goddesses and their Religious Meaning*. Ph.D. Thesis, University of Chicago.

BRÜCKNER, HEIDRUN. 1999. »Thomas Mann's ›Transposed Heads‹ and Girish Karnad's ›Hayavadana‹: An Indian Motif Re-imported«. In: *Of Clowns and Gods, Brahmins and Babus. Humour in South Asian Literatures*. Ed. by Christina Oesterheld and Claus Peter Zoller. Delhi: Manohar, 118–145.

----. 2009a [1996]. »Divinity, Violence, Wedding and Gender in Some South Indian Cults«. Reprinted in: Id., *On an Auspicious Day, at dawn...Studies in Tulu Culture and Oral Literature*. Wiesbaden: Harrassowitz.

----. 2009b. »Karnataka«. In: *Brill Encyclopedia of Hinduism*. Vol. 1. Leiden: Brill, 201–220.

DALRYMPLE, WILLIAM. 2009. *Nine Lifes – In Search of the Sacred in Modern India*. London: Bloomsbury.

DIRKS, NICHOLAS. 2004 [2001]. *Castes of Mind. Colonialism and the Making of Modern India*. Delhi: Permanent Black.

GAIL, ADALBERT. 1977. *Paraśurāma, Brahmane und Krieger*. Wiesbaden: Harrassowitz.

HAHN, BENJAMIN. 2010. *Der Kult der Göttin Ellamma. Regionale Ausprägungen von religiöser Praxis und Selbstverständnis der Jogammas*. Unpublished Master Degree Thesis, Würzburg.

HARMAN, WILLIAM P. 1992 [1989]. *The Sacred Marriage of a Hindu Goddess*. Delhi: Shri Jainendra Press.

HILTEBEITEL, ALF. 1995. »Dying before the Mahabharata War: Martial and Transsexual Body-Building for Aravan«. *Journal of Asian Studies* 54, 2: 447–73.

MALLEBREIN, CORNELIA. 1993. »Die Göttinnen Renuka und Yellamma«. In: Id., *Die anderen Götter. Volks- und Stammesbronzen aus Indien*. Köln: Braus, 222–237.

MARGLIN, FRÉDÉRIQUE APFFEL. 1985. *Wives of the God-King. The Rituals of the Devadasis of Puri*. Delhi: Oxford University Press.

NAIR, JANAKI. [2011, in press]. »The Illicit in the Modern: Banning the Devadasi«. In: Id., *Mysore Modern: Essays in Social, Political and Cultural History*. Minnesota: Minnesota University Press.

SHULMAN, DAVID D. 1984. »Die Integration der hinduistischen Kultur durch die Brahmanen: ›Große‹, ›mittlere‹ und ›kleine‹ Versionen des Parasurama-Mythos«. In: *Max Webers Studie über Hinduismus und Buddhismus*. Ed. by W. Schluchter. Frankfurt: Suhrkamp, 104–148.

SRINIVAS, M. N. 1952. *Religion and Society among the Coorgs of South India*. Oxford: Oxford University Press.

----. 1976. *The Remembered Village*. Delhi: Oxford University Press.

STARK-WILD, SONJA. 1997. *Die Göttin Renuka in Mythos und Kultus*. Ph.D. Thesis, Heidelberg.

SUNKAPURA, M. S. (ED.). 1977. *Jōgati Hāḍu*. Dharwad: Karnataka Visvavidyalaya.

Gender in Folk Narratives with Special Reference to Tuḷuva Society, in the West Coast Region of Karnataka, India

B.A. Viveka Rai

Gender differences are produced through the division of labour found in every society. But once formed, they are reproduced and maintained through gender images appearing in cultural practices such as folklore, art and religion, even after the original division of labour has changed. Gender differences may thus be used to legitimate the unequal distribution of power, wealth and other resources in a society. They are conditioned by historical, economic and social developments and influenced by environmental factors. The role of folklore in the reproduction of gender images is greater in folk societies than in modern societies.

›Folk societies‹ are distinguished from ›modern society‹, mainly on account of the folk societies' oral traditions. A social structure with communal production and with common sharing is the distinctive feature of ›folk societies‹. Folk narratives, rituals, performances, belief systems are some markers of a shared folk tradition.

The approaches used in anthropology and literature studies to analyze the representation of gender and gender images, cannot be applied indiscriminately to folklore. The perspective and methodology of feminism in different disciplines, like literature, anthropology and folklore are different.[1] In Folklore, the focus is on variation and its reasons related to different social contexts. The visibility, invisibility and marginalisation of women can be understood with the variations in oral tradition, in time and space. Multiple kinds of documentation give empirical data for the identification and analysis of the changing roles of women in a given society.

The special conditions for the production and reception of folklore should be taken into consideration. Folklore is produced, performed and used in situations where performers and audience are in direct contact with each other. In the folklore process, there are factors which facilitate and enhance the reception of the messages (Honko 1991). These factors are even more pronounced in folk performances, in particular rituals and ceremonies, where the emotional involvement of the participants is greater than in everyday life. In folk societies,

1 See: *Folklore and Feminism.* Journal of American Folklore, Vol. 100 / 398 (Oct. to Dec. 1987).

women occupy three realms, namely home, workplace and ritual space. Sometimes home and work place are the same.

In the Tuḷuva culture as well, a folk culture from the southwest-coast of Karnataka, women participate in all the three realms, that is to say home, workplace and ritual space. The interrelated tensions between these three realms are responsible for the shaping of differently structured folk narratives. At home, women bear children and take care of the family. They are the producers and performers of folktales in Tulu known as *ajjikate* or grandmother tales. *Ajjikates* were identity symbols of women at home. *Ajjikates* confined to the realm of ›home‹, explain the predominant role of women in the production and narration of folktales, thereby giving women authority as tradition bearers at home. Men normally could not possess the repertoire of this folktale tradition and women were in the ›center‹ at home, not just for cooking and cleaning but for producing and transmitting ›folktales‹, an important genre of oral tradition. Women were recognized and respected for their repertoire of folktales, a respect which men lacked.

The idea or message conveyed in folktales is often feminine in content. Tales begin like this: »Once upon a time, there was a grand old lady [...]« or »There was an old woman in a village [...]«. In many of these tales, the dreams and aspirations of the family are fulfilled by the youngest daughter. Quite often this youngest daughter is not only the heroine of the tale, she also manages to achieve the realization of set goals all on her own.

There are several other motifs that mark the power of women in folktales: A man fails in accomplishing the goal, but a woman – his wife, sister or daughter – succeeds in doing so. In many tales, a woman appears as a symbol or representative of intellectual power. Often the minister's daughter is such a character. She plans the strategies and takes upon herself all the risks involved in achieving a particular goal. Finally, she emerges victorious.

Tuḷuva women working in the paddy fields sing work songs, like *kabita* (lively shorter work songs) and *sandis* (folk epics).[2] Traditionally, only women carry out two important activities of paddy cultivation, namely the pulling out and transplanting of the paddy seedlings. This is a reproductive process, wherein paddy crops and folk narrative songs are produced together. Women participate as a community in the paddy cultivation. This gives them confidence and results in a feeling of ›group identity‹. The *kabitas* or narratives they sing together while transplanting paddy seedlings represent Tuḷuva women in their various activities and aspirations. They all share the important idea that »women are always together in a group« [see ILLUSTRATIONS 1–3 and FILM CLIP 1].

The popular *kabita* »*ōbēlē*« [AUDIO 1] deals with the working situation in paddy fields. The word *bēlē* in Tuḷu means »work«. A landlord seeks the

2 For further explanation of these terms compare CLAUS, this volume, footnote 2, 3 and *passim* and RAI 1993.

help of a traditional labourer to get women to work in the fields. He goes to fetch the women labourers. At the end of the narrative the wife of the landlord becomes pregnant and the concluding part appreciates the girl child. The wishes of women are heard as a message like this: »Let new crops come up with the seedlings we have transplanted. Let the wife of our landlord become pregnant.« The themes of having plentiful children and crops are manifestations of the same ideology.

An interesting *kabita* »*yē dā balla magā dūji kemmairā*« [AUDIO 2], describes a magnificent bull, the different parts of its body, its gestures and its various actions. At the end of this *kabita*, there is a reference to this Dūji Kemmaira (magnificent bull), its waiting for the cows in hiding, and also to the appearance of calves. Though not in the text, in the actual singing context the women, at this juncture, catch hold of each other in fun and enjoyment. On enquiry I was told that they were mimicking the action of the tiger catching the cattle. This section conspicuously comes immediately after the mention of calves in relation to the admiration of the bull. Thus considering the text and its context, the *kabita* can be interpreted as a symbolic representation of the desire for mating and motherhood on the part of women.

There are many kabitas which just list the ornaments of women; except the words denoting the ornaments, the whole of such a text employs repetitive words in *kabitas* like, *e.g.* »*poṇṇu rāmasvāmi magalālɛ*«, »*tērɛḍɛ tēreḍḍenō*«, »*elyālɛ elya bāle*«, etc. [AUDIO 3–5]. Such *kabitas* are open-ended and they can be extended or contracted to any extent by adding or deleting the number of ornaments, depending upon the situation. The reference to various ornaments, in *kabitas* of this sort sung by women, is meaningful to them. Tuḷuva women normally love to have gold ornaments of different varieties, but cannot actualise their wishes because of their economic condition. Such *kabitas* fulfil their wish for gold ornaments.

There are other *kabitas* whose structure is very similar, but in which place names substitute for ornaments. The desire to go to the temple festivals of different places is the theme of another type of *kabita*. Here also the desire of women to go to different temple festivals is expressed in a repetitive style.

Kabitas are sung in the fields by women and mainly reflect women's aspirations, their desire for dress and ornaments, their wish to go to temple festivals, and their sexual desires. Some other *kabitas* reflect women's relationship with birds and plants. A *kabita* »*rāvō rāvu koroṅgō rāvandēnɛ dānɛbē*« [AUDIO 6] denotes the wish of women, to fly like birds. Here, a bird, *koroṅgu*, a fieldbird, is a symbol of flying from one's normal place. This gives an indication of women to come out of their homes and to have freedom like a bird.

Going for work, travelling together to participate in a village festival, the wish to get married, a desire for dress and ornament and the symbolic representation of women's urge to be emancipated are some of the themes of these *kabitas*. The theme of ›going out‹ for temple festivals is one kind of liberation for women in villages. It gives them freedom to chat freely with fellow women, to relax and also to comment on men's activities. Going out for work is another such outlet for women in villages, who are normally confined to their homes under the control of men. Working in paddy fields gives women liberation from the controlled atmosphere of home and a chance to open up for association and sharing with other women of the villages and thereby to get a sense of community.

While pulling out the paddy seedlings for transplantation, women sing *sandis* (folk epics), which often stress the tragic aspects of the heroine's life (*e.g.* CLAUS 1991). Although such epics are recited in other contexts, too, the role of women as the producers of folk epics comes out most clearly within the space constituted by their workplace, *i.e.* the paddy fields.

In contradistinction to the *kabita* work songs, folk epics, such as *pāḍdanas* and *sandis*, are sung in ritual contexts as well, for instance the *bhūta* festivals. The narratives about the origin and dissemination of a *bhūta* (local deity) are sung by a woman, while a male member of her family is the impersonator and performer of the deity in these ritual performances. Prior to the theatrical performance, when the actor is being made up and dressed, a female family member of the male performer, perhaps his mother, wife, sister or daughter, sings portions of the folk epics so as to create the right atmosphere for the performance. She also prepares the costumes on the spot. The processes of singing and preparing costumes take place simultaneously. Again, this is a reproductive process, wherein epics and costumes, which are essential for the ambience and success of the ritual, are produced by women. But from the audience's point of view, the roles of women in such rituals appear insignificant. Women are not visible and their role is seen as marginal in the theatrical *bhūta* performance, where the male performer stands in the centre and most of the rituals and performances focus on him. His visual and aural glorification drowns out the voice of the female singer. Although hidden from the public view, women are the tradition bearers of the folk epic and have an equal share in the performance.

Research on folklore in the Tuḷuva region during the past three decades has contributed to a better understanding of the identity of women in relation to the transmission, production and performance of folk narratives. Documentation of Tuḷu folk epics, folktales and *kabitas* from women singers / performers has also created a greater awareness among the womenfolk themselves with regard to their own resources and has kindled their interest in the preservation of their tradition. For instance, Kargi Muṇḍāldi, the Tuḷu folk epic singer with whom Peter J. Claus worked, has now been recognized as a resource person for folk literary criticism.[3] Giḍigere Rāmakke Mugērti, a resourceful folk epic singer, became well-known after her Siri epic had been documented and published by

3 Compare CLAUS, this volume.

A. V. Navada (NAVADA 1999). She has been nominated as a member of the Tuḷu Academy by the Government of Karnataka.[4]

Only recently, documentation of *bhūta* performances has also focussed on the role of women in these performances. Such a comprehensive, ›thick‹ documentation goes beyond the conventional emphasis on male performers and, instead, features women as producers of folk epics and artefacts connected to such rituals. The focus of cameras on such female singers has not merely a technical aspect, but also an ideological one. The importance of the role of women in *bhūta* ritual performances becomes visible only in the total documentation of such performances. This was illustrated during my fieldwork in 1989 when the Finnish-Indian folklore training program occurred in a place where a festival was organized for the female deity Ullāldi. Professor Bente Alver from Bergen, Norway, and I were jointly leading the fieldwork team. The festival rituals started at eight o'clock in the evening. The male performer danced throughout the night. In the morning, there were only a few people to watch the conclusion of the ceremony. When he fainted at this stage, it was his mother who took care of him – a fact that is corroborated by our footage. Thus our visual documentation was able to add a new insight to our understanding of *bhūta* ritual performances, namely that women do play a role in performances which normally are considered to be the prerogative of males.

Modernity

Here I will briefly discuss the impact of modernity and the role of women in folklore with particular reference to Tuḷuva society. The practice of telling a folktale at home has vanished to a large extent. The reasons are manifold: The disintegration of joint families, whereby grandmothers no longer have direct access to their grandchildren, and formal school education, where the burden of extensive curricula has come to occupy the time and mind of children. The role of women in work places, such as paddy fields, has also been affected negatively since there has been a drop in paddy cultivation in Tuḷuva society. But even then, women are still indispensable when it comes to the pulling out and transplanting of paddy seedlings, as no modern machine can replace them.[5] Modernity has had conflicting effects on ritual performances, such as the *bhūta* festivals. Money plays a major role in the sustenance and growth of *bhūta* festivals in the Tuḷuva region. The number of performances in a year has increased enormously

4 A lengthy version of the Siri epic as performed by Gopala Naika has been published in Tuḷu and English by Lauri Honko in collaboration with Ch. Gowda, A. Honko and V. Rai (see HONKO 1998a). It was published along with a volume by L. Honko on »Textualising the Siri Epic« (HONKO 1998b). On the Siri complex cp. also CLAUS 1975 and 1999.

5 There are rare occasions where you see women using mobile phones in the paddy fields, the only modern items I could detect in a paddy field.

over the last twenty years. Indirectly, this has helped to improve the economic position of the families of the performers.

Media coverage of ritual performances has influenced both the content and form of the traditional performances. These have been revitalized to suit the tastes of a ›modern‹ audience, *i.e.* there is more emphasis on the theatrical, spectacular, ceremonial and ›showy‹ aspects of the ritual, flashy costumes, playing of film-music before and in between the ritual performances, and less emphasis on direct and personalised verbal exchanges with the deities concerning family and village affairs. The coverage of ritual events in local newspapers and the electronic media has provided an identity to the traditional performers, especially the women. Local Tuḷu language TV channels like Namma Kuḍla in Mangalore City telecast various folk narratives and performances, thereby enhancing the identity of artists and providing them publicity outside their own immediate performance area. Whereas this is concerned with mainly voice recordings and their broadcasting, things are different with live performances involving the exposure of the artist's or possessed individual's body in public rituals. In this area, a vulgarisation of folk performances can be observed.

Performances have been taken out of the traditional contexts to cater to the needs of a modern audience, as if they were commodities for sale, such as putting bits and pieces of ritual performances on a theatre stage. With other rituals, such as female possession in Siri festivals, the impact of changed attitudes of the audience is even more adverse, to the point of making the rituals and the women involved objects of ridicule.

Siri festivals

In Siri festival performances women get possessed en masse. In the mass possession space, women get transferred and transformed from the mundane realm into the mythical characters of the Siri epic. In this epic, Siri is the central protagonist. She is also an identity symbol of women. She protests and revolts against male dominance and becomes a mythical icon of feminine power. During the Siri festival, women belonging to various castes, regions and cultures join together as a community and take on the same group identity. All these women transcend their home and workplaces to constitute a larger family of women aspiring emancipation from the spaces of home and work. They become members of a mythical family who get possessed in a ritualistic space where they sing the lines of the folk epic and enact the mythical roles. The tensions created in their home and work spaces get released in this sacred space [see Film clip 2]. But these women have to go back again to the other spaces of home and work. The conflict and links that exist between these three realms is a matter for investigation of women's role in performance. Harmony can be achieved through the mental management of these three realms together.

A woman's appearance in the ritual space, which is public, is considered as an obligation and as a condition for proper existence in the other two spaces [see ILLUSTRATIONS 4–6].

But this kind of Siri festival should be looked into from the perspective of changing audiences as well as their changing tastes and beliefs. The traditional audience had faith in the system and the arrangement between the performers and audience was a harmonious one. In contrast, the modern audience is critical and judges the entire ceremony from a more secular and rational point of view. Some family members of Siri women object to what they call a public show where ›their women‹ get possessed and behave in an ›abnormal‹ manner in a public place in front of a not so ritual-committed and supportive audience. Modern audiences, who are exposed to many media performances and who do not share the belief system that underlies these possession cults, behave in an impolite and sometimes vulgar manner. On the other hand, male relatives feel that the participation of female family members places them and their families in an awkward situation. This new trend has led women to opt out of the public possession performances and restrict their participation to hand-offerings to the main deity of the place. But even then these kinds of mass possession rituals continue to have the support from the organizers of such festivals who want to maintain their authority and continue their religious obligations through this public event. In addition, the performers and their family members continue to believe in these possession rituals, because they say that »they cool down the heat of their vertex«.

I interviewed about 50 Siri women between 1990 and 1995, mainly in the Belthangadi region of Coastal Karnataka, both in ritual contexts and at their homes [ILLUSTRATION 7].[6] These women work in coffee estates, in paddy fields and also as daily wage labourers. At home, they are under pressure from male members of the family, especially the husband, and sometimes the mother or mother-in-law; they wish for a change in their life wherein they can get an identity of their own. At the work place, too, women are often treated as inferior to men and even now their wages are lower than those of male labourers. They do not have power, privileges or an identity of their own, either at their home or at their places of work. It is in the sacred space provided by the Siri rituals that they can acquire an individual identity as well as a group identity. By moving from the secular to the sacred world, where male members of their family and men in their workplace consider them as icons of deities and pay them due respect, such women obtain a kind of security that extends into their normal life. Against this background, recent developments are a drawback for many women. When they become objects of ridicule for ›modern audiences‹ and withdraw from the public possession rituals, they are deprived of an important means to develop their own identity.

6 See HONKO 1998.

These women were performing in the Siri festivals within a time span of ten to thirty years. Interviews of these Siri women were conducted at their home, at the workplace, mainly the paddy fields and during the intervals in the Siri festival. The personal interviews at their home, individually, in the absence of their family members, particularly the men, revealed many varied reasons for their participation in the Siri ritual and performance. Physical illness, harassment by husband and mother-in-law, not having children, death of children, misbehaviour of husbands due to excessive consumption of alcohol and husbands not caring for the wishes of their wives are some factors which made the women seek an outlet to escape the pressure in the family and bondage at home. When a woman is inducted into a Siri cult group, then it is almost like a permanent membership. Such Siri women believe in the system and practice of the cult. Many of them during the interview mentioned to me the problem of feeling heat on their vertex (head) and said that by participating in the Siri festival they felt coolness on their head. It is a kind of cultural purgation for them. One factor which adds to this is that affiliation to a Siri group gives Siri women a kind of freedom, emancipation from the bondage at home. Coming out of the home realm, and fellowship with women having similar restrictions at home, forms a group or community of women, leading to a ›group identity‹. This kind of emancipation may be temporary but it has effects in the home also. This is an important factor to understand the relationship between these three realms, *viz.*, home, workplace and ritual space. I was told by some Siri women during the interview that, after they became ›Siri women‹, the harassment by their husbands at home diminished. Women as ›Siri‹ are normally respected beyond the ritual spaces, even at their homes and in their villages.

Conclusion

Reproductive processes with women in the central roles as producers, like transplanting the paddy crops and producing the field songs, preparing the costumes and singing the epic (*bhūta* festivals) are discussed in this paper. With this background, I would like to emphasize that women do participate actively in the production of songs, performances and rituals. But the audience does not validate their role, because the women are less visible. In the case of the public performances, such as the *bhūta* festival, the focus is on the male performer who enjoys greater visibility and status. This raises the question whether there is a division of (artistic and reproductive) labour at work here, where singing and making artefacts are delegated to the women and impersonation, which requires the exposition of the body, to men.

With reference to the Siri cult, the recent developments and problems addressed above might have to do with changing attitudes vis-à-vis the visual display of a woman's body in a public space, often a suffering body whose mimics and movements do not accord with conventions of normal ›decent‹ female behaviour. The context is one of affliction and healing of the individual person, not of communal, public and theatrical display of the local *bhūta* deities.

Women from the *bhūta* performing families reciting *pāḍdanas* at public festival rituals are, again, different from the Siri women, because they are in their ›normal‹ state of mind and in control of their body. The male performers who wear the costume and makeup of deities behave in a stylised, choreographed way and do not exhibit their own, ›private‹ personality. Women as skilled singers of *pāḍdanas* whose recitation may be broadcasted over the radio are considered folk artists. They will sing the Siri epic outside the context of the Siri festival, in an unpossessed state. The portions of the epic as recited in a possessed state during the rituals would never be recorded for broadcasting, although the singers may be the same persons. Therefore, women may gain more recognition as performers, *e.g.* in the ›modern‹ context of radio broadcasting, and at the same time may face more difficulties in another context, such as the Siri rituals.

The roles of women in social space and ritual space may be in conflict or complement each other. The complexities of such roles and their interrelation can be understood when we analyze the documentation of the different spaces separately as well as in relation to each other.

So the interrelations among the three realms which I have introduced in the beginning of my paper – home, workplace and ritual space, are substantiated with the illustration of women in Tuḷuva culture. Opening up of more space for women in all three of these realms can only give more freedom and identity for them, which we scholars theorize as ›emancipation‹.

In the light of empirical research regarding the role of women in folk narratives, I feel that the concept of ›emancipation‹ should be redefined by distinguishing between the point of view of the performer and that of the audience. Differences in gender and class of the audience, too, contribute to constructing the meaning of ›emancipation‹ of women. Emancipation as a social reformative activity always enjoys the hegemonic power of the promoters. Emancipation from within should be understood both from the experience of participation in performances and from the documentation of the ›mental texts‹ of the women performers.[7] Rather than considering ›emancipation‹ as a social activity of the outsider, I would like to stress here the transformation of mind and body of the performing women as a way to emancipation. To me a continuous dialogue between these ideas will be most revealing in our exploration of a new set of methodologies to investigate the nature of women's emancipation and how the performance of folk narratives and rituals contributes to bringing it about.

7 For the concept of »mental text« see CLAUS 1989 and 2000 and HONKO 1998b.

References

Brückner, Heidrun. 2009. *On an Auspicious Day, at Dawn…: Studies in Tulu Culture and Oral Literature.* Wiesbaden: Harrassowitz.

Claus, Peter J. 1975. »The Siri Myth and Ritual: Description of a Mass Possession Cult of South India«. *Ethnology* 14, 1: 47–58.

Claus, Peter J. 1989. »Behind the text: performance and ideology in a Tulu oral tradition«. In: *Oral Epics in India.* Ed. by Stuart H. Blackburn et al. Berkeley: University of California Press, 55–74.

----. 1991. »Kin Songs«. In: *Gender, Genre, and Power in South Asian Expressive Traditions.* Ed. by Arjun Appadurai et al. Philadelphia: Univ. of Pennsylvania Press, 136–177.

----. 1999. »Ritual Transforms a Myth«. Online-publication: http://class.csueastbay.edu/anthropology/claus/kumar.htm (2007/11/21).

----. 2000. »Mental Text«. *Indian Folklife* (Chennai) 1, 1: 12-13.

Folklore and Feminism. 1987. *Journal of American Folklore* 100, 398 (Oct.–Dec. 1987).

Honko, Lauri. 1998a. *The Siri epic as performed by Gopala Naika.* 2 Vol. Helsinki: Suomalainen Tiedeakatemia.

----. 1998b. *Textualising the Siri epic.* Helsinki: Suomalainen Tiedeakatemia.

----. 1991. *The Folklore Process.* Folklore Fellows' Summer School Programme (Turku, FFSS 1991).

Navada, A. V. (Ed.). 1999. *Siri pāḍdana. Giḍikere Rāmakka Muggērti kaṭṭida.* Hampi: Kannada University.

Rai, B. A. Viveka. 1993. »The Genres of Tulu folk-poetry: An introduction«. In: *Flags of Fame. Studies in South Asian Folk Culture.* Ed. by H. Brückner et al. Delhi: Manohar, 269–282.

----; Rajashree. 1997. *Tuḷu Kabitagaḷu.* Mangalore: Mangalore University.

----. 1985. *Tuḷu Janapada Sāhitya.* Bangalore: Kannada Sahitya Parishat.

Audio Files

Six audio files are published online together with the Tuḷu text and an English translation: *http://www.indologie.uni-wuerzburg.de/women_performers/contributors/rai/audio_files/.*

Audio File 1: *ō bēle ō bēle* – »Oh work oh work«. Main singer: Jainabi (Kaniyooru, Beltangady); supporting singers: Minka (Kaniyooru, Beltangady), Geetha (Kaniyooru, Beltangady).

Audio File 2: *ē dā bala maga dūji kemmairā* – »Hey! Come on, son, charming bull«. Singers: Nagamma (Budoli); Peraja (Bantvala Taluk); Girija (Chikkapadnuru); Mani, Kemmayi (Puttur Taluk).

Audio File 3: *poṇṇu rāmasvāmi magalālɛ* – »She, the daughter of Ponnu Ramasvamy«. Singer: Girija (Chikkamudnur), Kemmayi (Puttur Taluk).

Audio File 4: *tērɛdɛ tēreḍḍenō* – »Among the chariot festivals, the superior chariot festival«. Singer: Shila (Kaniyuru, Beltangady).

Audio File 5: *elyālɛ elya bālɛ telikkēda mōnedālɛ* – »Young girl, the young child, with smiling face«. Main singer: Minka (Kaniyuru, Beltangady); supporting singer: Gita (Kaniyuru, Beltangady).

Audio File 6: *rāvō rāvu koruṅgō rāvandēnɛ dānɛbe* – »Fly, oh fly, crane; without flying what can I do?«. Singers: Nagamma (Budoli, Peraja); Mani (Bantwala Taluk).

Filmography

Two film clips are published online: *http://www.indologie.uni-wuerzburg.de/women_performers/contributors/rai/film_clips/*.

Film Clip 1: *Hii Joo Racing Buffalo* (translation of the song is given online).
Film Clip 2: *Siri Festival at Nidgal, Belthangady, Dakshina Kannada, Karnataka, India.* Documented for Siri Oral Epics Project, Kalevala Institute, Turku, Finland, on 30.03.1991.

Photographies

Six illustrations are published online: *http://www.indologie.uni-wuerzburg.de/women_performers/contributors/rai/illustrations/*. All the photographs are taken from the following book: Lauri Honko: *Textualising the Siri epic.* Helsinki, Suomalainen Tiedeakatemia, Acad. Scientiarum Fennica, 1998.

Illustration 1: The Siri epic sung in the work context. Gopala Naika joins the women plucking seedlings.
Illustration 2: The seedlings are planted to the accompaniment of work songs.
Illustration 3: Documenting the singing in the paddyfield on a narrow embankment.
Illustration 4: The invocation of the divine Kumara in Niḍgal. Gopala Naika (second from the left) and his three assistants.
Illustration 5: The Siri row. Photo by Lauri Honko.
Illustration 6: The relinquishing of areca flowers and possession at the end of the ritual.
Illustration 7: Viveka Rai interviewing a lady.

Siri Revisited

A Female ›Mass Possession Cult‹ without Women Performers?

Lea Griebl and Sina Sommer

This paper deals with observations made during a month long fieldwork workshop held in Udupi, Udupi District, Karnataka in March 2008.[1] Compared to archival footage of the Regional Resources Centre for Folk Performing Arts (RRC) covering the Urmbitoṭṭu Siri jātre (Siri festival) of 1989, nineteen years earlier, the Urmbitoṭṭu Siri jātre we witnessed on February 21st 2008 was different in many ways. Most striking was the fact that the number of women getting possessed during the *jātre* was far less as compared to earlier years. This paper examines this issue and deals with possible reasons for the declining number of Siri women involved in the service (*sēve*). We begin with a brief description of the international fieldwork workshop mentioned above, followed by an overview of the Siri cult, with particular emphasis on two aspects we would like to take a closer look at – the Siri epic (*pāḍdana*) and its representations at the annual Siri festival (*jātre*). Subsequently, we will describe our own observations beginning with an outline of the 2008 Siri festival (*jātre*), followed by a discussion about public (*jātre*) and private exercise (*illecci dalya*) of religious duty. The last and most extensive part of the article deals with the Siri women performing their service (*sēve*) at the annual Siri festival and the possible reasons for the decline in their numbers.

1. Setting and Methodology

The research was carried out as part of the international fieldwork workshop at Udupi (see fn. 1). The main focus of the workshop was on the Siri- and the Kōṭi-Cennaya-tradition. The Siri jātre at Urmbitoṭṭu on 21st February 2008 was the first event of the workshop attended by the entire group, which was divided into different teams. One team concentrated on video documentation, another one on photography and the third one was responsible for note-taking.

1 The international workshop on fieldwork organized by the University of Würzburg, Germany (Heidrun Brückner) in collaboration with the Regional Resources Center for Folk Performing Arts (RRC), Udupi, and the National Folklore Support Center, Chennai, and conducted by Peter J. Claus provided us with the opportunity to study the Siri Cult. We specially thank Peter J. Claus, S. A. Krishnaiah and T. K. Bhat.

In the following weeks two groups were formed to do practical fieldwork, one focusing on Kōṭi-Cennaya and the other on Siri, in which we took part. While the Kōṭi-Cennaya group concentrated on the complete documentation of an annual village festival about which there was not much information available, the Siri cult has been well-researched already leaving not much room for new discoveries. However, the earlier work on the Siri cult is about ten to twenty years old. Using this background information, our ›Siri group‹, consisting of four German[2] and three Indian students[3], studied the video documentation available at the RRC archives and visited important sites of Siri worship in Udupi District. We also conducted interviews with several women involved in the cult. Combining these different sources of information, we came to realize that a lot of changes have taken place during the last twenty years. Therefore we decided to focus on a comparison between the *jātre* at Urmbitoṭṭu as observed on 21st February 2008 and the earlier video-documentation taken in 1989[4] and preserved at the RRC archives in order to gain new insights, and find out what kind of changes had occurred over the last twenty years.

2. *Introducing the Siri cult*

The term Siri can be used to refer to a single deified human being, named Siri, but it can also refer to a family of deities including Siri, or to a group of goddesses, the Seven Siris[5]. In this paper we concentrate on two dimensions of the Siri cult of Tuḷunāḍu[6]: a textual dimension, which is based on the mythic story of the Siris (*pāḍdana*), and a ritual dimension, which includes an annual festival (*jātre*) with mass possession of the participants by the Siri spirits (CLAUS 2008: section one).

The Siri pāḍdana

The *Siri pāḍdana* is an oral narrative of epic length in Tuḷu. It is well-known as a morality tale throughout Tuḷunāḍu amongst Tuḷu speakers as well as Kannaḍa speakers of all castes. The *pāḍdana* is mostly sung by women while transplant-

2 Johanna Kutzer, Lea Griebl, Sarah Merkle, Sina Sommer, all of the University of Würzburg, Germany.
3 Maya Hemant Krishna, Sowparnika Balaswaminathan, Wekowe u Tsuhah, of the Dakshina Chitra Institution, Chennai.
4 For a clipping of the 1989 documentation see FILM CLIP 1
5 The seven Siris are Siri, Sonne, Ginde, Abbaga, Dāraga, Dāru and Sāmu.
6 The term Tuḷunāḍu comprises the Tuḷu speaking area of coastal Karnataka.

ing paddy in the fields.[7] Due to the fact that the *Siri pāḍdana* is a sacred narrative of the earthly lives of the Siri spirits rather than a historical account, following CLAUS 1999, it will be referred to as a myth. The dominant atmosphere of the *Siri pāḍdana* is one of tragedy because her husband and other men in the epic transgress the values that Tuḷu-society Siri stands for. Siri's claims to respect (*mariyāde*) and honour remain unanswered. She uses her power of truth for revenge and the reinstatement of the social values of the local community. Due to its oral transmission there are various versions and variations of the Siri epic[8] and while some do not differ much in the main content, in some others the heroine is not even called Siri (Claus, personal communication).

The *pāḍdana* starts with the supernatural birth of Siri from an areca flower [see ILLUSTRATION 1], which the old, childless Berma Alveru, usually called »Ajjeru« (grandfather), had received as *prasāda* from his ancestral god Bermeru. After her marriage to Kāntu Pūñja, who insults and mistreats her, Siri gives birth to a boy child, Kumāra. Siri curses the land of her birth and travels south together with her maid servant Dāru and her newborn son. Foreseeing his mother's second marriage to a man of another community Kumāra objects to their association with another caste. Therefore, after crossing a river and reaching a foreign land, Siri transfers her son into *māya*[9], *i.e.* into an invisible realm. According to some versions, having crossed the river, Kumāra and Siri both become *māya*. Other versions of the story include the two succeeding generations: Siri remarries and gives birth to a daughter, Sonne. Just like Siri herself, Sonne's twin daughters Abbaga and Dāraga are born after their parents have made a vow (*parake*) to give an offering to god Bermeru, but fail to keep it. While Sonne and her husband are away from home in order to make arrangements for the twins' wedding, god Bermeru appears in the guise of a poor Brahmin and provokes Abbaga and Dāraga into playing a game of *cenne* although this had been prohibited by their parents. As the Brahmin tricks them into playing *cenne* they start quarreling. Abbaga kills her sister by hitting her on the head with the *cenne* board and subsequently commits suicide in a well. Some versions of the *pāḍdana* continue with the return of Sonne and her husband. Finding Abbaga and Dāraga dead they remember their unfulfilled vow to Bermeru and solicit him to bring their daughters back to life so that Abbaga and Dāraga can get married [For the family tree of the Siri family see ILLUSTRATION 2].

7 According to CLAUS 1999, one distinctive feature of the *Siri pāḍdana* is the fact that though it is mainly sung by women during paddy transplantation, some men from different castes also know and sing it. See also RAI in this volume, especially for *kabita*.

8 For a full version of the *Siri pāḍdana* see HONKO 1998. Honko along with V. Rai and Ch. Gowda recorded, transcribed and translated the Siri epic as sung by the Kumāra Gopala Naika. For a shorter outline of the *Siri pāḍdana* see GOWDA 2005, 131–136.

9 See BRÜCKNER 2009: 44 for the use of the terms *māya* and *jōga* in Tuḷu.

The Siri jātre

The Siri *jātre* is an annual festival which can be regarded as the climax of religious practice conducted by the devotees of the Siri cult, where many people gather – active participants and other visitors – at about fifteen to twenty places in Dakṣiṇa Kannaḍa / Tuḷunāḍu called *ālaḍe*[10]. On this occasion, the members of the cult get possessed by the Siri spirits (CLAUS 1999). Though a textual link between Śiva and Siri is missing, many of the *ālaḍes* where Siri *jātres* take place are associated with Śaiva temples (CLAUS 1975: 53; 2008: section one). The earliest Siri rituals can be traced back to the 16th century and to a place called Nandolige, though scholars assume that Siri rituals at Hiriyadka and Brahmavara are even older (BHATT 1969: 16; see also BHATT 1975: 359). In spite of several differences between the *jātres* at different *ālaḍes* the rituals have certain elements in common: a row of women standing on a long strip of purified, new white cloth (*dalya*) spread on the ground facing one or several men, the Kumāras, who wear a red or white waist-cloth and keep pacing back and forth. The Siri women on the *dalya* usually wear white saris although this tradition is not followed by all women at all *jātres / ālaḍes*. The Siri women and the Kumāra(s) hold areca flowers (*piṅgāra*) in their hands. Verbal communication between the participants is always in the form of song. The verbal exchanges contain phrases from the *pāḍdana*[11] and are preceded and interspersed by invocations (CLAUS 2008: Section one). Except for the Kumāras, who are sometimes professionals, the participants who get possessed by the female spirits of the *Siri pāḍdana* are lay persons from different castes, different backgrounds and different villages who have hardly any relationship with one another in everyday life (CLAUS 1993: 336).

Though *jātres* at different *ālaḍes* have some elements in common, there are also striking differences between the overall rituals at different centers. One of the major Siri jātres is held at Nandolige, where according to the *pāḍdana*, Siri's daughter Sonne grew up. On the full moon days between February and April thousands of people gather in groups consisting of twenty to thirty individuals[12] at traditionally allocated places around the large Mahāliṅgeśvara temple. They get possessed and the groups carry out their ritual activities simultaneously. In the following weeks, additional rituals are held at nearby shrines built at places of importance in the Siri myth, for example at Urikitōṭa.

10 *Ālaḍe*, a kind of *bhūta* shrine often referring specifically to a *brahmasthāna* or to a complex of five or more *bhūta* shrines, especially of Brahma, Nāga, Kṣētrapāla, Raktēśvarī, Nandigōṇa and others, see UPADHYAYA 1988.

11 GOWDA 2005: 158 calls the portions sung at the Siri ritual as »Siri sandi«. *Sandi* is often used synonymously with *pāḍdana*. It can also refer to a section of a *pāḍdana*.

12 These groups are also called *dalya* after the purified cloth on which the women stand.

Here, Sonne's daughter Abbaga is said to have committed suicide by jumping into a well after having murdered her twin sister Dāraga while playing the game of *cenne*. At Urikitōṭa, a ritual is held in daytime that looks more like a *bhūta kōla*[13] than the Siri ritual described above, since only three people briefly get possessed by the spirits of Abbaga, Dāraga and Kumāra. They recite parts of the *Siri pāḍdana* and the devotees make offerings to the Siri deities. Some devotees will also bring relatives who have been experiencing involuntary possession in their everyday life and, though there is no larger *dalya* group present, identification of the spirit will take place. Similar to what happens in a *dalya*, the person will be encouraged to get possessed, identify herself as one of the Siri spirits and if this is the case, will be asked to return annually to the Siri ritual to make an offering.

During the *jātre* at the Vīrabhadra temple at Hiriyaḍka, only about half of the participants get possessed by Siri spirits and practice their ritual in the way described above. The other participants get possessed by one or several other spirits, like the Chikkus who closely resemble the Siri spirits, or by goddess Mahākāli and they perform their ritual possession on their own. They neither gather in groups nor are they accompanied by a Kumāra.

Both Niḍgal and Urmbitoṭṭu claim that they are original sites of the events of the Siri myth. Though it is said that at both places annual *jātres* have a long history, the Siri jātres there are presumably of relatively recent origin. What is unique about both *jātres* is that before the *dalya* is held, the *cenne* game, during which, according to the *pāḍdana*, the twins become *māya*, is enacted by people possessed by Abbaga, Dāraga and Kumāra[14] (CLAUS 2008: section one; 2004: 37 p).

The term Siri jātre cannot be generalised, as there is no homogeneity within the rituals at the *jātres* held at different centres. Rather there are some common elements which appear in all the Siri jātres. But, as stated above, there are also many differences in the way the overall rituals are performed due to the variability of oral traditions in general and because of the local temple administrations and their influence on the structure of the rituals.[15]

13 An annual festival ritual with costumed impersonations of local deities (*bhūtas*).

14 For a detailed description of the enactment of the *cenne* game at Urmbitoṭṭu Siri *jātre* and a discussion of the dramatization of the twins' death in relation to the Siri myth and the ritual see CLAUS 1999.

15 See also RAI's general description of the Siri jātre in this volume, especially his FILM CLIP 2.

3. 2008 Fieldwork observations

The jātre at Urmbitoṭṭu[16]

To give a comprehensible description of the location of the Siri jātre the festival area has to be viewed in two sections: the large open space located on one side of the temple compound and the temple complex of the Mahālingeśvara temple itself. The entire area, including the open field and the temple complex, is situated close to the village of Urmbitoṭṭu. The field, again, can be subdivided into separate areas. At the far end, as viewed from the temple, an elevated stage for various types of performances had been erected and a small area had been set aside for a small market with stalls and shops. The central part housed temporary bhūta shrines and shelters with sitting arrangements for the patrons and musicians. The area closest to the temple complex included the *gobbuḍa kaṭṭe*[17] an elevated platform used for the performance of the *cenne* game. Furthermore, close to the platform, and towards the temple a fenced shrine with nāga stones is found. The Mahālingeśvara temple complex is situated at the end of the area just described.

On February 21st 2008 (about 9 p.m.) the Siri jātre at Urmbitoṭṭu commenced with the ceremonial procession carrying the paraphernalia such as the *cenne* board from the *guttu* farmhouse of the chief patrons to the festival area. The patrons' family, the two Siri women (acting as Abbaga and Dāraga in the *cenne* game), and the *mūla* Kumāra (chief Kumāra), as well as the *pātri* (possession priest) were part of the procession. The first major ritual event is a *raṅga pūja* at the temple [see Illustration 4]. It is followed, about midnight, by the impersonation of the *bhūta* Maisandāya (buffalo spirit), in front of his shrine in the centre of the open field next to the temple. After one hour of preparation, including various rituals and the acts of putting on make-up and costumes, the dancer gets possessed by the *bhūta* Maisandāya, for about 15 minutes [see Illustration 5]. The scene then shifts back to the temple, where the *mūla* Kumāra initiates the possession of two Siri women and also gets into a state of possession. The women being possessed by the twins Abbaga and Dāraga, the *mūla* Kumāra, and the *pātri* move to the *gobbuḍa kaṭṭe* to play the traditional *cenne* game of the *pāḍdana* [see Illustration 6]. Sitting between the two women the *mūla* Kumāra supervises the game and leads the recitation of the *pāḍdana*. Unlike the fatal ending of the game in the *pāḍdana*, the *mūla* Kumāra, in the ritual enacted, interferes and stops the one twin from hitting the other with the *cenne* board [see Illustration 7]. The group makes their way back

16 For an overview of the location of the Siri jātre at Urmbitoṭṭu see the map drawn during fieldwork [Illustration 3].

17 *Gobbuḍa kaṭṭe* (also *cenne gobbuḍa kaṭṭe*), a platform located in the middle of the Urmbitoṭṭu *jātre* area used in the ritual *cenne* game of the twins Abbaga and Dāraga.

to the temple and the Kumāra formally brings the possession to an end. In the next stage of the Siri rituals, the *mūla* Kumāra and six Siri women line up in front of the Śiva temple and start getting possessed. This is the first group (first *dalya*). Then, the *mūla* Kumāra moves to the *sthala* Kumāra (subordinate Kumāra) to initiate his possession and the possession of the second group (second *dalya*) of another five Siri women, taking place in front of the *nāga* shrine [see ILLUSTRATION 8]. Since our group left the Siri jātre about 5 a.m. (February 22nd) the events that followed could not be recorded. People told us that a *bhūta kōla* for Pañjuli (boar spirit) would be the last event concluding the festival rituals.

It is worth noting that throughout the night, even while the rituals described above were being conducted, an entertainment programme, which attracted a much larger audience, was being presented on a large stage at the other end of the field. Because of the use of microphones and amplifiers, the sound of the stage performances dominated the whole place and drowned the sound of the ritual performances. This is a recent development made possible by modern technology and perhaps indicates a shift in the interest of the audiences involved. The whole festival was filmed and later compressed into a short clip [see FILM CLIP 2].

Jātre[18] *and illecci dalya*

As a counterpart to the annual festival, a couple of *illecci dalyas*[19] take place all through the year in private houses [see ILLUSTRATION 9]. They are attended only by Siri women escorted by family members, sometimes their parents, but in the majority of cases by their husbands. Visiting an *illecci dalya*, as well as the Siri jātre, we became aware of their different organisation, the one being rather a private ritual and the other a public one. After several conversations with Chinnappa Gowda as we were writing this paper at Würzburg, we have come to assume that the annual Siri rituals originally may have been held exclusively on a household level with several Siri women and Kumāras assembling at the homes of the Kumāra or one of the Siri's to fulfill their religious duty. Against this background the Siri *jātre* could be viewed as a pilgrimage event, in contrast to the domestic ritual. As suggested by Chinnappa Gowda, over the years, temple authorities may have encouraged the groups who used to gather at conveniently located places or at sites of epic importance, to assemble on the temple premises, thereby turning the private gathering more and more into an institutionalised temple ritual. In this way, the ›private‹ ritual may have become

18 Due to the huge variety and differences in the *jātre* at different *ālades* the following observations can refer only to the Urmbitoṭṭu Siri jātre we actually witnessed and compared to archival footage; Our findings cannot claim validity for any other location.

19 *Illecci dalya*: *dalya* in the house; ›private‹ *dalya*.

a ›public‹ festival event. Due to this development and for several other reasons, the number of visitors may have increased over the last decades. Another explanation could be found in the structure of the *jātre*, which consists of a temple festival at the Śiva temple, the Siri possession ritual, as well as *bhūta kōlas*, all in the same large compound. Many people attend the Siri possession ritual but an equally high number of people join the event because of god Śiva's temple festival. Simultaneously, cultural programmes and dance performances are presented on a large, elevated modern stage at the other end of the compound.

Thus, the Siri jātre may have evolved from a household level ritual with few participants into an annual event with a large number of devotees and other visitors. But it may be assumed that the key features of the ritual are the ones still practiced in the form of the *illecci dalyas*.

New perspectives

1. Only recently Dalits are allowed as participants in most of the temple complexes at the *jātre*, even though they usually do not avail themselves of this possibility for different reasons. In this connection, we observed a certain correlation between the caste of a woman and the Siri character by whom she gets possessed: If Dalit women participate actively in the Siri ritual, they mostly get possessed by Dāru, Siri's servant, whereas Billava and Bant women often get possessed by Siri or one of the characters related to her. One of our informants, a Dalit woman experiencing possession by Dāru, told us that she, as a Dalit, has the obligation to serve other castes. Dāru and a Dalit woman, the former in a literal, and the other one in a figurative sense, are servants by occupation. Accordingly, there is also a social hierarchy concerning the Siri characters and their possession media.

2. At the beginning of the workshop, the German students expected that Siri women would be dealing with their individual problems during possession (*darśana*). In conversations with Siri women it became clear, though, that they are not expressing their personal emotions, but the emotions of the Siri character they are possessed by. The women consider this as a service (*sēve*) to god which endows them with strength and spiritual support.

3. As preparation for the workshop we had read summaries and translations of the *Siri pāḍdana* which is centered on females. We therefore assumed that the women, who have the leading role in the epic, have the same important role in the ritual as well. However, observations of the actual rituals suggest that men acting as Kumāra priests play the major role within the ritual. Thus, the *pāḍdana* is female dominated whereas the ritual is male domi-

nated. We are unable to say whether this is a more recent development and what the reasons are to account for it.

4. Another observation we made was the fragmented recitation of the *pāḍdana* by women in a state of possession. In conversations with several Siri women they explained that during possession (*darśana*) they are capable of reciting parts of the *pāḍdana* but not outside the ritual context. Most of them asserted that they received this ability naturally during possession and attributed it to god. Among the women interviewed only one said she was capable of reciting the whole *pāḍdana*. We were told that nowadays the number of women able to sing entire *pāḍdanas* is decreasing.

5. Though the Udupi Fieldwork workshop 2008 yielded many interesting findings and new insights, what seemed most striking to us was the fact that the number of women getting possessed by the Siri spirits during the *jātre* was much less than we had expected. These expectations were based on information gathered in the lectures during the initial week of the workshop and on papers by scholars like Claus and Gowda (Claus 1993, 1997, 2004; Gowda 2005) as well as on archival footage available in the RRC covering earlier Siri jātres. All the materials we used for preparation suggested a mass possession of women at the *jātre*. With this anticipation in mind we were very surprised to find only eleven Siri women in Urmbitoṭṭu participating actively in the *dalya*. Concurrently many of our female interview partners actually were Siri women and mentioned that they do not go to have *darśana*, *i.e.* get possessed, during the Siri jātre, but rather prefer to give *kāṇike*, an offering containing a certain amount of money, to the temple instead. As a consequence, one can say that a women's expressive tradition is changing rapidly. In the next paragraphs possible reasons for the decline of the Siri women's *sēve* in terms of getting publicly possessed by one of the Siri spirits during the Siri jātre and the increasing popularity of giving *kāṇike* instead will be presented and discussed.

4. *Possible reasons for the decline of female possession at the Siri jātre*

Behaviour of audience / changing audience

First of all, as discussed above, the Siri jātre probably has not always been a public affair as it is today. Initially, it was a private ritual at the household level which was attended only by people who actually were connected to the cult – the Kumāras and the Siri women, as well as their relatives, who came to support them. Hence, people witnessing the possession part of the ritual all had background knowledge about the Siri cult and were involved in the ritual directly or at least indirectly. Only when the management of different temples in the region began to attach the Siri ritual to the temple institutionalising it as a festival ritual (*jātre*) and combining it with different kinds of entertainment programmes like stage-shows, markets and food stalls, did more and more people started coming to the »Siri jātre« without having any connection to the cult itself or to the Goddess.

Lacking knowledge about the Siri tradition and worship nowadays most members of the crowd attend the festival as mere spectators. The sight and behaviour of possessed women might seem strange and cause confusion to a person lacking any background knowledge about the ritual context. These spectators will look for a way to explain or justify their experience at the *jātre* and might end up deriding and criticising the practise of mass-possession in public by women.

Another possibility is that spectators only attend the festival attracted by its ›sensational‹ content with the intention of having fun at other people's cost and laughing about the participants. While getting possessed in public the women behave in a way which the spectators could interpret as indecent or even obscene. Indeed, during our investigations, participants of the Siri jātre reported incidents of mockery, especially by male youth spectators. As a result, one possible explanation for the fact that fewer women actually get possessed during the ritual might be that the Siri women, and also their families, fear being viewed with ridicule or facing libel and slander by the audience while being in a state of mind in which they cannot control themselves. Hence, the behaviour of an insensitive crowd at the Siri jātre might be an important reason for the lack of women participating in the public possession rituals during these festivals, and, consequently, the repression of women's expressive culture.

Media representation

Secondly, and closely linked to the first possible explanation, the influence of the mass media, especially television, might play an important role in the decline of the Siri women's *darśana*. Generally, modern mass media and especially TV have a potent manipulative force: by choice of subjects, mode of presentation, emphasis and rating they convey certain codes of conduct, values and norms for desirable behaviour in very subtle ways and through this mechanism can influence the attitude and also the behaviour of the audience. Thus, another possible reason for the decline of the number of women having *darśana* at the Siri jātre is the incompatibility of this religious practice with urban middle class norms conveyed by and reinforced through TV.

More closely linked to the Siri cult itself is the following observation: in recent times, several TV features covering the Siri cult have been broadcasted.

Footage of Siri jātres has appeared on local TV channels as part of popular documentation serials called *Crime Story* and *Crime Diary* suggesting that the cult had some connection with illegality. The title of the serials already shows the programme makers' general attitude towards the Siri cult: Both clippings we viewed during the workshop were not at all sober and neutral reports, but rather products of sensationalism. Little background information about the cult was given, and the participants were portrayed in a very unfavourable light. A short excerpt of the TV serial *Crime Story*, available at our visuals, shows the front credits and a brief introduction of the Siri cult given by the commentator [see FILM CLIP 3]. The lurid title *Crime Story* is highlighted by dramatic sounds emphasising the crime factor followed by the subheading »Siri Coming! Siri Coming!« (Original title: »*Siri bandaḷō Siri*«) which directly links the activities of the Siri cult with crimes. In this excerpt the way of presenting the cult, *e.g.* voice and emphasis of the commentator, is more sensational than the facts can stand up to. The programme starts with the commentary about origin and development of the Siri cult and is illustrated by sequential clips of possessed women, one following the other, without any reference to the possession ritual.

Both serials are good examples of showing the manipulative power of modern mass media. Completely deprived of its (textual, ritual and cultural) context and laced with some sensational comments, the Siri cult is presented to the audience trying to convey urban middle class norms and shaping the public opinion. As a result, the ›modern‹ urbanised middle class audience not familiar with the Siri tradition might react with lack of appreciation at best, and with abhorrence of the uncivilized and backward practices of rural India's people in the worst case.

The TV clippings on Siri were not only watched by uninvolved urban audiences, but also by many of our informants actively participating in the Siri ritual. Though many of the performers commented that they do not care about the media representation it is quite likely that the TV clippings on Siri have a deterrent effect on potential participants in the Siri *darśana*. Their husbands and families being aware of the public opinion, might discourage them from taking an active part in the ritual. Though all Siri women consider it their duty to come to the *jātre* and provide service to the goddess, they might prefer giving *kāṇike*, a practice widely accepted, instead of having *darśana* which, from an ›enlightened‹ middle class point of view, is something undesirable and backward. Media projects the Siri cult in an inexpedient way by criticising its ›low content‹ and projecting the cult and its participants as backward. It shows that television, too, contributes towards placing the Siri jātre in an unfavourable light and might lead to discouraging women from participating in the rituals, thus stifling this expressive culture of women.

Changing perception of the relationship between Siri and Kumāra

A special relationship which is often eyed with suspicion by outside observers is the close contact of the Siri women and the Kumāra. In the epic context Kumāra is the brother, son or uncle of the female characters of the *pāḍdana*. The family bond between them could be transferred to the relationship of the Siri women to their Kumāra in day-to-day life. The Siri women hardly know each other unless they meet by chance, but in the majority of cases they just meet at the Siri jātre and hardly know each others' names, but only their Siri characters.

This is in contrast to the extraordinary relationship of the individual Siris to their Kumāra. The bond between them is a lifelong bond. The Kumāra is invariably connected with the Siri women of the *dalya* he is responsible for and from time to time he pays a visit to the several Siris and acts as an adviser and confidant in case of problems.

When the Siris and the Kumāra get possessed, he takes the leading role in keeping the ritual within its limits. While interacting with the Siris he is in close contact with them – emotionally as well as physically. Thus, he firmly holds their hand to help them get into trance. Outsiders observe this physical contact between Kumāra and Siri with distrust partly because they don't know the background of this relationship. Moreover, touching a person of the other sex in public is still a delicate issue in Indian society, especially in rural areas, and is viewed by the general public as having sexual connotations. During our workshop, we sometimes heard oral comments describing the physical contact between Kumāra and Siri as a public display with sexual undertones. According to this opinion, the Siri who is touched by the Kumāra, a man who is not related to her through blood or marriage in real life, loses her honour and thereby disgraces her family. This perception is also gaining ground in the closer circle of participants. More and more families do not want their female members to participate actively in the possession ritual, but recommend them to give *kāṇike* instead, because of the impure image projected onto the Siri women.

The danger for the women lies in the disrepute, which they potentially invite by participating in the ritual. As they and their families want to keep their reputation intact, many women prefer to join private *dalyas* on a small scale where they are not showcased or give up their active participation in the possession rituals altogether. Many husbands do not want their wives to participate in the ritual anymore as they do not want to invite malicious gossip with regard to the reputation of their wives. In the state of possession, the Siris do not have control over their actions. Without being aware of it they shake their bodies in quivering movements hitting themselves with bunches of areca flowers and often having their hair untied and disheveled. This visual imagery underscores the uncontrolled state of the women and is accordingly an expression of their vulnerability, as well as liberation from rules of expected behaviour. In such moments, the women are liable to the gaze of male voyeurs. Most probably husbands let the importance of how other men might ogle their wives take precedence over the perceived beneficial outcomes of their wives' participation in the rituals encouraging the latter to discontinue their participation. This danger increases because of more visitors at the *jātre*. Husbands and close family members may have problems, too, with the relationship between the Kumāra and Siri, in particular as this relationship is seen by outsiders as having a potential sexual content.

Changing status of women in society

A third possible explanation for the decline of *darśana* at the Siri jātre is the change of women's roles in society. In this context, an earlier, but still existing approach to the nature of spirit possession has to be presented and discussed. There has been – and sometimes still is – a tendency in research (especially from the field of medical anthropology) about spirit possession to reduce this phenomenon to a pathological state. According to this view, spirit possession is associated with abnormal behaviour and associated as psychiatric disorder caused by anxiety, depression etc. (*e.g.* CARSTAIRS, KAPUR 1976: 106). This view is strengthened by the fact that spirit possessions often start with various expressions of anguish and frequently end with a »cure« (CLAUS 1984: 61).[20] It projects the notion of oppressed and psychologically troubled women, who are seeking relief in the possession at the annual Siri jātre as a kind of a local psychotherapy. One of the objectives of our fieldwork was to find out whether the spirit possession actually had a cathartic effect and is a platform for women to address their personal problems which they cannot discuss with their husbands and families.

In case this assumption would have proved valid, one could interpret the decline in the number of women getting possessed at the Siri jātre as the result of the improving situation of women in the family and society: the ›valve‹ provided by possession is no longer needed by many women due to their better status and improved opportunities to speak out and address their problems within the scope of their everyday lives. In that case it would be possible to reason that, as a result of women's emancipation through feminist advocacy, better education and employment opportunities for women, which have led to their empowerment both at a micro-level (within the family) and a macro-level (within society), the general situation of women has started to change for the better. As many women have a strong voice in their day-to-day lives and are no longer oppressed by the male members of society, there is no more need of the

20 This view has been contested in recent publications. For a critical overview and discussion on literature of possession see SCHÖMBUCHER 1993.

catharsis they experience during possession and it is sufficient for them to offer *kāṇike* as a service to god.

In spite of the fact that the view of seeing possession as an outlet for repressed emotions appears widespread amongst the new Indian middle classes, this interpretation soon turned out to be wrong, one-dimensional and oversimplified. The medical / psychological perspective is a Western one; it completely neglects the cultural concepts and ideologies of the people involved. For the Siri women their *darśana* is a highly religious phenomenon of spiritual origin (CLAUS 1984: 63). Not a single one of our informants ever mentioned selfish motives of getting cured from individual problems through possession. They did not address any personal problems during the *darśana* at all. They considered their *darśana* as service (*sēve*) to the goddess lending their bodies to the Siri spirits and, by doing so, acting as the spirits' vehicles to manifest themselves in the profane world. After a troublesome time of uncontrolled individual possession, which they experienced at their homes, the Siri women promised to participate annually in the *jātre* and serve the Siri spirits as vehicles or media. By fulfilling this promise and by allowing the spirit willingly to fully possess them without them trying to resist, the troublesome condition of uncontrolled possession is resolved.[21]

From an emic perspective, spirit possession can be valued as a connection between the individual and the moral order of her / his society. According to CLAUS (1984: 63) the emotions from which possession arises are common to all societies, only the way in which they are handled differ: »They arise under a number of situations, largely culturally conditioned, in which the individual feels himself / herself outside of the order of moral expectations in which he / she has been conditioned to see himself« (CLAUS 1984: 63). In Tuḷu ideology this crisis manifests itself in the encroachment of spirits from the domain of *māya* on the domain of *jōga* (the ordered world of humans). The supremacy of an ideal order over the crisis situations of daily life is questioned or reasserted periodically by individuals or larger social groups. Along this line of thinking spirit possession can be regarded as »a symbolic medium through which the individual (or group) re-adjusts himself to an appropriate order« (CLAUS 1984: 63). In the case of the Siri cult, women offer their bodies as vehicles to the Siri spirits who according to the *pāḍdana* themselves maintained female virtues in their own lives. Doing so, the women hope for spiritual support and protection against threats both from worldly struggles and supernatural enemies (CLAUS 1979: 38).

It becomes obvious that reflecting upon spirit possession from a strictly medical perspective and explaining the decrease of women's *darśana* in the Siri jātre as a result of the improving status of women is insufficient as it completely

21 Initial resistance against the possession followed by total surrender and promise to serve the spirit / goddess is a phenomenon described in much of the literature about possession in India and Sri Lanka, *e.g.* SCHÖMBUCHER 2006.

neglects the emic, socio-religious perspective. The merely medical problem-cure-paradigm does not do justice, neither to a complex and multidimensional phenomenon like spirit possession, nor to the women in question as it reduces their *sēve* to an attempt of curing themselves from imputed psychological problems instead of acknowledging it as a religious expression. Thus (from our point of view) the decline of the number of women having *darśana* cannot be explained simply by a decreasing need for a platform to express one's own feelings due to an improved status of women.

Nevertheless, the impact of the changing status of women, and especially of educational opportunities for women, on the decline of *darśana* at the Siri jātre and the increasing popularity of giving *kāṇike* instead should not be denied here. Actually, it seems quite likely, that changes in the status of women in society have an effect on the practice of *darśana*. But we propose a different approach: these factors should be presented focusing on a social mode of impact instead of a medical one.

As stated above the status of women in Tuḷuva society has changed. This fact is reflected in phenomena like changed womens' property rights, right to vote, feminist movements, employment opportunities, improved access to education and information for women. Education and the mass media, in particular, have shaped the understanding of womens' role in society and have become pivotal in conveying role models for socially encouraged and accepted behaviour.

Apart from knowledge transfer education always – directly or indirectly – conveys certain moral values, norms and codes of conduct and thus is a highly sensitive and political issue.

Hence, education plays a crucial role in the conservation or the abasement of local culture and tradition. One has to be extremely sensitive implementing education especially in rural parts of India as education towards modernity can easily lead to some sort of ›cultural imperialism‹ of western, urban values:

It remains to be researched whether women's education in Tuḷunāḍu and also mass media accessible to women through education transmit certain ›modern‹, urban middle class expectations and norms with regard to the behaviour of women and aim to culturally mainstream them rather than to implement critical thinking and general emancipation. Should this assumption prove valid it is quite likely that education, too, plays an important role in the decline of *darśana* at Siri jātres. According to the hypothesis of a biased educational system which keeps women in leading-stings promoting ›modern‹ values at any cost, it is plausible that people become alienated from their own traditions and culture resulting in a feeling that taking part in the Siri ritual and having *darśana* is socially inappropriate and a sign of backward behaviour. In that way insensitive education can discourage the Siri women from taking part actively in the Siri ritual and can lead to depreciation of the Siri ritual amongst the general public as something that does not fit the modern world. As we have not examined the way education is implemented in Tuḷunāḍu these interdependences between education and the decreasing number of women getting publicly possessed in the Siri jātre can only be assumed and need further substantiation.[22]

5. Conclusion

Our 2008 fieldwork shows that the number of women actively participating in the Siri jātre by having *darśana* had decreased considerably as compared to earlier *jātres*. This fact becomes significant, in particular in the context of women's participation in performance rituals, when one realizes that there was no evidence for the decline of the *jātre* or the cult as a whole. Many of our (female) informants explained that they preferred giving *kāṇike* (a ›disembodied‹ material gift apparently having higher prestige) instead of having *darśana* (a personal, ›embodied‹ gift of lower prestige) in public. Observations at the Urmbitoṭṭu Siri jātre do not point at the decline of the cult, but rather to a cult undergoing change: The mode of service (*sēve*) to the goddess is changing from having *darśana* to giving *kāṇike*. In this article we have presented possible reasons for the changes in the Siri cult – changes which appear to have led to a declining number of women participating in the Siri possession rituals and, consequently, to women being increasingly cut off from an expressive medium that they considered as their exclusive way of serving the Goddess, because ›modern‹ society struggles accommodating this particular way of female worship with its projected images of desirable feminine behaviour.

First of all, the *jātre* appears to have developed from a private, small-scale household-level ritual into a public Śaiva temple festival. The presence of uninvolved spectators, who do not possess adequate background knowledge about the cult, in what has now evolved into a practice of worship open to be viewed by the general public and mass media can lead to a misapprehension of the events that can be observed during the *jātre*. There are instances of spectators perceiving the *jātre* as mere spectacle and making fun of the participants. Presenting oneself in a state of possession to an audience which does not perceive the *jātre* as a ritual of high religious significance but as mere entertainment may make the Siri women and their families feel uncomfortable and may prompt them to give *kāṇike* instead.

The spread of public misconceptions has been promoted, too, by the mass media, which have represented the Siri rituals and the participation of women therein in a sensational and unfavourable way. TV serials, such as *Crime Story*,

22 By no means the importance of education for rural women as a fundamental human right should be questioned here; the crucial point is the mode of implementation: It has to enable the persons in question to consciously and independently make their own decisions rather than to adjust them to the cultural mainstream.

pretend there is a link of the cult to some sort of crime. The women are shown in a state of uncontrolled possession. This portrait of a possessed woman, who waves her body and shakes her untied hair, is exposed to the public, to non-related spectators and in particular to young males, who eyeball the possession rituals with voyeuristic intention.

A similar issue was picked up by parts of a reinforced conservative society, which began to consider the physical contact between Kumāra and Siri in a state of possession as a potentially sexual one, or at least as a way of immoral behaviour. Such notions further discourage public *darśana* of the Siri women. The display of female bodies in public is no longer desirable and incompatible with the ›modern‹ (*i.e.* neo-conservative) picture of an ideal woman.

Such new role models, also conveyed by mass media, tend to be incompatible with *darśana* as a mode of worship. One of the key factors in this development might be the changed position of women in society as the result of the impact of modern education contributing to the increasing preference of giving *kāṇike* instead of having *darśana* as a mode of *sēve* in the Siri ritual. Since we did not examine the mode of implementation of women's education in Tuḷunāḍu, this linkage can only be regarded a hypothesis. In case further investigation can prove a connection between spoon-feeding education and a decline of local traditions, this insight would once again approve the importance of research in the field of culture-sensitive education.

All the factors mentioned above contribute to a more or less negative image of the Siri women's possession and thus may have lead to the recent decline of Siri women's *darśana* we observed at the Urmbitoṭṭu Siri jātre in 2008. The possession as a personal, embodied gift has been replaced more and more by the impersonal, material, dis-embodied option of giving *kāṇike*. By replacing the mode of *sēve* and not abolishing it completely the *sēve* is still seen as a must and indicates the belief in the Siri cult is still strong. It has to be emphasized again that the numerical decline with respect to women's *darśana* is no indication of the decline of the Siri cult as a whole but only points to changing modes of public worship as part of normal processes of cultural and social change.

References

Bhatt, Gururaja. 1969. *Antiquities of South Kanara.* Udipi: Prabhakara Press.

----. 1975. *Studies in Tuḷuva History and Culture.* Manipal: Manipal Press.

Brückner, Heidrun. 2009. *On an Auspicious Day, at Dawn...: Studies in Tulu Culture and Oral Literature.* Wiesbaden: Harrassowitz.

Carstairs, George M.; Kapur, Ravi L. 1976. *The great universe of Kota: Stress, Change and Mental Disorder in an Indian Village.* London: The Hogarth Press.

Claus, Peter J. 1975. »The Siri Myth and Ritual: A Mass Possession Cult of South India«. *Ethnology. An International Journal of Cultural And Social Anthropology* 14: 47–58.

––––. 1979. »Spirit Possession and Spirit Mediumship from the Perspective of Tulu Oral Traditions«. *Culture, Medicine, and Psychiatry* 3: 29–52.

––––. 1984. »Medical Anthropology and the Ethnography of Spirit Possession«. In: *Contributions to Asian Studies.* Ed. by K. Ishwaran and Bardwell L. Smith. Leiden: E. J. Brill, 60–72.

––––. 1993. »Text Variability and Authenticity in the Siri Cult«. In: *Flags of Fame. Studies in South Asian Folk Culture.* Ed. by Heidrun Brückner, Lothar Lutze and Aditya Malik. Delhi: Manohar, 335–74.

––––. 1999. »Ritual Transforms a Myth«. *http://class.csueastbay.edu/anthropology/claus/kumar.htm* (access date: 19th March 2009; an earlier version of this paper was presented under the same title at the South Asia Conference, Madison, WI, 1991 and published on the Internet in 1994).

––––. 2004. »The Drama Unfolds: Tuluva Myth and Ritual in Its Western Stage«. *Indian Folklore Research Journal* 1, 4: 36–52.

––––. 2008. »Before The Text. Siri Myth and Ritual from Field to Media. Section One: Overview of the Siri Cult«. *http://class.csueastbay.edu/anthropology/claus/Siri/SiriSection1.htm* (access date: 19th March 2009).

GOWDA, CHINNAPPA. 2005. »Siri: The Tulu Oral Epic. Text, Textualisation and Performance«. In: *The Mask and the Message. A Collection of Research Papers on various Aspects of Tulu Culture and Folklore.* Ed. by Chinnappa Gowda. Mangalagangothri: Madipu Prakashana, 121–138.

––––. 2005. *The Mask and the Message. A Collection of Research Papers on various Aspects of Tulu Culture and Folklore.* Mangalagangothri: Madipu Prakashana.

HONKO, LAURI. 1998: *Textualizing the Siri Epic.* Helsinki: Suomalainen Tiedeakatemia Academia Scientiarum Fennica.

SCHÖMBUCHER, ELISABETH. 1993. »Gods, Ghosts and Demons: Possession in South Asia«. In: *Flags of Fame. Studies in South Asian Folk Culture.* Ed. by Heidrun Brückner, Lothar Lutze and Aditya Malik. Delhi: Manohar, 239–267.

––––. 2006. *Wo Götter durch Menschen sprechen. Besessenheit in Indien.* Berlin: Reimer.

UPADHYAYA, ULIYAR PADMANABHA (ED.). 1988. *Tulu Lexicon.* Vol. 1. Udupi: Rashtrakavi Govinda Pai Research Centre.

LIST OF VISUALS

ILLUSTRATIONS 1 and 9: Photographs taken at the *illecci dalya* by Lea Griebl and Sarah Merkle (March 2008).

ILLUSTRATIONS 2 and 3: Charts drawn during the workshop by Sina Sommer.

ILLUSTRATIONS 4–8: Photographs taken at the Urmbitoṭṭu Siri jātre by Lea Griebl and Sarah Merkle (February 2008).

FILM CLIP 1: Clipping of the Urmbitoṭṭu Siri jātre video-documentation taken in 1989. Original available at the RRC Archive, Udupi.

FILM CLIP 2: Summery clip of the Urmbitoṭṭu Siri jātre fieldwork material 2008.

FILM CLIP 3: Short excerpt of the TV Serial *Crime Story*.

Subhadra Redux

Reinstating Female Kutiyattam

Diane Daugherty

In 2001 a grant from the American Institute of Indian Studies allowed me to commission performances of »Subhadra's Entry and Nirvahana« (see RAJAGOPALAN 1997: 61–87 for an English translation). In this essay I will describe female *kutiyattam* at the time the text came into my hands. Then, focusing on the four women who have defined contemporary female *kutiyattam* performance, I will chart the growth that took place in the dozen years between the manual's acquisition and production. Finally, I will discuss the process for staging an item of *kutiyattam* that has not been staged in living memory and, therefore, has no pre-set choreography.[1]

Subhadra-Dhananjaya, a five-act Sanskrit play based on the love story of Subhadra and Arjuna, is attributed to a tenth century Kerala monarch, Kulasekhara Varman. A *nirvahana* is a character's reflection on past events. Anonymous practitioners of *kutiyattam* inserted *nirvahana* into the dramatic text hundreds of years ago. In this flashback the performer plays multiple roles – recreating divinities, demons, soldiers, sweethearts, animals – even inanimate objects that figured earlier in the story. An acting manual (*attaprakaram*) for a *nirvahana* contains verses to be sung by women seated stage right and explications of the verses. These inspire the performer who elaborates each verse by blending a codified sign language system of the hands, face and eyes with stylized movement *before* it is sung (see MOSER in this volume).

Kutti Nangiaramma

Every five years, Act I of *Subhadra-Dhanajaya* plays for eleven nights in the Thrissur Vadakkunathan (Shiva) Temple theatre (*kuttambalam*) [see ILLUSTRATION 2]. On the ninth night, a curtain is held for Subhadra's entrance. When it is removed spectators see a quaking »maiden« standing on a stool. Subhadra is in the clutches of a demon who snatched her and flew off. The demon drops her when he sees Arjuna aiming an arrow at him. Arjuna catches her as she falls

1 Some artists have refined the rendering of a piece and younger artists strive to approximate their interpretation.

from the sky (jumps from the stool). They take one look at each other and fall in love. Neither knows the other's identity. While Arjuna and his sidekick talk, Subhadra mysteriously disappears.[2]

The only other female role in the temple's repertoire is Lalitha – the gross demoness, Surpanakha, disguised as a beauty – in *Surpanakhankam* (see JONES 1984 for an English translation).[3] Kutti Nangiaramma played both of these parts until she passed away in 1984 in her late seventies. Her family (Meledath) had the right to perform the female roles, keep the rhythm (*tala*) by striking small cymbals, chant, and drum in the Thrissur temple theatre.[4] Because she was not formally trained there was, L.S. Rajagopalan has noted, »a tendency to make her role as short as possible« (RAJAGOPALAN 1997: 16). Her age also factored in keeping her part brief. L.S. Rajagopalan remembers hoping that the curtain would be whisked aside to reveal a young woman playing Subhadra. He was repeatedly disappointed to see the senior Nangiar with whom it was impossible to believe anyone could fall in love at first sight (Rajagopalan, personal communication). The actor who played Rama to the older woman's Lalitha confided his discomfort when he had to address her as *sundari* or beautiful one (Ammannur Madhava Chakyar, personal communication).

Like a handful of other dedicated women, despite age and minimal training, Kutti Nangiaramma continued to fulfill her obligation to annually present *nangiar kuttu*, a genre of *kutiyattam* in which one actress tells the story of the god Krishna (DAUGHERTY 1996 and MOSER in this volume). G. Venu, a *kutiyattam* expert who performs, directs, and manages two institutions, has remarked that because of her makeshift costume and lack of acting ability »they performed the Koothu with the doors of the Koothambalam shut since they thought that nobody should see their miserable condition« (VENU 2002: 54).

C.K. Jayanti remembers Kutti Nangiaramma as a »courageous« person. When, as a child, Jayanti first sat with Nangiaramma to keep the *tala*, the senior woman told her: »A Nangiar is a very powerful person. If a Chakyar makes a mistake, a Nangiar can stop the performance and ask him to correct his error. Also, should you have to use the toilet let me know and I will stop the performance.« (C.K. Jayanti, personal communication).

2 We learn in *Subhadra's Nirvahana* that Krishna sent Garuda to rescue her; see RAJAGOPALAN 1997: 51–58 for a detailed description.

3 »The Surpanakha Act« (*Surpanakhankam*) is the second act of *Ascharyachudamani* (»The Wondrous Crest-Jewel«). Based on the *Ramayana*, it is attributed to the 9th (?) century Kerala playwright, Shaktibhadra. Each of its seven acts is performed as a separate entity.

4 A Nangiar is a member of a temple serving caste (Ambalavasi) whose hereditary occupation was portraying virtuous female characters, marking the beat with small cymbals, and singing for *kutiyattam*. The men of her community (Nambiar) played a drum (*mizhavu*) that looks like a huge metal jar. They were also makeup artists and stage managers. Taking the male roles in *kutiyattam* was the job of another Ambalavasi subcaste, the Chakyar.

Nangiaramma died from injuries sustained when a bus struck her en route to a temple performance. No woman in her family was equipped to take her place and offer *nangiar kuttu* in Vadakkunathan Temple theatre.

Usha Nangiar

In June 1989 L.S. Rajagopalan and I met with the late Nangiaramma's family and the Devaswom Board that governs Vadakkunathan Temple activities to arrange for a special performance of *nangiar kuttu* in the *kuttambalam* by Usha Nangiar. Usha – a college graduate in math / science who trained in *kutiyattam* since childhood – had recently decided to make *kutiyattam* performance her career. On 30 July 1989, a Nambiar from the Meledath family ceremonially struck the metal drum (*mizhavu*); then Usha's father, Chathakudam Krishnan Nambiar who was an accomplished *mizhavu* player, took over. Two women, Thankam, a relative of the late Nangiar, and Rethy, Usha's cousin, kept the rhythm (*tala*) and sang the verses (*sloka*) while Usha acted a portion of the »The Birth of Kamsa« from *Sri Krishna Charitam* – Krishna's Story (see *slokas* 3–5 in Paniker 2005: 57–58 and Rajagopalan 1997: 98–104 for English translations). The highlight of the piece was the dressing of Suraseni (Kamsa's mother) by her two maids. Suraseni's request, »Oh please adorn me«, signaled the acting of one of *kutiyattam*'s set items, *koppu aniyal* [see film clip 7 by Johan for a male acting this item]. This was the first performance Usha had given outside of Ammannur Gurukulam, her home institution, and was probably the first time in a century that a *well-trained* Nangiar had presented *nangiar kuttu* on a temple stage. Commissioned outside the time that *nangiar kuttu* falls in Vadakkunathan Temple's schedule of rituals, it blurred the line between *nangiar kuttu* as temple-based theatre and as a concert performance form.

A few weeks earlier, during the mid-July break in the 1989 southwest monsoon, after the coconut palms had been greened by six weeks of rain, L.S. Rajagopalan – my friend, guide for my research, and translator – and I were making the rounds to interview *kutiyattam* performers and to ask if they had any manuals pertaining to female roles [see illustration 1]. We had just come upon an acting manual for Subhadra's *nirvahana* in Act V of *Subhadra-Dhananjaya*. The *attaprakaram* (manual) was copied in a child's school notebook. This was just the sort of discovery I had dreamt about – unearthing a score for a female performance that had fallen out of the active repertoire.

Mid-summer 1990, I asked Usha to present another portion of *Sri Krishna Charitam* in the Thrissur temple theatre. On 29 July 1990 she showed *Ugrasenabandhanam* (»The Imprisoning of Ugrasena«) (*sloka* 8–11 in Paniker 2005: 60–62). At that time the various episodes of *Sri Krishna Charitam* did not have the code names they do today. The manual (*attaprakaram*) sent by Ammannur Madhava Chakyar several days before the performance was titled: »How

Kamsa Became the King of Mathura«. The manual noted that Kamsa's preparation for war (*patappurappad*) should be shown, but did not give any details. L.S. Rajagopalan offers this description of *patappurappad*:

> A soldier enters, tightens his belt and gets ready to do exercises. He takes his weapon and exercises with it. Like this, other soldiers enter one after another and show exercises with the weapon of their choice, like the sword, the spear, the mace, bows and arrows, and so on. Then horses, elephants and chariots enter and soldiers exhibit feats standing on them. Then various instruments of the military band come, the Cenda drum, the Maddalam, the Timila, the Conch, the Kombu (horn), the pipe, cymbals and so on and the mode they are played is demonstrated. (RAJAGOPALAN 1997: 109)

Several months later Usha offered *nangiar kuttu* in its traditional slot in Vadakkunathan Temple's ritual cycle, beginning the day before *Sri Krishna Jayanti* (Krishna's birthday) and running for the next six days. During the next seven years she worked her way through all of the verses of Sri Krishna Charitam. The half dozen Nangiars who still offered annual temple performances in 1990 covered, at most, the first thirty-five of more than two hundred verses.[5] The balance of the acting manual was unexplored territory.

In 1991, as the senior student at the Ammannur Gurukulam (Training Center), Usha was entrusted with training new disciples including Saritha, Aparna, and Kapila. For years she had the benefit of association with her famous *guru*, Padmabhushan Ammannur Madhava Chakyar. He was the last survivor among the three male actors recognized as consummate artists in the second half of the 20th century. She also gained stage experience because of G.Venu's energy and commitment. Venu had, since 1976, been bridging the gap between the feudal milieu in which Madhava Chakyar grew up and modernity. He established an annual *kutiyattam* festival in Irinjalakuda, arranged performances in other parts of India, and organized foreign tours.

After Usha's marriage, Aparna Nangiar took over playing the female roles in *kutiyattam* and offering *nangiar kuttu* in Vadakkunathan [see ILLUSTRATION 3]. Sree Sankaracharya University of Sanskrit, Kalady, named Usha to the Department of Theatre faculty in 1997. The responsibilities of the job, the birth of a daughter, and her father's critical illness took their toll. In December 2000, during the preparation of the candidature file that would result in UNESCO designating *kutiyattam* a masterpiece of humanity's intangible heritage, rumors began to circulate that Usha Nangiar's performing career was in jeopardy. Anxious that this would not be the case, I proposed that she stage »Subhadra's Nirvahana« [see ILLUSTRATIONS 4–10]. The performances relaunched her career.

5 Usha's *guru*, Ammannur Madhava Chakyar, used a palm-leaf manuscript that has 216 verses (PANIKER 2005: 55–159). Narayanan Nambiar collated manuscripts held by several families and published a 217-verse manual in Malayalam (NAMBIAR 1984).

She has since restored many characters to the *kutiyattam* stage including Mandodari (2003), Katyayani (2003), Menaka (2004), and Draupadi (2005).

Kalamandalam Girija and Kalamandalam Sailaja

I had seen *kutiyattam* and *nangiar kuttu* for the first time in 1988, the year before I came upon the manuscript for Subhadra's *nirvahana*. Kalamandalam Girija, the first woman outside of the traditional community to be trained in *kutiyattam*, honored Marlene Pitkow's and my request to perform an athletic item from *Sri Krishna Charitam*.[6] Girija chose the first section of »The Birth of Kamsa« that includes Ugrasena (Kamsa's father) preparing to go hunting. A king preparing for a hunt is virtually the same as a king preparing for war (*patappurappad*). Readying to hunt involves »describing various weapons, hunting materials like nets, various mounts like the horse, the elephant. This procession for hunting takes a long time to act«, comments Rajagopalan, »but it is interesting to watch« (RAJAGOPALAN 1997: 103). With exhilaration I realized that the performance manual for *nangiar kuttu* demanded that a woman's body be strong and agile.

Several months later Kalamandalam Sailaja staged the second part of »The Birth of Kamsa«. The *bhava* (state of emotion) that Sailaja showed when Sauraseni realizes she has been tricked into having sex with a wily demon is still vivid in my mind's eye twenty years later. Female *kutiyattam* performance requires not only a flexible body, but also finely tuned facial and eye muscles.

In 1965 their *guru*, Painkulam Rama Chakyar, had bravely agreed to head a *kutiyattam* department at Kerala Kalamandalam (Arts Academy). The taboo on staging *kutiyattam* outside a temple had been challenged a decade earlier. Providing training in a state-supported institution to students who were not from the traditional communities for the express purpose of performing *kutiyattam* on the concert stage ruffled lots of feathers. Of the first batch of students only one, Sivan, was not from a performing family. But then the Nangiar trainee, Rukmini, decided the program was not for her and dropped out. After discussions with Girija's father, Rama Chakyar asked her if she would be interested in learning *kutiyattam*. She joined Kalamandalam's *kutiyattam* unit in 1971.

Sailaja, who also is not a Nangiar, joined Girija in the *kutiyattam* classroom in 1974. Their *guru* taught them Subhadra and Lalitha's parts. He cast them as Sita in *Jatayuvadham* and *Surpanakhankam*, Vijaya in *Toranayuddham*, and

6 At the time Marlene Pitkow and I were studying the all-female Tripunithura Kathakali Kendram Troupe (see DAUGHERTY and PITKOW 1991). Men take all the roles in *kathakali* including the female roles (see PITKOW this volume). *Sri Krishna Charitam* was composed for and performed by female actors. We wondered what challenges for women's bodies it contained.

Tara in *Balivadham*. The female students also played roles in *Svapna-Vasavadatta* and *Naganandam*. [This list is not inclusive.]

Kalamandalam premiered its signature production, an adaptation of the farce *Bhagavadajjukam*, in 1976. In the »Garden Scene« (*Udyanavarnanam*), which Painkulam Rama Chakyar choreographed specifically for Girija and Sailaja, the two women sing in unison, show the *mudras* (hand gestures) simultaneously and dance together [see ILLUSTRATION 11]. When you mention the »Garden Scene« to a *kutiyattam* aficionado, his eyes widen and he gets a wistful expression on his face. Thirty years later it is still a crowd-pleaser as was demonstrated when Girija and Sailaja performed on 14 January 2006 during the »International Seminar on Kutiyattam and Asian Theatre Traditions« held in Thiruvananthapuram, Kerala and on 25 March 2006 for the Bank Employees' Art Movement, Kochi (GOPALAKRISHNAN 2006a; SADASIVAN 2006).

Painkulam Rama Chakyar taught the entrance piece for *nangiar kuttu* (*Chedi Purappad*) and the description of the garden in the »Entry into Vrindavana« episode of *Sri Krishna Charitam* (*sloka* 80 in PANIKER 2005: 92). He »intended to take up *Sri Krishna Charitam* in detail«, but died (in 1980) before he could do so (Vasudevan Namboodiripad, personal communication). Girija performed »Entry into Vrindavana« at Kalamandalam in 1984.

Girija, Sailaja and the two male acting students, Sivan Namboodiri and Kalamandalam Rama Chakyar (Painkulam Rama Chakyar's nephew) were given teaching posts at Kalamandalam. Girija told me and confirmed to K.K. Gopalakrishnan that they worked as a team to develop those portions of *Sri Krishna Charitam* that had »potential for acting« using the *attaprakaram* published in 1984 by P.K. Narayanan Nambiar, the senior member of the *kutiyattam* faculty who taught drumming (K.K. Gopalakrishnan, personal communication). At the request of the Sangeet Natak Akademi, the Kalamandalam *kutiyattam* faculty jointly choreographed a thirty-minute version of *Putanamoksham* (»Putana's Salvation«) in 1986. This was expanded to a ninety-minute version that played at Margi in 1990. They also jointly choreographed »The Birth of Kamsa« that Marlene Pitkow and I saw in 1988 and *Kaliyamardanam* (»The Defeat of Kaliya«) which Girija performed at Guruvayur Temple in 1992.

Because the faculty was on vacation, Girija worked alone when I asked her to prepare *Kamsavadham* (»Slaying of Kamsa«) from *Sri Krishna Charitam* and »Lalitha's Nirvahana« in *Parnasalankam* (»The Act of the Leafy Hut«) for documentation in 1993.[7] Vasudevan Namboodiripad, who was superintendent

7 *Parnasalankam* is the first act of *Ascharyachudamani* (»The Wondrous Crest-Jewel«) by Shaktibhadra. *Surpanakhankam* is the second act. Lalitha has a *nirvahana* in both acts. Painkulam Rama Chakyar taught »Lalitha's Nirvahana« in *Surpanakhankam*. A character's *nirvahana* in a later act includes all of the verses from that character's *nirvahana* in earlier acts. So, the *nirvahana* that Girija learned for Act II would have included the *slokas* in the Act I *nirvahana*. She did not have classroom notes to rely on for *Kamsavadham*. In choreographing this she drew on two decades of involvement in *kutiyattam* and her dra-

of Kalamandalam for many years and a close associate of Painkulam Rama Chakyar, watched rehearsals with me and made suggestions.

In the 1990s Kalamandalam became a residential performing arts high school. The carrot of earning an SSLC (Secondary School Leaving Certificate) while training in an art form did not attract the male students who it was hoped would respond, but did appeal to female students. With classrooms packed, Girija and Sailaja seldom perform outside of Kalamandalam. When they do, however, they demonstrate that trained female *kutiyattam* artists – the mothers of grown children – can leave an audience breathless. I am thinking, particularly, of Sailaja's stunning performance as Lalitha in the *Ascharyachudamani Festival* sponsored by Sangeet Natak Akademi (National Academy of Music, Dance, and Drama) in December 2005.[8] Though in her mid-forties, she has full control of the muscles in her exquisite face and is able to powerfully perform the choreography for the disguised Surpanakha's resumption of her true demonic form.

Margi Sathi

Another girl who was not from a traditional performing family, Sathi, joined Kalamandalam in 1976 and trained for eight years, first under Painkulam Rama Chakyar and then under Girija. In 1988, the year that he secured a Ford Foundation Grant, D. Appukuttan Nair invited Sathi to join Margi, an institution in Thiruvananthapuram founded by arts enthusiasts. »Narayanan Nambiar had given me a copy of his book, *Srikrishnacharitham Nangyarammakkoothu* (NAMBIAR 1984), because he had used my picture in it. I really didn't know what nangiar kuttu was«, she confessed to me, »but I told Appukuttan Nair I would like to learn to perform it and he agreed« (Margi Sathi, personal communication).[9]

In 1991 the persuasive Appukuttan Nair received a special grant from Sangeet Natak Akademi, Delhi for developing Margi as a center that would provide regular performance opportunities to trained *kutiyattam* artists. He decided to

matic imagination. – I had seen »Lalitha's Nirvahana, Act I« and *Kamsavadham* performed at Margi. But, Appukuttan Nair (see next section) was very strict. With the exception of Sangeet Natak Akademi, Delhi, he did not allow shooting of photos or videos of the company. – »Lalitha's Nirvahana, Act II«, is not performed when the Ammannur family stages *Surpanakhankam* in Vadakkunathan Temple. Theatre scholar Farley Richmond, who published an interactive multimedia CD-Rom on *kutiyattam* (RICHMOND 2002), included »Lalitha's Nirvahana« when he commissioned a full staging of *Surpanakhankam* at Kilimangalam in October 2007. Margi Sathi acted the *nirvahana*.

8 *Ascharyachudamani* (»The Wondrous Crest-Jewel«) is a seven-act play by Shaktibhadra based on the *Ramayana*. The acts are performed as separate entities. *Surpanakhankam* is the second act.

9 Sathi left Kalamandalam before Girija's performance of »Entry into Vrindavana« from *Sri Krishna Charitam* in 1984.

stage all seven acts of *Ascharyachudamani* and all 217 verses in Nambiar's manual (*attaprakaram*) for *nangiar kuttu* (NAMBIAR 1984). Margi gave weekly performances; one performance a month was devoted to *nangiar kuttu*. Although Sathi and Usha Nangiar were simultaneously shaping performance scores for episodes in *Sri Krishna Charitam*, they rarely saw each other's interpretations because they lived a seven-hour train journey apart. The two women independently developed different, but equally skillful renderings.[10]

Appukuttan Nair asked Ammannur Madhava Chakyar to provide manuals for three acts of *Ascharyachudamani*: Act I, *Parnasalankam*, which features »Lalitha's Nirvahana«; Act III, *Mayasitankam*, in which two actresses are onstage at the same time playing Sita and False Sita; and Act VII, *Agnipravesankam*, which centers on Sita's ordeal by fire. The other four acts were in the active *kutiyattam* repertoire. In 1991 the only role invariably embodied by an actress was Lalitha in *Surpanakhankam* (see JOHAN in this volume for a description of the portrayal of Sita by the actor playing Rama).

Margi Sathi played the lead female roles in the prologue, the interludes, and six acts of *Ascharyachudamani*. (Act VI, *Anguliyankam*, is a male solo performance.) Margi Usha, who trained at Kalamandalam and joined Margi in 1992, played the supporting roles. There came a time when Sathi had played Sita so often that she begun to imagine what Sita's *nirvahana* would have been like. She culled verses from various sources and, in 1999, published *Sree Rama Charitam Nangiarammakoothu: Stage Manual*. This work, coupled with the strong performances she had turned in for over a decade, won her the Kerala Sangeetha Nataka Akademi award in 2003.

The Subhadra-Dhananjaya Project

Appukuttan Nair commissioned Ammannur Madhava Chakyar to provide an acting manual for *Subhadra-Dhananjaya*, Act II. It was completed, after Nair's demise (1994), at the behest of P. Rama Iyer, who had worked closely with Nair. In 1998 when Rama Iyer told me about the manual, I conceived of the Subhadra-Dhananjaya Project. Producing Act II and staging Subhadra's Act V *nirvahana* would extend the active repertoire and add to the roles for female actors [see ILLUSTRATION 12].

Margi staged Act II in twelve performances between 26 January and 20 September 2001. At that time there were only a few ›scenes‹ in which two female characters appeared: several scenes in *Bhagavadajjukam*, notably the »Garden Scene«; Mandodari and her maidservant in *Asokavanikankam*; Sita and Maya Sita in *Mayasitankam*; and the contemporary staging of the scene in *Surpana-*

10 For Sathi's performance of »The Slaying of Kamsa« see INVIS 2003. For »Krishna Stealing the Gopis Clothes« see MARGI 2000.

khankam with Sita and Lalitha (see JOHAN in this volume). One ›scene‹ in *Subhadra-Dhananjaya* Act II added significantly to this list.

Arjuna is wandering in a garden when he hears women's voices coming from an arbor. He peeps into the arbor and sees the woman he rescued from the demon. Arjuna eavesdrops while Shatpadika persuades her distraught friend, Subhadra, to confide in her. Subhadra finally reveals that she is in love with two men: Arjuna and the man who saved her from the demon (UNNI, SULLIVAN 2002: 150–152). Surprisingly, Shatpadika, the *chedi* (a serving maid who is also a friend) has more lines of dialogue than the heroine (Subhadra). But the actress playing Subhadra has the challenge of showing ›love-sickness‹, and subtly reacting to her friend's entreaties.

As staged at Margi, focus in the scene was either split between the female and male characters or solely on the female characters. Per *kutiyattam* convention, Arjuna left the stage when he wasn't needed and the focus was entirely on the two women.[11] He returned just in time to overhear Subhadra's confession and realize that the woman he saved is in love with him twice over. At this point, though, he doesn't realize that the woman he saved is Subhadra [see ILLUSTRATIONS 13–14].

Three female characters – Subhadra and her two *chedis* (friends / maids) – were onstage frequently during the Act II *kutiyattam* (acting the playwright's text together) [see ILLUSTRATION 15]. In the summer of 2001 it was a rarity for three female actors to appear simultaneously on the *kutiyattam* stage.[12] Bear in mind that some forty years earlier *two* male actors had staged *Subhadra-Dhananjaya*, Act II at the Vellur Temple in one night.

Act II was part of temple ritual at Vellur until the early 1930s. Guru Moozhikulam Kochukuttan Chakyar played Kaundinya, the vidushaka (jester) – as he did in the Margi performances – in a failed attempt to revive the tradition in the late 1950s. Scholars dub the snippets of manuals for performances in the Vellur Temple the »Vellur Fragments«. The »fragment« for *Subhadra-Dhananjaya*, Act II presented to me by the Potiyil Chakyar family says that two actors handle all of the roles. It notes that the »verses (*slokas*) and prose passages of Balarama, Sri Krishna, Kanchukiya, Subhadra and Chedi are heard and acted« by the actor playing Arjuna.

The actor rolls his head to signal that he is going to use the convention of hearing and acting (*kettaduka*) in order to deliver lines of a character who is not embodied onstage. The drumming stops and the female vocalist, seated

11 In scenes with several characters, a performer subtly leaves the stage and returns just before his line, yet the audience is to imagine that the character has been onstage the whole time. The theory is that fewer actors allow the spectators to focus on the remaining performer(s) and, practically, allow more space onstage for the other performer(s).

12 Several weeks later in Thrissur when Usha Nangiar played Malayavati in *Naganandam* she was accompanied by her two friends / maids. Since the premiere of *Shakuntala* in 2002 at Irinjalakuda, it is not so uncommon to have three female characters onstage.

stage right, chants the lines. Then, changing the direction in which he is looking, repositioning himself onstage slightly, assuming a different stance, and / or adjusting his costume, he acts the meaning of the lines. Resuming the character of Arjuna, he gestures: »Is that what was said?«[13] In the past the technique was frequently employed to account for missing female characters. At Vellur four male characters were also missing.[14]

My notes from interviews with Ammannur Parameswaran Chakyar and Ammannur Madhava Chakyar on 13 and 14 January 2001 suggest that *kettaduka* was adopted in a production of *Subhadra-Dhananjaya*, Act II requested by the Cochin royal family at Tripunithura sometime in the 1940s. The actor playing Arjuna and the female vocalist(s) would not have been so busy as they were in Vellur because, although there were no women, there were four men in the cast.

Like many *kutiyattam* actors, Madhava Chakyar, who played Arjuna in the Tripunithura production, slips between genders uncannily (see SULLIVAN 2001). Yet, it is very difficult for me to imagine that staging the »puja scene« at the end of Act II using *kettaduka* (hearing and acting) could have the impact that the scene did with women taking the three female roles.

Subhadra is in a fix at the end of Act II. She has fallen in love with a *sanyasi* (celibate mendicant). Unaware that the *sanyasi* is Arjuna in disguise, she believes that she is in love with three different men. On 20 September 2001 Sathi as Subhadra, assisted by her two *chedis*, acted performing *puja* to the *sanyasi* by pouring water over his feet [see ILLUSTRATION 16].[15] One *kutiyattam* scholar who was seated near me sighed and remarked: »Beautiful.« When the distraught Subhadra dropped the vessel containing perfumed water, there was a collective gasp from the audience. We do not know when this scene was last staged with three women. Subhadra's *nirvahana* in Act V of *Subhadra-Dhananjaya* also had not played in living memory until 2001.

13 Multiple role-playing (*pakarnattam*) happens seamlessly in *nirvahana*. The performer slips from one character to another making the same physical adjustments I mention. But, each character change is not punctuated by chanted dialogue.

14 In January 2007, after a staging of *Balivadham* at Irinjalakuda in which all seven characters were embodied, K.R. Narayanan (Kidangur Ramanchakyar Narayanan) reminisced about the staging of *Balivadham* at Vadakkunathan by two actors in the 1960s. Tara's lines were heard and acted by Bali and chanted by the female vocalist. All other characters were cut. An uncostumed actor, who was hunched over and covered by a cloth, delivered one important line of Rama's. Unfortunately, no one can clarify what cuts and conventions were involved when two actors played *Subhadra-Dhananjaya*, Act II at Vellur.

15 Reference ILLUSTRATIONS 9 and 10 for this scene in *nirvahana*.

Subhadra's Entry and Nirvahana, Act V

The first rehearsal for Subhadra's entry (*purappad*) began auspiciously. An oracle of the goddess, Bhagavathi, was visiting houses in Usha Nangiar's semi-rural neighborhood. That day I was able to hold and photograph a centuries-old palm-leaf *attaprakaram* (acting manual) for Subhadra's entry and *nirvahana* that Usha had borrowed from Ammannur Gurukulam [see ILLUSTRATION 17]. This one included guidance for acting the verses, but did not contain the *slokas* (verses). Thankfully the hand-written manuscript for Subhadra's entry and flashback (*nirvahana*), which I obtained in 1989, gave both the verses and explications. Usha later located a second palm-leaf that contained only the verses. This separation makes sense. Two different women needed the material: the vocalist needed the verses and the actress needed the inspiration for showing their meaning.

We decided that there would be five performances: one devoted to Subhadra's entry (*purappad*) and four to *nirvahana*. Using copies of the 1989 *attaprakaram* (manual) that I had presented to them, both Usha Nangiar and Margi Sathi began the preparation process by writing their own *attaprakaram*. Usha's acting of *sloka* 10 in »Subhadra's Nirvahana: First Day« is an example of the license an artist may take in departing from the received *attaprakaram*. This *sloka* also appears in the manual for *nangiar kuttu* (PANIKER 2005: 151).

> Hearing of Arjuna's valor and good qualities, etc.
> Subhadra, the sister of Krishna, became lovesick
> With her heart placed in him
> Put on a bodice inscribed with his ten names and placed it on her breasts.[16]

The manual for »Subhadra's Nirvahana« offers this guidance for showing the meaning:

> At that time, hearing about the valour, beauty and other qualities of Arjuna, Subhadra became lovesick. *She* got the ten names of Arjuna painted on her brassiere and wore it on her chest (RAJAGOPALAN 1997: 66).

In the manual Usha wrote, Krishna orders a breast cloth with the ten names of Arjuna embroidered on it and sends it to his sister, just as he does in the manual for *nangiar kuttu* (PANIKER 2005: 150). L.S. Rajagopalan asked Usha why she deviated from the manual that she received from me: »Why couldn't you do it

16 Translated by L.S. Rajagopalan.

the way this fellow had it?«[17] Usha did not answer. But, she did not really have to for *kutiyattam* grants mature artists liberties.

Kutiyattam is an art of creative elaboration that leaves the artist free to imaginatively alter his / her own performance of the score not only between rehearsal and performance, but also from performance to performance. Usha was more likely to depart from the acting manual and from what she had rehearsed than was Sathi, perhaps because Usha worked independently while Sathi checked with her *guru* [see ILLUSTRATION 18]. Usha's performance was, invariably, different than its rehearsal. She told me that as she was performing she would get so deeply into it that she would spontaneously make alterations. The decisions she made, most typically to cut secondary characters' dialogue, always made excellent performance sense. A commission by the owner of a gallery in Fort Kochi gave Usha the opportunity to repeat three of the project's performances and (re)imagine her earlier interpretation of the score.

Both Usha Nangiar and Margi Sathi performed »Subhadra's Nirvahana: Third Day« and »Subhadra's Nirvahana: Fourth Day«. The similarities and differences between the two interpretations of the same source material by two artists who have the form's gesture vocabulary equally at their command were fascinating [see ILLUSTRATIONS 19 and 20].

You've Come A Long Way, Ladies

G. Venu remembers a performance that is the antithesis of the superlative ones I have been describing:

> I remember once seeing a *kutiyattam* performance where it was a new actress who appeared as Lalitha in »Soorpanakhankam«. It was obvious that she had only a few months' training. She had not participated in rehearsals or been involved with other actors. She did not even have any understanding or insight about the character she was presenting. When it was time for Lalita's entrance, an elderly man escorted her to the stage. When she finished reciting the verses a man came and took her back (VENU 2002: 17).

Kalamandalam Girija, Kalamandalam Sailaja, Margi Sathi, and Usha Nangiar inherited female *kutiyattam* in a deteriorated state. Their creativity and technique have brought their art to the highest standard. The mark that the next generation, including Kapila and Aparna Nangiar, must live up to is set very

17 We do not know who »this fellow« is. Usha Nangiar does not think a performer authored the manual or more opportunities for artistic elaboration would have been included. It was, we speculate, the work of a Nambiar who was a Sanskrit scholar and a bit of a poet – clever enough to turn Subhadra's prose dialogue into poetry (*slokas*).

high. The timing of my involvement in female *kutiyattam* was fortunate. I was not only privileged to be able to witness vestiges of *nangiar kuttu* offered as temple ritual, but also allowed to participate in the resuscitation of female *kutiyattam* performed on the concert stage.

I am very optimistic about the future of *kutiyattam*. G. Venu and Ammannur Parameswaran (Kuttan) Chakyar are grooming a vibrant young company in Irinjalakuda. Kapila and Aparna Nangiar are members. In the first draft of this article, written in 2006, I identified these two women as the »next generation« of female performers. Now, in 2008, I can add three names to the list of emerging female artists: Indu G., Kalamandalam Sindu and Kalamandalam Krishnendu.

L. S. Rajagopalan's quip that »we need to place the Nangiar on the endangered species list« summed up the grim future of temple-based *nangiar kuttu* in the early 1990s (DAUGHERTY 1996: 64). Strictly speaking this prediction was accurate if applied to orthodox temples where only members of the hereditary community can perform. But, today, most temples are not concerned about the background of the artists. In 2006 the Sreekrishna Swamy Temple at Ambalapuzha revived its twelve-day festival of *Sri Krishna Charitam*. It began, per the temple's ritual schedule on September 13, the day before *Ashtramirohini* (Krishna's birth star). Three participants were Nangiars; eight were not. A similar balance between traditional and nontraditional performers prevailed when the festival was staged again in September 2007. In November 2007 the Tiruvarpu Krishna Temple near Kottayam requested Usha Nangiar's performance – the first performance of *nangiar kuttu* in that kuttambalam since 1934. Temple officials hope she will work with them to reinstate the performances of *Sri Krishna Charitam* that were once part of their temple's April festival.

Female *kutiyattam*, particularly solo female *kutiyattam*, is thriving. If you are willing to travel up and down the length of Kerala (some four hundred miles) you can see at least half a dozen performances by female actors a month. The sponsors include temples that have *kutiyattam* or *nangiar kuttu* as part of their ritual schedule; temples where *kutiyattam* or *nangiar kuttu* is being presented for the first time; performing arts institutions; civic organizations; and individual art lovers. My six months in Kerala each year are strenuous, but stimulating.

References and Bibliography

DAUGHERTY, DIANE. 1996. »The Nangiar: Female Ritual Specialist«. *Asian Theatre Journal* 13, 1: 54–67.

----; MARLENE PITKOW. 1991. »Who Wears The Skirts in Kathakali?«. *TDR* 35, 2: 138–156.

GOPALAKRISHNAN, K. K. 2006a. »Exploring Koodiyattom«. *The Hindu* (27 January).

----. 2006b. »At the Crossroads«. *The Hindu* (26 March).

INVIS. 2003. *Nangiar Kuttu*. DVD. Thiruvananthapuram: Invis Infotech.

MARGI. 2000. *Documentation of Koodiyattam.* 3 DVDs. Thiruvananthapuram: Margi Theatre.
NAMBIAR, NARAYANAN. 1984. *Sreekrishnacharitam Nangyarammakkoothu.* Trichur: National Book Stall.
PANIKER, NIRMALA. 2005. *Nangiar Koothu.* Rev. Ed. Irinjalakuda: Natana Kairali.
RAJAGOPALAN, L. S. 1997. *Women's Role in Kutiyattam.* Chennai: The Kuppuswami Sastri Research Institute.
RICHMOND, FARLEY. 2002. *Kutiyattam: Sanskrit Theatre of India.* Multimedia CD-Rom. Michigan: University of Michigan Press.
SADASIVAN, T. K. 2006. »Classic play for all seasons«. *The Hindu* (31 March).
SATHI, MARGI. 1999. *Sreerama Charitam Nangiarammakoothu.* Kottayam: Current Books.
SULLIVAN, BRUCE M. 2002. »Skirting the Issue: Gender and Identity in Kutiyattam Sanskrit Drama«. *Notes from a Mandala: Essays in Honor of Wendy Doniger.* New York: Seven Bridges.
UNNI, N. P.; BRUCE M. SULLIVAN. 2001. *The Wedding of Arjuna and Subhadra: The Kutiyattam Drama Subhadra-Dhananjaya.* Delhi: Nag Publishers.
VENU, G. 2002. *Into the World of Kutiyattam with the Legendary Ammannur Madhava Chakyar.* Irinjalakuda: Natana Kairali.

ILLUSTRATIONS

All the photographies are published online: *http://www.indologie.uni-wuerzburg.de/women_performers/contributors/daugherty/illustrations/.*

ILLUSTRATION 1: L.S. Rajagopalan, September 2005 (Photo: Diane Daugherty)
ILLUSTRATION 2: Vadakkunathan Temple Theatre (Photo: Diane Daugherty)
ILLUSTRATION 3: Aparna Nangiar showing the snake Kalia in *nangiar kuttu*, September 2001 (Photo: Diane Daugherty)
ILLUSTRATION 4: Usha Nangiar as Subhadra crying for help in »Subhadra's Nirvahana: First Day«, June 2001 (Photo: Diane Daugherty)
ILLUSTRATION 5: Usha Nangiar standing on the stool as Subhadra, »Subhadra's Nirvahana: First Day«, June 2001 (Photo: Diane Daugherty)
ILLUSTRATION 6: Usha Nangiar as the divine bird Garuda in »Subhadra's Nirvahana: First Day«, June 2001 (Photo: Diane Daugherty)
ILLUSTRATION 7: Usha Nangiar as Garuda coming to Subhadra's rescue, »Subhadra's Nirvahana: First Day«, June 2001 (Photo: Diane Daugherty)
ILLUSTRATION 8: Usha Nangiar as Garuda returning Subhadra to her palace. »Subhadra's Nirvahana: First Day«, June 2001 (Photo: Diane Daugherty)
ILLUSTRATION 9: Usha Nangiar as Subhadra doing *puja* to the *sanyasi*, »Subhadra's Nirvahana: Second Day«, September 2001 (Photo: Diane Daugherty)
ILLUSTRATION 10: Usha Nangiar as Arjuna blessing Subhadra, »Subhadra's Nirvahana: Second Day«, September 2001 (Photo: Diane Daugherty)
ILLUSTRATION 11: Kalamandalam Girija (left) and Kalamandalam Sailaja (right) in »The Garden Scene« November 2001 (Photo: Diane Daugherty)
ILLUSTRATION 12: The author and P. Rama Iyer, September 2001 (Photo: Shibu Lal)
ILLUSTRATION 13: Subhadra (Margi Sathi) tells Shatpadika (Margi Usha) of her love for Arjuna in Subhadra-Dhananjaya, act II, August 2001 (Photo: Shibu Lal)

ILLUSTRATION 14: Arjuna (Margi Raman Chakyar) eavesdrops on Subhadra (Margi Sathi) and her Chedi (Margi Usha) in Subhadra-Dhananjaya, act II, August 2001 (Photo: Shibu Lal)

How Kūṭiyāṭṭam Became ›kūṭi-āṭṭam‹, »Acting Together«

Or: The Changing Role of Female Performers in the Naṅṅyār-Kūttu Tradition of Kerala

Heike Moser

This essay is based on more than 15 years of fieldwork and research in Kerala / Southwest India. From 1995 to 1997 and again in subsequent years I was a student at Kēraḷa Kalāmaṇḍalam and studied the traditional Sanskrit theatre Kūṭiyāṭṭam with a special focus on the female solo form Naṅṅyār-Kūttŭ. Being a foreigner and becoming a Kūṭiyāṭṭam actress made me not only part of the tradition but also one more sign of its drastic change. The hypothesis formulated here gives a possible historical explanation for the exceptional status of Naṅṅyār-actresses in Kerala's Sanskrit theatre Kūṭiyāṭṭam. I presented parts of this paper in lectures at Thiruvananthapuram, Würzburg and Lyon.[1] It is a more elaborate distillation of thoughts already published in German as part of my PhD dissertation MOSER 2008.

Kūṭiyāṭṭam – ›combined acting‹, ›acting together‹, ›inter-play‹ – is the name given to India's sole surviving traditional Sanskrit theatre [ILLUSTRATIONS 1a–1c]. Combined acting takes place on many levels – for example, high-caste actors of the Cākyār community act together with similarly highly placed actresses of the Naṅṅyār caste (a very rare combination on the traditional Indian stage).

Kūṭiyāṭṭam is indigenous to the south-west Indian state of Kerala and springs from this unique culture. Down to the 1950s Kūṭiyāṭṭam was – and had been at least for the last few centuries – exclusively performed in prosperous brahmanised temples as a ritually important theatre of the elite (brahmins and nobles). For a variety of reasons Kūṭiyāṭṭam declined over recent decades. In the 20th

1 4th June 2005, lecture: *The Changing role of women in the Naṅṅyār-Kūttŭ tradition of Kerala* at the »Third International Colloquium ›Perspectives of Indian Studies‹ – Changing Roles and Perceptions of Women Performers in Indian Culture« at Würzburg University, Dept. of Indology. – 14th January 2006, lecture: *How Kūṭiyāṭṭam Became* kūṭi-āṭṭam *(Acting Together): A possible explanation* at the »International Seminar on Kutiyattam and Asian Theatre Traditions« organised by the UNESCO and the Indian Council for Cultural Relations in Thiruvananthapuram. – 23rd April 2007, lecture: *The changing role of female performers in the Naṅṅyār-Kūttŭ tradition of Kerala* at the Université Jean Moulin Lyon 3, Centre d'Études et de Recherches sur l'Occident Romain as part of the international colloquium »Les théâtres indiens et leurs fonctions. Interactions entre art, société et religions«.

century, temples once rich in real estate lost their holdings in the wake of land reforms and performances were drastically cut. Also, the new times produced fewer Sanskrit scholars, such as could properly follow a theatre of the educated elite and develop an appreciation of its subtly mediated messages.[2] In order to survive, Kūṭiyāṭṭam had to quit the protective environment of the temple playhouse (*kūttampalam*) with its scholarly public and present itself on ›secular‹ stages to audiences who were uneducated in the traditional sense [ILLUSTRATIONS 2a–2f].

›Stepping beyond‹ these traditional temple-theatre-houses occurred just about 60 years ago. Nowadays pupils from other castes, even foreigners like me, are inducted into this theatrical art: In 1995 I was the first foreigner to debut (*araṅṅēṟṟam*); I performed in the *kūttampalam* of Kēraḷa Kalāmaṇḍalam the story of Pūtanamōkṣam, taken from the so-called Naṅṅyār-Kūttu˘ [ILLUSTRATIONS 3a and 3b].

What is Naṅṅyār-Kūttu˘?

Naṅṅyār-Kūttu˘ is the flashback (*nirvvahaṇam*) of the Cēṭī in the beginning of the second act of King Kulaśekhara Varmman's play *Subhadrādhanañjayam*. ›Naṅṅyār‹ are the traditional actresses of Kerala's Sanskrit theatre Kūṭiyāṭṭam, ›kūttu‹ is in this context an elaborate solo sequence.

Retrospective views of single characters – male or female – are a common technique in the Kūṭiyāṭṭam complex. Please see the diagram published online [ILLUSTRATION 4]:[3] The dramatic text [*0*] is abandoned after reciting the first sequence (often only the first portion of it) of the character's dialogue. *Anukramam* [*blue-coloured/1*] takes us ever further back in time by repeating the question ›And what came before that?‹ – back to where the story of each retrospective view starts [*grey square*]. Then there comes a break: *saṃkṣēpam* [2] begins far back in time, often with the creation of the world, and moves forward in big steps up to the same event where *anukramam* stopped. Here *anukramam* and *saṃkṣēpam* meet in time and space [*grey square*] and the particular story, *nirvvahaṇam* proper or *ślōkārttham* [*green-coloured/3*], is told elaborately by gesturing and moving slowly back – or better forward – to the exact point where the dramatic text [*4 or 0*] was abandoned. For these flashbacks Sanskrit (and rarely Prakrit) verses are either composed or borrowed from various classical texts. These verses are woven through a *nirvvahaṇam* like a red thread. They are not recited by the actor or actress but by the cymbal-playing *Naṅṅyār*,

2 Even earlier the number of genuine Sanskrit scholars was not that great; many *Nampūtiri* brahmins were able to recite the Veda and a number of Sanskrit texts, but were quite unable to understand their proper meaning. The role of the Malayalam-speaking *Vidūṣaka* has become primarily that of a ›translator‹.

3 See also JOHAN in this volume, especially her diagrams.

sitting at the side of the stage to show that here an inserted portion is being enacted and not the drama proper.

In my PhD thesis I demonstrated that the so-called Naṅṅyār-Kūttŭ is just such a flashback. Here the character of the Cēṭī inserts in all detail the story of the god Kṛṣṇa up to that point in the second act of the play *Subhadrādhanañjayam* where Kṛṣṇa's dear friend Arjuna-Dhanañjayan marries Kṛṣṇa's sister Subhadrā. The actress performs more than 200 *nirvvahaṇam*-verses in solo performance. For several days she has to portray the demons, gods, humans and animals of Kṛṣṇa's story all on her own, only accompanied by drums played by male members of her family and another Naṅṅyār, who plays the cymbals and recites the *nirvvahaṇam* verses [ILLUSTRATIONS 2e and 5; FILM CLIPS 1 and 2].
This flashback was introduced most probably in the 16th/17th century as part of the *kṛṣṇa-bhakti* movement in Kerala – depending on its content it may also be called *Śrīkṣṇacaritam*. We have no earlier evidence of such an elaborate flashback or enactment of the stories around Śrīkṛṣṇa. Neither the Kūṭiyāṭṭam-patronising King Kulaśēkhara, who authored the drama *Subhadrādhanañjayam*, nor Vyaṅgyavyākhyā, a detailed commentary on the same, nor *Naṭāṅkuśa*, ›the hook of the actor‹, a detailed critic of Kūṭiyāṭṭam from the 15th century, mention any performance of *Śrīkṛṣṇacaritam* or Naṅṅyār-Kūttŭ.

Was the performing of Naṅṅyār women introduced to Kūṭiyāṭṭam together with this Śrīkṛṣṇacaritam / this flashback of the Cēṭī?

Definitely not. In Kerala, the oldest inscription mentioning performing Naṅṅa(i) is from Cōkkur and dates from 898 AD.[4]

Mindful of these sources, we must always be aware that ›Naṅṅai‹ means ›young woman‹ in general, *i.e.* may have been used for other women than today's Kūṭiyāṭṭam-performing Naṅṅyār.[5]

Rāghavavāriyar and Rājangurukkaḷ list in their *Kēraḷacaritram* the terms »Naṅṅai«, »Naṅṅaiyār«, »Naṅṅacci« and »Kūttacci« as denoting women performing on stage (Rāghavavāriyar, Rājangurukkaḷ 1992 [1991]: 147–149).[6] Let me give a short account of these inscriptions:[7]

4 The spelling of names, titels, places, etc. correspond to the writing used by the secondary sources cited. The Tamil alphabet has no »ś«, but some authors writing in Malayalam language and script have ›corrected‹ terms like »Cākkaiyar« and »Cākkaiyaṉ« to »Śākyar« and »Śākkai«.

5 See for example SŌMAN 1996: 506; he gives more variants: *Naṅṅamma, Uṇṇinaṅṅa, Naṅṅēma.*

6 See also RĀGHAVAVĀRIYAR, RĀJANGURUKKAḶ 1992: 54–56.

7 The following indications are from RĀGHAVAVĀRIYAR, RĀJANGURUKKAḶ 1992 [1991]: 147–149. The spelling of names, titels, places, etc. correspond to the writing used by them.

1. The Cōkkur inscription mentions payment being made in the form of paddy and land-tenure to the Naṅṅayār of Ciṯṯarai. The inscription does not mention for what kind of service such payment was due. The inscription dates from the 15th year of the reign of King Kōtaravipperumāḷ (or 898 AD). Today we still find place-names like Naṅṅapaṟampŭ or Naṅṅaccikkunnu occurring close by the Cōkkur temple.[8]

2. Just two years later, in 900 AD, an inscription from Neṭumpuṟam tells us for the first time of a Naṅṅai, who was paid for an unspecified performance: She is mentioned in connection with paying (*āniyam*) *kāndarppi* performers and *naṭṭuvar* teachers. Three classes of performing Naṅṅai are distinguished: *uttama*, *madhyama* and *adhama*. What kind of distinction is meant is unclear; it could refer to ritual status, knowledge or the kind of service offered.

3. The account-books of Neṭumpuṟam-Taḷi mention in the 11th year of the reign of King Bhāskararavi (978 AD) the land-tenure of »Tribhūvana-mahādēvi Ciritara-naṅṅacci«. The honorary title of queen, *mahādēvi*, may point to a close relationship, or *sambandham*, on the part of this Naṅṅacci to the royal family. Such marriage-like relationships seem not to have been unusual, as witness the well-known legend that King Kulaśēkhara Varmman had just such a *sambandham* liaison with a performing artiste.

4. A copperplate from Tiruvalla (or Tiruvallavāḷ)[9], dated to the 11th/12th century, mentions Tēvaṭicci and Kūttacci together with musicians. T. A. G. RAO cites in his *Huzur Office / Treasury Plates* a copperplate from the Viṣṇu temple of Tiruvalla: in line 350 he mentions »Iḷaṅkuṉṟanāṭṭu Naṅkaiyār« and »Iḷaṅkuṉṟanāṭṭu Nampiyār«,[10] in line 252 another »Naṅkaiyār«[11] and in line 233 the place name »Naṅkaiyārvaḷāḷ«[12].

5. The next evidence comes from the Śiva temple of Talapulli (Cochin district), being an inscription written in the 11th century in the reign of Kovindēśvaran Koḍai. It tells of the handing over of rice to »Naṅgaimār«.

8 *Paṟampŭ* is a mountain, a garden, or a dry and cultivated, raised piece of land; *kunnŭ* is a hill.

9 TAS / T.A.G. RAO 1992 [1908]: 131 pp.

10 TAS / T.A.G. RAO 1992 [1908]: 159, 189 and figure xxii (b); cited in Tamil script, the ›malayalamised‹ spelling reads »Iḷaṅguṉṟanāḍu Naṅgaiyār« and »Iḷaṅguṉṟanāḍu Nampiyār« (the facultative spelling »Naṅgaiyār« is also given in the examples below).

11 TAS / T.A.G. RAO 1992 [1908]: 161 and 186.

12 TAS / T.A.G. RAO 1992 [1908]: 169 and 185.

It is mentioned in Hema Govindarajan's epigraphical collection of the performing arts in South India.[13]

6. The next inscription to come down to us was written at the time of King Vikramacōḷa. It mentions payment being made in the form of land-tenure to Ēḻunāṭṭu˘ Naṅkai for performing Śānti-Kūttu. The inscription is engraved in one of the outer walls of the Vyāghrapurīśvara-temple in Tiruvengavasal (Pudukottai).[14] In the same wall another inscription mentioning payment for performing Śānti-Kūttu was engraved during the reign of King Tribhuvanacakravartin Rājādhirājadēva II.[15] It is not known wether this »Ēḻunāṭṭu˘ Naṅkai« is an ancestor of the still existing Nampyār-/Naṅṅyār family of Ēṭanāṭṭu˘ who continue to perform Kūṭiyāṭṭam today [ILLUSTRATIONS 6a–f].[16] The place-names seem to be linguistically very close, if not identical – however, in the absence of incontrovertible proof, the question must remain open.

7. About 1100 a description from Nallūr (Viḷvaraṇyēśvara temple) mentions for the first time the terms »Naṅgai« and »Śākkai« together.[17] The *Annual Report on South Indian Epigraphy* gives the following information:

> Damaged. Seems to record the appointment of Būmāḻvi, daughter of Poṟkōyil Naṅgai, as the dēvaraḍiyāḷ of the temple for performing śākkai on festival occasions and to sing the Tiruvembāvai (Kaḍaikkāppu), before the deity on certain terms (details lost) on the demise of one Uḍaiyanāchchi alias Kulōttuṅgaśōḻamāṇikkam, daughter of Tiruvēmba-Naṅgai. (ARSIE 1952: 94, »Remarks« on inscription no. 160)

Interesting but also doubtful is the statement that a Naṅgai was performing something called *śākkai*. Unfortunately the verification of the translation cannot be checked, because the original wording is not given in print and I have not so far been able to gain access to the original. Still, this is the earliest reference of the terms denoting today both male and female performers of Kūṭiyāṭṭam.

13 GOVINDARAJAN 1993: 92 [referring to: *Epigraphia India* 28, 37: 220, line 10; original unpublished].
14 ARSIE 1915: 30, inscription no. 253 and N.V.K. WARRIER 1964: 117, fn. 12.
15 ARSIE 1915: 30, inscription no. 254.
16 See also JOHAN in this volume, especially her ILLUSTRATIONS 8, 9, 12–15 and FILM CLIP 4.
17 GOVINDARAJAN 1993: 161 [referring to: *TAS* 4/7; original unpublished].

Did these Naṅṅai or Naṅkaiyār already perform Kūṭiyāṭṭam? Are the male actors, the Cākyār, mentioned too in these inscriptions?

According to the inscriptions known to us, ›Naṅṅai‹ seem to have performed in Kerala some kind of Kūttu without any ›Śākkai / Cākyār‹ up to the 11th century. But one has to be careful with this kind of information and bear in mind that the basic meaning of Naṅṅai is young woman; so these Naṅṅai are not necessarily identical with the modern, Kūṭiyāṭṭam-performing Naṅṅyār.

We find much epigraphical evidence of performing ›Śākkai‹ in Tamil Nadu up to the 11th century:[18]

1. In the Tamil classic Śilappadikāram (dating from the 2nd to the 5th century AD) is a reference to kōṭṭiccēdam kūttu performed by Kūttaccākkyar from Paṟaiyūr (part 28, lines 76–79):

   pāttaru nālvakai maṟaiyōr paṟaiyūr
   kūtta ccākaiya nāṭalin makiḻntava-
   nētti nīka virunila māḷvōn
   vēttiyan maṇṭapa mēviya pinnar
   (ILAṄKŌ AṬIKAḶ 1997: 617)

   Sri L.S. Rajagopalan directed my attention in a personal conversation to the lines immediately following this famous reference, where the red eyes of the Cākyār are mentioned. Usually red eyes are interpreted as a sign of the hero being in love, but in connection with Kūṭiyāṭṭam the unique Keralite tradition of colouring the eyes with the help of *cuṇṭapūvu*˘ springs to mind [ILLUSTRATION 7]. Kunjunni Raja doubts that this passage can be seen as describing what we today call Kūṭiyāṭṭam, since it is the »forceful *tāṇḍava* dance of Śiva« that is described (KUNJUNNI RAJA 1994 [1960]: 4–5), nor can he see any parallels with a Kūṭiyāṭṭam performance. Another problem is the reference to the sound of anklets – no anklets except for special characters like Jaṭāyu und Śūrpaṇakhā are used in Kūṭiyāṭṭam. Still, it is the earliest reference we have to a performing Cākyār; the way he performs these days may have changed drastically.

2. A Tamil inscription dated 994 AD on the wall of the Śiva temple of Gōmuktīśvaram (Tiruvāḍutaṟa) in Tanjore district mentions the payment of seven *acts* (*aṅka*) *ār[i/ī]ya-kūttu* in the form of land tenure *śākkaikāṇi* (or *nrityabhōga*).[19]

18 The spelling of names, titels, places, etc. correspond to the writing used in the secondary sources.

19 ARSIE 1926: 26, inscription no. 120 and SASTRI 1955 [1935]: 575. – See also JONES 1967: 14 and N. VANAMAMALAI 1974 [referring to: R. NAGASAMY (ed.). *Collected Inscriptions of the Thanjavur Temple.* Mandavalli / Madras: Department of Archaeology].

3. In the year 1041 another Tamil inscription informs us of *Śākkai Mārāyaṉ Vikramaśōḻaṉ, who was paid for performing Śākkai-Kūttu˘* in the Kārkōṭakēśvara temple at Kamarasavalli (Trichinopoly district).[20]

4. The fourth reference is engraved in the Nāganāthasvāmī temple in Mānambādi (Tanjore district), dated 1088: land was given for performing Tamiḻa-Kūttu˘ (»*tamu[sic? i?]ḻak-kūttu*«) five times in the Kailāsamuḍaiya-Mahādēva temple at Vīranārāyaṇapuram (Miḻalainādu).[21] That ›Ārya-Kūttu˘‹ may denote Sanskrit drama and ›Tamiḻa-Kūttu˘‹ »a special form with Tamil translation«, as JONES suggested (1967: 15), are only assumptions. Till today there are passages in Kūṭiyāṭṭam which are called ›Nampyār-Tamiḻ˘‹.[22] And till today we have texts in Sanskrit and Prakrit as well as texts in Malayalam – once called Tamil, from which it originated – examples being passages recited by the Viḍūṣaka, by Vasantakan in *Mantrāṅkam*, or by the demoness Śūrpaṇakhā.

5. The fifth reference is to Alayūr Cākyār and the payment he received for performing Śākkai-Kūttu˘. It is dated to the 6th year of the reign of King Parakēsarivarman and associated with the Trichinopoly district (Vaṭamūlēśvarasvāmi-Temple, Kilapaluvur, Udaiyar-palaiyam):

> Registers a grant of 1.5 kaḻañju of gold and three kalam of paddy to a certain Alayūrch-Chākkai to enact three scenes of the *śākkai-kūttu* on the Aśvati day of the festivals in the month of Aṟpaśi at Tiruvālanduṟainallūr. (ARSIE 1927: 58, »Remarks« to inscription no. 250)

All the above literary and epigraphical references to performing Śākkai / Cākyār are situated in modern Tamil Nadu. Up to the 12th century there is no evidence of performing Cākyār in Kerala. But from the 12th century on the contrary is true: from now on inscriptions referring to performers called Cākyār are found in Kerala *only*, while no inscriptions from later than the 12th century are known to us from Tamil Nadu.

The earliest epigraphical reference in Kerala to a Cākyār is dated to about 1172. It is a copperplate of the Dēvidēvēccuvaram temple near Kilimānūr pal-

20 ARSIE 1915: 16, inscription no. 65; the spelling corresponds to the writing used in ARSIE. – See also C.H. RAO 1930, JONES 1967: 14–15, GOVINDARAJAN 1993: 161, N.V.K. WARRIER 1964: 117, fn. 12. – In the Tamil lexicon *Divākaram,* the entry for »Śākkaiyār« reads as »the name of an official of the King«. This could be a link to the honorific title »Cōḷan« / »Cōḻaṉ«, signifying that the »Śakkai« may have been given by the king. – See also JONES 1967: 15 [referring to: M. RAGHAVA AIYANGAR. 1950. *Some Aspects of Kerala and Tamil Literature.* Part 2. Trivandrum: University of Travancore (Travancore University English Series, 8)].

21 ARSIE 1934: 15, inscription no. 90. – See also SASTRI 1955 [1935]: 574 and S.R. KRISHNAMURTHI 1966: 163 (Annexure II, no. 90, 1932).

22 *Nampyār tamiḻ* 1990.

ace, giving information about the *virutti* of the »Śākkaimār« who performed »Śākkai-Kūttuˇ«.[23]

The term *kūttu* is used within the Kūṭiyāṭṭam complex as in Naṅṅyār-Kūttuˇ, Cākyār-Kūttuˇ, Mantrāṅkam-Kūttuˇ or Aṅgulīyāṅkam-Kūttuˇ, but when referring to sources not clearly related to Kūṭiyāṭṭam we always have to bear in mind that *kūttu* denotes in Tamil as well as in Malayalam every kind of performance, play, dance (*i.e.* Tōlpāva-Kūttuˇ, Terukkūttu). We find innumerable references using this term, so there is no point listing them all here.

Let me sum up the results of the present evaluation of epigraphical references to the performing tradition of the Naṅṅyār and Cākyār:

1. From at least 900 AD we have written evidence that Naṅṅai were performing in temples in the area of modern Kerala. In these early inscriptions nothing is mentioned about how they performed and what they performed.

2. From the Saṅgam period up to the 11th/12th century AD we have evidence of performing Śākkai in the area of modern Tamil Nadu.

3. From the 12th century on we find inscriptions mentioning performing Śākkai in Kerala; at the same time, references to performing Śākkai in Tamil Nadu cease.

4. In the 12th century we find for the first time Śākkai and Naṅṅai being mentioned together. Moreover, the source is a clearly Keralan one.

What I conclude from these observations is that performing Cākyār may have spread from Tamil Nadu to Kerala only during the 11th century. Up to then there existed in Kerala some kind of performing art carried out by Naṅṅai. It seems to me that what were essentially two performance traditions joined during the 11th and 12th century to form *kūṭi-āṭṭam* – ›performing together‹.

This theory draws substance from two orally transmitted legends: Kūṭiyāṭṭam-performing families tell of a far-reaching reform of the then existing theatre being undertaken by King Kulaśēkhara Varmman. The dates of this king are unclear, he either lived in the 9th/10th centuries or in the 11th/12th centuries[24] – precisely when the two theatrical traditions seem to have amalgamated and – of course – undergone a reform required by these new circumstances.

23 TAS / K.V.S. AIYAR 1923: 28–29. – See also JONES 1967: 16–17.

24 For the problems in dating King Kulaśēkhara Varmman see *e.g.* UNNI; SULLIVAN 2001: 49–52 or MOSER 2008: 75 pp.

The second legend tells of the first Cākyār actor, who came from Tamil Nadu to Kerala as part of the retinue of a Perumal king and who introduced their theatre tradition to the local stage.[25]

So Naṅṅyār, Nampyār and Cākyār may have started to perform together in the 12th century AD and may have formed, by combining their already existing performing traditions, what we call today Kūṭiyāṭṭam, ›combined acting‹. Even though the standard repertoire consists of classical Sanskrit plays, a Dravidian name may have been chosen for this new kind of performance, because it developed in a clearly Dravidian setting, even including long textual parts in Malayalam (*i.e.* by the Vidūṣaka) or a dialect of Tamil (*Nampyār tamiḻ* 1990). It is unique and remarkable for the whole of the Indian subcontinent that in a traditional, non-folk theatre men and women act together on stage – performing ›*kūṭi-āṭṭam*‹ in a literal sense.[26]

If there is anything to this hypothesis, Kūṭiyāṭṭam may ›only‹ be about 800 to 900 years old – although clearly its roots are much older and may include two performing traditions: one indigenous to Kerala and once performed by the community of Naṅṅyār and Nampār only; and one imported from the neighbouring areas of modern Tamil Nadu, along with its performers, the Cākyār.

This model of combining two – previously independent – performing artforms may even help explain the strong epic elements in the present dramatic tradition of Kūṭiyāṭṭam: As explained above, Kūṭiyāṭṭam inserts long flashbacks, *nirvvahaṇam*, into its dramas, and has a penchant for elaborate explanations of certain *ślōkas*. The performer acts as a storyteller and takes the role of all characters present in the inserted passages (*pakarnnāṭṭam*). He (or she) often sits on a stool, moving hands and face only [ILLUSTRATIONS 5 and 9c; FILM CLIP 1]. Cākyār are traditionally equated with *sūtas*, or epic bards:

Hermann Gundert notes in his dictionary:

> *sūtan* [...] 2. the son of a Kṣatriya from a Brahmani = cākyār a bard (GUNDERT 1991 [1872]: 1061)

Thurston derives »Chākkiyar« from »Slaghyavākkukār«:

> *Chākkiyar* [...] Slaghyavākkukār (those with eloquent words) (THURSTON 1909/2: 7)

Even in a modern Malayalam dictionary we find the entry:

25 In *Kēraḷōlpatti* he is a bard (*sūta*).

26 In other theatrical forms – Kathakaḷi or Yakṣagāna or Rāmlīlā – men would, or even still do, present all roles on stage, both male and female. See also PITKOW in this volume.

cākkiyār, cākyār n. (hist.) member of a Kerala community of professional and traditional expounders of the epics (MĀDHAVANPIḶḶA 1995 [1976]: 375)

Rangacharya writes in his *Drama in Sanskrit Literature*:

> It was thus the post-epic Sūta [...] that originated dramatic representation; the recitation of the epic [...] is the Bhāratī stage; [...] (RANGACHARYA 1967 [1947]: 39)

Even today we observe the tradition of *Māvāratabhaṭṭēri* or *Māvāratapaṭṭan* (*Mahābhāratabhaṭṭatiri*) – these may be something of a missing link between mere oral story-telling and the acting-out of a story. They sit on a stool in the temple on a kind of stage and read or recite passages from the *Mahābhārata*. It takes only a very small step more for them to start acting on the stool, illustrating the words with facial expressions and gestures – a technique still very typical of today's Kūṭiyāṭṭam [ILLUSTRATIONS 1a–1c, 5 and 9c; FILM CLIP 1].

So Cākyār seem to have been traditional experts in reciting the epics like bards, *sūtans*. They seem to have been originally ›those with eloquent words‹ [ILLUSTRATION 9b]. Unfortunately we have no hints as to how the performing tradition the Naṅṅyar practised before the 11th/12th century looked like. Did they add the more dramatic elements to today's Kūṭiyāṭṭam? We cannot even hazard a guess, too vast is our ignorance.

Does Naṅṅyār-Kūttuˇ somehow reflect the performance of the Naṅṅai, who seem to have performed alone on stage? Is Naṅṅyār-Kūttuˇ not after all the »oldest women's theatre in the world« as announced recently in Mumbai?

No, most probably it isn't. If it is indeed true that two performing traditions have fused, we cannot now reverse the process. Today Naṅṅyār-Kūttuˇ is performed in exactly the same way as any other flashback of any other character on the Kūṭiyāṭṭam-stage. The techniques are identical to, say, the *nirvvahaṇam* flashback of the male characters of Śrīrāman or Rāvaṇan or the female character of Subhadrā.

The roots of Naṅṅyār-Kūttuˇ as part of the Kūṭiyāṭṭam-complex are quite old, we can follow them back to the 11th/12th century or even – within certain limits – to the 9th century. Naṅṅyār-Kūttuˇ itself, narrating the story of Śrīkṛṣṇa, is no older than about 400 years.

So maybe Naṅṅyār-Kūttuˇ is not the »oldest women's theatre in the world«; but it is undoubtedly experiencing at present a growing independence and popularity. Its highly stylised mime and body-language attracts a large audience in India and abroad.

Since Kūṭiyāṭṭam left the environment of conservative temples in the 1950s, especially the representation of female characters has undergone far-reaching reform. In the mid-1990s I had the opportunity to interview not only the Kūṭiyāṭṭam actresses who perform in the reformed style (including a renewed costume and make-up), but also to observe and question elderly Naṅṅyār ladies, who still serve in certain temples and enact part of the annual ritual calender not for the sake of aesthetic delight.

To illustrate the obviously big differences between Naṅṅyār-Kūttŭ performed as a ritual and Naṅṅyār-Kūttŭ performed as an art-form, I have posted some pictures and film clips online [ILLUSTRATIONS 2e, 5, 6a–e, FILM CLIPS 1–3]. These photos and video-recordings were taken in 1995/96. Subhadra Naṅṅyār [ILLUSTRATION 8 and FILM CLIP 3], the most learned of the traditionally performing Naṅṅyār, died in 1998, and others stopped performing soon after the recordings were made – so these documents already possess historical value.[27] Seeing the way these elderly Naṅṅyār ladies perform, we must bear in mind that they studied and acted at a time when Kūṭiyāṭṭam was slowly vanishing and Naṅṅyār-Kūttŭ was often being performed mainly for ritual and not aesthetic reasons. At least the already mentioned text *Naṭāṅkuśa* from the 15th century shows that Kūṭiyāṭṭam was not always performed in such a ›poor‹ way. If it had not done what any living art-form does, namely adjust to evolving circumstances, it would have already vanished centuries ago. Still these pictures give us a valuable window into an earlier way of enacting Sanskrit dramas in the Kūṭiyāṭṭam style, as compared to the modern performances we can witness nowadays on stages in Delhi or Paris.

The costume and make-up used are already history, as are certain movements like jumping without lifting the legs too high because of the skirt that opens to the front. Still, this gives us a hint of an original ›immobility‹ on the part of women performers developing – by degrees – into ›mobility‹, a hint of how women came to embody radical change:[28]

Women were traditionally mainly ›voice‹ on the Kūṭiyāṭṭam stage:[29] Female roles were minor, short and, at least for the last two or three centuries, without lengthy elaborations; often they were sitting on a stool and gesturing with the hands only [FILM CLIP 1]. The principal part of the Naṅṅyār on stage consisted in reciting verses during the long *nirvvahaṇam* flashbacks of the male characters (*i.e.* more than 500 verses in *Mantrāṅkam*, 3rd act of *Pratijñāyaugandharāyaṇa*).

27 Of the interviews and demonstrations recorded on audio and video in 1995/96 only clippings from three examples are given here online. Please contact the author for further information.
28 See HANNE DE BRUIN's introduction to this volume.
29 I thank VIRGINIE JOHAN for this wonderful verbalisation; for more details see her article and multimedia in this volume.

Naṅṅyār were performing on immobile stages (*kūttampalam* theatre halls in about a dozen conservative temples) in an immobile way (reciting verses; or, when acting, sitting often on the stool; or, when moving, using small movements only without lifting the legs too high because of the costume, etc.) for a selected, similarly immobile audience (traditionally consisting of Brahmins, nobles and notables from the neighbourhood of the temple where the performance took place). A traditional *kūttampalam* performance was more a performance in extended domestic space than one in real public space. Beginning some 50–60 years ago, the whole genre has been opening up by playing on new stages in a more and more globalised setting. Accordingly, the status of the performing women has changed – and is still changing – a lot. For Naṅṅyār in the old system it was no problem to combine a decent life with performing in a protected space. But with Kūṭiyāṭṭam becoming a mobile genre, there are many new challenges the actresses are facing, with the borders between fame and shame becoming rather porous – as witness performing with new male colleagues from other families and castes, instead of performing with relatives; travelling overnight, or for several nights, to new secular stages everywhere in the world, instead of to two or three temples nearby; catering to new audiences with new tastes, instead of to a small group of high-caste, personally known spectators; pondering and reflecting on the new understanding of Kūṭiyāṭṭam and Naṅṅyār-Kūttuˇ as art-forms demanding much more mobility on and about the stage; dealing with the new context of Kūṭiyāṭṭam and Naṅṅyār-Kūttuˇ, one that is both commercialised and institutionalised; and, finally, finding a husband who will tolerate all these innovations.

New mobility in new public spheres? – The 20th and 21st centuries

To give an overview of how fast Kūṭiyāṭṭam and Naṅṅyār-Kūttuˇ have changed and how radical these changes have been over the last five to six decades, I will now summarise the key way-stations:[30]

A simplified Cākyār-Kūttuˇ performance by Paiṅkuḷam Rāma Cākyār in 1949/1951[31] was followed in August 1956 by the first full-fledged Kūṭiyāṭṭam play ever to be performed outside of a temple. Here *Subhadrādhanañjayam* act 1 was performed over six nights in the palace of the Sāmūtiri of Kōḻikkūṭṭu by Paiṅkuḷam Rāma Cākyār and his group.[32] This pioneering step into new public spheres heralded performances outside of Kerala (1961 in Madras, Delhi and Benares by the group of Māṇi Mādhava Cākyār) and even outside of India

30 Of course this list is not complete, it just mirrors the most important steps. For more details see Moser 2008: 60–74.

31 The year is not clear; for details see Moser 2008: 52–53.

32 For more details see Moser 2008: 54.

(1980 in Warsaw and Paris by the group of Paiṅkuḷam Rāma Cākyār) [ILLUSTRATIONS 9a–f].

In 1965, a chair for Kūṭiyāṭṭam was established at the Kērala Kalāmaṇḍalam arts academy, the appointment going to Paiṅkuḷam Rāma Cākyār. In that same year, the latter accepted for the first time a male student from another caste than Cākyār, Śivan Nampūtiri [ILLUSTRATIONS 9g and 9h]. Together with the *miḻāvu*-drum maestro P.K. Nārāyaṇa Nampyār, Rāma Cākyār developed a novel teaching technique as well as breaking new ground with a systematised curriculum. A year later, in 1966, the first conference to concern itself with Kūṭiyāṭṭam was held at Kērala Kalāmaṇḍalam. Over the following two decades costume and make-up were refined and the first students from abroad accepted (Maria Krzysztof Byrski, Clifford Reis Jones and Farley Richmond). In 1984, P.N. Girija, the first non-Naṅṅyār-Kūṭiyāṭṭam actress, performed for the first time a part of Naṅṅyār-Kūttŭ on a secular stage (*Vṛndāvanavarṇanam* at Kērala Kalāmaṇḍalam) [ILLUSTRATION 9i].

Well trained by Ammannūr Mādhava Cākyār, Uṣa Naṅṅyār set out in the year 1989 – with the support of Diane Daugherty – to perform a full cycle of Naṅṅyār-Kūttŭ in the reformed, more ›mobile‹ style, the venue being the traditional *kūttampalam* of the Vaṭakkunāthan temple in Tṛśśūr [ILLUSTRATIONS 2e and 5]. In 1995, Kalāmaṇḍalam Sōphi was the first woman to perform a male role on stage (Lakṣmaṇa in *Jaṭāyuvadham* [ILLUSTRATION 9j]) and I myself was the first foreigner to make a stage-debut *araṅṅēṯṯam* [ILLUSTRATION 3a].

Just two years later, in 1997, Uṣa Naṅṅyār forfeited her right to perform in the Vaṭakkunāthan temple by marrying a Nāyar, who is lower in ritual status. This even found its way into the international edition of *India Today*, under the by-line: »Dance of Codes: Nangiarkoothu, one of the oldest dance forms, [...] caught in a caste controversy as its best performer is banned« (RADHAKRISHNAN 2002). In 1990, Mārgi Sati wrote and published a new, elaborate flashback for Sītā in act three of Bhavabhūti's *Uttararāmacaritam* (SATI 1999). In 2001, UNESCO awarded Kūṭiyāṭṭam the title: »Masterpiece of the Oral and Intangible Heritage of Humanity«.

In the past two decades numerous plays were revived or newly adopted;[33] papers, books, VCDs, DVDs, films and multimedia CDs were published (even online); conferences were held, new institutions founded and new ways explored. Especially the female performers of Naṅṅyār-Kūttŭ are on their way to conquering new stages all over the world, as they courageously test the flexibility of an old tradition. In December 2009 and January 2010, for example, I personally witnessed such new stories as *Narasiṃhāvatāram* and *Ammakallu* being performed by trained Kūṭiyāṭṭam-actresses like Kapila and Indu – using the basic techniques of Naṅṅyār-Kūttŭ, but bringing in new elements: *e.g.* showing the tongue in vigorous scenes, reciting their text themselves [ILLUSTRATION 9k].

33 See also DAUGHERTY in this volume.

What defines – or validates – Kūṭiyāṭṭam and Naṅṅyār-Kūttu˘, what makes a performance good and what gains an actor or actress merit is not only changed by outside conditions but, even more, changes from the inside: The FILM CLIPS 1 and 2 shown online are exemplary and show women performers from traditional Naṅṅyār-families performing parts of Naṅṅyār-Kūttu˘ in the same year (1996). Both women know each other well. The elder one, Ēṭanāṭu Sarōjini Naṅṅyār, performs in the above-mentioned ›immobile‹ way, but, for all that, admires Uṣa Naṅṅyār's ›mobile‹ artistry; Uṣa Naṅṅyār, for her part, respects Sarōjini Naṅṅyār's vast knowledge in being ›voice only‹[34]. Sarōjini Naṅṅyār highly approves Uṣa Naṅṅyār's virtuosity in using her face and body on stage, although she herself never learned to do so. This validation from the inside, as it were, leads to new roles for the actresses, in the sense of becoming more flexible and mobile in mind and body. What, then, is ›tradition‹ from an inside perspective? Kūṭiyāṭṭam and – being part of it – Naṅṅyār-Kūttu˘ can be construed as a kind of meta-level, a tradition or *paramparā*, a reservoir containing oral, visual and written sources that can change and develop – within certain limits.[35] It is an omnipresent, abstract blueprint that can accommodate even major change. Crucial here are the boundaries of such a tradition. They seem to be invisible but very well defined and embedded, owned and controlled by the performers and by their (growing) community. The lively discussions in the community about where these boundaries lie are as gripping as they are in need of detailed research. The past few decades have had, and the next few decades will have, a deep impact on Kūṭiyāṭṭam, similar to that of the probable formation of ›performing together‹ in the 11th/12th century – but, in any case, as a living tradition and a genuine ›Masterpiece of the Oral and Intangible Heritage of Humanity‹ Kūṭiyāṭṭam, of this we can be sure, is able to cope with these new challenges and grow new futures.

LIST OF ABBREVIATIONS

ARIE Annual Reports on Indian Epigraphy (Madras, New Delhi)
ARSIE Annual Report on South Indian Epigraphy (Madras, New Delhi)
TAS Travancore Archaeological Series (Trivandrum)
[see: T.A.G. RAO 1988]

34 See JOHAN in this volume, especially her ILLUSTRATIONS 14 and 15 and FILM CLIP 4.
35 For the concept of the existence of a (hypothetical) oral reservoir, see DE BRUIN 1999: 163–168.

Works cited

[Annual Report on South Indian Epigraphy / ARSIE]. 1915. *G. O. No. 1260, 25th August 1915. Epigraphy. Recording, with remarks, the progress report of the Assistant Archaeological Superintendent of Epigraphy, Southern Circle, for the year 1914–15.* Madras: Government of Madras [/ Department of Archaeology] [reprint 1986 in: Annual Reports on Indian Epigraphy / ARIE (1915–1917). New Delhi: Archaeological Survey of India].

[Annual Report on South Indian Epigraphy / ARSIE]. 1926. *Annual Report on South-Indian Epigraphy for the year ending 31st March 1925.* Madras: Government of India [reprint 1986 in: ARIE (1922–1925). New Delhi: Archaeological Survey of India].

----. 1927. *Annual Report on South-Indian Epigraphy for the year ending 31st March 1926.* Madras: Government of India [reprint 1986 in: ARIE (1922–1925). New Delhi: Archaeological Survey of India].

----. 1934. *Annual Report on South Indian Epigraphy for the year ending 31st March 1932.* Madras: [Government of India] [reprint 1986 in: ARIE (1930–1934). New Delhi: Archaeological Survey of India].

----. 1952. *Annual Reports on South Indian Epigraphy for the years 1939–40 to 1942–43.* Ed. by C.R.Krishnamacharlu and N.Lakshminarayan Rao. Delhi: [Government of India] [reprint 1986 in: ARIE (1939–1944). New Delhi: Archaeological Survey of India].

Aiyar, K.V. Subrahmanya. 1923. *Travancore Archaeological Series [TAS].* Vol. 4, 1. Trivandrum: Govt. Press.

De Briun, Hanne. 1999. *Kattaikkuttu. The Flexibility of a South Indian Theatre Tradition.* Groningen: Egbert Fortsen.

Govindarajan, Hema. 1993. *Dance Terminologies. Their Epigraphical Interpretation.* New Delhi: Harman Publishing House.

Gundert, Hermann / Guṇṭarṭṭ˘, Herman. 1991 [1872]. Malayāḷam-Iṅglīṣ Nighaṇṭu. Kōṭṭayam: Ḍi. Si. Buks (Hermann Gundert Series, 1).

Iḷaṅkō Aṭikaḷ. 1997 [1975]. *Cilappatikāram. Tamiḻ˘ mahākāvyam.* Ed. with comm. by Nenmāṟa P. Viśvanāthan Nāyar. Tṛśūr: Kēraḷa Sāhitya Akkādami.

Jones, Clifford Reis. 1967. *The Temple Theatre of Kerala. Its History and Description.* University of Pennsylvania [unpubl. PhD-thesis].

Krishnamurthi, S.R. 1966. *A Study on The Cultural Developments in the Chola Period.* Annamalainagar: Annamalai University.

Kunjunni Raja, K. 1964 [1960]. *Kutiyattam.* An Introduction. New Delhi: Sangeet Natak Akademi.

Mādhavanpiḷḷa, C. 1995 [1976]. *En Bi Es Malayāḷam English Nighaṇṭu.* Kōṭṭayam: Nāṣanal Bukk Sṯṯāḷ.

Moser, Heike. 2008. *Naṅṅyār-Kūttu˘ – ein Teilaspekt des Sanskrittheaterkomplexes Kūṭiyāṭṭam. Historische Entwicklung und performative Textumsetzung.* Wiesbaden: Harrassowitz (Drama und Theater in Südasien, 6).

[Nampyār tamiḻ]. 1990. *Nampyār tamiḻ (rāmāyaṇa tamiḻ).* Ed. by P.K. Sumatikuṭṭi. Tiruvanantapuram: Oriental Research Institute and Manuscripts Library, University of Kerala (Tiruvanantapuram Malayāḷagranthāvali, 171).

Radhakrishnan, M.G. 2002. »Dance of Codes. Nangiarkoothu, one of the oldest dance forms, is caught in a caste controversy as its best performer is banned«. *India Today [International]* 36: 51.

Rāghavavāriyar, M.R.; M.P. Rājangurukkaḷ. 1992 [1991] Kēraḷacaritram. Śukapuram / Kottayam: Vaḷḷattōḷ Vidyāpīṭham / Current Books.

Rangacharya, Adya. 1967 [1947] *Drama in Sanskrit Literature.* Bombay: Popular Prakashan.

Rao, C. Hayavadav[*sic*:n?]a. (Ed.) 1930. Mysore Gazetteer. Vol. 2, 2. Bangalore: Govt. Press.

Rao, T. A. Gopinatha. (Ed.) 1921. *Travancore Archaeological Series [TAS].* Vol. 2, 3. Trivandrum: Government Press.

----. (Ed.) 1988 [1908]. *Travancore Archaeological Series [TAS].* Vol. 1. Thiruvananthapuram: Govt. of Kerala, Dept. of Cultural Publications.

----. (Ed.) 1992 [1908]. *Travancore Archaeological Series [TAS].* Vol. 2 and 3. Thiruvananthapuram: Govt. of Kerala, Dept. of Cultural Publications.

Sastri, K. A. Nilakanta. 1955 [1935]. *The Cōḷas.* Madras: University of Madras (Madras University Historical Series, 9).

Sati[, Mārgi]. 1999. *Śrīrāmacaritam naṅṅyārammakkūttˇ. Avataraṇaprakāram.* Kōṭṭayam: Kaṟanṯ Buks.

Sōman, P. 1996. »Dēvadāsikaḷ illātta kēraḷasaṃskāram«. *Vijñānakairaḷi* 27, 8: 499–509.

Thurston, Edgar. 1909. *Castes and Tribes in Southern India.* 9 Vol. Madras: Govt. Press.

Unni, N. P.; Bruce M. Sullivan. 2001. *The Wedding of Arjuna and Subhadrā: The Kūṭiyāṭṭam Drama Subhadrā-Dhanañjaya. Text with Vicāratilaka Commentary, Introduction, English Translation & Notes.* Delhi: Nag Publishers.

Vanamamalai, N. 1974. »State and Religion in the Chola Empire: Taxation for Thanjavur Temple's Music and Dance«. *Social Scientist* (Trivandrum) 27 (?), 3, 3: 26–42.

Warrier, N[erukkavil] V[ariyathu] Krishna [= N. V. Kṛṣṇavāriyar]. 1964. »Kūṭiyāṭṭam«. In: *Paripprēkṣyam.* Tṛśūr: Kaṟanṯ Buks, 116–129.

Basic literature on Kūṭiyāṭṭam in English language

Brückner, Heidrun. 2000. »Manuscripts and performance traditions of the so-called ›Trivandrum-Plays‹ ascribed to Bhāsa – A report on work in progress«. *Bulletin d'Etudes Indiennes* 17–18 (1999–2000): 501–550.

Byrski, Maria Christopher. 1967. »Is Kudiyattam a museum piece?«. *Sangeet Natak Akademi Journal* 5: 45–54.

Daugherty, Diane. 1996. »The Nangyār: Female Ritual Specialist of Kerala«. *Asian Theatre Journal* 13, 1: 54–67.

----. 2000. »Fifty Years On: Arts Funding in Kerala Today«. *Asian Theatre Journal* 17, 2: 237–252.

Jones, Clifford Reis. 1967. *The Temple Theatre of Kerala. Its History and Description.* University of Pennsylvania [unpubl. PhD-thesis].

----. 1984. *The Wondrous Crest-Jewel in Performance. Text and Translation of the Āścaryacūḍāmaṇi of Śaktibhadra with the Production Manual from the Tradition of Kūṭiyāṭṭam Sanskrit Drama.* Delhi: Oxford University Press.

Kunjunni Raja, K. 1964 [1960]. *Kutiyattam.* An Introduction. New Delhi: Sangeet Natak Akademi.

Moser, Heike. 2000. »Mantrāṅkam. The Third Act of Pratijñāyaugandharāyaṇam in Kūṭiyāṭṭam«. *Bulletin d'Etudes Indiennes* 17–18 (1999–2000): 563–584.

----. 2007b. »To enjoy playing with play. Or: He by whose goodness I was redeemed, having slipped through the clutches of the demon and fallen ...«. In: *The Power of*

Performance. Ed. by Heidrun Brückner, Elisabeth Schömbucher, Phillip Zarrilli. Delhi: Manohar, 209–234.

PANCHAL, GOVERDHAN. 1984. *Kūttampalam & Kūṭiyāṭṭam. A Study of the Traditional Theatre for the Sanskrit Drama of Kerala.* New Delhi: Sangeet Natak Akademi.

PANIKER, NIRMALA. 2005 [1992] *Nangiar Koothu. The Classical Dance-Theatre of the Nangiar-s.* Second Revised Edition. Irinjalakuda: Natana Kairali (Documentation of Kutiyattam Series, 2).

PAULOSE, K. G. (ED.). 1993. *Naṭāṅkuśa. A Critique on Dramaturgy.* Tripunithura: Govt. Sanskrit College (Ravivarma Samskṛta Granthāvali, 26).

----. 2000a. *Bhagavadajjukam in Kūṭiyāṭṭam. The Hermit and the Harlot – the Sanskrit farce in Performance.* Delhi: Bharatiya Book Cooporation.

----. 2000b. *Bhīma in search of celestrial flower. Nīlakaṇṭhakavi Kalyāṇasaugandhikavyāyoga.* Sanskrit Text with English Translation. Delhi: Bharatiya Book Cooporation.

----. 2006. *Kutiyattam Theatre:* The Earliest Living Tradition. Kottayam: DC Books. [including VCD].

----[; MARGI MADHU]. 2003. *Improvisations of Ancient Theatre.* [Documentation of the text and performance of Kaanchukeeyam, from a 11th century Sanskrit text]. Text and performance Margi Madhu. Tripunithura: International Centre for Kutiyattam.

RAJAGOPALAN, L. S. 1997. *Women's role in Kūḍiyāṭṭam.* Chennai: The Kuppuswami Sastri Research Institute.

----. 2000. *Kūḍiyāṭṭam: Preliminaries and Performance.* Chennai: Kuppuswami Sastri Research Institute.

RICHMOND, FARLEY. 1990. »Kūṭiyāṭṭam«. In: *Indian Theatre. Traditions of Performance.* Ed. by Farley Richmond, Darius L. Swann, Phillip B. Zarrilli. Honolulu: The University of Hawaii Press, 87–117 [reprint Delhi: Motilal Banarsidass (Performing Arts Series, 1)].

----. 1999 [1993]. »Kutiyattam«. In: *The Cambridge Guide to Asian Theatre.* Ed. by James R. Brandon. Cambridge: University Press, 97–99.

----. 2002. *Kutiyattam. Sanskrit Theater of India.* Multimedia CD-ROM. [Ann Arbor:] University of Michigan Press (Digital Publishing at The University of Michigan Press).

SANGEET NATAK AKADEMI. 1995. *Kūṭiyāṭṭam.* Ed. by K. Ayyappa Paniker. Sangeet Natak Akademi Journal 111–114 [special issue].

UNNI, N. P. (ED.). 1987. *Kulaśēkhara Varman's Subhadrādhanañjayam.* Delhi: Nag Publishers.

---- (ED.). 1998a [1974]. *Mattavilāsa Prahasana.* Delhi: Nag Publishers.

----; BRUCE M. SULLIVAN. 1995. *The Sun God's Daughter and King Saṃvaraṇa: Tapatī-Saṃvaraṇam and the Kūṭiyāṭṭam Drama Tradition. Text with Vivaraṇa Commentary.* Delhi: Nag Publishers.

----; ----. 2001. *The Wedding of Arjuna and Subhadrā: The Kūṭiyāṭṭam Drama Subhadrā-Dhanañjaya. Text with Vicāratilaka Commentary, Introduction, English Translation & Notes.* Delhi: Nag Publishers.

VENU, G. 1989. *Production of a play in Kūṭiyāṭṭam. Text and translation of the first act of Abhiṣeka Nāṭaka of Bhāsa with the Kramadīpika (production manual) and the āṭṭaprakāraṃ (acting manual) from the Sanskrit Drama Tradition of Kerala.* Irinjalakuda: Natanakairali (Documentation of Kūṭiyāṭṭam Series, 1).

----. 2002. *Into the world of Kutiyattam with the legendary Ammannur Madhava Chakyar.* Irinjalakuda: Natanakairali (Documentation of Kūṭiyāṭṭam Series, 3).

----. 2005. *Kathakali, Kūṭiyāṭṭam and Other Performing Arts. Fifty Years of Theatrical Exploration.* Irinjalakuda: Natanakairali.

FILMOGRAPHY

The three film clips are published online: *http://www.indologie.uni-wuerzburg.de/women_performers/contributors/moser/film_clips/*.

FILM CLIP 1: *Ēṭanāṭu Sarōjini Naṅṅyār* ([Moser Hi8 25.2], 3:18 min.):
Annual ritual performance of Naṅṅyār-Kūttu˘ in the *kūttampalam* of Tirumaṇḍāṅkunnu Bhagavati Kṣētram at Aṅṅāṭipuṟam (3 days, daily about 8–8:30 am); see also ILLUSTRATIONS 2c, 2f and 6d. Clipping of day 2, 27.03.1996: end of *saṃkṣēpam*, acting and recitation of verse 1.
Cēṭi: Ēṭanāṭu Sarōjini Naṅṅyār, *miḻāvu* (drum): Nārāyaṇa Nampyār (Sārojini Naṅṅyār's son), *tāḷam* (cymbals): Kōmāḷam Naṅṅyār; Sarōjini Naṅṅyār recites herself, because Kōmāḷam is not capable to do so; being a ritual performance a Naṅṅyār by birth has to play the cymbals.

FILM CLIP 2: *Cāttakkuṭam Uṣa Naṅṅyār* ([Moser Hi8 40], 5:47 min.):
The episode *Pūtanamōkṣam* of Naṅṅyār-Kūttu˘ performed by Cāttakkuṭam Uṣa Naṅṅyār at the Nehrucenter at Mumbai, 07.10.1996. Clipping of Kṛṣṇa drinking milk from Pūtana's poisoned breast and the death of Pūtana.

FILM CLIP 3: *Villuvaṭṭattu ›Subhadra‹ (Pārvati) Naṅṅyār*, ([Moser Hi8 22.2], 2:35 min.):
Interview of Villuvaṭṭattu ›Subhadra‹ (Pārvati) Naṅṅyār by Uṣa Naṅṅyār and Heike Moser in Subhadra Naṅṅyar's house at Iriññālakuṭa, 23.09.1995; see also ILLUSTRATION 8. Clipping of the recitation and demonstration of verse 30 Naṅṅyār-Kūttu˘ and the text of the heroine in the play *Nāgānanda* just before the famous ›hanging scene‹.

PHOTOGRAPHIES

The 31 photographies are also published online: *http://www.indologie.uni-wuerzburg.de/women_performers/contributors/moser/illustrations/*.

ILLUSTRATIONS 1a to 1c: *Kūṭiyāṭṭam – ›combined acting‹, ›acting together‹, ›inter-play‹:*
1a: *Kalyāṇasaugandhikam*, Tirunakkara *kūttampalam* (Kōṭṭayam), Ammannūr Cāccu Cākyār Smāraka Gurukulam, 08.12.1996 [photograph: Moser I.96.29-37]
1b: *Nāgānandam* [1957] [photograph is taken from: K. P. NĀRĀYAṆAPPIṢĀRŌṬI: »Nāgānandaṃ kūṭiyāṭṭam«. In: *Mātṛbhūmi āḻcappatippu* 27.10.1957: 25]
1c: *Śūrpaṇakhāṅkam*: Rāma (Śivan Nampūtiri) and Sīta (Mārgi Sati) [original: Kuñju Vāsudēvan, collection Moser]

ILLUSTRATIONS 2a to 2f: *Kūttampalam – traditional theatre halls in Kerala temples:*
2a: exterior view of the *kūttampalam* of Vaṭakkunāthan temple, Tṛśśūr, 1995 [photograph: Moser I.95.5-31a]
2b: exterior view of the *kūttampalam* of Peruvanam temple, Peruvanam, 20.08.1995 [photograph: Moser I.95.1-34a]
2c: exterior view of the *kūttampalam* of Tirumaṇḍāṅkunnu Bhagavati Kṣētram, Aṅṅāṭipuṟam, 26./27.3.96 [photograph: Moser I.96.02-17]
2d: interior view of the *kūttampalam* of Peruvanam temple, Peruvanam, 20.08.1995 [photograph: Moser I.95.4-32]

2e: Uṣa Naṅnyār performing Naṅṅyār-Kūttu˘ in the *kūttampalam* of Vaṭakkunāthan temple, Tṛśśūr, 17.08.1995 [photograph: Moser I.95.8-13a]
2f: Ammannūr Paramēśvara Cākyār in the role of the Sūtradhāran, performing in the *kūttampalam* of Tirumaṇḍāṅkunnu˘ Bhagavati Kṣētram, Aṅṅāṭipuṟam, 1996 [photograph: Moser I.96.02-03]

ILLUSTRATIONS 3a and 3b: *Heike Moser performing Kūṭiyāṭṭam (stage debut as first foreigner in 1995):*
3a: Araṅṅēṯṯam (stage debut) of the author (Heike Moser) performing Naṅṅyār-Kūttu˘ in the *kūttampalam* of her school, Kērala Kalāmaṇḍalam, 18.09.1995 [photograph: Kuñju Vāsudēvan, collection Moser I.95.09-04]
3b: Heike Moser in the role of Laḷita in *Śūrpaṇakhāṅkam* at Paḷuṅkil Śivanārāyaṇakṣētram, Kiḻlimaṅgalam, 01.01.1996 [photograph: M. N. Nārāyaṇan, collection Moser I.96.01-11(neg)]

ILLUSTRATION 4: *Nirvahaṇam – insertion of flashbacks in Kūṭiyāṭṭam* [graph: the author]

ILLUSTRATION 5: *Naṅṅyār-Kūttu˘:* Uṣa Naṅnyār performing Naṅṅyār-Kūttu˘ in the *kūttampalam* of Vaṭakkunāthan temple, Tṛśśūr, 17.08.1995 (Tāḷam: Aparṇṇa Naṅṅyār, Miḻāvu: Nārāyaṇa Nampyār). [photograph: Moser I.95.8-12a]

ILLUSTRATIONS 6a to 6f: *The Nampyār- / Naṅṅyār-family of Ēṭanāṭṭu˘ (Taṅkam Naṅṅyār and Sarōjini Naṅṅyār are sisters):*
6a: Taṅkam Naṅṅyār, performing Naṅṅyār-Kūttu˘ at Mārgi, Tiruvanantapuram, 14.07.1995, using the old makeup: Her face is coloured deep red and surrounded by a black line; the ›cap‹ is made of cardboard, covered with red cloth, silver ornaments and fresh flowers. [The reformed makeup has omitted the black line, the face is bright yellowish; the headgear and the ornaments are mode of wood on a permanent base (standard since about 1984; see ILLUSTRATIONS 1c, 3a, 3b, 5 and FILM CLIP 2).] [photograph: P.L. Shaji, collection Moser I.95.23-24(neg)]
6b: Taṅkam Naṅṅyār, demonstrating Naṅṅyār-Kūttu˘ at her house in Ēṭanāṭu, 10.08.1996, again using the old makeup and ornaments. [photograph: Moser I.96.10-02]
6c: Taṅkam Naṅṅyār, demonstrating Naṅṅyār-Kūttu˘ at her house in Ēṭanāṭu, 10.08.1996 (on her left: Heike Moser, right: Uṣa Naṅnyār), showing not only the traditional makeup, but also the old type of costume: it is without blouse and just a cloth covering the legs – similar to the one, the male characters wear (open in front with a kind of wrap-over trousers underneath); rice-paste covers the upper arm, legs and feet. The modern costume uses long trousers and a kind of long, wide, entirely closed skirt, allowing the women more movements and jumps without daring glimpses (standard since about 1984; see pictures 1c, 3a, 3b, 5 and movie 2). [photograph: Moser I.96.10-19]
6d: Sarōjini Naṅṅyār, performing Naṅṅyār-Kūttu˘ at Aṅṅāṭipuram, 27.03.1996, using the old makeup and ornaments but the modernised, closed skirt (see FILM CLIP 1). [photograph: Moser I.96.2-11(dia)]
6e: Sarōjini Naṅṅyār, performing Naṅṅyār-Kūttu˘ at Tṛppūṇittuṟa, 31.08.1995, showing the old makeup and ornaments. [photograph: Moser I.95.06-06]
6f: Sarōjini Naṅṅyār's son Nārāyana Nampyār together with her father (his grandfather) Viluvaṭṭattu Rāvuṇṇi Nampyār; both are experts of the *miḻāvu*-drum, played exclusively for Kūṭiyāṭṭam, 1996. [photograph: Moser I.96.19-24]

ILLUSTRATION 7: *Red eyes, caused by inserting the premature seed of the cuṇṭapūvu˘ flower:* Kalāmaṇḍalam Rāma Cākyār as Bhrāntan in *Mantrāṅkam*, performed at Paḷuṅkil Śivanārāyaṇakṣētram, Kiḷḷimaṅgalam, 26.05.1996. [photograph: Moser I.96.09-07]

ILLUSTRATION 8: *Viluvaṭṭattu ›Subhadra‹ (Pārvati) Naṅṅyār (1917–1998):* Interview with Viluvaṭṭattu ›Subhadra‹ (Pārvati) Naṅṅyār by Uṣa Naṅṅyār and Heike Moser at her house in Iriññālakuṭa, 23.09.1995 (see FILM CLIP 3). [photograph: Moser I.95.13-30]

ILLUSTRATIONS 9a to 9k: *Kūṭiyāṭṭam and Naṅṅyār-Kūttu in new public spheres (20th / 21st centuries):*

9a: Paiṅkuḷam Rāma Cākyār, Māṇi Mādhava Cākyār, Ammannūr Mādhava Cākyār – the »trinity of Kūṭiyāṭṭam«. [Courtesy: V.T. Induchudan (Ceṟuturutti), collection Moser]

9b: Paiṅkuḷam Rāma Cākyār as Vidūṣaka in *Subhadrādhanañjayam*, act 1, Kūṭalōṭṭupurttumana temple, 1979. [Courtesy: Krishna Nair Studio (Ṣoṟaṇūr), collection Moser]

9c: Paiṅkuḷam Rāma Cākyār as Arjuna-Dhanañjayan in *Subhadrādhanañjayam*, act 1. [Courtesy: Krishna Nair Studio (Ṣoṟaṇūr), collection Moser]

9d: Māṇi Mādhava Cākyār, his daughter Amminikuṭṭi and his son (?), performing *Subhadrādhanañjayam* at Lucknow, 1964. [Courtesy: P.K. Nārāyaṇa Nampyār (Kiḷḷikkuṟuśśimaṅgalam), collection Moser I.2000.05-03a(neg)]

9e: The first Kūṭiyāṭṭam-tour abroad: Paris 1980. [Courtesy: Śivan Nampūtiri (Ceṟuturutti), collection Moser]

9f: The first Kūṭiyāṭṭam-tour abroad: *Jaṭāyuvadham* at Paris 1980 (Rāvaṇa: Kalāmaṇḍalam Śivan Nampūtiri, Jaṭāyu: Kalāmaṇḍalam Rāma Cākyār, *miḻāvu*: Kṛṣnan Nampyār and P.K. Nārāyaṇa Nampyār). [Courtesy: Gilles Tarabout (Paris), collection Moser]

9g: Kalāmaṇḍalam Śivan Nampūtiri, showing the gesture for Garuḍa. [Courtesy: V.T. Induchudan (Ceṟuturutti), collection Moser]

9h: Kalāmaṇḍalam Śivan Nampūtiri as Arjuna-Dhanañjayan in *Subhadrādhanañjayam* (acting »playing the *vīṇā*«). [Courtesy: P.N. Girija (Ceṟuturutti), collection Moser]

9i: First performance of an episode of Naṅṅyār-Kūttu˘ on a secular stage and first performance of an episode of Naṅṅyār-Kūttu˘ by a non-Naṅṅyār: P.N. Girija shows *Vṛndāvanavarṇṇanam* (here: *Mayilāṭṭam*) in December 1984 in the *kūttampalam* of Kēraḷa Kalāmaṇḍalam. [Courtesy: Krishna Nair Studio (Ṣoṟaṇūr), collection Moser]

9j: Kalāmaṇḍalam Sōphi acts fort he first time as a woman in a male role in Kūṭiyāṭṭam: she performs as Sūtan / Māyā-Lakṣmaṇa in *Jaṭāyuvadham* in the *kūttampalam* of Kēraḷa Kalāmaṇḍalam, 09.11.1995. [photograph: Moser I.95.19-4a]

9k: Kapila G. Vēṇu shows the new piece *Narasiṃhāvatāram* in Naṅṅyār-Kūttu˘ stile; the main technical innovations are that she recites the text herself and that she shows her tongue on stage when portraying Narasiṃha (ITFoK'09 – Afro-Asian theatre festival, Tṛśśūr, 21.12.2009). [photograph: Moser P1000182.JPG]

Women's Musical Knowledge and Power, and their Contributions to Nation-Building in Kerala, South India

A Case Study of Kaikkottukali[1]

Christine Guillebaud

The issue of gender raised recently in ethnomusicology, too, opens up new theoretical considerations for the study of musical performances, such as the questions as how music creates asymmetric power settings and gender conflicts, maintains social and sexual order or, on the contrary, works as an agent of change, contestation and inversion (KOSKOFF 1987; HERNDON, ZIEGLER 1990). While some authors consider music as a social space for the construction of inter-gender relationships, others focus on their own position as female scholars during fieldwork, as conditioned by the music repertoire they study and the socio-political settings (BABIRACKI 1997). Yet none of these studies explores the question of the authority of musical knowledge that different groups of performers possess. What exactly constitutes authority in a musical context? Who are its agents and what constitutes the economy of power that informs the aesthetic codification of music?

Music and caste

The link between musical authority and caste organisation is central to the Indian context. If musical knowledge is related to social hierarchy, one should look more carefully at the status of the musicians who produce it. This observation is particularly relevant for ›professional music‹, performed as a specialised activity by representatives of a particular caste and patronised by the members of other castes, who often tend to be of a higher status than the performers themselves.[2]

1 I would like to thank Hanne M. de Bruin for the care she took in reading this article and for her insightful comments.

2 Among the local castes of musicians which have been documented, I would like to mention the musician-genealogists, the Manghaniyars and Langas of Rajasthan (KOTHARI 1972, 1973, 1990), the temple musicians in Kerala (TARABOUT 1993), the musician-tailors of Nepal (TINGEY 1994) and the specialists of domestic rituals in Kerala (GUILLEBAUD 2008).

Among India's great diversity of musical repertoires and musical theories, those rooted in the classical musical systems representing the »Great Tradition« – both North Indian (Hindustani) and South Indian (Carnatic) – are the most socially valued (BABIRACKI 1991). Classical music is an »elite art« that legitimates its superiority over other musical traditions by claiming to follow the rules and praxis laid down in the written treatises on music (QURESHI 1991, 2000). Moreover, the classical musical system might be labelled as a »dominant musicology«, because of its rationalization of musical concepts, an important step in the process of theorizing about music. Many consider such an analytical-theoretical approach, which takes its origins and authority from classical sources, the only valid way to study the vast diversity of musical practices in India (GUILLEBAUD 2005).

In the case of low caste musicians, it is rather difficult to study their music with the tools offered by the classical musical theory, because the concept of *raga* and the analytical rationalization of rhythmic classifications (*tala*) that form part of the classical system do not find a place in the musical knowledge of these low caste performers or, at least not in such an analytical way. In addition, the ultimate aim of their music appears to be the attainment of ritual efficacy rather than a unique aesthetic satisfaction. As a component of ritual actions or as a service dedicated to local deities, it is embedded in a complex interplay between ritual officiants, patrons, gods and devotees. Differences in the objectives of these particular forms of music are reflected in the nature of the musical knowledge and its application by the exponents. For this reason, high caste people perceive low caste performers often as unable to theorize about what they perform. Specialists of classical music, who often belong to the higher castes, deny low caste musicians any form of musical authority in order to establish themselves as experts: they are the ones who ›know‹ how to analyze musical structures, whereas the low caste musicians are considered ›performers‹ only.

The Kaikkottukali example

In the case of non-professional music, as for the group dance *kaikkottukali* (»play of clapping or beating hands«), the construction of musical authority seems to vary according to gender and age – important criteria that determine the status of an individual in the local society. Yet, caste as a criterion is not completely absent. The same musical repertoire performed by different castes can change considerably in its codes of execution. And those who are considered the experts as regards the possession of musical knowledge (*e.g.* men, women, old people) vary from one caste to another. In this article, I will highlight *kaikkottukali*, a dance traditionally performed by women in Kerala, to illustrate differences in the execution of this particular form in relation to the social status of its performers. The performance of *kaikkottukali* is characterized by a highly flexible nature that allows for changes in the aesthetic features of the performance according to place, context and status of the performers.

A preliminary ethnographic exploration will provide an insight into the social relationships, in particular those involving caste and gender, which traditionally have shaped the aesthetic codification of this dance. Thereafter, I will examine how both the social reform movement and the nation-building process in Kerala in the 20th century, have contributed to the creation of new forms of leadership in the context of musical performance and the possession of musical authority.

In the ethnographic depictions of folklorists of the early 20th century (ANANTHAKRISHNA IYER 1912; THURSTON, RANGACHARI 1909), *kaikkottukali* is introduced as a ›feminine‹ speciality, mainly performed by Brahmins and Nayars both of which are socially dominant castes in Kerala. When I started my fieldwork on *kaikkottukali*, local scholars provided me with contacts of women performers who were considered the best regional ›experts‹. All of them were Namputiri Brahmins, but their styles of singing were very different. One singer, called Savitri, who had a professional training in classical music, performed *kaikkottukali* music with a vocal technique rich of melisms and ornaments. Another Brahmin woman, a housewife also called Savitri, had a huskier voice. She did not use any melodic embellishments. Both informants considered these aesthetic contrasts simply as individual variations, which they attributed to their different musical backgrounds. Their discourse about *kaikkottukali* agreed on the fact that both considered this dance to be typically ›feminine‹ and typically ›brahmin‹, that is to say a typical art form among Antarjanam (»people living / being inside«), the local name to refer to Brahmin women.[3]

Kaikkottukali generally is performed as a group dance form inside the house during domestic festivals (marriages, ritual celebrations, such as Onam and Tiruvatira[4]) or during informal meetings when members of a family or an entire neighbourhood get together. These occasions for dancing and singing together are part of a feminine sociability and are generally accompanied by other domestic activities, such as culinary preparations and collective baths with water plays (*tudichu kuli*). Most women associate *kaikkottukali* with prosperity. They perform in order »to have a good husband«, a recurrent theme of the songs most of which are about the love between the god Krishna and the shepherdess Radha.

3 Until the middle of the 20th century, Brahmin women were not allowed to leave the familial premises. Their social interactions with people outside the house were limited and strictly regulated.

4 Onam and Tiruvira are two important festivals in Kerala. The dance, which is a part of the festival celebrations, is also called *tiruvatirakali* (»play of Tiruvatira«).

1. Performance and power

The *kaikkottukali* dance is widespread among Brahmin women, but it is performed in similar contexts by members of low caste communities, in particular Toddy tappers (Ilava) and Washermen (Mannan), too. However, women belonging to these castes generally are not considered as ›experts‹ in singing and dancing by Kerala society. It should be pointed out that high caste women most of the time are unfamiliar with *kaikkottukali* practiced by low caste women. However, if they know about it, they do not acknowledge the musical skills of these lower caste women, in addition to perceiving the body postures, manner of carrying out gestures and rendering of songs in a very negative way. The following ethnographic observations of *kaikkottukali* performances enable us to identify important contrasts between the aesthetic codes used by high caste and low caste groups of performers. The descriptions focus on stylistic variations and different ways in which these two distinct groups validate the musical knowledge, authority and skills of the performers.

My first description concerns a performance held in a Namputiri Brahmin house and the second a village festival, which took place in a quarter inhabited by Toddy tappers and Washermen in 2004. The comparison shows to what extent voice culture, musical forms and choreographic postures are ruled by heterogeneous codes and norms.

The performance in the Namputiri house takes place in the domestic sphere and does not require a public audience [see FILM CLIP 1]. The performers share a common physical and emotional experience. Their purpose is to be together, to sing and dance in a collective way. The musical form is responsorial[5]: two women render simultaneously each line of the song while the entire group repeats the same verses. However, all participants perform identical body movements. The musical tempo, the intensity and the pitch are progressively ascendant and provide an indicator of a collective arousing. Voice and movements are used as sensitive media to express feminine sociability.

The musical authority of this performance may be questioned because of its intimacy in the family setting, its domestic location and the absence of a public audience. In this Brahmin area, the *kaikkottukali* repertoire is the prerogative of women. The oldest lady of the family generally is considered the main possessor of musical knowledge. For example, she decides which songs should be performed and she should be able to recall the lines and appropriate words if other participants forget them. In addition, the distribution of musical parts transposes such hierarchical roles. The solo singers direct the text, the melodic line, the steps and the general movement. As the repositories of musical authority, they call themselves the »troupe leaders«. However, this term has come in

5 Ethnomusicological term describing the musical process of alternance, generally between a solist and a choir.

vogue recently, in particular in the context of Radio and TV programs of folk music (GUILLEBAUD 2008: 118–155) held by the State Government to promote a ›keralite‹ local heritage, something to which I will come back below.

The second performance of *kaikkottukali* I observed was held in a quarter of Toddy-tappers and Washermen [see FILM CLIP 2]. It consisted of dancing in front of an audience mainly composed of villagers. Songs and body movements were performed by women only, but the general organisation of the dance was determined in detail by men. Men were instrumental in deciding in advance how many musical pieces had to be performed. They addressed the solo singer, considered to be the most experienced of the group, and cued her to begin the dance by counting with intensity: »One, two, three, four!« The use of the English language appeared to be a way to exert their authority over the form and content of the performance.

This collective dance is performed with the aim of achieving prosperity, too. But unlike the previous example where the dance was executed by Brahmin women inside their houses, here the dance was a public event in which all members of the local families participated. Even though women can and do dance among themselves, generally at night after finishing the domestic tasks, men perceived these activities rather as informal ›rehearsals‹ in preparation for the public village festivals than as performances proper.

In public performance contexts, men standing outside the circle of women performers can also sing the *kaikkottukali* repertoire. Most of the times their musical skills are basic and their pitch quite imprecise. They themselves are aware of the fact that they don't perform as ›beautifully‹ as the women and »don't know the lines« so well. They usually follow the song texts written down in small notebooks by their spouses or sisters and use microphones in order to occupy the sonic space – yet another way to underline their authority over the women's performance.

The low caste women used a completely different aesthetics from the Brahmin women, in particular with regard to their gestures and postures. Their chests were comparatively inclined, arms moved in a slower motion. Some scholars have analysed the steps and gestures of *kaikkottukali* as one of the main sources that went into the making of the classical dance Mohiniyattam in Kerala (VENU / PANIKER 1995: 31; VENU 1990: 95). This general statement cannot be extended beyond the unique aesthetics of the dance as used by the Brahmin women. Indeed, Brahmin women often considered the performances of *kaikkottukali* by other castes as a degenerated form of the dance, a »non-original *kaikkottukali*« or a »poor dance performed by illiterate people who don't know anything« and »just imitate Brahmins«. Such depreciating statements are very common among Brahmin women. The differences observed in aesthetic codes, and their validation by the Brahmin women performers who are considered to be ›more knowledgeable‹ with regard to the ›right‹ form and content of the dance, contribute to the creation of unequal power settings.

Brahmin women performers themselves invoked the issue of gender in their definitions of what is a ›good‹ or ›correct‹ *kaikkottukali* dance. The fact that men from low castes take part in the songs, or dance with women during the last part of village ceremonies is seen as particularly objectionable by high caste women. An example of a mixed performance recorded in 2004 [see FILM CLIP 3] shows the extent to which the dance *kaikkottukali* mediates a village's sociability. The performance takes place at the end of a local village festival and brings together male and female performers in a common dance. The low caste community, too, has its ›group leaders‹: two male performers who are responsible for the annual organisation of the local festivities and participate themselves with vigour in the dance event. Public participation is intense among other members, too: all villagers attend the dance and clap their hands in a common rhythm. The dance ends with a collective shout (»*ayayo*!«) and in a joyful atmosphere, which is not necessarily the case during ›feminine‹ public performances recorded previously in the same low caste village [see FILM CLIP 2].

In the eyes of Brahmin women, a dance in which the genders mix is definitely distasteful. But even more than hurting their aesthetic feelings, the negative perception they harbour of the dance when performed by low caste people appears to follow from the apparent mixing of genders displayed on such an occasion[6]. In contrast, low caste participants do not perceive the performance of *kaikkottukali* as a privileged means for feminine sociability, but as a community celebration for villagers belonging to the same locality. »We have a good cooperation!«, the inhabitants willingly admit.

We may conclude that the same dance is performed in different ways according to the perceptions and performance needs the participating castes have with regard to the dance and with regard to the performance contexts in which it takes place. Among Brahmins, *kaikkottukali* contributes to the creation of a special, idealized feminine image, in addition to ascertaining Brahmin women's sociability within their own community, while among low castes, it mediates village sociability as a whole. The experts of musical knowledge vary also from one caste to the other. Among Brahmins, female gender and age of the group leaders set the authority, while among low castes, musical authority is fundamentally conceived as masculine.

2. *Kaikkottukali as an instrument to facilitate social reform movements*

During the beginning of the 20th century Kerala witnessed the birth of a number of social reform movements, many of which were caste based (CHERIAN 1999: 452). These reform movements had not only their impact on traditional believes,

6 See also SEIZER (2005) on the inappropriateness of the ›mixing of genders‹ in the lowly validated form of Tamil Special Natakam.

customs and power relations in Kerala, but affected also the musical scene and the ways in which particular forms of music and dance, such as *kaikkottukali*, were being used by the Namputiri Brahmins as the cultural emblems to define a new progressive caste identity.

Yogakshema Association of Namputiri Brahmins and the position of women

Through the advent of the social reform association Yogakshema in 1908, Namputiris realized that some traditional customs resulted in injustice, in particular for their women: due to the law of primogeniture, only few women could marry and this caused an increase in spinsterhood and, when the husband was much older, widowhood. A a matter of fact, this law dictated that only the eldest son was entitled to marry within his own caste, stimulating others to marry outside their caste and depriving the children of these outside alliances of their father's property. The Yogakshema, through its journal *Unni Namputiri*, spread new ideas among the Namputiri community, which resulted in an unprecedented awakening. The journal published articles criticizing established customs and drew attention to the educational backwardness of the community, which were instrumental in initiating different kinds of reform[7]. These reforms provided the members of the Namputiri caste, whether male or female, with the right to get married inside their caste and legalized the equal inheritance of children of the family property.

The Yogakshema Association is today a registered society and has three sections: the General Government Board represented by different committees or units in each district (*jilla* committees), a Ladies Wing (*vanita sabha*) and a Youth Wing (*yuvajana sabhā*). The Ladies and Youth sections of the Association are concerned with family issues and deal with children's affairs. They hold cultural activities (arts, sports and games), are involved in charity through providing, for instance, scholarships to students and grants for marriages. Each unit sells food items made by the ladies of the unit under the label *Janani products*.

The Yogakshema reform movement has been decisive for the emancipation of Namputiri women. Gradually, women gave up traditional customs, such as the carrying of a leaf umbrella (*marakkuda*) and wearing of a blanket covering the body (*ghosa*), and began to reject domestic restrictions (SHEEBA 2001: 931). These changes reflect the rise of political consciousness among women and their participation in social reform movements (see VELAYUDHAN 1994). In addition, literary works, such as Lalithambika Antarjanam's writings, highlighted the resistance of the Antarjanams against existing customs and attempted to reframe subjection of women in new terms through focusing on their right to express their sexuality and through re-interpretating »mythological women« in

7 The Tiruvitamkur Malayala Brahman Regulation in 1930 and thus, the Madras Nambudiri Acts in 1933 (VASANTHA 2000: 752–763). For an historical account of the Yogakshema association and the social reform movement among Brahmins, read *http://www.namboothiri.com/articles/yogakshemamahaasabha.htm*.

the light of contemporary values (SHEEBA 2001: 934–936). Gradually, male-female relationships were re-negotiated.

Kaikkottukali as a ›Brahmin‹ art form today

Even today the theme of gender relationships remains in vogue in the Yogakshema association. The *kaikkottukali* dance is used as a medium for the empowerment of women. Every year, a dance competition is held during which different groups of performers trained in their locality as »yogakshema troupes« come together. The teams of each unit participate in an annual competition and the best are selected and sent to the district and state festivals. Judges from outside the association, mainly Brahmins, but not especially from the Namputiri caste, are appointed. The competition is held according to the ages of the performers and involves other art forms, too.[8] During the year, older ladies (called »grandmothers« or *mutassi*) organize meetings of *kaikkottukali* in villages to rehearse for these competitions, but also to perform during the traditional ritual functions (marriages, temple festivals etc.). According to Pushpakumari, the Secretary of the Ladies Wings in 2006, and a *kaikkottukali* singer:

> We work to encourage women [to engage in *kaikkottukali*] for their empowerment (*strisakti karanam*) and prosperity (*vanita vibhavam*), not only physically but also mentally. Art forms are introduced to have a healthy mind and body, also for children. Competitions are held in October, on the second Saturday and Sunday. It is called *tauryatrikam*[9]: melody (*raga*), cycle (*tala*), rhythm (*laya*), expression (*bhava*). It is a Sanskrit word. Dance forms such as Tiruvatira [*kaikkottukali*], Mohiniyattam, Bharatanatyam, Kathakali, Ottan tullal [different forms of dance and drama] are represented. All generations participate and all families attend the competition. It is good for mental refreshment and entertainment. All members of the community get closer. The association works to unite people and preserve traditions. (Pushpakumari, Interview 2006)

By organizing new performances, the Yogakshema association has introduced the dance into the public sphere. And, among the art forms promoted through the association, *kaikkottukali* is particularly enhanced, as a group leader told me:

> *Kaikkottukali* is very important because religion and life style are connected. The dance is originally an offering of the Goddess Parvati to Lord Siva (Parvati *sumangali*). It is Siva's birthday's celebration by his wife [...][10]. They represent a model couple

8 Besides the main traditional dances, other arts forms are encouraged as mimicry, cinematic dance and human painting (called »tableaux«) consisting of a group of people arranged as a collective of fixed poses exhibiting mythological scenes and current social and political issues.

9 Tauryatrikam can be explained as »music, dance and playing of instrument combined« (C. Madhavan Pillai: *Malayalam-English Dictionary*, 1999: 510).

10 According to this original myth, the Goddess cooked traditional preparation using plants and roots, which she had collected in the forest (OMANA 2000).

> for our community. Both Siva and Parvati are made from each other. They represent social equality. Art form is our advice. Real life is in Kailasam [mythical location of God Siva and Parvati]; it is our model life! (Shobana, Interview 2006)

In addition to defining *kaikkottukali* as a typically ›brahmin‹ and ›feminine‹ art form, the dance also implements new social and inter-gender relationships.

Such institutionalisation of *kaikkottukali* dance by the Yogakshema association has created new aesthetic codes and caused a new distribution of roles. Performances now take place on stage. The troupe ›leaders‹ stand backstage outside the circle of dancers. They use microphones to render the songs, while other participants are dancing in the foreground. Such separation reinforces the authoritative roles of the singers through performance itself and seems to be another form of appropriation of sonic space, as already mentioned in the case of low caste male ›singers‹. Besides, the musical and choreographic structures change because of this new stage display. The separation of dance and singing gives rise to greater independence and complexity of both forms of expression. The judges appointed by the Yogakshema for these annual competitions explain this evolution through referring to the technical constraints of having more physical distance between people on stage and audience:

> When ten people dance together, we cannot hear their voices. That is the reason why microphones are preferred. But this is only for the stage. Traditional steps, songs, body movements and rhythm are preferred. Songs have to be preserved in pure traditional style. (Shobana, Interview 2006)

The tension created by the evolution of aesthetic codes in response to a different perception of the artistic form and the role of women in it and in response to new performance venues, on the one hand, and, on the other hand, the prescriptive rules with regard to steps, movement and music as represented in the above discourse about ›tradition‹ are at the very core of the debate about the form and content of the dance among *kaikkottukali* performers. Such debates mainly involve Brahmin women, who were pivotal in reshaping the dance and adapting it to the stage's requirements and who made it into an important medium for social change for their community, in general, and for the empowerment of Brahmin women, in particular. The keen interest of the Yogakshema in promoting *kaikkottukali* as an instrument of social change for their own Brahmin community contributed to the establishment of the dance as a caste-based art form, despite the great diversity of practices of this form in Kerala, which was practiced other by castes, too. One may note that such institutionalization did not taken place among low castes for whom the social struggle dealt less with women's conditions, but with caste inequalities (Guillebaud [2010]). As mentioned earlier, *kaikkottukali* among low castes generally is performed as a village community art form involving both genders. This might be a possible reason to explain why the same dance form is a potentially less powerful medium to contribute to the shaping of a ›feminine‹ identity within low caste communities. In comparison, Namputiris have appropriated *kaikkottukali* as ›their‹ art form, because of a better organisation of their caste and a better representation of the artistic features defining the ›femininity‹ of Brahmin ladies. Here, the contemporary history of a particular performing arts form perfectly fits with the history of local power dynamics.

3. *Performing the Nation*

The appropriation of *kaikkottukali* by the Namputiri (women) community has not been without repercussions in the wider contemporary Kerala society. When the Brahmins were reshaping the dance to suit their own requirements, the Kerala Government was building a wider cultural and political framework to promote local arts as typically ›keralite‹.

Since 1956, the date of the creation of the Kerala State, *kaikkottukali* has undergone important changes in its execution modalities and performance venues. The communist government of Kerala has promoted it as a ›national‹ repertoire, together with other forms of local music and dances.[11] This political project intends to advocate a kind of ›keralite‹ cultural unity, which transcende the hierarchical splits brought about by caste and religion. The Government was instrumental in devising a wide-ranging cultural policy, which favours the creation of new spaces for the celebration and organisation of festivals in cities, in addition to creating »Tourism Week Celebrations« in Trivandrum, the capital of Kerala. Many musical troupes from all over Kerala are invited to participate in such celebrations held on the occasion of the Onam festival[12]. They receive payments for their stage performances, which are dedicated to all citizens who are invited to »rediscover« their own »cultural heritage« (TARABOUT 2005: 199). Indeed, local music has become a privileged tool for the process of nation building. *Kaikkottukali*, which was earlier associated with ritual and domestic life, has became a public cultural event to commemorate the national history of Kerala and its recent political unity.

11 The Kerala Communist Party (KCP) was elected for the first time in 1957, one year after the creation of this new State in independent India. Marxists have ruled the region in coalition with other parties and alternately with Congress-led coalitions.

12 *Onam* (full name *Tiruvonam*) derives its name from a »constellation« (*naksatra*). The festival celebrates the mythological King Mahabali whose reign is associated with prosperity. The date of the feast is calculated according to the lunar mansions and takes place during the solar month of »Lion« (Cinnam, mid-August / mid-September). For further readings on this festival, see KURUP 1966, MARAR 1979, KUNJAN PILLAI 1981.

A dance for the younger generation

In addition to the organisation of cultural celebrations in cities, the government promotes the dissemination of Kerala's cultural heritage through performances in schools. The younger generation is invited to participate in different competitions patronised by the Education Ministry and local bodies, such as the municipal corporation, district organisations, etc. Even more so than promoting the local exponents of these art forms, such events intend to initiate a new transmission process of musical knowledge through inviting students, irrespective of their caste and religion, to learn different Kerala performing arts forms and to perform them in competitive contexts. This young generation is advertised as the main bearer of the Keralite cultural heritage with the aim is to allow a new social category, »Youth«, to emerge as the main driving force behind national culture and as a valid alternative to earlier categories defined by caste and / or religious identities.

Among school competitions, the »Kerala State Youth Festival« (renamed in 2006 *School kalotsvam* / School arts festival) is the most important. It is held once a year, every time in a different city in Kerala and receives extensive media coverage. The art forms showcased during this festival are performed exclusively on a stage. In the case of *kaikkottukali*, two main singers stand backstage, keeping the pitch with a *sruti-box* and the rhythm with small cymbals. The student troupes do not have authoritative ›leaders‹ and musical roles are attributed according to the individual abilities of the performers. Students are trained to represent the school they belong to. They perform independently of their caste origin or gender; sometimes initiating new, unexpected performance settings, for instance those featuring girls who have mastered and perform – sometimes at technically very advanced levels – instruments, which in the past were reserved exclusively for male performers and ritual performance venues.

These public performances of Kerala's national culture by schools are highly competitive. Rivalry between individual schools have motivated parents to become involved in the rehearsal processes and to spend considerable budgets on the appointment of individual tutors for their children.

The troupes do everything to attract the attention of the judges and to affirm their originality among hundreds of other groups. For example, new steps and dance postures are created, other styles of dancing are introduced, which are mainly borrowed from South Indian classical dances and mixed with the basics of *kaikkottukali*. These changes have given rise to intense debates among specialists about the correct, or the ›traditional‹, way to perform this dance. The mixing of *kaikkottukali* with elements borrowed from classical South Indian dances certainly captures the attention of the public and the judges. On the other hand, it is especially this strategy (and the inclusion of novel elements), which is most strongly criticized by local performers, in particular those who are involved in Yogakshema units. The Kerala State Youth Festival thus plays a role in renewing the dance, at a sociological as well as at an aesthetic level, too, and being open to all castes, religions and genders, links up with the basic principle on which the government has built its policy of ›preserving‹ music. »Modification and innovation in order to preserve« could be the motto of this national event. When considered as a way of preserving Kerala's national heritage, this type of competition revolves around the evaluation of performances, not in term of ›authenticity‹, but according to their potential degree of transformation. This innovation process not only sustains the dance, but also legitimises the process by roping in the participation of new ›institutional‹ repositories of musical authority, such as established artists and professors, members of the principal government institutions involved in the arts, such as the Sangeet Natak Akademi or the Kalamandalam Kerala State Academy of Fine Arts.

Finally, I would like to mention the rising interest from video companies in recording *kaikkottukali* performances as releasing them as commercial videos. Recently, the first video CD of *kaikkottukali* performed at the Youth Festival held in Calicut in 2005 was released in two volumes [see ILLUSTRATION 1]. It consists of a selection of the best groups of dancers chosen according to technical criteria, such as the complexity of choreographic sequences and their variety.[13] Such video CDs are purchased by many students who use them as a support for their training and as sources to copy new ideas from which they then use in their own performances.

An extract of such a recording shows a troupe of young ladies performing *kaikkottukali* during the »8th Kerala State Higher Secondary Youth Festival« [see FILM CLIP 4]. It clearly shows the attention paid by the performers to the dance movements. Most probably, the singing was pre-recorded so as to perfectly coincide with the performance's duration.[14] The choreographic sequences are particularly complex. The dancers move in different rhythms and in various directions both to the back and the front of the public. The bending of the legs and waists are emphasized (to the ground level) and the arm movements have been particularly extended. Every choreographic part is directed with a single unique aim in mind: to focus the public's (and the judge's) attention on the complexity of the movements. Performances such as this one provide a new definition of *kaikkottukali* as a purely visual display.

As compared to *kaikkottukali* performed in different domestic contexts, which I have described earlier, the ›competitive‹ style of *kaikkottukali* has undergone important aesthetic changes and elaborations. In addition, the traditional forms of sociability that used to be actualised through the dance performance

13 These videos are anonymous. The names of performers or troupes are not mentioned.

14 Because of the increasing number of participants, the Youth Festival Organisation Committee has recently adopted new rules for the duration of performances. The shortening of the performances to few minutes has generated new aesthetical changes, such as the replacement of background singers with pre-recorded music. The choreographies, which now have become the core of the performance, are subject to new developments and innovations.

and that emphasized Brahmin femininity and / or the cohesion of a low caste village community have been reshaped to fit a new ›national‹ framework, which organises the social relations of individuals and groups in a different way. While earlier musical knowledge was divided on the basis of hierarchical criteria, such as caste, age and gender, the cultural policy of the Kerala government promotes a national unity based on a ›common‹, shared musical heritage, irrespective of caste and / or religion and represented by the Keralite youth. Aesthetically speaking, the paradigm offered by the Government of Kerala seems to favour – consciously or unconsciously – a mainly ›classical‹ model, which commands a higher status and authority.

4. *Performers' self reflexivity of their own performances and musical knowledge*

The emergence of new performance contexts and principles of aesthetic codification have resulted in novel representations of the musical and choreographic culture, in particular of also by the high castes *kaikkottukali* performers themselves. These representations involve complex claims with regard to the musical authority of *kaikkottukali*. Nowadays many singers advertise their knowledge of the genre in order to valorise their own caste, and their own (high caste) femininity. The publication of several works about *kaikkottukali*, consisting of compilations of songs and / or directions for the dance in Malayalam, the local language, shows how high caste women performers reaffirm their leadership and their status as the ›authentic‹ bearers of *kaikkottukali* and *kaikkottukali* aesthetics.

These printed books represent an extensive corpus of knowledge, which is indicative of the self-reflexivity of these high caste performers and their individual response to the demands of contemporary reforms, including novel performance venues and public stage arrangements. The authors introduce themselves not only as ›performers‹, but also as ›experts‹ in song and dance. In addition, these publications reveal that Brahmin exponents and exponents of other high castes, in particular Nayars, are engaged in processes of distinction of their respective practices of *kaikkottukali* and the cultural context in which they perceive it to be embedded from each other in order and from other low caste forms in order to ›prove‹ the legitimacy of their caste claims to musical authority and ownership of the form.

For instance, a book published in 2003 by Cheruvakara Parvathi Antharjanam with the title »Traditions of Brahmin Ladies« (*antarjanannalute acaranusthanannal*) [see ILLUSTRATION 2 and 3], features song texts and sketches of *kaikkottukali*, in addition to the main culinary preparations and domestic rituals associated with Brahmin family festivals. Such a process of safeguarding and valorising ›traditional‹ material is mainly carried out by women with a high social status, such as NAYAR 2004 and WARRIER 1999 [see ILLUSTRATIONS 4–7]. Yet, the perception of Namputiri Brahmin women of the publications by »Nayar« and »Warrier« women of slightly lower (caste) status remains negative. They reveal a strong caste competition within the public sphere with regard to their respective claims to being the (only) ›legitimate‹ representatives of *kaikkottukali* in whom the authority and knowledge about the art form are vested.

As far as the low caste performers, such as the Ilava (Toddy tappers) and Mannan (Washermen) are concerned, such self-reflexivity takes the form of writing down the song texts in small notebooks. The notebooks are used as memory aids when learning the song texts and as a way of transmitting them to other members of a family or a village. The comparatively lower economic status of these performers considerably limits any attempt at a wider dissemination of these notebooks. As a matter of fact, they are never published and if they would had been, they would have a lesser status in terms of musical authority. However, these low caste performers, too, lay claim to the originality of their performances, in particular when compared to the performances and dance style used by high caste women and students in school festivals. Low caste performers tend to qualify such performances as an ›imitation of Bharatanatyam‹, the South Indian classical dance. Most probably, the argument of ›greater originality‹ enables them to counteract the negative appreciation, which their performances and these notebooks have in the eyes of high caste performers and the implicit denigration by the government establishment. As mentioned earlier, the contemporary validation of *kaikkottukali* involves a highly complex intertwinement between social status, the possession and authority of the musical knowledge, authenticity or originality as possessed by the exponents of specific high caste and lower caste groups.

With specific reference to the women performers, we may conclude that they have tended to use their cultural forms in order to renegotiate and to raise their status in the local society. Depending on their caste, they have been trying to strengthen their authoritative position in the context of nation building and as a response to the powerful impetus of an ›egalitarian‹ governmental cultural policy. However, the social power exercised by Brahmin women seems to have emerged as the dominant form in terms of aesthetic codification. This process appears to have been helped by the promotion and dissemination of their performances through privately produced commercial recordings.

Through the publication of printed books, and, more recently, through the release of musical albums [see ILLUSTRATIONS 8–11] and dance videos [see ILLUSTRATION 12], they have been able to reach wider audiences and publicize ›their‹ point of view of what *kaikkottukali* should be – its form, contents and the specific cultural values associated with its performance. It shows their very easy integration of print and image technologies in the way to diffuse their knowledge today. The videos CD's feature performances by ›troupes‹, which have been recently constituted on the basis of friendship relations or neighbour-

hood connections, which, I spite of the governments promotion of equality, generally remain caste-based.
An extract of a video CD, released in 2006 [see FILM CLIP 5], shows a *kaikkottukali* dance recorded at the gate of a Brahmin family property (*illam*). The place is decorated sumptuously and the location is explicitly mentioned with the name of the performers. Two troupes, »under the direction of Kannipayoor Sreelatha and Narayanan Namboothiripad in collaboration with the *Kaikkottukali* Art Association (*Kala Kendra*) of Tripunithura, jointly present the traditional dance of Kerala«. Their purpose is to introduce the public to a ›traditional‹ art form. The performance is embedded in a colourful frame added at the time of editing: different food items (bananas, coconut, betel leafs etc.) are displayed on a green background next to small photos representing miniatures of dancers performing Mohiniyattam, the classical dance of Kerala. Such editing intends to display *kaikkottukali* as a typically ›keralite art form‹, which is explicitly connected with domestic everyday life. It emphasizes the ritual content of the ›traditional‹ performance, in addition to its ›auspicious character‹ and ›prosperity‹ – bananas, coconuts and betel leafs are also items offered during domestic rituals, while associating the dance to the other respectable art form, as Mohiniyattam, the Kerala classical dance. The main singers stand backstage and use microphones, while the dancers move in the front part of the stage. In contrast to performances previously described, this troupe is accompanied by two instruments: the hour-glass drum *itakka* – usually used in Kerala temples music – and a barrel drum or *mridangam*, used mainly in the classical music of South India. These additions are significant: while they enrich the music and its rhythmic organisation and timbre, they also mark the performance as a classical and a ritual one. The public is invited to discover a very ›ancient‹ tradition displayed together with other respected art forms and carried out by local celebrities. Such *kaikkottukali* video releases are dedicated to a new audience mainly consisting of members of the urban middle class, and, more recently, of upper caste migrants settled in the Gulf countries. These video albums claim to offer ›authentic‹ musical pieces of *kaikkottukali*, a ›fact‹ usually indicated on the video jackets, and have found a wide reception among the Kerala diaspora in search of their cultural roots.

Conclusions

An investigation of the *kaikkottukali* dance reveals the complexity of the relationships between musical performances, the (re)constitution of aesthetic knowledge and the (changing) ownership of musical authority in relation to changing social and political power dynamics in Kerala society. In this article, I have examined the ways in which the performance of *kaikkottukali* by different groups, in particular the lower caste toddy tappers and washermen and the women of the high caste Brahmin, and to some extend Nayar communities, have resulted in different kinds of aesthetic change. These changes have been validated and used differently by representatives of these communities as well as by the Kerala government, fostering the differences in cultural interests that came to the fore simultaneously.

The exploration of musical and choreographic codes, which I have attempted here, shows a process of crystallisation where the conflicting values of a caste-based society that organized musical knowledge in hierarchical terms and the cultural policy of a communist government, which aimed to diffuse egalitarian values were accommodated and reformulated to provide Kerala as a newly created State with its own ›traditional‹ cultural identity. While the high caste Brahmin women, aided by social reforms within their own caste favouring women, were able to reaffirm their (caste) identity and superiority in and through their performances of *kaikkottukali*, this appears not to have been the case for women exponents belonging to the lower castes.

REFERENCES AND BIBLIOGRAPHY

ANANTHAKRISHNA IYER, L. K. 1981 [1912]. *The Cochin Tribes and Castes.* 2 Vol. New-Delhi: Cosmo Publications.

ANTHARJANAM, CHERUVAKARA PARVATHI. 2003. *Antarjananannalute acaranusthannal.* Vadanamkurussi: published by the author.

BABIRACKI, CAROL. 1991. »Tribal Music in the Study of Great and Little Traditions of Indian Music«. In: *Comparative Musicology and Anthropology of Music: Essays on the History of Ethnomusicology.* Ed. by B. Nettl and P. V. Bohlman. Chicago: The University of Chicago Press, 69–90.

----. 1997. »What's the Difference? Reflections on Gender and Research in Village India«. In: *Shadows in the Field. New Perspectives for Fieldwork in Ethnomusicology.* Ed. by G. F. Barz and T. J. Cooley. New York: Oxford University Press, 121–136.

BHATTATIRIPAD, V. T. 1990. *V. T. Bhattatirippayute kathakal.* Trichur: Kerala Sahitya Academy.

CHERIAN, P. J. 1999. *Perspectives of Kerala History. The IInd Millenium.* Kerala State Gazetteer Vol. II, Part II: Government of Kerala.

GUILLEBAUD, CHRISTINE. 2004. »Musique et société en Asie du Sud«. *L'Homme* 171–172: 499–512.

----. 2005. »Le croisement des musiques classiques et populaires. L'exemple de la catégorisation au Kerala (Inde du Sud)«. In: *Musiques. Une Encyclopédie pour le XXIe siècle. Vol. III: Musiques et cultures.* Ed. by J.-J. Nattiez. Paris: Actes Sud, 672–699.

----. 2008. *Le chant des serpents. Musiciens itinérants du Kerala.* Paris: CNRS Editions (Collection »Monde Indien«). [+ 1 DVD-Rom]

----. 2010 [forthcoming]. »Music and Politics in Kerala: Hindu Nationalists versus Marxists«. In: *The Cultural Entrenchment of Hindutva.* Ed. by D. Berti, N. Jaoul and P. Kanungo. Routledge, 23 p.

HERNDON, MARCIA; SUSANNE ZIEGLER. 1990. *Music, Gender and Culture.* ICTM Study Group on Music and Gender. Berlin: International Institute for Comparative

Music Studies and Documentation / Wihelmshaven: Florian Noetzel Verlag (Intercultural Music Studies, 1).
KOSKOFF, ELLEN. 1987. *Women and Music in Cross-Cultural Perspective.* Urbana: University of Illinois Press.
KOTHARI, KOMAL. 1972. *Monograph on Langas: A Folk Musician Caste of Rajasthan.* Borunda, Jodhpur: Rajasthan Institute of Folklore.
----. 1973. »The Langas. A Folk-Musician Caste of Rajasthan«. *Sangeet Natak* 27: 5–26.
----. 1990. »Patronage and Performance«. In: *Folk, Faith and Feudalism.* Ed. by N.K.Singh and R.Joshi. Jaipur (Institute of Rajasthan Studies), New Delhi: Rawat Publications, 55–66.
KUNJAN PILLAI, S. 1981. »Onam. Kerala's festival of Peace and Prosperity«. *Malayalam Literary Survey* 5, 3–4: 3–6.
KURUP, A.M. 1966. »Onam. A Festival of Kerala«. In: *Census 1961.* Vol. I: Monograph Series, Part VII, B2. New Delhi.
MARAR, T.R.K. 1979. »Onam. The National Festival of Kerala«. *Malayalam Literary Survey* 3, 3: 2–10.
MENON, A. SREEDHARA. 1979. *Social and Cultural History of Kerala.* New Delhi, Bangalore: Sterling Publishers.
MENON, SRIDEVI. 1993. »Strikalute natotikkalakal«. *Samskarakeralam* (April-June): 57–67.
NAMBOODIRIPAD, E.M.S. 1984. *Kerala Society and Politics.* Delhi: National Book Centre.
NAYAR, DRAUPADI G. 2004. *Tiruvatirayum strikalute mattu vratanusthanannalum.* Kottayam: Current Books.
OMANA, K.N. 2000. »Tiruvatirakali«. *Kodungallur kunjunni tampuran smaraka nritta natya sastra silpasala* 12–14: 67–74.
PARAMESVARAN NAIR, P.K. 1967. History of Malayalam Literature. Madras: Sahitya Akademi.
QURESHI, REGULA. 1991. »Whose Music? Sources and Contexts in Indic Musicology«. In: *Comparative Musicology and Anthropology of Music: Essays on the History of Ethnomusicology.* Ed. by B.Nettl and P.Bohlman. Chicago: The University of Chicago Press, 152–168.
----. 1995. »Recorded Sound and Religious Music: The Case of Qawwali«. In: *Media and the Transformation of Religion in South Asia.* Ed. by L.Babb and S.Wadley. Philadelphia: University of Pennsylvannia Press, 139–166.
----. 2000. »Confronting the Social: Mode of Production and the Sublime for (Indian) Art Music«. *Ethnomusicology* 44, 1: 15–38.
RAHEJA, GLORIA G. 2003. *Songs, Stories, Lives. Gendered Dialogues and Cultural Critique.* New Delhi: Kali for Women.
SEIZER, SUSAN. 2005. *Stigmas of the Tamil Stage. An Ethnography of Special Drama Artists in South India.* London, Durham: Duke University Press.
SHEEBA, K.M. 2001. »Contextualising Sexuality: Antarjanams in the 20th century, Nambudiri caste order of Keralam«. In: *Proceedings of the India History Congress. Millenium 61th Session (Kolkata 2000–2001).* Ed. by R.Chaterjee. Kolkata: Indian History Congress, 930–938.
TARABOUT, GILLES. 1993. »Corps social, corps humains, corps des dieux. A propos d'une caste de musiciens en Inde du Sud«. In: *Jeux d'identités. Etudes comparatives à partir de la Caraibe.* Ed. by M.J.Jolivet and D.Rey-Hulman. Paris: L'Harmattan, 235–258.

----. 2003. »Passage à l'art. L'adaptation d'un culte sud-indien au patronage artistique«. In: *L'esthétique. Europe, Chine et ailleurs*. Ed. by Y. Escande and J.-M. Schaeffer. Paris: You-Feng, 37–60.

----. 2005. »Malabar Gods, Nation-Building and World Culture on Perceptions of the Local and the Global«. In: *Globalizing India. Perspectives from Below*. Ed. by J. Assayag and C. J. Fuller. London: Anthem Press, 185–209.

THURSTON, E.; K. RANGACHARI. 1965 [1909]. *Castes and Tribes of Southern India*. 7 Vol. New York: Johnsons Reprint Corporation.

TINGEY, CAROL. 1994. *Auspicious Music in a Changing Society. The Damai Musicians of Nepal*. London: SOAS (Musicology Series, 2).

VASANTHA, KUMARI. 2000. »The Madras Nambudiri Act (XXI of 1933). A Study of the Nambudiri Customs of Malabar in the Light of the Judicial Findings Antecedent to the Act«. In: *Proceedings of the India History Congress. Diamond Jubilee 60th Session (Calicut 1999)*. Aligarh: Indian History Congress, 752–764.

VELAYUDHAN, MEERA. 1994. »Changing Roles and Women Narratives«. *Social Scientist* 22, 1-2: 64-79.

VENU, G. (1990). *Puppetry and Lesser Know Dance Traditions of Kerala*. Irinjalakuda: Natana Kairali.

----; NIRMALA PANIKER. 1995 [1983]. *Mohiniyattam. The Lasya Dance*. Irinjalakuda: Natana Kairali.

WARRIER, SRIDEVI. 1999. *Tiruvatira Nrttapathanam*. Trivandrum: published by the author.

DISCS:

2003. *Avani. Tiruvatirappattukal*. Sung by Chitra. 1 CD Malayala Manorama Music. Cochin.

2004. *Atiratinkal. Tiruvatirappattukal*. Sung by Urmila Unni. 1 CD Ragasudha Music. Cochin.

2004. *Tiruvatirappattukal*. Dance Master: P. S. Sahadevan. 1 CD Wilson Audios. Ernakulam.

2004. *Avanitinkal. Tiruvatirappattukal*. Sung by Varija Menon. 1 CD Bayshore Records. Chennai.

FILMS:

2005. *8th Kerala State Higher Secondary Youth Festival. Tiruvatira vol. 1*. 1 VCD M.C. Videos. Irinjalakuda.

2005. *8th Kerala State Higher Secondary Youth Festival. Tiruvatira vol. 2*. 1 VCD M.C. Videos. Irinjalakuda.

2006. *Tiruvatira. Tiruvatirakalippattukkal*. Sung by Thripunithura Tiruvathira Kala Kendra, Kannipayoor Sreelatha and Narayanan Namboothiripad. 1 VCD Metro Vision. Ernakulam.

FILMOGRAPHY

The film clips are published online: *http://www.indologie.uni-wuerzburg.de/women_performers/contributors/guillebaud/film_clips/*.

FILM CLIP 1: Kaikkottukali Performance in the Courtyard of a Brahmin House, Irinjalakuda (2004). 3:50. Image: Christine Guillebaud, CNRS.

FILM CLIP 2: Kaikkottukali Performance in a Village of Toddy-Tappers and Washermen, Kadavaloor (2004). 3:53. Image: Christine Guillebaud, CNRS.
FILM CLIP 3: Mixed Performance of Kaikkottukali in a Village of Toddy-Tappers and Washermen, Kadavaloor (2004). 2:23. Image: Christine Guillebaud, CNRS.
FILM CLIP 4: Commercial Video CD of a Youth Festival (extract 10:00): 8th Kerala State Higher Secondary Youth Festival. Tiruvatira. Vol. 2.1. VCD M.C. Videos: Irinjalakuda (2005).
FILM CLIP 5: Video CD of Kaikkottukali (extract 1:10): Tiruvatira. Tiruvatirakalippattukkal. Sung by Thripunithura Tiruvathira Kala Kendra, Kannipayoor Sreelatha and Narayanan Namboothiripad. 1 VCD Metro Vision: Ernakulam (2006).

ILLUSTRATIONS

The illustrations are published online: *http://www.indologie.uni-wuerzburg.de/women_performers/contributors/guillebaud/illustrations/*.

ILLUSTRATION 1: Commercial Video CD. 8th Kerala State Higher Secondary Youth Festival. Tiruvatira. Vol. 2.1. VCD M.C. Videos: Irinjalakuda (2005).
ILLUSTRATION 2: Traditions of Brahmin Ladies. By Cheruvakara Parvathi Antharjanam (2003). Book Front cover.
ILLUSTRATION 3: Traditions of Brahmin Ladies. By Cheruvakara Parvathi Antharjanam (2003). Book Back cover.
ILLUSTRATION 4: Tiruvatira and Other Feminine Ritual Arts. By G. Draupadi Nayar (2004). Book Front cover.
ILLUSTRATION 5: Tiruvatira and Other Feminine Ritual Arts. By G. Draupadi Nayar (2004). Book Back cover.
ILLUSTRATION 6: Tiruvatira. Studies on dance. By Sridevi Warrier (1999). Book Front cover.
ILLUSTRATION 7: Tiruvatira. Studies on dance. By Sridevi Warrier (1999). Book Back cover.
ILLUSTRATION 8: Kaikkottukali CD Album. Atiratinkal. Tiruvatirappattukal. Sung by Urmila Unni. 1 CD Ragasudha Music. Cochin (2004).
ILLUSTRATION 9: Kaikkottukali CD Album. Avani. Tiruvatirappattukal. Sung by Chitra. 1 CD Malayala Manorama Music. Cochin (2003).
ILLUSTRATION 10: Kaikkottukali CD Album. Avanitinkal. Tiruvatirappattukal. Sung by Varija Menon. 1 CD Bayshore Records. Chennai (2004).
ILLUSTRATION 11: Kaikkottukali CD Album. Tiruvatirappattukal. Dance Master: P.S. Sahadevan. 1 CD Wilson Audios. Ernakulam (2004).
ILLUSTRATION 12: Video CD of Kaikkottukali. Tiruvatira. Tiruvatirakalippattukkal. Sung by Thripunithura Tiruvathira Kala Kendra, Kannipayoor Sreelatha and Narayanan Namboothiripad. 1 VCD Metro Vision: Ernakulam (2006).

Poetic-Painful Lives of Women Performers Vis-à-Vis High-Caste Moral Modernity

as Remembered by Kamalabai Gokhale, and Retold by Brigitte Schulze

Brigitte Schulze

Prologue

Actress Kamala Gokhale[1] was a human being who, against all odds, was strong enough to safeguard her individual human dignity as a woman performer on the stage and the silver screen in then colonial Bombay and Maharashtra. One of the most beautiful tributes to Kamala Gokhale surely is Reena Mohan's film *Kamalabai* (1991). My original idea for this book about women performers in India was to write an essay about how filmmaker Mohan[2] captured the self-assertive and forthright woman Kamalabai. At the age of ninety-five, Kamalabai received me at her tiny Pune apartment, listened and spoke to me when I conducted my research on the silent cinema and theatre in Pune (SCHULZE 1995a). Mohan has given us an extremely honest and intense film. For different reasons it was not possible to carry out this plan.

Instead, through this unconventional medium of a »photo-essay«[3] I wish to reflect on Kamalabai's life and invoke in the reader something that I learnt from ›Dadasaheb‹ Phalke's idea of the beauty and truthfulness of the art of the mute film (SCHULZE 2003): to appeal to our eyes with pictures; to create a vision of the true beauty of Kamalabai who enacted the poetics of humanness and who

1 See ILLUSTRATION 1–4.

2 Reena Mohan had completed her film studies at the Film and Television Institute of India (FTII) and left Pune before I started my research on the sociology of Indian silent cinema there and the National Film Archive of India (NFAI). We did not meet then. After 1995, when I got in touch with Mohan, she was kind enough to provide me with very interesting material from the research she had conducted for her documentary film. Several of the photographs showing Kamalabai during performances and in her private life, which are documented in this essay, I owe to Mohan's kindly shared research work. However, Mohan could not reconstruct the exact date and context in which most of the photographs had been taken, neither could I.

3 The photographs can be accessed online: *http://www.indologie.uni-wuerzburg.de/women_performers/contributors/schulze/illustrations/*.

endured the pains inflicted by the socio-political circumstances under which she lived and worked. However, she never remained silent but was quite outspoken about the injustices of the modern entertainment industry and its use of theatrical performances as a political instrument. Kamalabai, with her trained and strong voice and her lean and tall stature, defied any of the accepted role models of female modesty and silent suffering.

When the journalist Vaijayanti S. Tonpe asked Kamala Gokhale: »And wouldn't people of today like to know what it was like to be the first Indian cine actress. What it was like to work with Dadasaheb Phalke?«, she replied with her bluntly ironic realism exposing the hypocrisies of the media and the state:

> Why do they want to know? [...] Does the Sarkar [the state government, respectively those who decide about the cultural policy and the politics of culture] care if I'm dead or alive [able to earn my daily bread]? You say that I am the first Indian cinema actress [Gokhale played the female lead in Dhundiraj Govind Phalke's second long film of 1914, see below] that is true. You say I worked with Dadasaheb Phalke, that too is true, but of what use is that to me today? They [the state] have a prestigious award [the »Dadasaheb Phalke Award« established in 1970] in the name of my guru [Phalke who remained unrecognised as the remarkable humanist cine-artist that he was, died in poverty in 1944, cp. SCHULZE 2003]. Everyone reveres him as the father of the film industry. And no one has even bothered to find out if any of his associates are alive still, leave alone give us an award, all of us who contributed to making his visions come true in the days of the film industry's infancy. How many people know that Dadasaheb's daughter [Mandakini, who played Shri Krishna in Phalke's films of the late 1910s] is still living in Nasik? And, they [the state, respectively the appointed committee] are giving the award to people like Ashok Kumar and Lata Mangeshkar who are very competent people and deserve every praise in their sphere of work, but they don't even know if Dadasaheb was dark or fair. (TONPE 1991: 65)

The poetics in the life of Kamalabai were a concrete creative act directly linked to her individuality. They were an outcome of her disciplined learning and training – an expression of her maturing humanness. In contrast, her pains as a woman performer – and this is what I am trying to highlight in this tribute to Kamalabai – resulted from the wider socio-political context into which she was born as a pauper, and which she, therefore, could not escape. The capitalist nature of the emerging public spheres of the performing and cinematic arts as a mass media market had a far-reaching impact on its workforce and its consumers. Two dimensions stand out here: 1. Commercial theatre and cinema (as well as other art forms) had to compete with each other in order to be attractive to the spectators-consumers; all artists were wageworkers whose well being depended on the spectators' willingness and ability to pay for their performances; 2. The growing importance of theatre and cinema as mass media made them attractive instruments for certain influential groups in society to popularise their interests and ideologies.

Consequently, the Marathi theatre in Bombay / Maharashtra – as much as the Bengali theatre in Calcutta / Bengal – was an arena for the contestation of nationalist politics of identity, and of the respective morality that went with these political ideologies. Despite their local and historical differences, the characteristic shared by the different representations of a »suitable« Indian, Marathi or Bengali identity was the projection of the idea of »respectable [Indian] womanhood« (KUMAR 1993: 32–73).

Act 1
Kamalabai: a working woman torn between the public and the private, struggling to perform humanness instead of casteist Indianness

Kamala Gokhale was born around 1900 (SCHULZE 1995a). She was the first child of Durgabai Kamat, who, from the moment she became a mother, had to earn a living by singing, making music, and acting on the stage. Kamala's father failed throughout his life to even partly sustain his wife and their four children.

Little Kamala first appeared on stage when she was four or five years old. At thirteen she was cast as Mohini, the celestial temptress, in Dhundiraj Govind Phalke's second long narrative film *Bhasmasur Mohini* (1913–14), in which Kamalabai's mother played the goddess Parvati. Soon afterwards Kamalabai was married and became the second wife of Raghunathrao Gokhale, the younger brother of the owner of a Marathi theatre company.

Wife and husband, both working as actors, lived and worked together in harmony. Towards the end of the 1920s, Raghunathrao Gokhale suffered a stroke when he was about to enter the stage. Kamalabai remembered having taken over and enacted her husband's male role on that fateful evening as »the show must go on« (BAHADUR, VARANASE 1980: 23–24). Shortly thereafter Raghunathrao Gokhale breathed his last.

As part of her theatrical practice, Kamalabai used to act male and female parts.[4] However, this did not mean that she, as a woman and an artist, could express herself freely, nor that she could ignore the social and economic pressures under which she had to work.

Contemporary emancipatory social movements and theatre

After 1913, the politics of social emancipation in Maharashtra gained momentum in three different phases (1913 until 1920, 1920 until 1937–39, after 1939), which were quite heterogeneous in nature. The assertive, male working classes of Bombay, which retained strong rural links, saw the Indian high castes and classes rather than the British colonial power as their main tormentor. Conse-

4 See ILLUSTRATION 5: Kamalabai playing a male role in K.N. Asnodkar's *Durangi Dunya*, 1924.

quently, the Non-Brahmin Movement's struggle for emancipation was directed against these high castes and classes. This struggle was reflected in the different agit prop theatres or *Satyashodak Samaj Tamashas* and, at a later moment in time, in the Textile Workers' theatre. All these theatre forms drew on rural folk traditions, which had their origin in the last decades of the 19th century, but each of which developed its own particular contents and styles (OMVEDT 1976; JADHAV 1989; CHANDAVARKAR 1994; SCHULZE 2003: 109–252).

In contrast to Bombay, Pune was a stronghold of Chitpavan Brahmins. Under the charismatic leadership of Bal Gangadhar Tilak they turned modern Marathi literature, the press and theatre into integral elements of their mass agitations (CASHMAN 1975). In the mid 1910s famous dramatists, like Krishnaji Prabhakar Khadilkar and Krishnaji Hari Dixit, made the Marathi theatre into a mouthpiece of Tilak's propaganda for »self-rule« and *swadeshi*. Through this propaganda two major adversaries were addressed: the Non-Brahmin Movement and the lower classes with their democratic humanism, on the one hand, and, on the other hand, the colonial British rulers and their racist ideologies terming Indians »immature« and, therefore, unfit for self rule.

Of a very different nature were the social struggles and the cultural politics played out in the rural areas of the Deccan, in particular its southernmost regions, such as Satara. Here the majority of peasants lived under depressing feudal conditions and had to endure the often wilful cruelty of high-caste landowners and money lenders. Interestingly, the agit prop *tamasha* of the Non-Brahmin Movement founded by Jyotirao Phule and sustained by low caste urban and rural leaders played a major role in instigating the rebellions of oppressed peasants (OMVEDT 1976; SCHULZE 2003).

The complex situation outlined above provided the larger political and ideological back drop for the modern urban-based Marathi Theatre, which Tilak transformed into a platform for his identity politics (TILAK 1922 [1918]). While these politics unveiled British colonial racism, they also opposed the democratic workers' struggles and the Non-Brahmin Movement (SCHULZE 2003: 171, 184–252) – a fact that is mostly overlooked.

Ambedkar's contemporary critique of caste and (high-)caste morality

B. Ambedkar, who followed in the footsteps of Jyotirao Phule, was one of Tilak's most radical and uncompromising critics. In his essay *Annihilation of Caste* (1936), Ambedkar unmasked India's casteist politics and demanded to oppose the Brahmin-defined caste hierarchy that kept in tact a system of purity and pollution. Ambedkar convincingly argued that the caste system and its social impact was profoundly inhuman and undemocratic destroying any possibility for a creative collaboration and communication between women, men and children in India.

Free spirited, humanist artists, like Kamalabai and Dadasaheb Phalke, had to endure both the effects of poverty linked to class and the social stagnation and ethical poverty produced by a debilitating caste ideology:[5]

> There was no special treatment for anyone in Phalke's unit. The rules were the same for all members. Everyone lived and ate together, and the expenses were borne by the company [...]. Yet, there was a five-fold difference in payments: the maximum was Rs. 50 per month and the lowest Rs. 10 per month. When the film [we worked for] was finished, Phalke took us to Bombay for the first showing at Coronation Theatre. After that I left the company. [...] Phalke was in difficulties. He had an intense, ambitious vision, and he had gone abroad [England] to learn film making and pursue his dream. When he returned, the Nasik Brahmins insisted on his performing prayaschita, since Phalke [a Brahmin] had crossed the seas. Otherwise he would have been ostracised. Moreover, Phalke was a very honest person, meticulous with accounts, but his financiers [Maharashtrian industrialists] were dishonest and they ditched him. Phalke was deep in financial troubles when I left, but he treated me with great affection and gifted me eight tolas of gold, two thousand rupees in cash and four sarees. Moreover, I was itching to get back to the theatre – acting and singing. You see, it gets into your system – into your guts. (Kamalabai as quoted by BAHADUR, VANARASE 1980: 24)

Kamalabai was from a higher caste background. However, because of her poverty and widowhood she could not fulfil the socially accepted role model of confinement to the private sphere as would have been appropriate for women of her caste. She was forced to work in modern commercial theatre companies where she was exposed to the forces unleashed by different social agents involved in the contestation of political, economic, moral and cultural power. Earlier theatre forms in Maharashtra, in particular the rural based and widely non-monetary *tamasha* folk theatre with its humorous bards and expressive dance and mime, could sustain their artists only as long as the peasant and rural environments were intact. With the disintegration of the complex village economy and as a result of the migration of peasants to factories in the cities, the *tamasha* groups, too, were pushed into the urban cosmos of work for wages.[6]

By the 1920s, the forced adjustment of such groups to the new urban commercial entertainment industries had resulted in a vulgarisation of the original *tamasha* (ABRAMS 1974; GARGI 1991; SCHULZE 1995b). Therefore, Kamalabai, and other women performers like her, shared the same fate as other poor women of having to cope with the existing powers shaped by the economics and morals of a competitive society.

5 See ILLUSTRATION 6: Kamalabai as Surma in *Nama Nirala* in the 1930s and ILLUSTRATION 7: Phalke checking a film strip in his Nasik studio; a still from Phalke's instructive film titled *How Films Are Made* (1917) of which only fragments survive and are kept at the NFAI, Pune.

6 See BANERJEE 1989 for the analysis of respective developments in Bengal.

Act 2
The Kamalabai persona: torn between gender constructions of Indian male- and femaleness[7]

Adarkar's »In Search of Women in History of Marathi Theatre, 1843 to 1933« provides a resume of the image which society had of a woman in the world of theatre in those days (ADARKAR 1991). This idea oscillated between the actress defined as a prostitute – by definition without any morals – and a *neetiman* / ›moral‹ woman. Those who thought that women were necessary for the ›art of theatre‹, but who did not want *kulin* (upper-caste) women to lose their morality, ›consented‹ reluctantly to letting prostitutes enter the stage on the condition that they were ›*neetiman*‹: »fitting the moral standards of society. If not, there was the risk that these same prostitutes would spoil the morality of the men in the theatre companies.« (ADARKAR 1991: WS-89)

ADARKAR 1991 identifies two distinct phases with regard to the entrance of women on the public stage: the first phase is from 1915 to 1925 and the second from 1925 to 1933.

Referring to the first phase, which he calls the »latter half of the ›golden era‹ of theatre«, he says that the enactment of female roles by males was appreciated. However, as the result of the exposure to western literature and western thoughts and the increased visibility of educated women in society, the possibility of ›*kulin*‹ women enacting female roles in the theatre was considered for the first time. The public debate focused on whether *kulin* women should, or should not, enter the theatre and replace the male actors performing female roles. (ADARKAR 1991: WS-89)

However, there were possibilities to modify the definition of who w(c)ould count as a *kulin* woman, and who would not. And, interestingly enough, it was economic necessity, which made it possible to disconnect ›*kulin*-ness‹ from birth, and reconnect it to an upper-caste's assessment of a woman's moral behaviour: »There was a class of *devdasis* from Goa [in Maharashtra] who had concubine status. They had a high standard of artistic talents, especially in music, which the theatre trade could not afford to waste. In order to be able to be called ›*neetiman*‹, with high morals, they could be pressurised to follow a life style prescribed by the middle class patriarchy.« (ADARKAR 1991: WS-89–90)

Adarkar's work makes a particularly fascinating study, if read together with Kamalabai's experiences and memories. It aptly shows how small and politically controlled the social and ethical spaces were where women could act, in the double sense of the word: as a free individual who would search for ways of expressing her creativity and humanness in the social sphere, and as an actress who would be able to follow her inclination to professional self-expression

7 See ILLUSTRATION 16: Kamalabai in S. Khandekar's *Rankache Rajya*, 1928.

within a democratic public sphere. Nonetheless, if this kind of democratic space was aggressively and violently denied to women like Kamalabai, we researchers could, if sensitive to discovering the subjective and subaltern agency, identify traces of millions of little rebellions that went unregistered in the historiography of the nation.

Adarkar provides an example of an interesting ›female rebellion‹ against the modern Brahmin / middle class guardians of Maratha morality and their ideological desire of supremecy vis-à-vis women, low castes, Dalits and Muslims in the period from 1925 to 1933 (cp. SCHULZE 2003: 149–181).

In 1933 a periodical named *Sanjiwani* initiated a debate about women and theatre (ADARKAR 1991: WS-90). Though the discourse was dominated by men, six upper-class women argued strongly in favour of what they saw as a natural urge of any woman to express herself as a creative actress on stage. Amongst these six women there was one who spelled out her aversion against any kind of high-caste male interferences in very explicit terms. Adarkar lists some of her points:

> Women should accept and encourage free mixing of men and women to overcome inhibitions. It is a matter of our own opinion and not of the society. There are some very bold statements by Yamunabai Dravid regarding Khadilkar, the famous playwright and Balgandharva. According to her, playwrights cannot portray women characters and Khadilkar is no exception. She criticises the way in which Khadilkar, in the play Maneka, has insulted womanhood and motherhood by making Maneka run after Rishi Vishwamitra [...]. She says: ›Every woman has an urge to become a mother but certainly women are not so crazy as to run after a man. How can a male writer like Khadilkar understand this? No wonder that a male actor like Balgandharva is not ashamed to portray this Menaka.‹ She adds that Rukmini and Draupadi portrayed by Khadilkar in his famous play *Swayamwar* are similarly ›male nayikas‹ [...]. Many women thought it would be ideal if both the partners were in the field of theatre, not necessarily as husband and wife. That any art form requires total dedication therefore the women should marry only if she can select a husband who also respects and loves arts, otherwise one should remain unmarried to serve the theatre. (ADARKAR 1991: WS-90)

Some thoughts about the aggressive high-caste ›Indian femaleness‹ performed by female impersonators (males performing female roles):[8]

> In my time we faced fierce opposition particularly from actors who were playing female roles on the stage. We were their first natural enemies. They hated us. Some companies actually would not have women performers as a matter of policy. Like Bal Gandharva [...]. He wanted my husband to join his company for major male roles opposite his female roles, and when my husband accepted only on the condition that my mother and myself should also be taken in the company, Bal Gandharva refused, saying that no woman will ever appear in his stage productions. Of course, he could not hold on for very long to this policy, but that is another story. (Kamalabai as quoted by BAHADUR, VANARASE 1980: 25)

8 See ILLUSTRATION 9: Bal Gandharva in *Swayamvar*.

The construction of Indian / Marathi femininity, and in particular also of the notion of ›respectability‹, both of which were derived from a high-caste patriarchal vision of appropriate womanhood, revealed the total disregard for the position of women performers, such as Kamalabai, and the problems they faced in actual life. In how far the performance of such ›ideal womanhood‹ by female impersonators was also the result of the competition, which male performers of female roles experienced from real women performers remains a moot point.[9]

Bal Gandharva was the most famous impersonator of appropriate femaleness in the 1910s and early 1920s. B.G. Tilak admired him and referred to him as the »celestial singer«. As a member of the Gandharva Natak Mandali, Bal Gandharva celebrated his greatest triumph on the stage as Bhamini, Shakuntal or Subhadra in classics, such as *Manapman*, *Swayamvar* and *Shakuntal*, adapted by K.P. Khadilkar and A. Kirloskar to the then current Hindu nationalist politics. His portrayal of Indian womanhood was such that many high-caste / middle class modern women copied his hairstyle, body language, manners and wardrobe (Nadkarni 1988; The Marathi Theatre 1961: 23–24; Hansen 1998: 2295–2297). In this way the high-caste, patriarchal construct of ›respectability‹ and proper Indian / Maharatta / Hindu womanhood penetrated as much women's private lives, as their public life-worlds, and thus exerted a strong impact on the socio-political agency of women.[10]

During the colonial times Indian artists and audiences were controlled by the censorship of the colonial administration. Public performances were subjected to it from the mid 19th century onwards when the Indian Press Act, the Indian Performance Act, and finally the Indian Cinematograph Act were in force.

The censorship of the colonial state fostered its own ideological concepts of Indianness, which took into account the political needs of those days. Thus, the British colonial state was another powerful agent in the contestation of Indianness and appropriate Indian femaleness (cp. Mohan, Choudhuri 1996; Schulze 2002).

Act 3
Kamalabai's and Dadasaheb's enactment of passionate humanness in Phalke's films

> I worked with men keeping control on my senses. I was a widow, a young widow at 28. It was a matter of just one slip. But I had my children, my mother and a brother-

9 See illustration 10: Bal Gandharva (right) in Khadilkar's *Manapman*, date unknown.

10 See illustrations 11 and 12: *Tamasha* artists in Pune 1995, seen with social worker Sushma Deshpande who had started an initiative to rise public awareness about the economic marginalization and the prevailing ostracism of *tamasha* women performers.

> in-law, and the liabilities of debts from my husband's theatre company, which had failed. Actually I had to liquidate all my assets to meet part of the debts and I had to earn further. I had to treat the other men like ›cold stones‹ [...]. I was bent upon keeping the respect of the family. This was my one aim in life and I was working in a profession where laxity of behaviour was possible, even expected, though not sanctioned. So I traversed a narrow path, using my skills in theatre for earning my livelihood, clearing my liabilities and building a secure home for my children. All this had been tough, but anything worthwhile would be tough. [...] Theatre acting is done within norms of restraint. It is symbolic, particularly in love scenes. On the stage you can keep your distance, decide your limit and say that I would go no further than holding hands [...]. But, in a love scene in a film, you have to embrace – really embrace – the other fellow in front of the camera. Otherwise, it would make no sense. (Kamalabai as quoted by BAHADUR, VANARASE 1980: 25)

Due to her precarious status as a young widow, a mother and an actress, Kamalabai preferred to keep her physical distance, and to remain in control of the realism of her acting. Stylisation as it was the norm in the Marathi theatre provided the best fusion between her passion for acting and her fragility as a working ›public woman‹.[11]

Realistic acting in cinema: unprecedented emotional experiences of humanness

Dhundiraj Govind Phalke strongly argued against the notion that ›acting‹ was just ›acting‹, and that a stage actor would make for a good cine-actor. Phalke's holistic philosophy of cinema (SCHULZE 2003: 9–27, 254–391) made it a distinctly different ›world‹ from that of theatre. Consequently, he was opposed to the idea that stylised stage acting would be appropriate for the medium of film. In his long article series »Bharatiya Chitrapat« (*Indian Moving Pictures*, 1917–18) he wrote that he always wanted women to act the female parts in his films. It was only after a long and unsuccessful search for a woman fit for the role and willing to act under the constraints of the public morality that he chose Anna Hari Salunke, a young waiter, whom the film pioneer discovered in Bombay's red light area. »Dadasaheb« liked Salunke's effeminate beauty, his fine features, fragile stature and swift movements. To the fascination of his spectators A.H. Salunke was cast in two roles in *Lanka Dahan* (›Lanka Aflame‹, 1917): he played both Sita and Ram, and Phalke exerted all his technical skills to make the famous couple appear in the same frame.

Phalke described the essentially different natures of the cinema with its reproductive, photographic realism, and of the live theatre with its momentous and atmospheric character, where the recreation of a location or an act depended on

11 See ILLUSTRATION 13: Kamalabai and her first-born son Lalaji and ILLUSTRATION 14: King Harischandra and Queen Taramati in a last desperate embrace, still photograph from Phalke's second version of his film *Raja Harischandra* (1917).

the skill of the actor, his voice, the artistry of the props and backdrops, and the imagination of the spectator:[12]

> Cinema is a totally new phenomenon in India. There are many new suggestions, which come to me from time to time which do not evoke my curiosity at all. For instance, we are planning to use the story of Devyani for my next film. Some well-wishers suggest that it would be better if I were to take up: Vidyaharan by Khadilkar. Someone suggests the choice of Vidyasadhana by Dixit [...]. I do know that all these suggestions are made in good faith, and are due to high esteem for the original dramatic works. But the suggestion to film a play only because the play was applauded on the stage is as ridiculous as the suggestion that the speeches of Lokmanya Tilak and Annie Besant on the screen will make good films. The other day, I received an even stranger suggestion. The plays of Gandharva Company are being performed in Bombay these days. One of my well-wishers says: ›Come what may, but replace your actor playing female roles by Bal Gandharva and then it will be as effective as Devyani in Vidyaharan.‹ No one would question the good faith underlying these suggestions. But, surely it is unpardonable ignorance to prescribe a migraine pill for a stomach-upset, even if the suggestion is made in good faith. [...] We must bear in mind that the stage play is meant for our two ears while the screenplay is for our two eyes. (Phalke Centenary Celebration Committee 1970: 95)

References and Bibliography

Abrams, T. 1974. *Tamasha: People's Theatre of Maharashtra State.* Ann Arbor: UMI.

Adarkar, N. 1991. »In Search of Women in History of Marathi Theatre, 1843 to 1933«. *Economic and Political Weekly* (Oct. 26): WS-87–WS-90.

Ambedkar, B. 1936. *Annihilation of caste.* Ed. by Mulk Raj Anand. New Delhi.

Arte, S. B. 1918. »Mr. D. G. Phalke and his ›Hindusthan Cinema Films‹«. *The Modern Review for May*: 516–519.

Bahadur, S. and Sh. Vanarase. 1980. »The Personal and Professional Problems of a Woman Performer«. *Cinema Vision India. The Indian Journal of Cinematic Art* 1, 1: 22–25.

Banerjee, S. 1989. *The Parlour and the Streets. Elite and Popular Culture in Nineteenth Century Calcutta.* Calcutta: Seagull Books.

Cashman, R. I. 1975. *The Myth of the Lokamanya. Tilak and Mass Politics in Maharashtra.* Berkeley: UCP.

Chandavarkar, R. 1994. *The Origin of Industrial Capitalism in India. Business Strategies and the Working Classes in Bombay, 1900–1940.* Cambridge: CUP.

Deshpande, S. [undated, presumably around 1995]. *WHAY mi Savitribai – synopsis of a solo performance film on social reformer Savitri & Jotiba Phule.* Pune: unpublished manuscript.

Gargi, B. 1991. *Folk Theatre of India.* New York: Theatre Arts Books.

12 See illustration 15: Anna Hari Salunke as Sita in Phalke's *Lanka Dahan* 1917; illustration 17: Mandakini Phalke playing Lord Krishna in Phalke's *Kaliya Mardan* 1919; and illustration 18: Kamalabai Gokhale with her son Chandrakant to her left and grandson Vikram, both performing artists.

HANSEN, K. 1998. »Stri Bhumika: Female Impersonators and Actresses on the Parsi Stage«. *Economic and Political Weekly* (August 29): 2291–2299.
JADHAV, N.R. 1989. »Textile Worker's Theatre: A Cultural Perspective«. *Facts & News. National Centre for the Performing Arts Project: Theatre Development Centre* (»For Private Circulation Only«) 14, 4–8.
KHADILKAR, K.P. 1915. *Satwapariksha (Marathi)*. Pune: Chitrashala Press.
KUMAR, R. 1993. *The history of doing. An illustrated account of movements for women's rights and feminism in India 1800–1990*. New Delhi: Kali for Women.
KUMTAKAR, R.M. 1995. »Kamlabai Kamat, first woman artist of cinema«. *Screen* (Jan. 27): 10.
MASSELOS, J. 1984. »Spare time and recreation: changing behaviour patterns in Bombay at the turn of the nineteenth century«. *South Asia. Journal of South Asian Studies*: 34–57.
MOHAN, R. 1990. *[Undated interview with Kamalabai Gokhale]*.
----. 1991. *Kamalabai*. Documentary film.
----; D. CHOUDHURI. 1996. »Of Wayward Girls and Wicked Women. Women in Indian silent feature films (1913–1934)«. *Deep Focus* 6: 4–14.
MÜNSTERBERG, H. 1970 [1916]. *The film. A psychological study. The silent photoplay in 1916*. New York: Dover Publications.
NADKARNI, D. 1988. *Balgandharva and the Marathi Theatre*. Bombay: Roopak Books.
----. 1992. »A human document. A review of Reena Mohan's documentary on the Marathi actress, Kamalabai«. *Cinema in India* 3, 3: 16–17.
NADKARNI, M. 1988. *Bal Gandharva. The nonpareil thespian*. New Delhi: National Book Trust.
O'HANLON, R. 1985. *Caste, conflict and ideology. Mahatma Phule and low caste protest in nineteenth-century western India*. Cambridge, etc.: CUP.
OMVEDT, G. 1976. *Cultural revolt in a colonial society. The non-brahman movement in Western India: 1873 to 1930*. Bombay: Scientific Socialist Education Trust.
PHALKE CENTENARY CELEBRATION COMMITTEE (ED.). 1970. *Phalke Commemoration Souvenir*. Bombay, 87–102.
PHALKE, DH.G. 1917–18. »Bharatiya Chitrapat« (›Indian Cinema‹) I, II, III, IV, orig. Marathi. *Navyug* (Nov. / Dec. 1917; Feb. / Sept. 1918). English translation in: *The Raja Harischandra*. Film. Bombay, 1913 and Nasik, 1917.
----. 1914. *Bhasmasur Mohini*. Film. Nasik.
----. 1917a. *How Films Are Made*. Film. Nasik.
----. 1917b. *Lanka Dahan*. Film. Nasik.
----. 1919. *Kaliya Mardan*. Film. Nasik.
POPULAR BOOK DEPOT FOR MARATHI NATYA PARISHAD. 1961. *The Marathi Theatre*. Bombay: Popular Book Depot for Marathi Natya Parishad.
SCHULZE, B. 1995a. *Interview with Kamalabai Gokhale (Marathi), facilitated and translated into English by Aruna Damle, partly noted down and audio-taped by the author*. Pune: January 31.
----. 1995b. *Interview with Sushma Deshpande, social worker and artist, and Sakuntala, tamasha artist, at Lakshmi Theatre*. Pune: February 2 and 7.
----. 1995c. *Interview with Vishram Bedekar, Marathi writer, screen playwright and film director, noted down by the author*. Pune: February 1.
----. 1995d. *Photo-documentation and talk with Kshama Vaidya, homoeopathic doctor and amateur actress, about the revival of plays like Khadilkar's Manapman (Respect – Disrespect) at Pune's theatre Bharat Natya Sanshodan Mandir*. January 26.
----. 1997. *Visionen indischer Nationalkultur und eine vergessene Film-Geschichte 1912–18. Ein Beitrag zur Kinosoziologie*. 2 Vol. Vol. 1, Part 1: »›Raja Harischandra‹:

Rezeption und Aufführungskontext«. Frankfurt University, unpublished PhD dissertation.
----. 1999. »The first cinematic pauranik kathanak [by the filmpioneer Dh. G. Phalke 1912–17]«. In: *Narrative Strategies. Essays on South Asian Literature and Film*. Ed. by V. Dalmia, Th. Damsteegt. New Delhi: OUP.
----. 2002. »The cinematic ›Discovery of India‹: Mehboob's re-invention of the nation in Mother India«. *Social Scientist* 352–353: 72–87.
----. 2003. *Humanist and Emotional Beginnings of a Nationalist Indian Cinema in Bombay. With Kracauer in the Footsteps of Phalke*. Berlin: Avinus.
SUNTHANKAR, B. R. 1993. *Maharashtra 1958–1920*. Bombay: Popular Book Depot.
TAPPER, B. E. 1981. »An enactment of perfect morality: the meaning and social context of a South Indian Ritual Drama«. In: *Culture and Morality. Essays in honour of Christoph von Fürer-Haimendorf*. Ed. by A. C. Mayer. Delhi, etc.: OUP.
TILAK, B. G. 1922 [1918]. *Bal Gangadhar Tilak. His writings and speeches*. Madras: Ganesh & Co.
TONPE, V. S. 1991. »Kamalabai Gokhale. A Living Legend Speaks«. *The India magazine of her people and culture* 2, 9: 64–72.

ILLUSTRATIONS

The photographies mentioned in the text are published online: *http://www.indologie.uni-wuerzburg.de/women_performers/contributors/schulze/illustrations/*.

Acknowledgements:
ILLUSTRATIONS 1 and 2: Kamalabai Gokhale, photographed by the author, January 31, 1995.
ILLUSTRATION 3: Courtesy Reena Mohan.
ILLUSTRATION 4: Photographed by the author in the attic of the theatre house Bharat Natya Sanshodhan Mandir, Pune, February 5, 1995.
ILLUSTRATION 5: TONPE 1991: 67, from the play Durangi Duniya by Krishnajee Narayan Asnodkar.
ILLUSTRATION 6: TONPE 1991: 70, from the play Nama Nirala, Kamala Gokhale played the role of a female called Surma.
ILLUSTRATION 7: Courtesy National Film Archive of India (NFAI), Pune.
ILLUSTRATION 8: Photographed by the author.
ILLUSTRATION 9: THE MARATHI THEATRE 1961: opposite 57.
ILLUSTRATION 10: NADKARNI 1988, B. Gandharva in Khadilkar's celebrated Manapman.
ILLUSTRATIONS 11 and 12: Sushma Deshpande and *tamasha* artist Shakuntala photographed by the author in Pune 1995.
ILLUSTRATION 13: Kamalabai Gokhale and Lalaji, her first born. Courtesy Reena Mohan.
ILLUSTRATIONS 14 and 15: Courtesy NFAI, Pune.
ILLUSTRATION 16: TONPE 1991: 69, from the play Rankache Rajya by Sakharam Khandekar.
ILLUSTRATION 17: Courtesy NFAI, Pune.
ILLUSTRATION 18: TONPE 1991: 71.

Part III

Interpretation

The Good, The Bad, and The Ugly

Kathakali's Females and the Men who Play them

Marlene Pitkow

Introduction

Since the emergence of Kathakali in the late sixteenth century, a predominantly male community of patrons, composers, and artists has shaped the female characters. This essay explores how male artists have chosen to interpret the female roles through their largely exclusive enactment of them. Their impersonations articulate a male view of the female in her mythically divine and mortal forms. Furthermore, these representations reflect a uniquely Hindu-specific form of gender play in which both deities and demons transform their sexual identity at will.

Each of the three female character types in Kathakali has a direct homologue with a goddess construct or archetypal female figure in Hindu lore. Kathakali's noble heroine, designated by the category known as *minukku*, is analogous to Rama's wife, Sita, a model of goodness, chastity and inner strength. The *lalita*, who appears identical to the *minukku* in appearance, is in reality a seductress. She is a heavenly *apsara* or dancer who comes to earth to entreat men and satisfy her erotic desires. While *lalitas* make a pretense toward goodness, *karis*, or demonesses, who comprise the third category of female characters, constitute the true form of the *lalita* when undisguised. This role type is completely uncontrolled, always appearing alone, widowed or otherwise unmarried. Similar in iconography and behavior, there are strong parallels between *kari* and the goddess Bhadrakali – the destructive aspect of the goddess Kali.

Kathakali

Kathakali evolved from a variety of much older traditions, including a local form of Sanskrit drama, Kutiyattam, ritual enactments, and Kalarippayattu, a martial arts form native to this region. Literally meaning ›story-play‹, Kathakali combines a codified sign language system of the hands and face, strenuous and rhythmic movement and elaborate costumes and make-up to relate stories from the Hindu epics and Puranas. Two singers in alternation vocalize the poetic verses (or *padams*) in specific time beats, rhythms, and melodic structures while playing cymbals and gongs, supported by two percussionists playing the *maddalam*, a barrel shaped two-headed drum played with both hands, and *centa*, a cylindrical drum played with two sticks. The actor / dancers interpret the lines of verse, almost word for word, using stylized facial expressions and hand gestures. Abstract dance passages punctuate the lines and stanzas of verse.

Characters are grouped into several distinct make-up categories corresponding to the following stock character types: *minukku* (literally meaning shining and radiant) comprise the noblewomen, brahmins, and sages; *pacca*, or green, connotes heroes or those of divine or noble birth; *katti*, literally knife, stands for males of noble birth who also possess arrogant and hot-tempered natures; demons and demonesses are *chuvanna tadis* (red beards) and *karis* (black ogresses), respectively; forest dwellers and monkeys are *karutta tadis* (black beards) and *velluppu tadis* (white beards), respectively.

While women do perform the non-demonic female characters in the Sanskrit drama, Kutiyattam, and they are the exclusive participants in the regional dance style of Mohiniattam and in other important Hindu festival dances such as Tiruvatirakali and Kaikottukali, there is also a long-standing tradition in Kerala (and in India in general) in which men impersonate women in certain expressive performance genres including street processions, religious rituals, and dance-dramas like Kathakali.[1]

Historically, the ability to control women's purity had very much to do with whether or not women were free to perform in a genre. The social issues that primarily dictated their participation concerned the range of caste members allowed to both view and participate in these genres as well as the proximity of performance locale. Kutiyattam drew its performers from a closed unit of family members who came from a tightly knit cluster of upper level, ritually connected castes and there was little if any travel to other areas. In the martial arts tradition of Kalarippayattu, only girls in the ›pure‹ pre-menstrual state took part. The *kalari*, or place where Kalarippayattu was practiced, was also local.

1 Impersonation of female characters is certainly not unique to Kerala art forms nor to Indian performing arts in general. In Greek dramas, males controlled the stage; it was considered highly improper for females to participate in any public display. (See CASE 1985) In Shakespearean England, men took the female roles. The *onnagata*, female impersonator in Kabuki, is a respected and highly coveted role-type for a male player in Japan. In Western opera, there are many examples of men taking female roles. Females impersonating males also appeared to be a widespread practice in Western opera. In Mozart's *The Marriage of Figaro* and Richard Strauss' *Ariadne auf Naxos*, for example, we find the situation reversed with women playing the roles of young boys. However, it seems fair to say that impersonation of females has been much more widespread than its inverse, at least up to the eighteenth century even in the West.

By contrast, the larger Kathakali pool of actors were not at all necessarily related to each other and could have come from a much wider number of different subcastes. Another distinction concerns the fact that while Kalarippayattu and Kutiyattam practitioners performed in limited locales in a small number of nearby villages, Kathakali performers were itinerant ›troubadours‹ who performed outdoors, all night long, and at a variety of locations miles apart, and were therefore subject to much intermingling with a wide range of social classes.

The continued absence today of women in the mainstream of Kathakali is due to a number of reasons. To some extent the seventeenth century rules around ritual purity still persist, as well as an ingrained perception in Kerala society of the need to safeguard female sexual propriety. Moreover, a deeply rooted conservatism within the male leadership of Kathakali remains unchallenged to this day.[2]

However, despite their absence as actors, women are present in Kathakali as a multi-layered feminine construct, refracted across female and male characters in ways not true for men. Significantly, the *stri vesam* (actor of the female roles) does not strive to conceal his masculine identity in order to establish his virtuosity in interpreting the female roles in the manner of a Western drag performer or Japanese *onnagata*, for example. Instead, he allows space to embody and express his feminine aspect alongside the masculine. Not only does the Kathakali *stri vesam* actor take delight in the androgynous quality of his representation, but also actors of some male roles assume the feminine by mirroring her on their own bodies. I contend that this play with gender in Kathakali reflects and is sanctioned by a form of gender play that is a distinct feature of Hinduism. A closer examination of the female roles reveals which aspects of the feminine are highly revered and praised and which are feared and loathed.

The three types of female characters occupy three different points on a continuum. The noble maiden or *minukku* is a restrained character whose virtues are praised. She is beautiful to gaze upon, and behaves in a chaste and modest manner. In idealizing her, the actor confers on her a benign and divinely auspicious presence and she is rewarded for her devotion. The *lalita* character, a female demon in disguise as a maiden, enjoys a freer mode of behavior, often expressing her erotic desires. The *kari* – who is the *lalita* without her disguise – is a grotesque and vile creature exceeding all acceptable limits. She appears to the viewer as a degradation and mockery of her idealized counterpart / alter ego, the *minukku*. The *kari* represents a complete abandonment of any moral or sexual ethic and must be punished for her transgressions. Assuming her stage

2 For a fuller treatment of this subject, see PITKOW 1998: 48–105. On a collaborative Fulbright in Kerala in 1988, Diane Daugherty and I investigated and documented the existence of the all-female Kathakali troupe, the Tripunithura Kathakali Kendram Ladies Troupe. For a treatment of this troupe, which still performs to this day, see our article (DAUGHERTY, PITKOW 1991).

persona allows the actor to experience control over her treacherous and deceptive aspects.

Although the *kari* and her disguised double, the *lalita*, are flip sides of the same textual character, I treat them here as two distinct character types. This follows the established Kathakali practice of distinguishing the type of actor who plays them. More significantly, I want to foreground the male preoccupation with never being entirely sure who really lurks beneath the façade of the *minukku*.

The typology of female characters in Kathakali correlates with the wider Hindu worldview of the feminine. In numerous anthropological studies dealing with images of women and goddesses in India, scholars postulate a dualistic opposition, similar to what I have outlined above. On the one hand, there is the benign, married, high-ranking and controlled female; on the other, there is the female who is capricious, unmarried, powerful, low ranking and potentially destructive.[3]

In her examinations of the cultural construction of gender in Kerala, anthropologist Caroline Osella asserts that the category of ›woman‹ embodies an ambivalence which »refers both to general representations of womanhood and to specific male anxieties about identity and gender« (OSELLA 1993: 222). I would argue that the production of the female character types in Kathakali and their representations by men embody, articulate, and attempt to resolve these cultural and social ambiguities.

1. Minukku: Idealized Heroine

> The greater the austerity – the self-control of women, including their submission to men – the greater is their resulting power [...]. Men should control women if and when they [women] do not control themselves. But the self-controlled woman – the chaste, noble woman – will ultimately control all. (WADLEY 1980: 160)

Of Kathakali's three female role types, the *minukku* is the most emblematic of the *stri vesam* (female character or actor). Often seen in the protective company of her mate who asserts himself as a powerful stage presence, the *minukku* appears restrained and undemonstrative. While *minukku* maidens are in some ways subordinated to their male counterparts, it is their heightened sense of piety and devotion that generates their internal self-control and in so doing ensures the protection of her family.

3 See WADLEY 1980, O'FLAHERTY 1980 and KAKAR 1989.

1.1. Sita

The mythic model for the *minukku* is Sita, the iconic figure of chastity and faithfulness in Hindu lore. Sita's strict moral code, fasts, and other renunciations earn her a boon that if a man or demon were to touch her, they would burn to ashes. Thus, it is her purity and her great self-control that shields her from Ravana's advances. The Kathakali *minukku* maiden's subtle, contained, and controlled performances should be appreciated in this light. This photograph of the Kathakali hero and his heroine in classic pose typifies the traditional dynamics between the *minukku* maiden and her hero [ILLUSTRATION 1].

1.2. Mandodari

In her most pristine and idealized form, the *minukku* frequently appears in love scenes with the hero. The exceedingly slow set piece that is the centerpiece of this scene, the *patinna padam* (the *padam* in the slowest of tempos), eloquently illustrates her soft and understated attributes. The play, *Bali Vijayan (Bali's Victory)*, begins with such a romantic scene between the protagonists, in this case a *katti* or arrogant character, Ravana, and his wife, Mandodari.[4] The following is the full text of Ravana's love song:

> One with eyes comparable to lotus petals
> With face beautiful like the autumnal moon
> With beautiful gait which will remove the haughtiness
> Of a group of elephants in rut
> With teeth beautiful like jasmine buds
> My twenty arms and ten heads
> Out of eagerness to embrace and kiss you
> Among themselves I am to be the first, I am to be the first
> They are quarreling in an intense way.

Although the text is brief, the male character takes his time, allowing for the gradual unfolding of the mood of love and the erotic – *sringara*. Before interpreting the text through gestures, he establishes the dominant *bhava* (the root sentiment or emotion) of *sringara* only through his eyes, by performing the *nokkikannal*, literally meaning ›looking and seeing‹. All love scenes begin with this sequence derived from Kutiyattam.

Throughout Ravana's lengthy *padam*, Mandodari assumes a ›listening‹ stance. Her eyes are cast down in an expectant expression; her hands clutch the ends of her veil and rest on her hip. When Ravana first ›sees‹ her, he registers this by squinting his eyes and then opening them wider. As he visibly inhales, his

4 All scene excerpts discussed in this essay are based on performances and / or class demonstrations seen in Kerala in 1988 and 1990. I depend primarily on staged videotaped commissions taken by me in Kerala in July and August 1988 and in March 1990. Excerpts of these videotaped commissions appear on the provided website link.

eyes widen even further while he smiles broadly. He moves his head from side to side a few times, fluttering his eyebrows.

For the next several minutes (time in the *patina padam* is slowed down considerably), he extends this dance of the eyes. Still concentrating on her visage, he moves his eyes in an ever-quickening figure-eight pattern. His eyes enlarge again and in a wide stance, he draws his focus up to her head, then down through the center of her body to her feet, and back again to her face. When he returns his gaze to her face, his mouth widens in a grin, eyes soften, brows quiver more, and his head moves again from side to side. Please refer to a video excerpt of the *nokkikannal* as demonstrated by the famed Kathakali performer, Kalamandalam Gopi [VIDEO CLIP 1].

The actor takes a long time in this facial dance in order to accentuate his attention to the heroine, to elicit the proper sentiment of pleasure in the audience, and especially, to direct the audience's gaze to his own. Although the object of his delight is Mandodari, it is Ravana's performance of her that commands the spectator's attention.

Kathakali emanates from a deeply masculine ideology and evoking the rasa of *sringara* is reserved mainly for the male character. The *minukku* heroine is the consummate recipient of his praises. The heroine is essentially a romantic concept: »She is at once the inspiring source of love and the object of love.« (NAIR 1971: 200). Thus, this entire scene may be viewed as an exaltation of all that represents the ideal woman.

Moreover, the feminine is distributed across characters and is not just designated by characters called female. This mirroring and displacing aspect of the feminine is best illustrated in scenes with the *minukku* maiden. During Ravana's *padam*, he adopts a feminine quality in his movements. He sways his body with more fluidity in the love scene than he would when in battle or in the company of other male characters. His *kalasams*, or pure dance movements, are of the most delicate variety, characterized by extremely slow legato lunging rather than staccato stamping [VIDEO CLIP 2].

While the *minukku* character maintains a quiet and reserved profile, the spectator looks to the male for descriptions of her. The male character rhapsodizes on her physical beauty, often equating her body parts with natural objects. By associating her with fertile imagery, he enshrines her and glorifies her divine aspects. Ultimately and perhaps most revealingly, the focus of the viewer's attention is riveted to the hero who brings her to life on his body through his actions. The male character uses his body as the *canvas* on which he constructs her form and evokes the *rasa* of love and the erotic.

Once Ravana launches into the gestural part of the performance, he uses some of the text's metaphors to ornament his dance. To describe the fullness of her face, he shows the *mudra* for the moon. At other times, he elaborates further on the verse, momentarily *inhabiting* the essence of that which he describes. To show her lotus eyes, Ravana not only performs the *mudra* for lotus eyes, but he momentarily shifts his demeanor to *become* Mandodari with lotus eyes. He does this through softening his posture and expression, and moving in curving arcs, while holding the *mudra* of lotus eyes.

The actor may even go further by departing from the literal text to create a palimpsest of interlocking images. To show the gracefulness of her gait, which he compares to the elephant's, he acts out the *mudra* for elephant, and then poses in this animal's stance facing several directions to indicate many elephants. He then shows them being jealous because of the superiority of her walk, and indicates the elephants in turn quarreling, acting proud, and being humble. He ends with the simple elephant *mudra* once more, to signal for the musicians the completion of this embellishment [VIDEO CLIP 3].

The text gets extended again at the end of the *padam* – the centerpiece of the scene and the actor's tour de force – in which the ten-headed Ravana shows, solely with the use of rapidly shifting facial expressions, his different heads fighting with one another for the chance to embrace Mandodari.

In order to show his different heads quarreling with each other, the actor depicts each of the heads as a distinct *bhava* assuming them one after the other in quick succession with great virtuosic control over the minute muscles of his face. To show them quarreling, he first displays the *bhava* of anger or jealousy, the principal mood: he slowly inhales, his eyes widen, and the surrounding eye muscles – especially the upper cheeks – twitch. Then he shows each different sentiment in turn – *sringara* (love or the erotic); *vira* (heroic); *hasya* (sarcasm); *karuna* (sadness); *raudra* (anger); *bhayanaka* (fear); *adbhuta* (wonder); *lajja* (shyness); *paribhava* (the feeling of being hurt), then *sringara* again.[5] Only after showing each of the *bhavas* does he perform the *mudra* »they quarrel«, returning him to the actual text. In the following video clip, actor Kalamandalam Balasubramaniam demonstrates the sentiments *hasya* (satire) and *karuna* (sadness) in turn quarrelling [VIDEO CLIP 4].

In contrast to Ravana's flamboyant exhibitions, Mandodari's response, though twice as long in terms of the text, takes much less time to enact. As is typical of the *minukku* heroine, Mandodari maintains a low profile on stage and moves minimally. Her gestures are small and abbreviated and she performs them straight through without any embellishment. She impersonates nothing. When she praises Ravana, it is done with modesty and respect. Next to this ardent and extravagant figure, Mandodari is passively quiescent. She is simply herself – a reserved, chaste, self-controlled woman and a faithful wife.

In the *patinna padam*, the *minukku's* physical beauty is a paramount theme, and nature epithets are among the most common ways to describe and enshrine her. They are also meant to celebrate the life-giving aspects of the *minukku*

5 *Lajja* and *paribhava* do not traditionally belong to the group of nine *rasas*, but are considered to be subsidiary feelings. Here they are substituted for *bhibhatsa* (disgust) and *santa* (peace) which are not deemed appropriate *rasas* to show in this context. (KESAVAN 1980)

heroine – a very important facet of her association with the goddess Lakshmi, who is the symbol par excellence of fertility and prosperity.

The heroine here is best understood as a spirit essence which takes shape most fully in the minds' eye of both playwright and hero, and on the actor's body. She is an abstract embodiment of the male state of mind. In a bold statement, the celebrated female character actor, Kottakkal Sivaraman, states, »stri vesams are sheer tools for expressing the thoughts and emotions of the male characters. That is all the playwrights intended.« (personal interview, 1988) In order for the *sringara* to be experienced, the actor projects *his* image of the heroine onto her. In so doing, he »arrests the attention of the audience and intensifies their aesthetic participation in the dramatic process« (MILLER 1984: 21).

1.3. Damayanti

While the love scene reveals a passive and idealized *minukku*, there are many *minukku* characters depicted in Kathakali who attain special powers because of their chaste behavior and steadfast piety. Often, a *minukku* heroine is put to a test to prove the depths of her faithfulness and purity. Like Sita, whose piety ultimately protects her from Ravana, the heroine experiences a similar fate in the ever-popular series of plays dramatized in Kathakali, *Nala and Damayanti*. Damayanti has been exiled to the forest along with her husband Nala. Finding herself alone in the forest, vulnerable and exposed, she is threatened by an evil forest dweller. Because of her strong devotion to the god Indra, he gave her a boon that she could burn to ashes anyone who tries to violate her vow of chastity to her husband. Thus, her mere look burns the forest dweller to death.

Damayanti's devotion is rewarded yet another time. She is at her *swayamvaram*, a marriage selection for royal women. Because of her extraordinary qualities, many of the gods are anxious to marry her. They decide to come to the *swayamvaram* all disguised as Nala, knowing that it is this mortal whom she wants. She courageously faces these masked gods and by the strength of her *sakti* gets the clarity she needs to be able to choose the one true Nala. Thus, in the paternalistic world of Kathakali, man not only must praise and idealize the virtuous woman, but he must also reward her piety, which serves to protect *him* as well.

1.4. Kunti

The *minukku* heroine is seen rarely alone or in the presence of others beside her mate. Kunti, the mother of the five Pandava brothers of the *Mahabharata* epic, is an important exception. In the frequently performed contemporary Kathakali play, *Karna Sapatham* (*Karna's Oath*), she appears as a strong, solitary *minukku* heroine. Kunti's character is central to the evolution of the plot. She is the revealer of the unexpected truth (to Karna, the male protagonist), and by doing so she answers the very fundamental questions and doubts that have preoccupied him. Despite her aging looks, her intensity and determination are imposing from the start. She wears a simple white costume – nothing of the shiny beauty of the younger *minukkus* [ILLUSTRATION 2].

Her appearance and demeanor reveal her position in life and society. She is a dignified queen, an aging woman and a widow. All of these traits put her in a special position: the queen in the hierarchy; the aging woman as a person freed from the ambivalence of sexuality; and the lonely widow freed to some extent from the influence of a man's power. Her unique status allows her to speak her own mind.

Karna Sapatham is a modern drama.[6] No mother / son relationship has ever been presented in Kathakali prior to this play. Although Kunti's character is sexually neutralized in her position as an aging mother and widow, the crucial importance of this character gives hope for creating more expansive roles for the *stri vesam*. Many Kathakali scholars and connoisseurs believe that Kunti is one of the fullest female characters. Perhaps because this is a recently created role without years of codification embedded in it, and because the character is an older woman, the actor can be freer in his interpretation.[7]

Whereas the *minukku* represents the auspicious female who is sexually ›safe‹ and in control of her own desires her evil twin – the *lalita* – signifies male dread and sexual temptation.

2. *Lalita: Disguised Double*

> By far the most effective weapon used by the gods to corrupt virtuous mortals is a woman – usually a seductive celestial nymph, but sometimes just Woman, the root of all evil in the misogynist, ascetic-oriented view of the orthodox Hindu. (O'FLAHERTY 1975: 36)

In the genres of Kutiyattam and Krisnattam, demonesses appear in disguised form as *lalitas*, beautiful maidens, and this practice has been carried over to Kathakali. Several plays feature these *lalita* roles. Of these, current Kathakali troupes perform three of them frequently: *Putana Moksam (The Salvation of Putana)* by Aswathi Tirunal; *Narakasura Vadham (The Killing of Narakasura)*,

6 Mali, the play's author, died only in the mid 1990s. The great majority of Kathakali playwrights wrote well before the 20th century.

7 As pointed out by South Indian performance scholar, Hanne de Bruin, the Kunti figure may not be the stereotypical *minukku*, »as she begot Karna prior to her marriage and her abandonment of this illegitimate son runs as a sad line throughout her life [...]« (April 2007). In further correspondence Hanne de Bruin notes: »The story of Karna and Kunti is very well-known and performed in other South Indian [...] traditions, such as the Tamil Kattaikkuttu (and as such seems to be part of the (oral) reservoir of themes underlying these interrelated traditions.« (May 2007).

by Karthika Tirunal; and *Kirmira Vadham (The Killing of Kirmira)* by Kottayattu Tampuran.[8]

When the demoness decides to undertake her mission of sexual depravity and evil, she transforms herself into a *lalita*, a disguise to hide her characteristically terrifying form. For this purpose she appropriates the appearance and demeanor of the *minukku*, her dramatic opposite. The *lalita* is the embodiment of dread, representing the confusion between what she appears to be and is in reality. Any woman could be a *lalita* in disguise – this is the perception of the Kerala man.[9]

The prominent Indian ethnopsychoanalyst, Sudhir Kakar, speaks of the Hindu male's dread of the female in this way. In his comprehensive analysis of Hindu myths, he concludes that the female is regarded with great ambivalence:

> She is both nurturing benefactress and threatening seductress. The image of the ›bad mother‹ as a woman who inflicts her male offspring with her unfulfilled, ominous sexuality is indirectly confirmed by the staunch taboos surrounding menstrual blood and childbirth throughout traditional India […]. Men have a mortal horror of being near a woman during the time of menstruation […]. Manu is customarily blunt: ›The wisdom, the energy, the strength, the might and the vitality of a man who approaches a woman covered with menstrual excretions utterly perish.‹ (KAKAR 1981: 93)

Kakar goes on to define the contradictory image which men hold of the female and which succinctly characterizes the Kathakali *lalita*:

> Underlying the conscious ideal of womanly purity, innocence and fidelity, and interwoven with the unconscious belief in a safeguarding maternal beneficence is a secret conviction among many Hindu men that the feminine principle is really the opposite – treacherous, lustful and rampant with an insatiable, contaminating sexuality. (KAKAR 1981: 93)

Lalita relates to *maya*, which signifies both an abstract concept as well as the goddess whose defining feature is illusion. As *maya*, the *lalita* is the embodiment of dread, and the confusion between what someone appears to be and is in reality.

According to anthropologist Gilles Tarabout who has done extensive research on the goddess in Kerala's rituals, the *yaksi* is clearly connected with the goddess in many cults and is included in the iconography of the goddess (TARABOUT

8 According to Kaimal, there are four other infrequently performed plays in the Kathakali repertoire which feature *kari / lalita* roles: Surpanakha of *Khara Vadham*, by Kottarakkara Tampuran which was revived by the Margi School in Trivandrum under the direction of its former director, the late D. Appukuttan Nair; Hidimbi of *Baka Vadham*, by Kottayattu Tampuran; and two modern plays which have had minimal exposure: V. Krishnan Tampi's *Tadaka Vadham* and *Surapadmasura Vadham* by K. C. Kesava Pillai. (KAIMAL 1986: 224)

9 Please refer to Caroline Osella's doctoral dissertation (OSELLA 1993) in which she discusses at length male dread and ambiguity of the female in Kerala.

1986: 217–220, 559).[10] In Kerala folklore, *yaksis* are special kinds of *bhutans*, or ghosts, of sexually unfulfilled women who have not found serenity in life and who die either before having had sex, before marriage, or before giving birth. Considered to be the spirits of these women, they return at night in the form of alluring women to seduce men and then transform themselves back into ogresses to devour them. Belief in the existence of *yaksis* in Kerala bears specifically on the *lalita* construction in Kathakali.

According to the Kerala art scholars, Betty and Clifford Jones, *lalitas* are »demonesses transformed for a time into magically beautiful women, women who are ›too beautiful‹ and *therefore suspicious*« (JONES 1979: 34; italics mine). Any woman could be a *lalita* in disguise. It is the chimerical nature of the *lalita* that underscores male anxiety around her: under any *minukku* could be lurking a *lalita* / ogress who could materialize at any time.

Belying her feminine form, the *lalita* seduces and coaxes her victim with what in a Kathakali universe represents masculine vigor. There is nothing in Kathakali's highly elaborated and defined movement lexicon that defines a feminine style of aggressive movement.[11] Therefore, in order for the ogress to show aggression – either in her true or disguised form, she can only do so in a way that signifies masculinity.

In contrast to the *minukku*, for example, the *lalita's* movements are large and sweeping. There is no demure restraint in any movement; even the minutest eye movement registers more strongly than would a virtuous *minukku's*. The eyes have more focused energy; the muscles around them hold more tension.

The challenge of the *lalita* actor, then, is to present simultaneously an idealized and benign image, while revealing from time to time to the audience her instinctual and subversive motivations. To successfully achieve this doubling effect, a mature and experienced actor must take the role. The beautiful maiden is a most tenuous disguise, and the *lalita* is always on the brink of turning back into her wicked self. In order to give a convincing performance as a beautiful maiden and yet to reveal the opposite, he must portray a paradox in his glances, level of movement energy, and in his execution of the *mudras*. He must project gracefulness and gentility, but also maliciousness.

Thus, the male actor playing the *lalita* practices multiple disguises: In form, the audience sees a beautiful woman, knowing that she is really a demoness and that ›she‹ is really a ›he‹. In behavior, the actor creates both the artifice of innocence as well as evil, and in movement, he slips back and forth between

10 I am grateful to Gilles Tarabout for pointing out to me the important links between the *lalita* type in Kathakali and the *yaksi* in an interview in Paris, France (April 1993).

11 Offering a wider South Indian context in which to view female representations, Hanne de Bruin notes that »heroic women do exist and the heroic appears to be part of many Goddess cults in South India«. She refers to the work of Alf Hiltebeitel on the Draupadi cult, the Yakshagana play »*Minakshi Kalyanam* where Minakshi is shown as a warrior« (personal correspondence, May 2007).

the feminine and masculine styles. Clearly, the *lalita* roles require the skills and talents of the most accomplished actors.

2.1. *Simhika*

In the play *Kirmira Vadham (The Killing of Kirmira)*, the demoness Simhika appropriates masculine behavior, gestures, movement size and energy levels, and movement conventions. Her behavior toward women, in this case, the quintessential *minukku* heroine, Draupadi, is analogous to a man's treatment of her. Throughout the *padam*, Simhika lavishes praise on Draupadi using the typical formula of the hero to the heroine – comparing parts of her body with aspects found in nature. As we have already seen, equating women's body parts to elements of nature is very much a male practice.

The scene we will look at takes place in the forest during the Pandava's exile. Simhika's mission is to avenge the murder of her husband, Sardula, by Arjuna. She plans to kidnap Draupadi and bring her to her brother, Kirmira, who will rape her. When Draupadi is alone, Simhika discards her *raksasa* form and presents herself to Draupadi as a beautiful courtesan.

Simhika has two *padams* in this scene separated by short responses from Draupadi. Her first *padam* provides the chance to determine for certain that Draupadi is alone, and to put her at ease about being in her company. In the second, she lures Draupadi, now seemingly in her confidence, towards the trap.

A *slokam*, a verse sung in Sanskrit, signals Simhika's entry in the play. The text poetically describes the *raksasa* taking her beautiful form at sunset, and then approaching the solitary Draupadi. The demoness has already exited from the stage (a different actor plays her) and in her place stands the transformed, radiant *lalita*.

In her entrance, Simhika indicates to the audience that she is pleased with her new form. In one cycle of beats in the slowest tempo, holding delicately the edges of her veil with both hands, she ascribes an arc with her eyes, her head slightly following the curve. In this way, she frames herself within her newly transformed, beautiful state. She follows this movement with a pleased, smiling look at the audience, eyes wide in a *sringara* expression – her head and torso swaying slightly from side to side. Then suddenly, she breaks this joyful action and narrows her eyes, peering with a quick darting action. She looks from side to side a few times to check that she is alone, and to intimate an undercurrent of malevolence. In the excerpt contained on video clip 5, actor Kottakkal Sivaraman shows instances of Simhika's stealth during a performance of the play *Kirmira Vadham* [VIDEO CLIP 5]. In her first *padam*, Simhika looks at Draupadi as a male would. She employs the same flattering metaphors and takes her time to gradually take in her entire form.

In the second *padam*, Simhika employs more nature metaphors to further flatter Draupadi and rid her of any suspicions that might remain with regard to her new acquaintance. In a richly poetic section, Simhika elaborates on Draupadi's flowing curls, associating them with a swarm of bees. This is one of a very few times in the entire Kathakali repertoire where a female character has the opportunity to elaborate on the text.

She continues with her flatteries, but now it seems that she has won the confidence of Draupadi. Knowing how fond Draupadi is of the Durga Temple which can be found in this forest, she coaxes her into going there for prayer. Simhika's description of the forest flora is enchanting. Walking hand in hand, they approach the temple. Ironically, this aspect of winning her confidence recalls the Sanskrit term *canniya visrambhanam*, or »winning the confidence of a lover«, which pertains exclusively to a male desire to win over his heroine. This confidence, however, proves to be short-lived as Draupadi soon begins to express fear and trepidation. She senses bad omens and tells Simhika that she wants to return. There is a struggle, and once Draupadi accuses Simhika of deceiving her, the spell is broken and Simhika can no longer keep up her *lalita* pretense.

During her transformation back to her true demonic self, the *lalita* performs a *kalasam*, a brief pure dance passage, in the masculine mode. She pulls her long stringy hair forward, and assumes the masculine stance signifying readiness to fight. With one arm raised high on the diagonal behind her, and the other on the opposite diagonal down in front of her she gestures: »I'm ready to take you now!« It is rather disconcerting for the spectator to see someone who looks like a *minukku* suddenly unleash such anger and force in her body [VIDEO CLIP 6, ILLUSTRATION 3]. At this pivotal moment, the *centa* drummer appears. This in itself constitutes a shift to the masculine realm, for in Kathakali the *centa* drum is considered too powerful and too inappropriate to be used to accompany any scene in which a female is present.

2.2. *Nakratundi*

In the play *Narakasura Vadham (The Killing of Narakasura)* the Nakratundi *lalita* is even more blatantly sexual and seductive than Simhika, since her primary motivation is sexual lust and her target, a man. The lascivious Narakasura orders his demoness servant, Nakratundi, to go to heaven to kidnap beautiful damsels for his diversion. When Nakratundi suddenly sees Jayanta, the son of the God Indra, she is overcome with an uncontrollable lust. Before approaching him to fulfill her desire, she uses her powers to transform herself into a beautiful maiden.

Her first entrance as the *lalita* begins with the same framing sequence as described for Simhika. She follows this with a set movement piece known as the sari dance. This alluring and sensual dance is unsurpassed in the entire Kathakali repertoire. The dancer's body sways languidly in a laterally flowing direction. With lilting steps, the dancer draws an arm up through the center of the body, wrist bent down, head and torso heaving up and down following the direction of the moving arm. In the excerpt shown here by today's top *stri vesam* actor Margi Vijayan, all is curving, circular and luscious, characteristic of the *lasya* or feminine mode of movement. Depending on which actor plays this role, the sari dance can sometimes seem overtly sexual, but it does not usually exceed the bounds of propriety. It certainly does not in this instance [VIDEO CLIP 7].

In the first stanza of her *padam* to Jayanta, Nakratundi shows no stealth toward the object of her attention, as does Simhika. She is forthright in her expression of lust. She comes right out and tells him that fate has brought them together and he will become her husband. To create a reminder of her artifice, she remembers to show some shyness. But her shyness borders on a burning lust which she finds almost impossible to contain. She clutches the ends of her veil, and then curls her fingers, stretching her arms up over her head – a movement convention signifying being hopelessly impassioned.

After they identify themselves – she claims a heavenly clan as her origins – she mimes being struck by the arrows of the love god and invites Jayanta to perform *kamakeli* (literally »love play«) without delay. The strength of her actions showing the *mudras* for »love play« rivals those of a male character doing the same stock movement. Her eyes seem to dilate with sexual arousal. Most male characters (especially *pacca* heroes and *katti* villains) show a more heroic expression on their face, and handle the ›pain‹ from the arrows with more restraint, befitting their regal natures, whereas *lalita* is more openly lustful.[12] Here, the *lalita* even exceeds the male hero in her sexual display and we see that the ill-fitting *minukku* disguise cannot contain her [VIDEO CLIP 8].

The *lalita* is the most significant bearer of ambiguity in Kathakali, which she manifests both dramatically and emotionally. Simhika shows the purely dramatic variety: at once she must maintain the modest demeanor of the *minukku* to deceive her victim while she projects hints of her evil spirit lurking beneath. This draws on the special skills of actors who master the alternation of subtly contrasting gestures to maintain the tension of the *lalita's* dual nature. The character of Nakratundi unleashes the full force of a *lalita's* seductive potential. She unabashedly attempts to seduce her victim sexually in ways that Simhika cannot, given that she plays opposite a woman. Nakratundi goes further than Simhika: she not only appropriates masculine behavior, but her sexually aggressive manner toward the male character creates a distinct reversal of (gender) roles, turning him temporarily into a stunned love object and a paralyzed recipient of her shockingly assertive behavior. He will, however, have his revenge on her eventually.

The gender slippages seen with regard to these *lalita* characters emphasize that, at least in the fantasy world of Kathakali, men can subsume within their own identities what they view as dangerous feminine desire, and thereby control it through their own representation.

12 In Trivandrum, Kerala, on March 31, 1990, I commissioned the brilliant *stri vesam* actor Margi Vijaya Kumar to demonstrate for me several versions of the same stock movements as they would be performed by *minukkus*, *lalitas* and male characters. This juxtaposition revealed striking movement contrasts between these character types.

3. *Kari: Outrageous Ogress*

The *kari* exceeds all acceptable boundaries. Usually appearing alone, widowed, or otherwise unmarried, she craves only to annihilate. She is an aggressive, dangerous, destructive, as well as low-class and preposterous creature.[13]

In utter contrast to the refined *minukku*, the *kari* roars and bares her teeth while strutting about the stage. She is everything that the respectful and self-controlled heroine is not. Her make-up, costume, movement and iconography clearly express this antithesis. Her immense headdress (one of the largest in the repertoire measuring about a foot tall) sits high above a ferocious face that is painted primarily in black. Her most flagrant features, however, are her black, exposed, bullet-shaped breasts [ILLUSTRATION 4].

With regard to both the *lalita* and *kari* characters, there is a dichotomy between what they think or project they are, and what the audience either sees or knows. Whereas the *lalita* looks beautiful to the audience, we know that she is really a demoness. The paradox of the *kari* is that although the audience sees a hideous ogress, the character herself believes that she is beautiful.

For all the savage pretense of her dramatic entrance replete with flaming torches, thunderous percussion, and her loud shrieks, she spends most of her stage time in farcical displays. Her outrageous clowning and mock ferocity undermine any sinister impact she might otherwise have. The audience laughs at the *kari* for believing that she is as lovely as the *minukku*.[14]

As noted earlier, beauty is essential to the *minukku* character. Most *kari* characters perform an extended preening dance that seems to be a play on the convention of beautification known as *koppanikkuka*. This set piece, derived from Kutiyattam, shows the noble maiden, helped by her attendants, bedecking herself with elaborate ornaments, clothes, and make-up. While performed in earnest, the *kari's* rendition of the *koppanikkuka* appears to the audience as highly comical and very much a mockery of the ›real‹ thing.

13 The *kari* characters in Kathakali are all modeled on the *raksasi* Surpanakha, the sister of the demon-king Ravana of the *Ramayana* epic. The first use of Surpanakha as a dramatic character is in the Sanskrit drama, *Ascaryachudamani (The Wondrous Crest Jewel)* of Saktibhadra. A fragment of this play performed in the Kutiyattam style features Surpanakha in both her *kari* and *lalita* forms. Surpanakha later appears as a character in the *Ramanattam* play *Khara Vadham*. *Ramanattam*, a cycle of eight plays on the story of the *Ramayana*, is a precursor to Kathakali. In the play *Kirmira Vadham*, playwright Kottayattu Tampuran invented the *kari* demoness Simhika, modeling her on the *Ramayana's* Surpanakha character.

14 As pointed out by Hanne de Bruin in an email correspondence (May 2007): »Marginalization of the ›demonic‹, whether male or female, through ridicule and laughter so as to avert the dangers it harbours appears to be a standard treatment in the South Indian cultural area. [...] See *e.g.* KAPFERER 1983 on demonic possession & performance in Sri Lanka or Surpanakha in Kutiyattam.« [Additional information by the author: KAPFERER, B. 1983. *A Celebration of Demons: Exorcism and the Aesthetics of Healing in Sri Lanka*. Bloomington: Indiana University Press.]

An example of this drawn out mime sequence occurs during Simhika's first appearance as the *kari* in the play *Kirmira Vadham*. While on route to kidnap Draupadi and before she transforms into the *lalita*, Simhika pauses to look herself over. After seeing her own reflection, she shrieks with horror and disgust and resolves to make herself more attractive. She combs her hair using her fingers, but cannot manage to untangle the mess. She sniffs her hands, yells, and mimes: »What is this awful smell?« [VIDEO CLIP 9]. She tries to apply sandal paste to her forehead but cannot find any water. After asking for some from a few people who all refuse her, she decides to extract milk from her breasts. After a few tries pressing, pumping, and pounding, she succeeds in getting a few drops, rubs them together with the sandalwood, and smears the paste across her forehead.

She looks at herself in the mirror and, horrified at what she sees, howls in disgust, wipes it off, and repeats the action more delicately. Finally, she dusts off her ornaments and places them on her arms, ears, and waist. She looks at herself and, pleased with her image, sways from side to side. Now she is ready to play. She tries to coax others to dance with her, but each one rebuffs her over-eager advances. Dejected, she goes off to play by herself. Playing ball is a popular maiden's pastime, so she tries again in vain to engage someone to play with her. She plays by herself for a while, but she throws the ball so hard (she forgets her own strength!), that it goes out of reach. Weary, she sits down, fans herself, and wipes away the sweat.

Simhika breaks every rule of decorum that we have come to identify with the *minukku*. While performing this sequence, Simhika bounces up and down and covers large areas of space with her giant, kicking steps. When angry, she bears her teeth and fangs and cries out. By contrast, a noblewoman's steps are always small and delicate. She would never show her teeth even when smiling, and would never express an unpleasant emotion. By smelling her odiferous hair, Simhika displays true vulgarity. She exceeds all limits of decency when she assaults her breasts in public.

The *kari* is not merely dismissed as a comic or marginal character, however. Her audacity is taken all too seriously in the end. During the battle with her enemy, he mimes cutting off her nose, ears, and breasts in a brief, stylized scene, after which she usually leaves the stage shrieking in agony. Not silenced at this point, she reappears onstage before an accomplice, begging him to avenge her mutilations.[15]

In this horrific scene, she appears in what is literally known as the »blood dripping costume« (*ninam anninja vesam*). All the lights are turned off. The *kari* enters through the back of the audience flanked by attendants carrying burning

15 In the text on which this story is based involving Surpanakha's disfigurement, only her nose is cut off. In Kutiyattam and Kathakali, the creators added an erotic dimension to the violent act by having her breasts cut off as well. (PANCHAL 1984: 95)

torches. Resin thrown onto the torches makes the flames suddenly blaze high into the air. A large cloth dipped into a dark red dye mixture is draped around the *kari's* body, covering her from the neck down to the ground, eerily looking like dripping blood. Where her nose, ears, and breasts would be, there are pieces of the same red cloth tied to look as if her tendons, blood vessels, and entrails are dangling from the raw wounds. She screams and howls in pain. Plaintive wails of »*ayyo ayyo*« can be heard. This scene always takes place at the end of the night – a time reserved for the most gruesome of acts [ILLUSTRATION 5].

The *kari's* punishment and plea for vengeance allow her at last to fulfill the expressive function of her character. Although she is made to look like a low class fool, this brutal scene at the end forces us to see her serious side. As the *minukku* evokes her characteristic *bhavas* of love, or *sringara*, so too must the *kari* evoke her characteristic *bhavas* – terror and revulsion (*bhayanaka* and *bibhatsa*). The doubled percussion instruments reach a new intensity and volume. As she moves slowly down a cleared pathway among the spectators, one gets an all too close view of her grotesque form while her screams of agony fill the air. Writhing in pain, she fans the bloodied floor-length cape.

My Kerala informant, L.S. Rajagopalan, notes that when this scene is performed in North Kerala, the *kari* enters »with a cock, the neck of which is partly cut and drips with the blood«. This practice is reminiscent of exorcist rituals conducted by certain castes in the north and central regions of Kerala. One of these rituals, Mudiyettu, which also involves the sacrifice of a cock and which propitiates the goddess, Bhadrakali (a local name for Kali), was an important early influence on the development of Kathakali.[16] During climactic moments in these rituals in which Kali is propitiated, and in the Kodungallur festival for the goddess Kurumba (another name for Bhadrakali), sacrificed cocks are brought in front of the shrine of Kali or the oracle representing her. There appears to be a link to Kali whose characteristic *rasas* are also *bhayanaka* and *bibhatsa* and who is »born from wrath, is horrible in appearance, and is ferocious in battle. Taking delight in destruction and death, she epitomizes the wild, fearful aspects of the divine.« (KINSLEY 1975: 92).[17] It is not clear whether any Kathakali

16 Personal communications with L.S. Rajagopalan in February and August of 1991 confirmed this for me. In February 1988, I witnessed a Mudiyettu performance in a remote village in central Kerala. For more on Mudiyettu, see CALDWELL 1999.

17 Regarding my comparisons between the *kari* demoness and the goddess Kali, it is important to consider the goddess as a multidimensional figure. Her baser aspect which is associated with the *kari*, is highly sexual and is sometimes propitiated in rituals by the lower castes who sing dirty songs and imbibe alcohol. This aspect should be differentiated from Kali's boon-conferring, transcendent, redemptive, and liberating side. While the *kari* is enslaved by her debased qualities and desires, Kali transcends them. As Rajagopalan explained in a personal communication: »Kali is the personified *tamasik* form of Siva. Normally the gods are benign and when their anger is roused they may show *rajasik* qualities as in righteous indignation – but you won't find the gods descending down to the *tamasik* level. For such occasions a new form would be created – like an *avatar*. So

troupes still perform the scene in this manner, but the practice points to an instance in which the kari's fearful and repulsive demeanor shows a strong link with the goddess Bhadrakali – the popular Kerala goddess propitiated by the lower classes [ILLUSTRATION 6]. The fact that this scene is time consuming, expensive, inconvenient to stage, and causes confusion in the viewers, are all cited as reasons for its omission (KAIMAL 1986: 183).[18] Like no other scene in Kathakali, this one should evoke extreme terror and revulsion, dramatically offsetting the preceding humorous tone of the story. The Kathakali biographer and chronicler, Aymenom Krishna Kaimal, feels it is unfortunate that this scene is often omitted because he thinks its graphic tone would so powerfully »create a feeling among the spectators that sinning will have its retribution« (KAIMAL 1986).[19]

It is not in the scope of this essay to offer a general discussion of the diverse classes that view Kathakali and the characters that appeal to different strata of Kerala society.[20] However, it is relevant to point out here that there is a strong identification for the lower classes with the *kari* characters. As a rule, the less educated classes that attend Kathakali performances are not very conversant with the subtleties of Kathakali's *mudra* language, and so they would be more apt to enjoy the *kari's lokadharmic* (realistic) modes of expression versus the *natyadharmic* (abstract) modes that the noble and villainous (but still higher class) characters employ. By definition *lokadharmic* actions are easier to understand for the uninitiated. One must take into account that the first aficionados of Kathakali came out of a feudal society in which only the upper classes had the leisure time in which to make a scholarly study of the intricate aesthetics of Kathakali as well as other classical art forms.

The *kari's* fate is not only dramatic. It also reflects a moral order that demands a rightful punishment for sexual aggression and audacious behavior by women. The *kari* is guilty both of social impropriety and sin. Her audacity in merely aligning herself with the *minukku*, in plotting to kidnap noble or divine women, and her oversexed nature do not go unpunished. Not only does she lust after

Siva created Bhadrakali [...]. Naturally Kali, as the *tamasik* version of Siva's consort, Sati, will be repulsive and ferocious.« (Rajagopalan, interview; 29 August, 1991) *Tamasik* and *rajasik* refer to two of the three *gunas* or essential qualities of which *sattvik* is the highest, purest and most spiritual. The *kari* possesses none of this quality, while the *minukku* possesses the most *sattvik*. Only the most debased figures contain *tamas* whereas noble people with streaks of evil or unleashed anger will contain *rajas*.

18 In a personal communication on 29 August, 1991, my informant, L.S. Rajagopalan suggested: »The idea of playing to the gallery is anathema. Educated people don't want it.« As suggested by Hanne de Bruin (May 2007) this change may reflect an attempt to make Kathakali a more ›classical‹ art form.

19 This passage from Kaimal's book was translated and excerpted for me in a personal communication with L.S. Rajagopalan on 29 August, 1991.

20 For an in depth discussion of this topic please refer to my doctoral dissertation (PITKOW 1998).

inappropriate love objects – men far above her own lowly rank – but she sins merely by showing lust at all. This then is her function in Kathakali: to provide comic relief and to instill by her transgression and punishment the rules of caste and sexual propriety. The fact that she always is viciously punished in the end for her extremely impertinent and polluting behaviors serves to enhance her scapegoat status further and perpetuate this moral imperative.

Conclusion

In this essay I have demonstrated how each of the three female character types in Kathakali – the *minukku*, *lalita*, and *kari* – reflect and play on the gender slippages involved in a male construction and impersonation of the feminine. As we have seen, the feminine, as a positive force embodied as the idealized *minukku* character type, is associated with well-being, harmony, prosperity, and auspiciousness. Her procreative abilities confer on her the power to maintain and continue life. As a dark and dangerous figure in thecase of the *lalita*, the female is unpredictable, sexually volatile, and potentially destructive as seen in the *kari* demoness. Male impersonation of these roles appears to be a strategy to harness these qualities within his own being.

It seems to me that self-containment (in terms of harboring the male and the female within oneself) is the goal, however unconscious it may be, for the actor of female roles in Kathakali. Indeed, among Hindu deities, androgyny is valued as a special and powerful quality. In Hindu mythology, the image of the combined man / woman is a frequent and significant theme. For example, the Hindu god Siva is the archetypal model who incorporates masculine and feminine aspects. In one of his most celebrated forms, he is Ardhanarisvara, half-man / half-woman, representing Siva united with his *sakti* (the feminine creative power embodied by Parvati). In one of the most dramatic examples of gender ambiguity and slippage enacted in the Kathakali idiom, the character of Ravana performs the Ardhanarisvara, alternating between Siva and his consort Parvati.[21]

In observing the Hijras, a cross-gendered sect living primarily in North India, ethnographer Serena Nanda states that the »[h]ijra role appears in a culture where gender roles for ordinary purposes are sharply hierarchical and quite well defined and differentiated, *yet admits gender overlap, gender transformations, and alternative genders in both myth and ritual*« (NANDA 1990: 140–141; italics mine). »Hinduism not only accommodates such ambiguities, but also views them as meaningful and even powerful.« (NANDA 1990: 20).

According to Osella, the ultimate goal for high caste men in Kerala, is to »seek to develop androgyny within themselves« and at the same time, paradoxi-

21 This piece is even more dramatic when performed in the Kutiyattam idiom. The Kathakali rendering is not nearly as elaborated.

cally, »to be the only true men [...] to have a completed body, like that of Ardhanari, [...] which is perfectly self-contained, holding within itself both matter [...] and energy [...]« (OSELLA 1993: 387). Androgyny, an aesthetic strategy for Kathakali actors, appears to be logical and accepted because of the Hindu deities who appear in androgynous forms; and it functions as a way of containing the aspects of feminine ambiguity within themselves. Furthermore, maintaining control over the feminine construction in Kathakali allows men to safeguard their own imaginaries of women.

Kathakali has been a male province for hundreds of years, and it is most probable that men will want to continue to preserve their domain. If Kerala society were to allow women full access to study Kathakali at the arts academies, and to perform all the female roles in the mainstream of Kerala culture, there is no doubt that these depictions would be called into question and radically reconfigured. It will be left up to future scholars to interrogate these new representations.

REFERENCES AND BIBLIOGRAPHY

CALDWELL, S. 1999. *Oh Terrifying Mother: Sexuality, Violence and Worship of the Goddess Kali.* New Delhi: Oxford University Press.

CASE, S. 1985. »Classic Drag: The Greek Creation of Female Parts«. *Theatre Journal* 37, 3: 317–327.

DAUGHERTY, D.; M. PITKOW. 1991. »Who Wears the Skirts in Kathakali?«. *TDR* 35, 2: 138–156.

JONES, C. R.; B. T. JONES. 1970. *Kathakali: An Introduction to the Dance Drama.* New York, San Francisco: Theatre Arts Books and American Society for Eastern Arts.

KAIMAL, A. K. 1986. *Kathakali Vijananakosham.* Kottayam: Sahitya Pavarthaka Cooperative Society. Portions translated from the Malayalam privately by L. S. Rajagopalan.

KAKAR, S. 1989. *Intimate Relations: Exploring Indian Sexuality.* New Delhi: Penguin Books.

KALADHARAN, V. 1990. »The Noble Nayika«. *Indian Express* (7 July).

KESAVAN, K. 1980. »The Sringara Padams of Kathakali«. In: *Kalamandalam: A Collection of Articles.* Kottayam: National Book Stall. Translated from the Malayalam privately by L. S. Rajagopalan.

KINSLEY, D. R. 1975. *The Sword and the Flute. Kālī and Kṛṣṇa, Dark Visions of the Terrible and the Sublime in Hindu Mythology.* Berkeley: Univ. of California Press.

MILLER, B. S. (ED.). 1984. *The Theatre of Memory: The Plays of Kalidasa.* New York: Columbia University Press.

NAIR, K. RAMACHANDRAN. 1971. *Early Manipravalam: A Study.* Trivandrum: Anjali Publishing Co.

NANDA, S. 1990. *Neither Man Nor Woman: The Hijras of India.* Belmont: Wadsworth Publishing Co.

O'FLAHERTY, W. 1975. *Hindu Myths: A Sourcebook Translated from the Sanskrit.* New York: Penguin Books.

OSELLA, C. 1993. *Making Hierarchy Natural: The Cultural Construction of Gender and Maturity in Kerala, India.* Unpublished Doctoral dissertation, London School of Economics, University of London.

PANCHAL, G. 1984. *Kuttampalam and Kutiyattam: A Study of the Traditional Theatre for the Sanskrit Drama of Kerala*. New Delhi: Sangeet Natak Akademi.
PITKOW, M. 1998. *Representations of the Feminine in Kathakali: South Indian Dance-Drama of Kerala*. Unpublished Doctoral Dissertation, Dept. of Performance Studies, New York University.
----. 2001. »Putana's Salvation in Kathakali: Embodying the Sacred Journey«. *Asian Theatre Journal* 18, 2: 238–248.
RAJAGOPALAN, L. S.; V. S. IYER. 1975. »Aids to the Appreciation of Kathakali«. *Journal of South Asian Literature* 10: 205–248.
TARABOUT, G. 1986. *Sacrifier et Donner a Voir en Pays Malabar*. Paris: Ecole Francaise D'extreme Orient.
WADLEY, S. (ED.). 1980. *Powers of Tamil Women*. Syracuse: Syracuse University Press.

Numerous interviews and correspondences took place between 1988–1997 with L.S. Rajagopalan and V. Kaladharan.

Film Clips and Photographies

Nine film clips and eight photographies accompany the text and are published online: *http://www.indologie.uni-wuerzburg.de/women_performers/contributors/pitkow/*.

Actresses on the Temple Stage?

The Epic Conception and Performance of Women's Roles in Kūṭiyāṭṭam Rāmāyaṇa Plays

Virginie Johan

Introduction

Reputed to be a model of Indian classical theatre, the Kūṭiyāṭṭam Sanskrit theatre of Kerala has had women on stage for about one thousand years.[1] Currently, the three main Kūṭiyāṭṭam schools (Kalāmaṇḍalam Kerala State Academy of Fine Arts, Ammannūr Cāccu Cākyār Smaraka Gurukulam and Natanakairali in Iriññālakuṭa, Mārgi in Trivandrum) all have good actresses playing women's roles. There are said to be five female characters: the *pañcakanyakaḷ*, »five virgins«, all of whom are married and among whom we find the three perfect spouses (*pativratāḥ*) of the *Rāmāyaṇa*: Sītā, Tārā and Maṇḍōdarī.[2] These three roles appear in the five *Rāmāyaṇa* acts performed on the stage of the Hindu temples where Kūṭiyāṭṭam was developed and performed exclusively by the *cākyār*, *nampyār* and *naṅṅyār* castes.[3] Four of these five acts are also enacted

1 In many ways Kūṭiyāṭṭam follows the *Nāṭyaśāstra* treatise on the theatre (dated back to about the 1st cent.), which notably describes how actresses should perform women's roles on the stage. Kūṭiyāṭṭam is known especially for its long history (see MOSER in this volume) and for its repertoire, consisting of separate acts from ancient Sanskrit plays, each becoming a mini-drama with a particular name. The performers also master the four acting techniques (*abhinaya*) involving voice, body, emotion, costume / make-up, as defined in the treatise. On the *Nāṭyaśāstra* see BANSAT-BOUDON 1992 and UNNI 1998. For a general discussion of Kūṭiyāṭṭam see *e.g.* JONES 1984, RICHMOND 2002, JOHAN 2002 and PAULOSE 2006.

2 *Ahalyā draupadī sītā tārā maṇḍōdarī tathā / pañcakanyāḥ smarennityaṃ mahāpātakanāśanaṃ.* – »Ahalyā, Draupadī, Sītā, Tārā and Maṇḍōdarī – by constantly remembering these five ladies, one can destroy even the greatest sin.« (UṢĀ NAṄṄYĀR 2003: 65)

3 Kūṭiyāṭṭam was part of the Sanskrit culture developed by the *nampūtiri* Brahmins in the temple complex, and the *cākyār*, *nampyār* and *naṅṅyār* castes, particular to Kerala, were included in the intermediary group of temple servants (*ampalavāsi*). They lead the »*kūttu*« year after year according to the prior programme (*aṭiyantaraṃ*), as a votive offering (*vaḻivāṭu˘*), or »to see« (*kāḻca*) at specific occasions (AMMANNŪR MĀDHAVA CĀKYĀR 1995 [1966]: 33). The performance can be Kūṭiyāṭṭam, as well as narrative mono-acting

on the secular stage.[4] In Kūṭiyāṭṭam, Sītā, Śrī Rāma's wife, is present in acts II, V and VI of the *Āścaryacūḍāmaṇi* (in the following: *Āśc.*), whereas Maṇḍōdarī, the spouse of the demon-king Rāvaṇa, is present (along with her maid), only in act V, and Tārā, spouse of the monkey king Bāli, only in the first act of the *Abhiṣēkanāṭakam* (in the following: *Abhiṣ.*) However, there are more than five women's roles in Kūṭiyāṭṭam: we also find Laḷitā (Śūrpaṇakhā in a seductive form) in ›her‹ act (Act of Śūrpaṇakhā, *Āśc.* II), and Vijayā, the doorkeeper of the Laṅkā palace (in the fifth and last of our Ramaite acts, *Abhiṣ.* III).[5] All are minor characters in the original Sanskrit plays where they speak in prose and Prakrit rather than in Sanskrit verse. In Kūṭiyāṭṭam, Sītā, Maṇḍōdarī, Tārā, Vijayā, Laḷitā and the maid are all treated as standard characters. This becomes evident from the fact that they bear no particular name and are indicated by the two same gestures [see ILLUSTRATION 1][6]. They also have the same basic emotional state (*bhāva*) – in the performer's Malayalam terminology, they are modest, shy, discrete (*lajja nāṇam*). When these roles are performed by actresses, as is usually the case on the secular stage, they also look the same: they are all of the *minukku*˘ type (with skin-coloured make-up), they all wear the same red blouse and headcovering (*muṭi*), they are all *strīvesam* (*strī* – woman; *veṣam* – role and, literally, costume). They are standard women's roles in standard costumes, embodied in a standard way in the current secular Kūṭiyāṭṭam practice.

However, if we look at the Hindu temple stage, the participation of women (*naṅṅyār*) is often limited to sitting as a (so-called) »singing / chanting *naṅṅyār*« [ILLUSTRATIONS 5 and 6], while a male actor, the *cākyār*, faces the central oil

forms such as the verbal Prabandham Kūttu of the *cākyār* masters, or the mimetic Naṅṅyār Kūttu of the *naṅṅyār* women (see DAUGHERTY 1996 and MOSER 2008, and their papers in this volume). In the largest temples, the performances are held in theatres designed specifically for *Kūṭiyāṭṭam*: the *kūttampalams* [see ILLUSTRATIONS 2–4]. Since the 1960s, thanks to the late Guru Paiṅkuḷam Rāma Cākyār, these arts have been opened up to the secular stage and other castes (RĀMAVARMMA 1978; see also DAUGHERTY in this volume), but only *cākyārs*, *nampyārs* and *naṅṅyārs* can perform in the *kūttampalam* (only very recently has a debate opened out regarding this rule).

4 These five acts come from two plays: (1) Śaktibhadra's *Āścaryacūḍāmaṇi* (»The Wondrous Crest Jewel«, ed. JONES 1984): act II is called »Act of Śūrpaṇakhā« (*Śūrpaṇakhāṅkam*), act V »Act of the Aśōka grove« (*Aśōkavanikāṅkam*), and act VI »Act of the ring« (*Aṅgulīyāṅkam*). (2) *Abhiṣēkanāṭakam* (»The Consecration«) attributed to Bhāsa (BRÜCKNER 1999–2000): acts I and III are known as the »Act of Bāli's death« (*Bālivadhāṅkam*) and the »Act of the battle at the door« (*Tōraṇayuddhāṇkam*) respectively; the Act of the ring is staged as a mono act, *kūttu* (»Kūttu of the ring«), only in the temples, whereas the four other acts can be performed on other stages.

5 Śūrpaṇakhā is not considered to be a woman's role and is performed by a male actor (RAJAGOPALAN 1997: 39–40).

6 The first gesture signifies »name«, and the other »respected woman«. In the second gesture, the position of the fingers (in *kaṭaka mudrā*) symbolises the feminine gender, while the movement evokes an embrace. Only Tārā is distinguished by being a female »monkey«.

lamp standing at the front of the stage.[7] In fact, while all the female roles mentioned above receive the same treatment on the secular stage, the performance practice of the temple stage distinguishes between them: some are embodied and others not. Only women who are independent and who play an important part in the action are played by actresses: Laḷitā, who asks Rāma to become her husband and whose mutilation by Lakṣmaṇa (in *Āśc.* II) leads to Sītā's abduction, and Maṇḍōdarī, who interferes with her husband Rāvaṇa and saves Sītā from death (in *Āśc.* V). In contrast, a woman who is accompanied by her husband, such as Sītā (in *Āśc.* II) or Tārā (in *Abhiṣ.* I), is not embodied, as is also the case with Vijayā (a minor role in *Abhiṣ.* III). Finally, since the fifth act (of Maṇḍōdarī) is rarely staged,[8] Laḷitā's role remains the only opportunity for the *naṅṅyār* to perform the *Rāmāyaṇa* plays in the *kūttampalam*. How can the relative absence of actresses from the Kūṭiyāṭṭam temple stage be explained?

The reduction of the number of performers to a minimum is a normal practice applied to all secondary roles and not only to those of women on the temple stage. First, this custom is linked to the dual nature of the Kūṭiyāṭṭam performer who is both actor and storyteller.[9] The *cākyār* uses and mixes these two skills during the Kūṭiyāṭṭam performance, in the dramatic structure as well as in the acting, by introducing a narrative retrospection (*nirvahaṇam*) into the dramatic text and by taking on (as a solo act) the various roles appearing in the story – this paper will provide more details about this dramaturgy, established in the performers' Malayalam texts: production manuals, *kramadīpika*, and acting manuals, *āṭṭaprakāram*.[10] Second, the reduction of the number of performers

7 L.S. RAJAGOPALAN refers to the »singing *naṅgyār*«(1997: 19). During all the Kūṭiyāṭṭam performances (on temple and secular stages), a female artist (the *naṅṅyār*) sits stage right (from the performer's view). She takes part in the performance as a musician and as a recitant. As a musician, she plays the small hand cymbals (*kuḻittāḷam*) and represents the *tāḷam* (basic rhythm) of the performance, creating the sound space for the performer, altogether with the male drummer, the *nampyār*, who sits backstage behind his *miḻāvu* (the big drum of Kūṭiyāṭṭam; see ILLUSTRATIONS 7–9). As a recitant, the *naṅṅyār* is *the voice of the performance,* when she chants the preliminary songs and subsequently the verses punctuating the narrative retrospection (*nirvahaṇam*) taking place within the dramatic text for several nights on the temple stage (see below, NOTE 10).

8 Only the *cākyārs* from the Ammanūr family perform this fifth act in the temples. They notably did so in 2008 in the Kūṭalmaṇikyam temple of Iriññālakuṭa. It was an important event because this act hadn't been performed since 1984 (when the performance was held in the same temple and Uṣā Naṅṅyār played the queen).

9 The mythical ancestor of the *cākyār* masters is a bard, Sūtan, to whom the *cākyārs* give life when they perform Cākyār Kūttu (the jester, *vidūṣaka*, is »*sūta bhāvi*«). The *cākyārs* are also closely linked to the Sūtradhāra (stage director and actor par excellence), given that they have the Sūtradhāra *puṟappāṭu*˘ (entry of the actor) as their first stage ceremony, *araṅṅeṭṭam* (see JOHAN 2010a).

10 These two types of manuals exist for each act of the repertoire. The production manuals give the general structure of the performance and the acting manuals its detailed subtext. In the temples, the *Rāmāyaṇa* performances follow this basic structure: a single character

(and perhaps the dramaturgy itself), is linked to the socio-economic conditions of production of the temple stage, particularly the diffuse light from the three flames of the oil lamp – it is said that »when two actors share the same light, the power of the performance is divided into two« – and the small fee given to the performers (that is also shared). Third, with respect to the absence of women's roles especially, *cākyārs* say that »there are not enough well-trained *naṅṅyār* able to perform«. This type of remark hides an entire social system, which creates obstacles to finding performers to conduct temple performances.[11] The problem seems quite old since the actor-protagonist of the *Nāṭankuṣa*, an anonymous critique of Kūṭiyāṭṭam dated back to about the 15th century, mentions that he performs alone »because he is alone«.[12] Finally, the conception of women's roles, resulting in a conspicuous absence of actresses from the temple stage, may reveal how much the *cākyārs*, who are originally *nampūtiri* Brahmins,[13] follow the ancient Hindu canons and what they have to say about the character of the Indian woman – a point I will develop below.

enters (*puṟappāṭu˘*), performs the beginning of the text of the act, and puts a ›verse in suspense‹. The next day, an ›actor-storyteller‹, dressed as the previous character, enacts the retrospection, *nirvahaṇam* (*i.e.* the history of this character and / or of the initial situation), using gestures following the acting manual, until he reaches the verse that was put in suspense earlier. The *kūṭiyāṭṭam* proper (literarily: acting – *āṭṭam*; with – *kūṭi*) starts: actors perform the Sanskrit text »together« using »combined acting«. This total performance (with *puṟappāṭu˘*, *nirvahaṇam* and *kūṭiyāṭṭam*) is usually found only in the temples. It lasts for five to sixteen nights in the case of the *Rāmāyaṇa* acts.

11 Since only the *cākyār*, *nampyār* and *naṅṅyār* castes can perform in the temples, it is important to understand the matrilineal system (*marumakkattāyaṃ*) by which they are bound together and maintain their status and different families (currently there are six main *cākyār* families). According to the caste rules, the *cākyārs* marry *illōṭamma* women (who have no role in theatre) who pass on their family name and *cākyār* (for sons) or *illōṭamma* (for daughters) status to their children; the *nampyār* and the *naṅṅyār* are to marry each other, and have *nampyār* or *naṅṅyār* children. If a *cākyār* marries a *naṅṅyār* (as is often the case), the children take their mother's caste. The women (*illōṭamma* or *naṅṅyār*) should not marry a man of lower status. Nevertheless, because nowadays many unions do not follow »the rule«, the system, despite being rigid in some cases (Daugherty in this volume), has been adapted to preserve the *cākyār* families: now, *illōṭamma* contracting hypogamic unions convey their status to their children. Anyway, the main problem related to transmission is that among the *cākyārs*, *nampyārs* and *naṅṅyārs* remaining, few are involved in theatre. Among them only some assume their ritual duty, and of those who do so not all are fully trained. For example, among the *naṅṅyārs* who perform in the temples, only Aparṇṇa Naṅṅyār [Illustrations 5 and 6] performs on an excellent level, whereas the other *naṅṅyārs* are acting out of ritual obligation.

12 *Nāṭankuṣa* IV.6: »*ekākitvād evam iti*« (ed. Paulose 1993: 34). In this very interesting text, the author, probably a Brahmin, criticizes the way the actors perform the Sanskrit drama. The actors try to clear themselves by explaining their dramaturgy (see the editor's introduction: xxi–xxix).

13 According to Subbaraya Iyer 1908 most of the temple servants were originally Brahmins who lost their status. Concerning the special case of the *cākyārs* and the excommunication process that some of them were subjected to, see A.M.N. Cākyār 1999.

Nevertheless, this article will favour a theatrical explanation for the question of the absence of actresses from the temple stage. It will examine how their absence has had both positive and negative effects, with respect to theatrical aesthetics, depending on the dramatic situation and the dramaturgical context investigated (which is not only limited to »*kūṭiyāṭṭam*« in the strict sense of the term). Limiting this study to contemporary performance and the five *Rāmāyaṇa* acts of the temple repertoire, I will investigate this question step by step while looking at the three main dramaturgic contexts that I distinguish in the temple performance (see DIAGRAM 1):

1. The *kūṭiyāṭṭam*, »acting together« of several performers in which actresses are supposed to take on the women's roles. Sītā's case will be studied here in detail.

2. The *nirvahaṇam*, narrative »retrospections« that are interwoven into the original dramatic play on the temple stage. The only feminine retrospections we find are those of Laḷitā and Maṇḍōdarī.

3. The *vistara* or mimetic »extensions«, which emerge within the dramatic *kūṭiyāṭṭam* and / or the narrative *nirvahaṇam*.

The absence of the actress on the stage provides good opportunities for understanding the aesthetic of Kūṭiyāṭṭam. Through the case of the women's roles, this paper will show how this theatre can be called ›epic‹, not only because it is narrative, but also in the Brechtian sense of the term. The investigation will be done principally on the basis of the stage manuals and film fragments.[14]

1. To embody or not to embody women's roles in kūṭiyāṭṭam? Sītā's Case

If the woman character »voiced« by the text is not embodied by an actress on stage, what then becomes of the role itself? Let us look at Sītā, a model Hindu

14 I have edited the films by freezing images, corresponding to the ›stop in time principle‹ that I identify in Kūṭiyāṭṭam (JOHAN 2008 and 2010b). Two original films have been provided by the Würzburg Indology Department (BRÜCKNER: 1999–2000). I thank H. Brückner and H. Moser for having allowed and helped me to copy some of the *Rāmāyaṇa* films of their collection in June 2002. I also thank the performers for agreeing to be filmed, for demonstrating some extracts for my (amateur) camera, and for their appearance in my audiovisual documentation. I am especially thankful to my *āśān*, Rāma Cākyār, who introduced me to and accompanied me into the world of Kūṭiyāṭṭam since 1998 and without whose knowledge and patience this paper would never had existed. Finally, I remember with gratitude the late Guru L. S. Rajagopalan, without whom Kerala will never be the same to me again.

woman who is the pretext of the *Rāmāyaṇa* epic and of the *Aścaryacūḍāmaṇi* plot (in the seven acts in which she appears).[15] The princess has special destinies on the temple stage, depending on the different situations in which she appears in. Let us start at the beginning, when she accompanies Rāma.

1.1. »She is always with Rāma«: Reflection and Substitution

According to the common performers' discourse, there is no need to play Sītā because »she is supposed to be always with Rāma« (RAJAGOPALAN 1997: 19). This perception of Sītā's role is typical of the *śiva-śākti* symbiotic relationship that partly supports the orthodox conception of the woman dependent on her husband – »she cannot go on living [without him]«[16]. This conception finds a deep echo in Kūṭiyāṭṭam practice, the woman accompanying her husband being performed by ›her male‹ or, more precisely, by the male actor playing the husband's role.[17]

Here the performer uses the famous mono-acting technique known as »substitution acting« (*pakarnāṭṭam*) by which he takes on several roles. Highly developed in the narrative retrospection context, this technique also enters into the »acting together«, *i.e. kūṭiyāṭṭam*, for replacing the secondary roles (male roles included).[18] This technique clearly remains the ›epic‹ way of acting that the German dramaturge Berthold Brecht sought for his theatre, and notably demonstrates an omnipresent distance between the actor and his role.[19] It involves different types of participation by the performer as actor, storyteller, and character (JOHAN 2010a, [2011]).

15 If Sītā is a pretext for the plot, it is because the epic first occurs at the macrocosmic level: Sītā's abduction (which leads to Rāvaṇa's death) is required because the gods decide to restore the *dharma* on earth.

16 *Vālmīki Rāmāyaṇa* II.26.5 (GOLDMAN, SUTHERLAND GOLDMAN 1996 [Vol. II]: 138).

17 For a discussion on men acting females see also PITKOW in this volume.

18 For example, in the Act of Bali's death (*Abhiṣ.*1), the actors who play the monkey brothers' roles (Sugrīva and Bāli) share the five other roles of the act (including Tārā's role, which also involves the chanting *naṅṅyār*).

19 Brecht wanted and referred to an ›epic theatre‹ (over against a ›dramatic theatre‹), comprised of several ›distancing effects‹. Three important concepts in his aesthetics are omnipresent in Kūṭiyāṭṭam: (1) the *distance from the events of the plot*, where the dramatic events are historicized (as they are in the Kūṭiyāṭṭam retrospections); (2) the *distance between the actor and his role*, where Brecht wants an »actor-demonstrator« who is not totally involved in »the character« (as is the case with the Kūṭiyāṭṭam actor-storyteller); (3) the *distance from the theatre itself*, where Brecht wants to reveal the theatrical and unreal aspect of theatre, for example while rejecting what the naturalistic aesthetic called the »quatrième mur« (the »fourth wall« between the performer and the public) – see below.

See the film extract from the Act of Śūrpaṇakhā [FILM CLIP 1]. We are in the *kūṭiyāṭṭam* dramatic time: the performer, Mārgi Madhu, has become the character Śrī Rāma who has chanted his first verse (*ślōkam*).[20] As a character, Rāma can chant, see, hear, and act.[21] Drawing on precisely these *powers*, Rāma is able to »reflect« (and bring to life) Sītā's presence.[22] For that, »he feels as if Sīta is here« (*sīta uṇṭānnu˘ bhāviccu˘*), »makes her sit on his lap« (*sītaye maṭiyilirutti*) and »embraces her with his left arm« (*iṭattu kaikoṇṭu tāṅṅi*).[23] Sītā appears as subordinate to Rāma, since the Kūṭiyāṭṭam convention dictates that minor characters are always on the left of major ones.[24] The princess, who appeared through Rāma's posture and eyes, must now answer her husband.

The so-called »hear and act« technique (*keṭṭāṭuka*) that is integral to the substitution acting makes it possible to render the text of an absent character. As the name implies, it consists of hearing (*keṭṭu˘*) and then of enacting (*āṭu˘*) the reflected character's lines. Thus, even if the actress is not on the stage, her role theoretically remains present through its text-in-performance. First, Rāma listens, conventionally looking down. Then the actor (and not the character) gives a signal to the drummer, using specific movements of the head. This ›key gesture‹, which reveals the actor's presence, signifies the beginning of the »heard and acted« portion, and is to replace the key gesture par excellence of the actor that usually »stops the drum« (*koṭṭuvilaccu˘*) to create the silence necessary

20 Śrī Rāma's first verse is known by (its first words) »*śailāyāmibhiḥ*«. It was put in suspense on the first day. Peacefully established in the Pañcavaṭī forest with Sītā, Rāma says that there are no demons in this place, which »bears a beauty like that of the gardens with which [he and Sītā] have long been familiar« (JONES 1984: 36), and asks Sītā to »consider« (*paśya*).

21 He can use the four *abhinayas* (*vācika*, *āngika*, *sāttvika*, *āhārya*) whereas in the retrospection (*nirvahaṇam*) the performer does not chant (*i.e.* does not use *vācika*) – only the *naṅṅyār* does. We recognize that the actor reaches the *kūṭiyāṭṭam* dramatic time and transforms himself into the character due to several conventional or key gestures (as *kuṇḍalamiṭṭumuṭiccu*), and especially because the hero starts to chant. The storyteller cannot chant because he does not have any ›human / character‹ ability (such as speaking, seeing, acting, etc.). Whereas the character is »first person«, the storyteller is »third person«, pure narration (on this subject see also *Naṭāṅkuśa* IV.5, ed. PAULOSE 1993: 30).

22 In the *Naṭāṅkuśa* the »reflected« character (*parāmṛśya*) – here Sītā – is opposed to the »imitated« character (*anukārya*) – here Rāma. Sītā is directly reflected (*pratyakśa-parāmṛśya*): seen by Rāma (*Naṭāṅkuśa* IV.9, ed. PAULOSE 1993: 38 and xxvi).

23 Quoted from the acting manual (*āṭṭaprakāram*) in the manuscript version of Rāma Cākyār (Paiṅkuḷam family) [Ms. *Śūrpaṇakhāṅkam āṭṭaprakāram*]: 61. In Malayalam, the female gender is not marked (by *ā* or *ī*) for women's names. I follow this rule when I quote the Malayalam text of the actor's manuals (and only in this case).

24 According to certain ancient prescriptions of Hindu iconography, Rāma has Sītā and Hanumān on his right (KAPUR 1993: 90). The proxemic rules of Kūṭiyāṭṭam appear to follow the current Indian (local) belief, according to which the right side is superior to the left (this is, for example, why people walk around the temple clockwise, showing the part of their body that is »placed on the right«, *pradakṣinam*, to the deity).

for the voice to be heard.[25] The character has a voice, but it is his own, and he cannot chant another character's lines (except when one of his verses directly quotes him / her). Here, as the lines belong to Sīta, a female character, it is the *naṅṅyār* who should chant the line, as prescribed at the beginning of the production manual (*kramadīpika*) of the *Āścaryacūḍāmaṇi*.[26] Nevertheless, the drum still plays after »the signal« and Sītā's lines are not chanted – as if they belonged to a male character (whose lines are never chanted by the *naṅṅyār* in the *kūṭiyāṭṭam* context). In fact, the Prakrit text disappears, and only the gestures explaining its meaning (*arttham*) evoke Sītā's presence. These gestures are based on the wording of the Malayalam acting manual (given below).

Why are Sītā's lines in act II never chanted? »This is the custom«, the artists I questioned replied. To enact the meaning of Sītā's lines, Rāma asks »What did Sīta say?« (*entāṇuˇ sīta paṟaññatuˇ*). At that moment the actor who is behind the character becomes Sītā or »as if he was Sīta« (*sītayāyiṭṭuˇ*).[27] The actor and only he has this power of transformation to become another character. We find a different type of key gesture here that involves a piece of the costume, in particular the skirt (*poynakam*). The actor pulls up a fold of the *poynakam* to symbolize that he becomes a woman. Since a character is usually designated by the performers as »a costume« (*veṣam*), the convention looks clever. With respect to the gesture (of pulling up a fold of the skirt) itself, it takes its inspiration from the way the traditional woman's dress is worn.[28] Likewise, other gestures involving the costume in Kūṭiyāṭṭam are also stylizations of local life habits.[29]

The actor can now enter freely into the substitution proper. He enacts Sītā by keeping the female posture fixed as gentle (with the feet joined together and the

25 It is the actor who stops the drum to let the character or the *naṅṅyār* chant (depending on whether the context is dramatic or narrative). This key gesture reveals the actor who is beside the character or the storyteller (depending on the context). The key movements of the head do not have any particular name.

26 *Strīgranthaṅṅaḷokke pāṭunna naṅṅyār collaṇaṃ iṅṅine vidhi.* –»The naṅṅyār who recites must recite all the lines of the female characters. This is the custom.« (Piṣārōṭi 1988 [1967]: 115; Jones 1984: 98). This convention applies to all female characters whose presence is created or reflected by a (male) antagonist. For Tārā's and Vijayā's lines (*Abhiṣ*.I and III), the sitting *naṅṅyār* chants the Prakrit text. A video extract from the Würzburg collection shows how, during the *Tōraṇayuddhāṅkam* (performance in the Vaṭakkunāthan temple of Tṛśśūr in 1995), the actor-master Ammannūr Kuṭṭan Cākyār interrupts his disciple for not letting the *naṅṅyār* chant.

27 Quoted from the acting manual [Ms. *Śūrpaṇakhāṅkam āṭṭaprakāram*]: 63. Here we find an example of the dramaturgical technique consisting of questioning. Questioning is a literary tool in Indian literature (and in the *Rāmāyaṇa* epic) to invoke stories and depictions; it is a practical way of teaching Sanskrit (well known to the *cākyārs*) in Kerala, and a main dramaturgic resort of Kūṭiyāṭṭam by which the performer distances himself from the events of the plot. For an account of the technique called *anukramam* see Moser 1999–2000: 566–567; Johan 2002: 376–377, 2004: 48–49.

28 This point is also discussed in the *Nātankuṣa* IV.7 (ed. Paulose 1993: 36, 127).

29 See below for an example applied to male characters (note 38) and a variant of the key-gesture (note 72).

hands holding the ornamental scarf – *uttarīyam*), by smiling in the modest (*lajja*) mood, and by adding the amorous look at the corners of the eyes (*kaṭākṣam*) with which Kūṭiyāṭṭam female characters look at their husbands. »Sītā« now »plays the meaning of [her] lines« (*enna vākyattinṯe arttham āṭunnu*) through gestures that correspond to the Malayalam text, word by word:

> *Oh my husband! I also feel great fascination because, after completing our forest life and reaching the kingdom, we will create astonishment among people of the harem by telling them of the miracles which happen in this forest.*[30]

The actor performs this in a slow, highly stylized way. Finally, he asks through gestures: »Is that what has been said?« Then he lets down the fold of his dress, and, sitting in a heroic posture, again becomes Rāma. Sītā's other lines (from the original dramatic text) will not be enacted.[31]

Theatrically fascinating as a perfect example of an epic theatre in which the actor distances himself from his role, this substitution technique seems appropriate for a minor role. That Sītā has no body and not even a voice may be because her words do not have any dramatic consequences. Furthermore, the fact that Sītā is not embodied and that Laḷitā (Śūrpaṇakhā) is may also be influenced by the orthodox Hindu mentality. As Kathleen K.M. Erndl says:

> Sītā and Śūrpaṇakhā exemplify two types of women who appear almost universally in folklore and mythology: Sītā is good, pure, light, auspicious, and subordinate, whereas Śūrpaṇakhā is evil, impure, dark, inauspicious, and insubordinate [...]. Sītā is the chaste good woman; Śūrpaṇakhā the »loose« bad woman. The good woman is one who remains controlled, both mentally and physically, by her husband [...]. [She] should never be independent. (Erndl 1991: 83)

Could forbidding the »good women« (like Sītā or Tārā) to appear »in the flesh« be a matter of respecting and exalting the modest behaviour expected of them? Could allowing the carnal embodiment of Laḷitā (Śūrpaṇakhā) emphasize the independence of this feminine figure and bring to light its dark destiny, which is to succumb to the masculinity she defies [Illustrations 10 and 11]?[32]

30 *allē āryaputran vanapradēśaṅṅaḷil uṇṭākunna aścaryyaṅṅaḷ okkeyuṃ vanavāsaṃ kaḻiññu rājyattiṅṅal cennu˘ antapuravāsikaḷāyirikkunna janaṅṅaḷōṭāyikkoṇṭu˘ paṟaññu˘ avarkku˘ vismayaṃ uṇṭākkanāyikkoṇṭu˘ enikkuṃ kautukaṃ bhāvikunnu˘* ([Ms. *Śūrpaṇakhāṅkam āṭṭaprakāram*]: 4–5). This meaning portion (*arttham*) is in fact a close translation of the Prakrit text. When the lines are chanted (in other situations), the *arttham* that follows clearly takes on a didactic dimension.

31 Thus, the remaining portion of the text belonging to Sītā in the original play will disappear in the *kūṭiyāṭṭam* performance, as is usual in the case of secondary characters.

32 According to Erndl, »[t]he ›bad woman‹ is punished in order to protect the good ›woman‹, or perhaps to serve as an example of what could happen to the ›good woman‹

Let us see now what happens to Sīta after her abduction when she is left alone. New reasons to exclude the actress from the stage are given, and new inventions confer new poetical relief to the role. Sītā finds what she was previously lacking – a voice.

1.2. »She is voice, only«: Vocalization

As Uṣā Naṅṅyār explained to me once, »Sītā is voice only« in the framework of a very particular *kūṭiyāṭṭam* within the very particular Kūttu of the ring (*Aṅgulīyāṅkam, Āśc.* VI). This *kūttu* is usually performed for twelve days in certain temples.[33] It is guided by Hanumān, messenger of Śrī Rāma, and Sītā's role appears through the *naṅṅyār's* voice in a way that also suits the plot's purpose.

In the play, Hanumān, bearing Śrī Rāma's ring, enters the Aśōka grove where Rāvaṇa holds Sītā prisoner. He discovers the princess, hides himself in a tree, listens to her lamentation, speaks to her, reveals himself, and salutes her: a conversation begins. Sītā wants to be sure that Hanumān is not a disguised demon and questions him. When she feels safe, she enquires about Rāma's reaction to her abduction. Hanumān answers, but she wants to know more, and asks repeatedly: »Then?« (»*tado tado*«). Hanumān again and again tells the stories that took place prior to their meeting. Sītā does not seem to have any other role than to enquire, to provide a motivation for telling the stories, this possibly being the reason why she has become a »voice only«.

In the *kūttu*, the text of the play provides the opportunity for a succession of skilfully intricate retrospections (*nirvahaṇam*) that cover almost all of the Kūṭiyāṭṭam *Rāmāyaṇa* repertoire and more (see the section below dedicated to retrospections and the schema of the *Aṅgulīyāṅkam kūttu's* complex structure with its commentary: DIAGRAM 3). The actor-Hanumān enacts the past stories as a storyteller, while the sitting *naṅṅyār* chants the 468 interpolated verses punctuating the extrapolations. Still sitting, she hides her mouth with the little cymbals in a conventional gesture signifying that she is »voice only«.[34] As the voice of the story enacted by the actor, she reminds me of the »muse« that the German poet Goethe dreamt of.[35]

if she decided to go ›bad‹« (1991: 84).

33 This study is based on the acting manual for act VI (PIṢĀRŌṬI 1988 [1967]: 184–404), the *Nampyār Tamiḻ* manuscript (presented below) and on the observation of the performance that Paiṅkuḷam Nārāyaṇan Cākyār directs every year in the Guruvāyūr temple (I witnessed the *kūttu* in 1999 and 2002, and wrote a special paper on it during the International Seminar of Kūṭiyāṭṭam held in Trivandrum on 13–14 January 2006).

34 The convention is also said to prohibit the recitant from spitting on the stage, since spittle is considered impure.

35 Goethe dreamt of »a rhapsode«, who was able to become invisible and to make »the voice of the muses« heard ... (BORIE, ROUGEMONT, SCHERER 1982: 153).

The text of the play itself – the dialogue between Hanumān and Sītā – is quickly performed thanks to a particular method of »combined chanting« (*kūṭicollal*), especially effective when many lines of the play are condensed, usually in the middle of the *kūttu*, and on the last day.[36] According to this method, which is not described in the acting manual, the *cākyār*, the *nampyār* and the *naṅṅyār* intervene [ILLUSTRATION 12].[37] The *cākyār* takes up Hanumān's character, standing in the posture of respect, with the five fingers bent into a fist before his mouth (*pañcapucchamaṭakki*), and the folds of his skirt (*poynakam*) tied.[38] He faces the sitting *naṅṅyār*, who chants the princess' lines in a way similar to [that] during the retrospection. Standing between the *cākyār* and the *naṅṅyār*, the *nampyār* interrupts the dialogue to make comments, thus creating a distancing effect from the *kūttu*, from the theatre itself. No gestures are used, only the combined chanting in a monotone and a quick recitation of the text. This acting technique suits the parts of the act which do not contribute to the progress of the plot but are merely a conversation recalling past events that have already been enacted during the previous retrospections (see DIAGRAM 3).

A better fit between the technique and the situation appears when the characters do not face each other, prior to »the Salutation« (*namaskāraṃ*) of Hanumān to Sītā, a famous moment in the Kūṭiyāṭṭam tradition, ending the first combined chanting [FILM CLIP 2].

From the tree in which he is hidden (the actor sits on the stool), Hanumān (Paiṅkuḷam Nārāyaṇan Cākyār) salutes Sītā:

Salutations to you, my lady!

The *nampyār* (Nārāyaṇan Nampyār) recalls which character speaks and translates each line into old, sanskritized Malayalam:

36 The daily division of the *kūttu* / the *nirvahaṇam* portions is not fixed; the only obligation is to perform all the verses within the twelve days allowed for the whole *kūttu*.

37 The acting manual does not include the two *kūṭicollal* texts, based on act VI (prose lines between VI.5–6 and VI.14–20 – see DIAGRAM 3). It prescribes the first combined chanting only, in those words: *tamiḻukalinnāl kūṭiccolli* – »the combined chanting comes after [two interruptions of the plot known as *Nampyār*] *Tamiḻ*« (PIṢĀRŌṬI 1988 [1967]: 265). At that time the *nampyār* drummer leaves his drum – the *cākyār* and the *naṅṅyār* leave the stage – and stands up near the so-called ›*nampyār* pillar‹ (in fact, at the front of the stage: ILLUSTRATION 13). He summarizes (speaking in a sanskritized Malayalam) the events that the actor previously enacted until he reaches the situation he interrupted. Then, the *cākyār* and the *naṅṅyār* come back onstage and resume their dialogue. Handed down through generations in the *nampyār* families, the *Tamiḻ* contains the text portions covered by the *kūṭicollal* technique.

38 The tied folds, along with the absence of the ornamental scarf (*uttarīyam*), symbolize that the character is always in action, while the fist in front of the mouth recalls the way people used to stand before *nampūtiri* Brahmins in daily life. The same meaningful conventions are used for Lakṣmaṇa's role, who, like Hanumān, is also Śrī Rāma's servant.

Śrī Hanumān said respectfully: »Salutations to you, princess!« So saying, Śrī Hanumān, son of the Wind, who was sitting [at the top of the śiṃśapa tree], presented the ring with his lotus-like-hand.

The *naṅṅyār* (Eṭanāṭu Sarōjini Naṅṅyār) does not move or change her posture when she recites Sītā's lines, in Prakrit:

Reveal yourself; come out from the hollow of the tree.

[Hanumān:] *As my lady commands.* (He comes down from the tree and makes obeisance).

Following the stage directions, the *cākyār* climbs down from the stool; Hanumān prostrates himself at Sītā's feet (*namaskāram*). The *nampyār* comments.[39]

The first combined chanting stops at this point. Because Hanumān and Sītā were speaking without seeing each other, their dialogue was the only way they could communicate with each other, and the fact that it is symbolically conveyed by voice only (without accompanying gestures), seems to suit the situation even more.

Let us look at a final interpretation for Sītā's absence of embodiment in the *kūttu* and a final example of impersonation.

1.3. »She is too beautiful«: Symbolization

Sītā is not always *only* a voice in the Kūttu of the ring. On the final day her presence is symbolically represented by a material object.

Hanumān then gives Śrī Rāma's ring to Sītā as a symbol of the success of his help: a sign of the future reunion of the couple, of Śrī Rāma's victory and of the dharmic cause.[40] At that very moment when Hanumān gives the ring (the *cākyār*'s ring is given to the *naṅṅyār*) – a famous moment known as »the gift of the ring« (*mōtiram koṭukkal*) – the *naṅṅyār* puts on what is called »Sītā's scarf« (*Sītā uttarīyam*), which is red like the blouses of women's characters. Symboli-

39 Text of act VI (according to JONES 1984: 76): »Hanumān: *svāmini tubhyamayam-añjaliḥ*. Sītā: *daṃsehi dāva attaṇo rūpam [...]*«. Nampyār's text (according to [Ms. *Nampyār Tamil*]: 16): »*uṇarttināl śrīhanumān svamini nintiruvaṭikkitallō añjali ennu colli karakamalamātratte pradarśippiccu˘irunnaruḷinan mārutātmajan śrīhanumān*«.

40 In the plot (*itivṛtta*) of the play, the sixth act is an aid (*prakāri*) to Rāma's success (*prāpti*) from Hanumān. The ring symbolizes this help. In the *kūttu*, the emphasis is put on what I call the ring cause (as the name given to the act implies). For example, in Hanumān's entrance (*puṟappāṭu˘*), when the bearer of the ring (*dhārayannaṇguliyaḥ*) pretends to put the jewel in the oil lamp, along with a piece of a cotton ball from his special blouse (*kuppāyam*), which may symbolize his own skin; or again, when the lengthiness caused by the discussion that follows the gift of the ring in the play (prose lines before VI.14) is avoided thanks to the (second) quick combined chanting (NOTE 37).

cally, the *naṅṅyār* becomes Sītā [see ILLUSTRATION 14]. This relation between Sītā's appearance and the gift of the ring may show how Sītā recovers her full identity, thanks to »the power of the ring« (*aṅgulīyakattinṯe māhātmyaṃ*) that connects her with Rāma.[41] This idea of transferring the power of presence through the ring that binds the lovers here confers a temporal and symbolic appearance on the princess [ILLUSTRATION 15].

So, Sītā's form changes according to the situation. Her symbolization (*samkalpam*) also changes. It reaches a high level when the princess faces the demon Rāvaṇa in the Act of the Aśōka grove (*Āśc.* V).

At that time Rāvaṇa (late Guru Ammannūr Mādhava Cākyār: ILLUSTRATION 16), completely lovesick, »enters the garden« where he imprisoned Sītā.[42] According to the artists, Sītā is not to be embodied because »she is too beautiful« – or more precisely, she is too beautiful in Rāvaṇa's mind. The demon slowly approaches a flame.

A branch represents the *śiṃśapā* tree at the foot of which the princess is sitting, a white piece of cloth (»double *muṇṭu*ˇ«) folded on the ground represents Sītā's purity,[43] and finally, a little lighted lamp Sītā herself. Whereas in the *Rāmāyaṇa* Sītā is described as »a flame extinguished«[44], the *cākyārs* depict her as she appears in Rāvaṇa's view: the flames symbolizing Sītā's beauty. We could also imagine the love fire that consumes Rāvaṇa[45] or, again, recall the divine dimension of Sītā-Lakṣmī, connected with the Lord Rāma-Viṣṇu through the fire-vehicle. As A. Kapur says:

> [T]he divine body is not an organ of sense in the same sort of way as is the human body. It is a sign for other meanings that seek to encompass the relation of the divine to the worlds of prayer, devotion, and desire. (KAPUR 1993: 88)

41 The *Rāmāyaṇa* says: »Taking her husband's ring and examining it, Jānakī was as joyous as if she had joined her husband« (*Vālmīki Rāmāyaṇa* V.34.3; GOLDMAN, SUTHERLAND GOLDMAN 1996 [Vol. V]: 207). The ring and woman's invisibility also has wider implications (see, for example, the *Śakuntalā* of Kālidāsa, and how this play is performed in Kūṭiyāṭṭam, under the direction of G. Vēṇu).

42 The »big entrance into the garden« (*valiya udyāna pravēśaṃ*) is the name given to the last night of the three *kūṭiyāṭṭam* nights ending this thirteen- to sixteen-night performance.

43 In the *Rāmāyaṇa*, Sītā puts a straw between Rāvaṇa and herself as a symbolic separation (*Vālmīki Rāmāyaṇa* V.19.2; GOLDMAN, SUTHERLAND GOLDMAN 1996: 169). In Kūṭiyāṭṭam, the white cloth is usually connected with purity, notably in the »Act of the crossing of the ocean« (*Samudrataraṇāṅkam*, *Abhiṣ.* IV), to represent the ritual *darbha* grass that surrounds Rāma who fasts [ILLUSTRATION 17]. In the Act of Bāli's death (*Abhiṣ.* I) it symbolizes Tārā who tries to prevent Bāli from fighting (see NOTE 52).

44 *Vālmīki Rāmāyaṇa* V.17.13 (GOLDMAN, SUTHERLAND GOLDMAN 1996: 165)

45 This love fire is performed during the »Kāma's arrows« (*kāmaśaram*) sequence (see NOTE 48).

All those objects are placed at the front of the stage, specifically »côté jardin«, near the singing *naṅṅyār*.[46] Sītā is thus on Rāvaṇa's right side (he enters from the left, as is the convention) and hierarchically superior to him. The demon sits in front of the white cloth which he must not touch, Sītā's purity separating him irremediably from his beloved. This symbolization is strengthened when combined with a scene of exceptional realism: the »seduction scene« (*cittavilōbhanam*) [FILM CLIP 3].[47]

Rāvaṇa describes Sītā from »head to foot« (*kēśādipādam*), stopping this systematic sequence momentarily when he »reaches the breasts«.[48] He then showers Sītā with concrete gifts. Facing the flames, he moves between the front and back of the stage using conventional steps and jumps (*cōṭu caviṭṭi*) showing the simultaneous desire for and impossibility of touching the beloved. The assistant (here Ammannūr Kuṭṭan Cākyār, nephew of the acting guru) furtively provides the material gifts needed, which Rāvaṇa puts one by one on the white cloth. He gives Sītā a purse and a sari, while Maṇḍōdarī and her maid, played by actresses standing »coté cour« (stage left, as inferior characters), watch the spectacle. He presents a white cloth (*muṇṭu*˘) a necklace, etc. But the princess stays as inflexible, as untouchable as before. Finally, Rāvaṇa continues with the description that he formerly interrupted, starting from the breast that made him so generous. Struck by Kāma's arrows, he swoons. A strong realism returns when he prepares some betel sweets for Sītā: this realistic action, which carries a sexual connotation and is performed in front of the symbol par excellence, clearly reveals that Rāvaṇa's wish will never come true. He may well implore but it will be to no avail:

> *True, the God of Love is taking away my life!*[49]

46 Kūṭiyāṭṭam's own (fictional) ›garden‹ is on the same side of the stage as the French ›garden‹ (*i.e.* the classical stage division: cour / jardin: stage left / right).

47 The name of the scene appears in the *kramadīpika* (PIṢĀRŌṬI 1988 [1967]: 154). The performance was held in the Natanakairali theatre of Iriññālakuṭa as a separate one-night *kūṭiyāṭṭam* piece, but the acting followed the usual temple practice.

48 What I call the systematic sequences are conventional and fixed mimetic portions that are known by particular names and regularly occur in the performances, notably for developing emotions. Into this category fall the depictions of »the five limbs« (*pañcāṅgam*) or »from head to foot« (*kēśādipādam*), that are generally followed by »Kāma's arrows« (*kāmaśaram*), and used to depict the beloved and to express amorous feeling. The present interruption of the *kēśādipādam* is prescribed in the *kramadīpika* and *āṭṭaprakāram* – a fact that shows its importance (PIṢĀRŌṬI 1988 [1964]: 155; ŚŪRANĀṬṬU 1968 [1957]: 109).

49 After he chants his line along with gestures, the actor performs the meaning through gestures, and repeats the line. The master here follows a Kūṭiyāṭṭam rule saying that »the text must always be chanted twice«. The origin of this rule can possibly be traced to the *Nāṭyaśāstra* (on the subject of *sāmānyābhinaya* see BANSAT-BOUDON 2004: 161–163). The *cākyārs* say the rule also comes from a habit according to which, when two characters speak together, the one who listens to the other usually leaves the stage and waits till the

Sītā speaks, thanks to the reciter's voice this time:[50]

No, my husband who is far more beautiful than Kāmadeva.

Listening to those harsh words, Rāvaṇa laughs sourly.[51]

The general absence of an actress playing Sītā on the temple stage prompts a rich panel of acting techniques and inventions each of which gives relief to the dramatic situation: appearing via Rāma's form when she is with her husband, via a voice when she questions Hanumān, via the feminine symbol of the scarf when she is given Rāma's ring, and via a flame when she is seen by Rāvaṇa, the imaginary Sītā of Kūṭiyāṭṭam remains close to the Hindu model of the good wife and the epic (and poetic) conception of her. Because it leads to innovations with respect to representing her symbolically, and because it enhances the skills of an individual performer, the exclusion of the actress on the temple stage can thus be welcomed, theatrically speaking. In contrast, the fact that the actress is required to give a female body to the independent women, such as Laḷitā and Maṇḍōdarī, may represent, respectively, the carnal nature of the demoness' love and the reality of the wife's, as opposed to the symbolic nature of Sītā. In this perspective, temple stage practice thus seems to result from a true reflection on women's roles, and not only from material, social and religious considerations that forbid them from being physically present on the stage.

Consequently, the fact that women's roles (Sītā's role in *Āśc.*II included) are nowadays systematically embodied on the secular stage seems to yield a reduction both of the powerful dramaturgy and the varied theatrical devices to express the feminine provided by traditional Kūṭiyāṭṭam. The role of Tārā provides yet another example that shows how using an actress leads to the loss of interesting conventions.[52]

second chanting to come back on the stage. This practical habit remains even if no second character is to come.

50 The production manual prescribes recitation (»*sītēṭe granthaṃ collippū*«, PIṢĀRŌṬI 1988 [1967]: 154) while the acting manual asks the actor to »hear and act« without specifying that the *naṅṅyār* chants the text (ŚŪRANĀṬṬU 1968 [1957]: 110; PIṢĀRŌṬI 1964: 47). Why does Sītā have a voice? To give more life to the flames? Because her words have a strong impact on Rāvaṇa? Further investigation should be made. One thing is sure: the aesthetic effect is powerful.

51 *Satyaṃ me jīvitam harati kāmaḥ / ṇa hi ṇa hi kāmādapi surūpo āyyaputto / hahaha.* (JONES 1984: 71, 235).

52 According to the production manual, in the Act of Bāli's death, Tārā is represented by a white cloth (which usually symbolizes purity). »The actor, Bāli, feigns the presence of Tāra by holding on with his own hand to the loose end of the white cloth with which the carved wooden stool [on which he is sitting] is covered. Feigning to see Tāra, Bāli looks to that side.« (VENU 1989: 54). To signify that (the reflected) Tāra leaves the stage, he pulls down the cloth that was previously folded up. This convention notably recalls the key gesture by which the actor temporarily embodies the heroines.

However, it is important to mention that this view is quite uncommon. Partisans of a theatrical »classicism« would prefer to see Kūṭiyāṭṭam in conformity with the *Nāṭyaśāstra*, in which a role (and a woman's role) is to be embodied. This view is represented well in the *Naṭāṅkuśa*, that implores the *cākyārs* to put actresses on stage again.[53] But this is no reason to ignore the omnipresent distance between the actor and his role: when the absence of the actress on the stage leads to the substitution solo-acting technique, it clearly reveals the typical ›epic‹ aesthetic of Kūṭiyāṭṭam.

Nevertheless, one must admit that the absence of women on the temple stage poses problems in the second dramaturgical context consisting of the retrospections.

2. *The difficulties in the suppression of the women's retrospections (nirvahaṇam) and the actresses' reactions*

The production manual for *Āścaryacūḍāmaṇi* testifies that Laḷitā and Maṇḍōdarī, embodied in the *kūṭiyāṭṭam* context, each have to develop a particular entry (*puṟappāṭu˘*) followed by a retrospection (*nirvahaṇam*) within the framework of a temple performance. The actress is supposed to find an occasion here for mono acting, as a character and as a storyteller. But in actual practice, these particular feminine parts are never enacted.[54]

The entry and the retrospection present the initial situation of the act and explore its history respectively. Usually, the entry is the expression of a particular character's feelings and thoughts. On the next day it then gives way to the retrospection, which is a further investigation of the character's story. The main part of the retrospection goes on for several nights and is called *ślōkārttham* (the meaning of the verses).[55] The storyteller enacts the past of the character of whom he wears the costume. In addition, he (as an actor using substitution

53 According to the author, all the »imitated characters«, female characters included, have to be represented on the stage in person. He deplores that »the role of the best of the monkeys [Hanumān] enters into the imitation of Sītā by pulling up a fold of his dress« – »*kapivarabhūmikāyām sītānukaraṇopakrame celāccalollambanam kriyate*« (*Naṭāṅkuśa* IV.7, ed. PAULOSE 1993: 36). Of course, the poetic effect communicated by the personification of Sītā by »Rāma« (in fact by the actor behind Rāma) that we explored above is not the same when another actor-storyteller (here »Hanumān«) assumes the role (as it happens during the retrospections inserted into the Kūttu of the ring).

54 One recent exception: in 2007, Mārgi Satī performed Laḷitā's *nirvahaṇam* of the Act of Śūrpaṇakhā in Kiḷḷimaṅgalam Vāsudēvan Nampūtirippāṭu˘'s temple (see DAUGHERTY in this volume).

55 For an account of the *nirvahaṇam* process, see Moser's graph (MOSER 1999–2000: 566). During the *ślōkārttham* nights, the actor visually explains the meaning (*arttham*) of fixed Sanskrit verses (*ślōkam*), taken from the previous acts of the play or from various narrative sources (often the Vālmīki epic, in the *Rāmāyaṇa* performances). On the stage, the seated *naṅṅyār* recites each verse after the actor has performed the meaning of it. In

acting) takes charge of the characters that this protagonist meets. The spectator slowly enters into the past story and penetrates the mind and the heart of its main character.

This dramaturgy, which distances itself from the events of the ›act-play‹ by notably going back to the epic, of course again brings to mind the Brechtian perspective. BRECHT wanted his audience to »learn much more about the character than it was written in the play« (1963 [1949] : 53). This is exactly what the Kūṭiyāṭṭam retrospections do.

For example, in her entry (*puṟappāṭu˘*) in act II, Laḷitā expresses her love for Rāma and explains how she previously met the prince. Then, in the retrospection (and *ślōkartthaṃ*), we learn how her husband died, how she crossed the three worlds to find another, how she fell in love with Rāma, how this love remained unrequited and how she went to Lakṣmaṇa who also rejected her (the retrospection here takes its source from the previous, the first act of the play). Finally, she decides to return to Rāma and we reach the initial situation of act II. When Laḷitā again approaches Rāma, we can imagine that her determination to obtain his love will lead to her final mutilation.

The retrospection takes what I call the ›colour‹ or ›point of view‹ of the principal character it is dealing with, and is followed by another entry and retrospection, giving another point of view, taking another colour – the schemas illustrate this idea (see DIAGRAM 2). In act II, according to the production manual (*kramadīpikā*), the (red, demonically coloured) Laḷitā-retrospection – quite short as it lasts only one night – is followed by the (green, heroic) entry and (longer) retrospection of Rāma himself (starting from the prince's birth until his coming to the forest). Śrī Rāma's *nirvahaṇam* for act II is based on Śrī Rāma's *nirvahaṇam* for act I, the production manual of which prescribes that the retrospection should not deal with the demoness' part.[56] But current practice follows an acting manual (*āṭṭaprakāram*) that totally modifies the performance's structure and that includes the forbidden portions.

In regular temple practice Śrī Rāma enters first, and only he develops a retrospection, whereas Laḷitā enters after Rāma, losing her own narrative part. First, we notice the inversion of the order of the entries. Dramatically, however, if Laḷitā would appear first (as the play and the production manual have it),

contrast to the drama proper where the recited text precedes the actor's visual elaboration here the *ślōka* chanted by the *naṅṅyār* summarises the actor's performance.

56 »*Jārastāvan ennu tutannīṭṭuḷḷa natētte kutiyattavum parṇṇaśālāṅkattil śrīrāmanu vēṇṭa.*« (PIṢĀRŌṬI 1988 [1967]: 128); C.R. Jones' translation explains: »[Śrī Rāma] should not perform the *nirvahaṇam* verse beginning ›*jārastāvadasau*‹ [*i.e.* verse included in Laḷitā's retrospection for act I and which is also the first verse of Laḷitā's retrospection for act II] and the following verses. The nirvahaṇam of Rāma does not include the acting together (by Lakṣmaṇa and Laḷitā) [*i.e.* a part that was performed earlier in act I].« (JONES 1984: 108).

Rāma's words – saying that the Pañcavaṭī forest is empty of demons – would create greater suspense because the spectator would know that his statement does not reflect reality. To make Laḷitā enter after Rāma suppresses the impression of impending danger, while giving more power to the male character. Second, Rāma's retrospection, shorter than the production manual's with its 32 verses, absorbs a major part of Laḷitā's *nirvahaṇam*.[57] This fact – that the actor performs Śūrpaṇakhās' part – violates the ›point of view‹ theory, since, on the one hand, Rāma does not know the demoness' story, and, on the other, his heroic nature (symbolized by the green colour) is opposed to the (red) demon's one. This two-coloured retrospection of Rāma – a unique case in the Kūṭiyāṭṭam *Rāmāyaṇa* plays – thus seems defective, and the suppression of Laḷitā's retrospection neither seems to serve the original dramaturgy of the play nor Kūṭiyāṭṭam dramaturgy. Why then is this done?

It could be because of the loss of the sections concerning women in the acting manuals (*āṭṭaprakāram*). The production manual (*kramadīpikā*) mainly provides information about the structure and the material aspects of the performance. When it deals with the retrospection, it gives only the first and last verses: the artist should refer to the acting manual in order to know the numerous verses in between and their Malayalam meaning. Currently, handwritten paper copies of acting manuals are used, but if they are not available the artist must search in the palmleaf manuscripts (*grantha*) – the *cākyār*'s »treasures« (in the words of Rāma Cākyār) that the ancestors copied and transmitted from one generation to the next within a family [ILLUSTRATIONS 18–20]. If the acting manual is lost, the retrospection is lost and, sometimes, the act itself. However, if the acting manual exists, the portion it deals with has a greater chance of remaining in the repertoire. This connection between the acting manual and acting practice is best seen in the *Rāmāyaṇa* repertory: the five *Rāmāyaṇa* acts that are performed in the temples do have their own ancient separate acting manuals, whereas the other acts that are not performed in the temples do not.

Why were the manuals lost? Surely because of the climate, but perhaps also because the acting portions themselves were no longer practiced – in the handwritten books that are currently used, the performers write down only the pieces they learn and act.

If the acting manual is lost, it becomes necessary to rewrite it in order to revive a play.[58] It seems quite possible that the late Guru Paiṅkuḷam Rāma Cākyār,

57 In fact, the second night of the retrospection is dedicated to Śūrpaṇakhā. It notably includes the verse known as »*jārastāvadasau*« (verse 3 of Śrī Rāma's retrospection) and Lakṣmaṇa's and Laḷitā's meeting (verses 11 to 22 of the retrospection according to the acting manual [Ms. *Śūrpaṇakhāṅkam āṭṭaprakāram*]).

58 For instance, this was done by Ammannūr Mādhava Cākyār and Ammannūr Kuṭṭan Cākyār, who rewrote the acting manual for the »lost« *Rāmāyaṇa* acts. Acts I, III, IV, VII

who reintroduced the women's roles on stage in the 1960s, noticed the dramaturgical inconsistency caused by the exclusion of Laḷitā's retrospection in act II. Early on he produced an acting manual reinstating Laḷitā's portions. Nevertheless, in spite of the fact that it was published twice (RAJAGOPALAN 1997; UṢĀ NAṄṄYĀR 2003), this version is used only by female students who start learning Kūṭiyāṭṭam.[59]

Maṇḍōdarī, who introduces the act in the play, encountered the same treatment as Laḷitā. According to the production manual for act V, she should start a triple-structured performance of which only the two male portions remain today.[60] The performer-scholar Uṣā Naṅṅyār tried to find her missing part in the palmleaf manuscripts. After having failed in this research, she reinvented the acting manual, creating new verses with the help of a Sanskrit scholar (UṢĀ NAṄṄYĀR 2003: 151–158). Yet Uṣā Naṅṅyār's creation has not been included in the temple performance of the Act of the Aśōka grove. It is performed as a kind of Naṅṅyār Kūttu by its author herself. We could think of this type of female mono acting, which is on the increase nowadays, as a beautiful response to the eviction of the female parts on the temple stage.

This trend, which consists of developing women's roles while creating new manuals, started in fact with Sītā and the actress Mārgi Satī. Of course, Sītā has no particular entry or retrospection in any play. Satī, who was well acquainted with the role because she played it in all the seven acts of the *Āścaryacūḍāmaṇi* play on the secular stage,[61] went beyond recreating a retrospection: she offered a forty-one-day *kūttu* to the princess (MĀRGI SATĪ 1999). Her *Śrīrāmacaritam* starts where Sītā's story ends, as dramatized in the *Uttararāmacaritam* play of Bhavabhūti (act III). The banished princess enters full of sadness, and questions the reason for her destiny of suffering. The answer involves enacting the full *Rāmāyaṇa* story.

Through mono acting, the actress not only gets to be the only performer on the stage and to assume all the roles to which she alludes – including the male

of the *Āścaryacūḍāmaṇī* were staged by the Mārgi group in the 1980s. Acts II, IV, V of the *Abhiṣēkanāṭakam* are staged by the Iriññālakuṭa group since the 1990s. In 2007, the troupe even performed the sixth and last act of the play.

59 Laḷitā's entry (including a part of the retrospection) is enacted for the first Kūṭiyāṭṭam stage (*araṅṅeṭṭam*) – Rāma Cākyār taught it to me for my initiation (held in 2001). It is not usually performed in the temple since the *naṅṅyārs* themselves have »the entry of the maid« (*cēṭī puṟappāṭu*) of the *Subhadrādanañjayam* play, which starts the *Śrīkṛṣṇacaritam* Naṅṅyār Kūttu, as the first stage scene.

60 They are the entry and the retrospection of Rāvaṇa, and then of his minister, which follow the queen's own entry and retrospection in the production manual (JONES 1984: 133–137).

61 Since Ammannūr Mādhava Cākyār wrote new manuals, the Mārgi artists have staged all the acts of the play. The »new acts« (*putiyāṅka*) are performed on the secular stage only (Satī, a Brahmin and not a *naṅṅyār*, cannot perform in the *kūttampalam*). The fourth act, Act of Jaṭāyu's death (*Jaṭāyuvadhāṅkam*), the shortest act of the play, is staged by all the Kūṭiyāṭṭam groups.

roles – but, above all, she also gets to develop that which is the masterpiece of Kūṭiyāṭṭam: extensions or *vistara* (that constitute the third dramaturgical context studied in this paper).

3. The power of extensions (vistara) or the exaltation of the feminine presence

When Satī wrote her *kūttu*, she selected the most flowery verses from all the *Rāmāyaṇa* sources she could find,[62] verses that would offer her the fullest opportunity to extend her acting skills in what the performers call extensions, *vistara*.

Extensions are pieces of pure mime that the performers develop as ›painters‹ and that enable them to create any object in the fictional and epic universe.[63] According to Rāma Cākyār they need only ›a hint‹ to emerge. Within the dramatic action – the entry (*puṟappāṭu˘*) or the *kūṭiyāṭṭam* proper – they take their starting point from a particular verse of the play that depict a scene, recall a previous (epical or mythical) event or evoke one of the numerous tropes of Indian literature. The performer then proceeds to enact the details of the scenes to which the selected verse alludes. These extensions can also occur within the retrospection (*nirvahaṇam*), where, depending on their content and their genesis, they can create flashbacks within the flashback (which the retrospection already is – see DIAGRAM 1).[64] In all contexts and cases they produce another type of ›stop in time‹ that benefits the extended time of the depicted scene.

Numerous and famous in the Kūṭiyāṭṭam field, the extensions are a repertoire themselves, each piece taking a particular name.[65] Some of them relive masculine and violent events, such as »the sleeping elephant swallowed by the snake« (*ajāgarakabaḷitam*; see JOHAN 2008), »hunting« (*nayattu˘*), »descent of the man-lion« (*narasiṃhāvatāra*), etc. A few other pieces, of particular interest to us, depict the feminine habits, such as »sports« (*krīḍā*) or »adornment« (*kōppaṇiyal*). These sequences can be used in different contexts and plays. Dramatically, they provide the deeper reasons for the fictional situation and intensify the aesthetic emotions.

Nevertheless, extensions are quite rare on the temple stage, notably because of the problematic lack of training of some performers who take up perform-

62 For example *Vālmīki Rāmāyaṇa*, *Adhyātma Rāmāyaṇa*, *Śrīrāmōdantaṃ*, *Raghuvaṃśa*, *Bhāṣā Rāmāyaṇa Campū*, etc.

63 The late Kūṭiyāṭṭam scholar, K.P.N. Piṣārōṭi (whom I had the chance to interview in 2002), himself compared the Kūṭiyāṭṭam artist enacting extensions to a painter: »When an artist is painting, he uses a colourful palette: the result – his painting – is for the art lover.«

64 A past event that creates a flashback within *kūṭiyāṭṭam* can also appear within the chronology of the retrospection.

65 This name can consist of the first words of the verse that inspired the sequence or an invented Malayalam title.

ance mainly as a ritual duty. Another reason for their omission or shortening might be the limited amount of oil available for the lamp.[66] Sometimes, within the ritualistic framework, the actor enacts the *vistara* very quickly, »as though his hands were burning« (to quote an apt expression by Rāma Cākyār). But in the Kūṭiyāṭṭam *Rāmāyaṇa* plays, we can still find great pieces that well-trained actors enact in detail. They are generally peculiar to one situation, like the concrete »building of the hut« (*parṇāśāla uṇṭakku*) opening the Act of Śūrpaṇakhā (*Āśc.* II), the poetic »Sugrīva's prediction« (*sugrīvapraśnaṃ*) ending Sugrīva's retrospection in the Act of Bāli's death (*Abhiṣ.* I), or the tremendous »death of the demons« (*rakṣōvadham*) closing the Kūttu of the ring (*Āśc.* VI). However, for the women characters in the *Rāmāyaṇa* (Maṇḍōdarī and Laḷitā) the tradition offers no occasion to act out extensions.

I will conclude this paper by looking at how the male actor-painter can make a purely female presence appear in two different extensions.

We will start with Sītā again. In the performance of the Act of the Aśōka grove (*Āśc.* V), the male actor playing Rāvaṇa's retrospection makes the princess omnipresent through reflection.[67] A particular extension, known as »drinking [the nectar of] the form« (*pānādrūpan*),[68] shows how Sītā is truly »too beautiful« in Rāvaṇa's mind. Everything starts when the demon (performed by the actor-storyteller) travelling in his aerial chariot (symbolized by the stool), sees the princess sitting on earth: we witness the love at first sight that Rāvaṇa feels for Sītā when he sees her (and makes her appear to us through his eyes). The problem (and the highlight of the scene) is that Rāvaṇa has twenty eyes and ten heads, each of which experiences one of the famous ten stages of love[69]. Since the ten heads desire Sītā at the same time, they start to fight among themselves until their owner gives each of them a particular part of Sītā's body to contemplate. Each pair of eyes individually and symbolically describes the form of the body part it has been given [FILM CLIP 4]. To enact this scene, the performer – in the

66 G. Vēṇu told me how Guruji (*i.e.* Ammannūr Mādhava Cākyār), frustrated by the lack of time, used to bring his own oil to the temple.

67 When he enters, Rāvaṇa is so lovesick that he confuses the moon with the sun. His retrospection takes five to eight nights: he falls in love with Sītā, who then haunts his spirit and nourishes his fantasies. I counted fourteen depictions of Sītā and ten »Kāma's arrows« sequences in the acting manual, and am tempted to rename this act the Act of love.

68 The extension has three parts, each separated by a verse, the last one (»*pānādrūpa*«, *Āśc.* III.21) giving its name to the sequence (ŚŪRANĀṬṬU 1968 [1957]: 26–28). The Kūttu of the ring includes this extension (PIṢĀRŌṬI 1988 [1967]: 365–367, verses 397–399), but it is never developed for reasons of time.

69 Ten stages of love are evoked in the *Nāṭyaśāstra* (*Nāṭyaśāstra*: XXIV.166–168; UNNI 1998: 667). A famous Kerala oral verse (»*cakṣu prīti*«) also depicts ten (slightly different) stages. Those that are described in Kūṭiyāṭṭam (and which, again, slightly differ from the previous ones) are enumerated in the verse (»*dhammillo*«) of the retrospection for act V (PIṢĀRŌṬI 1988 [1967]: 368). They consist in sighs, desperate, prostate, oscillating, yawning, rambling, speechlessness, meditating, shivering, being full of tears.

film Mārgi Madhu –, uses the daily eye exercises (*kaṇṇusādhakaṃ*), the formal movements becoming, in this context, an abstract choreography, a metaphor by which the eyes dance with ecstasy, and drink the nectar's beauty, recalling the verse from the *Rāmāyaṇa* of Kampaṉ describing Rāvaṇa in this same situation:

Why say his row of eyes were as ecstatic as a swarm of bees
whose humming is music when they settle and drink
from a spring full of flower nectar,
at her beauty as lovely as a peacock in the forest?
No! They were as ecstatic as his heart!
Are twenty eyes enough here for me to look at the body [of Sītā?][70]

Through Rāvaṇa's eyes, the spectator experiences the sight of Sītā and understands why the demon is so lovesick.

A last example, known as »adornment« (*kōppaṇiyal*), shows how a single performer can make three women appear from his own mind and body. Inspired by a verse of the *Subhadrādhanañjayam* play (RAJAGOPALAN 1997: 54–55), this extension also comes at the beginning of the performance of The Battle at the door (*Abhiṣ*. III), to explain how Maṇḍōdarī, who is fond of being adorned, does not pluck one single flower from Rāvaṇa's garden, even to perfect her ornamentation.[71] In the film the vistara is demonstrated by Ammannūr Mādhava Cākyār [FILM CLIP 5].

The scene takes place »one day« (*oru divāsam*). First, it is the storyteller who presents the characters to be performed: he uses a mixed gesture (*miśra mudrā*) – with one hand (in *sūcimukha mudrā*) signifying »one«, and with the other (in *kaṭaka mudrā*) indicating the female gender – thus designating »one maid«. Then only the actor (who has the power to act), enters the substitution. By pulling up a fold of his skirt (*poynakam*) he becomes the maid,[72] who takes her mistress in her hands: the performer takes hold of the imaginary shoulders and slowly draws them closer in front of the oil lamp. We understand that Maṇḍōdari has her back to us, facing the maid (the performer) who looks at

70 *Kampaṉ Rāmāyaṇa* VIII.8.28–29 (HART, HEIFETZ 1988: 222). There are many similarities in the way the Tamil Kampaṉ's *Rāmāyaṇa* and the *Aśōkavanikāṅkam āṭṭaprakāram* of Kūṭiyāṭṭam depict Rāvaṇa's lovesickness. Furthermore, there are close relationships between Śaktibhadra's play and Kampaṉ's text. Further research on this subject could contribute to the histories of South Indian literature and Kūṭiyāṭṭam.

71 The first verse of the act (»*yasyāṃ na priyamaṇṭanāpi*«), pronounced by the gardener Śaṅkukarṇa, leads to the sequence that proves how much the garden (destroyed by Hanumān) is precious to Rāvaṇa's eyes (JOHAN 2004).

72 The key gesture is slightly different from the one we previously observed: the Ammannūr guru takes the back fold, whereas Mārgi Madhu used the front one. According to Ammannūr Rajanīṣ Cākyār, who adopts his grand uncle's habit, »this gesture is more aesthetic and makes it possible to hide the legs«. In any case, it is similarly efficent.

her, arms crossed, as it is the custom in observation scenes.[73] The adornment can start.

The performer mixes the substitution and the reflection techniques together: through the first he portrays the two maids adorning their mistress and, through the second, the maids reflect the queen as seen through their eyes and represented by their gestures. »[Maṇḍōdarī] was thus gradually adorned in a fitting way«.[74] The precision of the stylized gestures (modelled on those used in the real world) and the intensity of the looks (incredibly attentive), confer a realistic tint to the adornment: any spectator who uses his imagination can easily follow the action and see the queen. The skilfulness of the enactment resides in the way the actor never becomes the mistress herself but uses the actions of the two women he momentarily portrays to make the queen appear. Thus, in spite of being alone, or more exactly because he is alone, the performer shows three women present on the stage.

After a slight last touch of kohl on the eyes the adorned woman is ready and the result simply is »beautiful« (as signified by the actor). This beauty increases when its nature changes, when the actor-master himself enters into an improvisation by which he clearly reveals his own presence. Fiction and reality mix. The performer looks at the audience using *rasadṛṣti* (glances full of *rasa*). We see how, as Brecht wanted, »the artist observes himself [turning] time and again to the spectator as though to ask him: ›it is exactly like this, isn't it?‹« (BRECHT 1963 [1949]: 121). As the actor indicates in the film: »What more could we expect?«

Performed by the Kūṭiyāṭṭam guru, this extension not only shows how the feminine ideal can emerge from a male actor in a very powerful way but, above all, how the epic – distancing – aspect of the art itself creates the marvellous *rasa* that is the culmination of the Indian – and the Kūṭiyāṭṭam – dramaturgy.

Conclusion

The absence of actresses on the temple stage is, to some extent, determined by material, economic and social factors. It also ensues from the Hindu conception of woman as subordinate to man. This seems consequential if one takes into account the devotional context of the performances, the performer's status and function, and, above all, the epic, dharmic subject of the fiction that is represented.

From a theatrical standpoint, the absence of actresses from the stage seems justified in the *kūṭiyāṭṭam* context, at least for Sītā's case. Also a part of the epic

73 *i.e.* the acting technique called »to look and see« (*nōkkikāṇuka*), used in the observation scenes (JOHAN 2006).

74 »*Iṅṅine kramēṇa tanmayatvaṃ varutti koṇṭŭ alankarippiccu.*« [Ms. *Tōraṇayuddhāṅkaṃ āṭṭaprakāram*: 2]

aspect of the aesthetic (as I call it, with reference to Brecht) and the mono-acting techniques that developed in the temples, this absence of the woman leads to dramatically powerful substitutes (modes of acting and symbolizations) that are able to convey the depth of the epic conceptions and the subtleties of the relations and situations between characters.

But the dramaturgical anomalies in the retrospections (*nirvahaṇam*) force us to acknowledge that the absence of women does not always result from a theatre aesthetics thought. The masculinization – whether deliberate or not – of Kūṭiyāṭṭam seems to have started quite early (as testified by the loss of acting manuals for the female roles). Quite ironically, this may have motivated the women, who have mastered the mimetic art for a long time (if we refer to the production manuals), to come out as actresses in an exclusively female art, Naṅṅyār Kūttu. It is amazing how, in this mono-acting form that leads male performers to the ornamentation in Kūṭiyāṭṭam, actresses can, conversely, become men and experience onstage things completely opposed to what is expected of them in real life – demons fight, chew tobacco, drink alcohol, etc.

Finally, the current practice of the actresses could be seen as a metaphor of the two faces of today's Kūṭiyāṭṭam. It brings out: (1) the continuity of the temple performances, maintained by a few *cākyārs*, *naṅṅyārs* and *nampyārs* who are still involved in their family duty – and among whom we find first-class artists (who also perform on secular stages); (2) the parallel processes of secularization and internationalization of the art, an inescapable development in today's context.[75] This situation – which itself brings to mind the two faces of Kerala as both a conservative and modern State – impacts the performers personally. For example, Aparṇṇa Naṅṅyār dedicates herself mainly to accompanying her father Ammannūr Kuṭṭan Cākyār in his *aṭiyantara* (performances to be held according to the temples' calendars), as a chanting *naṅṅyār*, despite also being a talented and fully-trained actress. Meanwhile, other artists who do not have the same obligations engage in tours and new productions without being allowed to perform on the temple stage. For example, the renowned actress Kapila Vēṇu [Illustration 21] once confessed to me that it was one of her dreams to act in a *kūttampalam*. To quote a final example, masters like Kalāmaṇḍalam Girija Dēvi or Kalāmaṇḍalam Śailaja have learnt the verses of the Kūttu of the ring without having had opportunity to chant them.

What will be the ways by which the artists will preserve both the ritualistic and artistic aspects of Kūṭiyāṭṭam, and the temple repertoire, in today's changing context? There is no doubt that the creativity of the contemporary actresses and their success on the secular stage are highlights in the development of

75 On the »globalization« process in the Indian performing arts, and particularly Teyyam, see Tarabout (2005).

Kūṭiyāṭṭam. But the temple repertoire, with the dramatic ingenuity I have sought to describe in this paper, with all its details and conventions, constitutes the basis. And the flower needs its roots to continue to grow.[76]

Bibliography

Ammannūr Mādhava Cākyār. 1976. »Kūṭiyāṭṭam kṣetraṅṅaḷil«. *Mārgi Souvenir*: 7–10. [English translation: 1995. »Kūṭiyāṭṭam in temples«. Transl. by S. Gopalakrishnan. *Sangeet Natak Akademi*, 111–114: 33–37].

Cākyār, A. M. N. 1999. *The Last Caste Inquisition (in Kerala). A Victim's Reminiscence*. Revised edition of *The Last Smārtha Vichāram*. Tripunithura: Padma C. Menon.

Bansat-Boudon, L. 1992. *Poétique du théâtre indien: Lectures du Nāṭyaśāstra*. Paris: École Française d'Extrême-Orient (Publications de l'EFEO, 169).

----. 2004. *Pourquoi le théâtre? La réponse indienne*. Paris: Mille et une nuits (Les quarante piliers).

----. (Ed.). 2006. *Théâtre de l'Inde ancienne*. Paris: Gallimard (La Pléiade).

Biardeau M.; M.-C. Porcher (Eds.). 1999. *Le Rāmāyaṇa de Vālmīki*. Paris: Gallimard (La Pléiade).

Borie M.; M. de Rougemont; J. Scherer (Eds.). 1982. *Esthétique théâtrale. Textes de Platon à Brecht*. Paris: Sedes.

Brecht, B. 1963 [1949]. *Écrits sur le théâtre*. Paris: L'Arche.

Brückner, H. 1999–2000. »Manuscripts and Performance Traditions of the so-called ›Trivandrum-Plays‹ ascribed to Bhāsa – A Report on Work in Progress«. *Bulletin d'Études Indiennes* 17–18: 563–584.

Daugherty, D. 1996. »The Nangyār: Female Ritual Specialist of Kerala«. *Asian Theatre Journal* 13, 1: 54–67.

Erndl, K. M. 1991. »The Mutilation of Śūrpaṇakhā«. In: *Many Rāmāyaṇas: The Diversity of a Narrative Tradition in South Asia*. Ed. by P. Richman. Berkeley, Los Angeles, Oxford: University of California Press, 67–88.

Goldman, R. P.; S. J. Sutherland Goldman. 1996. *The Rāmāyaṇa of Vālmīki: An Epic of Ancient India*. 5 Vol. Princeton: Princeton University Press.

Hart, G. L.; H. Heifetz (eds.). 1988. *The Forest Book of the Rāmāyaṇa of Kampaṉ*. Berkeley, Los Angeles, London: University of California Press.

Johan, V. 2002. »Kūttu, kūṭiyāttam: théâtres classiques du Kerala«. *Revue d'Histoire du Théâtre* 216: 365–382.

----. 2004. »Intrigue et représentation dans le théâtre kūṭiyāttam«. In: *Intrigue et représentation dans le théâtre sanskrit et le théâtre gréco-romain*. Ed. by M.-H. Garelli, V. Johan. Toulouse: Presses de l'Université de Toulouse Le Mirail (Les Travaux du CRATA), 39–76.

----. 2006. »Pour un théâtre des yeux: l'exemple indien«. *Coulisses* 33: 259–274.

----. 2008. »Préludes à une ethnoscénographie filmée de performances d'acteurs: l'exemple du kūṭiyāttam«. In: *Iconographie théâtrale et genres dramatiques*. Ed. by G. Declercq, J. de Guardia. Paris: Presses de la Sorbonne Nouvelle, 121–136.

76 This paper benefited from the attentive reading, suggestions and corrections of Heidrun Brückner, Hanne de Bruin and Heike ›Priya‹ Moser, to whom I express my gratitude. I am also very thankful to my friend Suzanne Lapstun for taking the time to read through my ›French-Indian-English‹. Of course, the content and final form of this paper, with its mistakes, engage only my responsibility.

----. 2010a. »L'Acteur indien: du corps enjeu au corps en jeu. Première scène, formation et omniprésence du corps-acteur dans le kūṭiyāttam du Kérala«. In: *Corps en jeu. De l'Antiquité à nos jours*. Ed. by M.-H. Garelli, V. Visa-Ondarçuhu. Presses Universitaires de Rennes (Collection Histoire), 271–285.

----. 2010b. »Stop-in-time Dramaturgy and Frozen Images: Editing Kutiyattam Performances«. In: *Colloque Arrêt sur images: pour une combinaison de la photographie et du film*. Paris, Quai Branly Museum, 9–10th april 2010: *http://www.quaibranly.fr/fr/programmation/manifestations-scientifiques/manifestations-passees/colloques-et-symposium/colloque-arrets-sur-images.html* [oral paper, published as podcast].

----. [2011; in press]. »›Même l'écureuil fait ce qu'il peut‹. Transmettre le savoir dans le théâtre kūṭiyāttam«. *Purusartha* 29 [volume ed. by M.-C. Mahias], Paris: Editions de l'EHESS.

Jones, C. R. (ed.). 1984. *The Wondrous Crest-Jewel in Performance: Text and Translation of the Āścaryacūḍāmaṇi of Śaktibhadra with the Production Manual from the Tradition of Kūṭiyāttam Sanskrit Drama*. Delhi: Oxford University Press.

Kapur, A. 1993. »Deity to Crusader: The Changing Iconography of Ram«. In: *Hindus and Others: The Question of Identity in India Today*. Ed. by G. Pandey. New Delhi [New York]: Viking, 74–107.

Mārgi Satī. 1999. *Śrīrāmacaritam Naṅṅyarammakūttu (avatāraṇaprakāraṃ)*. Kerala: Current Books.

Moser, H. 1999–2000. »Mantrāṅkam: The Third Act of Pratijñāyaugandharāyaṇam in Kūṭiyāṭṭam«. *Bulletin d'Études Indiennes* 17–18: 563–584.

----. 2008. *Naṅṅyār-Kūttu – ein Teilaspekt des Sanskrittheaterkomplexes Kūṭiyāṭṭam. Historische Entwicklung und performative Textumsetzung*. Wiesbaden: Harrassowitz (Drama und Theater in Südasien, 6).

Paniker, N. 1992. *Nangiar Koothu*. Irinjalakuda: Natana Kairali (Documentation of Kūṭiyāṭṭam Series, 2).

Paulose, K. G. (ed.). 1993. *Naṭāṅkuśa. A Critique on Dramaturgy*. Tripunithura: Govt. Sanskrit College (Ravivarma Samskṛta Granthāvali, 26) [Introduction: i–xxix; Sanskrit text: 1–97; Engl. transl.: 99–222].

----. 2006. *Kūṭiyāṭṭam Theatre. The Earliest Living Tradition*. Kottayam: D. C. Books.

Piṣārōṭi K. P. N. (Ed.). 1964. *Aśōkavanikāṅkaṃ kūṭiyāṭṭam sōvanīr*. Tṛśśivapērūr.

----. (ed.). 1988 [1967]. *Āścaryacūḍāmaṇi. Śaktibhadramahākaviyuṭe āścaryacūḍāmaṇi nāṭakavuṃ atinṟe abhinayattinuvēṇṭi raciccittuḷḷa kramadīpika, āṭṭaprakāram, tuṭaṅṅiya āṭṭakrama viśadīkaraṇaṅṅaḷuṃ*. Trichur: Sangeet Natak Akademi.

Rāmavarmma, K. T. 1978. »Paḻaya kala putiya vihāraraṅgaṅṅal«. *Mātṛbhūmi āḻcappatippu*˘ 56, 25 (3.09.1978): 6–13 and 56, 26 (10.09.1978): 43–48 [unpubl. transl. by M. V. Nārayaṇan: »Old Art, New Pastures«; courtesy: Kiḻḻimaṅgalam Vāsudēvan Nampūtirippāṭ].

Rajagopalan, L. S. 1997. *Women's Roles in Kūṭiyāṭṭam*. Chennai: The Kuppuswami Sastri Research Institute.

Richmond, F. 2002. *Kūṭiyāṭṭam. Sanskrit Theatre of India*. Interactive CD-ROM. Ann Arbor: University of Michigan Press.

Subbaraya Iyer, N. 1908. »The Antarallas of Malabar«. *The Indian Antiquary* XXXVII: 334–338.

Śūranāṭṭu, P. N. (ed.). 1968 [1957]. *Aśōkavanikaṅkaṃ āṭṭaprakāram*. Trivandrum: Kerala University (Bhāṣāgranthāvali, 95).

Tarabout, G. 2005. »Malabar Gods, Nation-Building and World Culture: on Perceptions of the Local and the Global«. In: *Globalizing India. Perspectives from Below*. Ed. by J. Assayag and C. J. Fuller. London, New York, Delhi: Anthem South Asian Studies, 185–209.

Unni, N. P. 1998. *Nāṭyaśāstra. Text with Introduction, English Translation and Indices*. 4 Vol. New Delhi: Nag Publishers.
Uṣa Naṅṅyār. 2003. *Abhinētri. Nāṭyavēdattile strīparvvaṃ*. Mumbai: Kēḷi prasiddhīkaraṇaṃ.
Venu, G. 1989. *Production of a play in Kūṭiyāṭṭaṃ (text and translation of the first Act of Abhiṣeka Nāṭaka of Bhāsa with the kramadīpikā (production manual) and the āṭṭaprakāraṃ (acting manual) from the Sanskrit Drama Tradition of India*. Irinjalakuda: Natanakairali (Documentation of Kūṭiyāṭṭam Series, 1).

Manuscripts

[Ms. *Śūrpaṇakhāṅkam āṭṭaprakāram*]. Handwritten manuscript of the acting manual of the Act of Śūrpaṇakhā (*Śūrpaṇakhāṅkam*, *Āśc.* II) [Malayalam], Koypa (Paiṅkuḷam) family, 1973: 1–74. Courtesy: Rāma Cākyār.
[Ms. *Tōraṇayuddhāṅkaṃ āṭṭaprakāram*]. Handwritten manuscript of the acting manual of the Act of the battle at the door (*Tōraṇayuddhāṅkaṃ*, *Abhiṣ.* III) [Malayalam], Ammannūr family, 4 pages. Courtesy: L. S. Rajagopalan.
[Ms. *Nampyār Tamiḻ*]. Handwritten manuscript of the *Nampyār Tamiḻ* in *Aṅgulīyāṅkam* [Malayalam], Eṭanāṭu family, 70 pages. Courtesy: Eṭanāṭu / Kalāmaṇḍalam Nārāyaṇan Nampyār.

Filmography

The film clips are published online: *http://www.indologie.uni-wuerzburg.de/women_performers/contributors/johan/film_clips/*.

Film Clip 1: *Keṭṭāṭuka* of Sītā by Śrī Rāman (Mārgi Madhu). *Śūrpaṇakhāṅkam*, Śiva Kṣētram, Veṅṅānallūr, 11.05.1996. Courtesy / Image: University of Würzburg, Indology Dept. Montage: V. Johan.

Film Clip 2: *Kūṭicōllal* of *Aṅgulīyāṅkam kūttu*, with Paiṅkuḷam Nārāyaṇan Cākyār, Eṭanāṭu / Kalāmaṇḍalam Nārāyaṇan Nampyār and Eṭanāṭu Sarōjini Naṅṅyār. Guruvāyūr Kṛṣṇa Kṣētram, *kūttampalam*, 02.12.2002. Image / Montage: V. Johan.

Film Clip 3: The seduction scene. *Aśōkavanikāṅkam*, Ammannūr Cāccu Cākyār Smaraka Gurukulam / Natanakairali, Iriññālakuṭa, 14.01.1995. Rāvaṇa: Guru Ammannūr Mādhava Cākyār; *tāḷam* and Sītā's voice: Aparṇṇa Naṅṅyār. Courtesy / Image: University of Würzburg, Indology Dept. Montage: V. Johan.

Film Clip 4: A short extract from *Pānādrūpan*. Private demonstration by Mārgi Madhu. *Miḻāvu*: Kalāmaṇḍalam Rajīv, Eṭanāṭu / Kalāmaṇḍalam Nārāyaṇan Nampyār; *iṭaka*: Kalānilayam Uṇṇikṛṣṇan; *tāḷam* and voice: Aparṇṇa Naṅṅyār. Muḻikulam, Jan. 2002. Image / Montage: V. Johan.

Film Clip 5: »Adornment« (*kōppaṇiyal*). Public demonstration by Ammannūr Mādhava Cākyār, Ammannūr Cāccu Cākyār Smaraka Gurukulam / Natanakairali, Iriññālakuṭa, 04.01.2001. Image / Montage: V. Johan.

PHOTOGRAPHIES

The photographies are taken by the author and published online: *http://www.indologie.uni-wuerzburg.de/women_performers/contributors/johan/illustrations/*.

ILLUSTRATION 1: Rāma Cākyār showing the gesture for Sīta (and for all woman characters, except Tārā), Arta, Paris, 19.02.1998.
ILLUSTRATION 2 TO 4: The Vaṭakkunāthan *kuttampalam* in Tṛśśūr. Outside: by night, under the rain, and inside. *Bālivaddhāṅkam*, Ammannūr *aṭiyantara*, 02.11.2009.
ILLUSTRATION 5 AND 6: The *tāḷam* and the voice of the performance: Aparṇṇa Naṅṅyār. *Ibid.*
ILLUSTRATION 7: *Miḻāvu* of the temple. *Ibid.*
ILLUSTRATION 8: *Nampyārs* playing *miḻāvu*. Eṭanāṭu / Kalāmaṇḍalam Nārāyaṇan Nampyār and Eṭanāṭu Rāmacandran Nampyār. *Ibid.*
ILLUSTRATION 9: The performance sound-space. Ammannūr Rajanīṣ Cākyār, Eṭanāṭu / Kalāmaṇḍalam Nārāyaṇan Nampyār, Indira Naṅṅyār.
ILLUSTRATION 10 AND 11: G.Vēṇu as Śūrpaṇakhā covered with »blood« (*niṇam*) after mutilation. *Śūrpaṇakhāṅkam*, Ammannūr Cāccu Cākyār Smaraka Gurukulam / Natanakairali (Iriññālakuṭa), 12.01.2003.
ILLUSTRATION 12: Combined chanting (*kūṭicollal*) of Hanumān (Paiṅkuḷam Nārāyaṇan Cākyār), Sītā (Eṭanāṭu Sarōjini Naṅṅyār) and the *nampyār* (Eṭanāṭu Rāmacandran Nampyār). The *naṅṅyār* conventionally hides her mouth behind the cymbals. *Aṅgulīyāṅkam kūttu*, *kūttampalam* of Guruvayur, 07.12.2002.
ILLUSTRATION 13: *Nampyār Tamiḻ* by Eṭanāṭu Rāmacandran Nampyār. *Ibid.*
ILLUSTRATION 14: Combined chanting (*kūṭicollal*) after »the gift of the ring«. *Ibid.*
ILLUSTRATION 15: Sītā's *uttarīyam*. *Ibid.*
ILLUSTRATION 16: Ammannūr Mādhava Cākyār as Rāvaṇa. *Aśōkavanikāṅkam kūṭiyāṭṭam* (*Āśc.* V), Ammannūr Cāccu Cākyār Smaraka Gurukulam / Natanakairali (Iriññālakuṭa), 11.01.2001.
ILLUSTRATION 17: Śrī Rāman (Sūreṣ Nampyār) undertaking a fast on the white cloth symbolizing the *darbha* grass. *Samudrataraṇāṅkam kūṭiyāṭṭam* (*Abhiṣ.* IV), Ammannūr Cāccu Cākyār Smaraka Gurukulam, Natanakairali theatre (Iriññālakuṭa), 10.01.2006.
ILLUSTRATION 18 AND 19: Kiṭaṅṅūr Kuṭṭapan Cākyār's *grantha* for *Aṅgulīyāṅkam*.
ILLUSTRATION 20: Four generations of stage manuals transmitted in the Paiṅkuḷam family: the *grantha* (Rāma Cākyār's ›treasure‹), and the handwritten books of Guru Paiṅkuḷam Rāma Cākyār, [Kalāmaṇḍalam] Rāma Cākyār and Kuṭṭañceri Saṅgīt Cākyār (disciple of Rāma Cākyār).
ILLUSTRATION 21: Kapila Vēṇu as Śakuntalā. Théâtre du Pommier, Neuchâtel, 29.09.2004.

DIAGRAMS: PERFORMANCES' STRUCTURES

The diagrams are publised online: *http://www.indologie.uni-wuerzburg.de/women_performers/contributors/johan/diagrams/*. See H.Moser's graph (MOSER 1999–2000: 566), whose form serves as the basis for these diagrams.

DIAGRAM 1: The three dramaturgical contexts *kūṭiyāṭṭam* (acting together), *nirvahaṇam* (retrospection) and *vistara* (extension).

DIAGRAM 2: Two different performance structures for the Act of Śūrpaṇakhā (*Śūrpaṇakhāṅkam*, *Āśc.* II):
2.1 according to the production manual (*kramadīpikā*),
2.2 according to the acting manual (*āṭṭaprakāram*) and the temple practice.

DIAGRAM 3: The performance structure and the retrospections in the Kūttu of the ring (*Aṅgulīyāṅkam kūttu*, *Āśc.* VI), according to the *āṭṭaprakāram* (PIṢĀRŌṬI 1988 [1967]: 184–404) and the temple practice.

The performance text starts in Kūṭiyāṭṭam style with Hanumān's entry (*puṟappāṭu*): »here and now« (»*samprati hi*«), Śrī Hanumān enters in Laṅkā. The first verse (»*maināka*ṃ *nāgakanyā*«) leads to Hanumān's retrospection (*nirvahaṇam*), particular to the *kūttu*. Knitted together by 156 verses, it takes four or five days to perform. Inspired by Vālmīki's epic, it mainly deals with Hanumān's story and thus takes »Hanumān's colour«. But its opening by the *Rāmāyaṇa saṃkṣēpam* (Rāmāyaṇa's summary), linked to Śrī Rāma's story, makes Hanumān appear as Śrī Rāma's messenger. Then, we gradually reach the text of the play. Hanumān enters in Laṅkā (»*laṅkāṃ prāpto 'smi*« *Āśc.* VI.1) and discovers the island's beauty. The »*yāni yāni*« verse in suspense (VI.2) launches the last part of the red demon-coloured *nirvahaṇam* used in the Battle at the door (*Tōraṇayuddham, Abhiṣ.* III), which shows how the demon's place consists of the divine Nandana garden (since this retrospection is short, it has no series of questions – *anukramam*).

Then Hanumān enters the garden – ritual dance (*kriya*). He discovers Sītā, listens to her lamentation and sings the praises of her beauty. This part, in prose, is done by a quick combined chanting – *kūṭicollal* – until Hanumān salutes Sītā through *namaskāraṃ*. Here the *Nampyār Tamiḻ* also enters into the performance for the first time.

Then, a verse (»*putaṃ punāsi*«, VI.6) in which Sītā is compared to the Ganges gives rise to the »Origin of the Ganges« and the »Origin of the Ocean« (*gaṅgayuṭe ulppattiyum sagarōlpattiyuṃ nirvahaḥam*), inspired by Vālmīki's epic and the *Brahmānda Purāṇa*.

We then reach the last, important part of the act: Sītā, who has some doubts about Hanumān's identity, asks the messenger how he met Rāma. To answer this question, Hanumān proceeds in three parts, including the previous acts of the play and different retrospections or part of retrospections found in the *Rāmāyaṇa* repertoire. These are all intricate in a complementary manner between two consecutive verses (VI.6–7).
(1) We start from the monkey side – Hanumān's side – with the origins of the monkeys (*vānarōlppatti*) and the first twenty-five verses of Sugrīva's retrospection found in the Act of Bāli's death (*Bālivadham, Abhiṣ.* I). But Sītā still asks: »Then?« (»*tado tado*«). Then Hanumān pronounces what we call the magic words of Kūṭiyāṭṭam: »at that time« (»*tatastasminkāle / samayatiṅṅal*«). Those words give birth here to the giant retrospection (*mahanirvahaṇam*, 187 verses):
(2) Starting, again, with the summary of *Rāmāyaṇa* (*Rāmāyaṇa saṃkṣēpam*), the retrospection first shows Rāma's side through the retrospection for act II of the play (including act I mixed with other sources), and act II itself (Act of Śūrpaṇakhā). It continues with Rāvaṇa's side through parts of the retrospections for act III and for act IV (including the first part of act III, *Āśc.* III.5–15) and finally, the retrospection for act V, including the second part of act III (*Āśc.* III.16–33) and act IV of the play.

Since the parts come in succession in a fluid manner, without returning to the drama except at the final retying point, this constitutes a giant retrospection, which ends when the demon-king Rāvaṇa keeps Sītā prisoner at the foot of the *śiṃśapa* tree, in the Aśōka grove.
(3) But Sītā still asks: »Then?« (»*tado tado*«). We then follow Śrī Rāma's reaction to the abduction through the last part of act III that began earlier (*Āśc.* III.34–42) and through Śrī Rāma's retrospection for *Abhiṣ.* I, linked to the end of Sugrīva *nirvahaṇam* that started the full process: Hanumān meets Rāma from the monkey side. He answers Sītā's question in this way.

Then, Hanumān's words and actions make Śrī Rāma enters into the *kūttu*: Hanumān describes Rāma (VI.7), performs the depiction »from head to foot« (*kēśādipādam*) of Śrī Rāma and ritual dance (*kriya*) again. He enacts Śrī Rāma's despair after Sītā's abduction till the princess asks him to stop (VI.8–13). He then gives the ring to Sītā – second *Nampyār Tamiḻ* and second and last combined chanting, *kūṭicollal*, until the last verse.

This last verse (»*rakṣōvadham*«) yields a special extension (*vistara*) that foretells the story's future: the Battle at the door (*Tōraṇayuddham*, *Abhiṣ.* III). The *nampyār* finally summarizes the whole *kūttu* through the *tamiḻ*.

Contributors

HEIDRUN BRÜCKNER (Würzburg): Heidrun Brückner is professor of Indology and South Asian Studies at the University of Würzburg, Germany. Her areas of research are Sanskrit drama, Hinduism and the history of Indology. She has authored books and articles on regional Hindu traditions and oral literature (*Fürstliche Feste*, Wiesbaden 1995; *On an Auspicious Day at Dawn ...*, Wiesbaden 2009) and edited 12 books including volumes on Performance Studies (with E. Schömbucher and P. Zarrilli: *The Power of Performance*, Delhi 2007), on 19th Century Indology (with Gabriele Zeller: *Otto von Boehtlingk – Briefe zum Petersburger Wörterbuch 1852–1881*, Wiesbaden 2007); on Indian drama and theatre (with K. Steiner: *Indisches Theater – Text, Theorie, Praxis*, Wiesbaden 2010) as well as a memorial volume (with Aditya Malik and Anne Feldhaus: *In the Company of Gods – Essays in Memory of Günther-Dietz Sontheimer*, Delhi 2005). *heidrun.brueckner@mail.uni-wuerzburg.de*

PETER J. CLAUS (Berkeley): Peter J. Claus is Professor Emeritus of Anthropology and Asian Studies at California State University East Bay, Hayward, California. His primary region of study in southern India has been the Tulu-speaking region of coastal Karnataka, but he has also done extensive work on the relationship between communities and performance traditions in the region along the Andhra Pradesh and Karnataka borders in an attempt to reconstruct the ethnohistory of the Golla communities. He has published several books and numerous articles on folklore and oral traditions of South Asia, including *South Asian Folklore, An Encyclopedia* (jointly edited with Margaret Mills and Sarah Diamond, Routledge 2004), *Oral Epics in India* (jointly edited with Stuart Blackburn, Susan Wadley and Joyce Flueckiger, University of California Press 1989) and *Folktales of India* (jointly edited with Brenda E. F. Beck, J. Handoo and P. Goswami, University of Chicago Press 1987). *peterclaus@netscape.net*

DIANE DAUGHERTY (London / Kerala / Pittsburgh): Since her early retirement in 1997, Professor Emeritus Diane Daugherty has lived in South India where she continues her research on Kerala performance. She is the recipient of a Fulbright Collaborative Research Scholarship, a Fulbright Senior Research Fellowship and an American Institute of Indian Studies Senior Research Fellowship in Performing and Creative Arts. She earned the Ph.D. in New York University's Department of Performance Studies; served as President of the Association for

Asian Performance; and as Associate Editor of Asian Theatre Journal. Her work on aspects of Indian performance has appeared in various journals.

didaugh@usa.net

HANNE M. DE BRUIN (Kanchipuram): Hanne M. de Bruin (b. 1959) studied Indian Languages and Cultures at the University of Leiden, the Netherlands. Since 2002 she works full-time as the facilitator and principal fund raiser for the Kattaikkuttu Sangam and Kattaikkuttu Gurukulam (*www.kattaikkuttu.org*) in Tamil Nadu, India. She is also a guest lecturer at the Indological Department, Julius-Maximilians Universität, Würzburg, Germany. Her books include *Kattaikkuttu – The Flexibility of a South Indian Theatre Tradition* (Gonda Indological Series 7, Groningen: Egbert Forsten Publications, 1999) and *Karna Moksham or Karna's Death – A Play by Pukalentippulavar, translation into English of an all-night Kattaikkuttu play* (Pondicherry: IFP, EFEO and IIAS, 1998). She has published articles on rural women performers, including the rural Devadasi tradition in North Tamil Nadu, and the history of the popular theatre in India. Hanne M. de Bruin is married to P. Rajagopal with whom she co-conceptualizes and co-directs new repertory for the Kattaikkuttu Gurukulam.

kattaiku@gmail.com

LEA GRIEBL (Würzburg): Lea Griebl (b. 1982) has studied Special Education For Mentally Handicapped Children, Speech Therapy, Paedagogy and Indology at Julius-Maximilians Universität Würzburg, Germany and graduated in 2010. During her studies, she frequently visited India: she attended Hindi classes in Varanasi (2006), took part in an International Workshop on Fieldwork and Archival Training at MGM College in Udupi / Karnataka (2008) and volunteered in a school for underprivileged children in Dehra Dun (2005, 2006, 2008). In 2008 she was awarded a DAAD-scholarship for doing field research within the scope of her M.A. thesis on women and literacy in India, which she submitted in March 2009. *leagriebl@googlemail.com*

CHRISTINE GUILLEBAUD (Paris): Christine Guillebaud is a social anthropologist and an ethnomusicologist. She is a Research Fellow at the (French Government) National Centre for Scientific Research (CNRS), and belongs to the Research Unit UMR 7186 »Research Centre for Ethnomusicology (CREM-LESC)«, located at the University of Paris Ouest-Nanterre. She is the author of the book *Le chant des serpents. Musiciens itinerants du Kerala / Song of snakes. Itinerant Musicians in Kerala* (CNRS Editions, with one DVD), recently awarded the prize »Coup de cœur Musiques du Monde 2009« by the Music Academy Charles Cros. *cguillebaud@free.fr*

VIRGINIE JOHAN (Paris): Virgine Johan is a scholar of theatre who studied at the Theatre Studies Institute of Paris III, New Sorbonne. She met her master

Rāma Cākyār and discovered Kūṭiyāṭṭam in 1998. She had her stage debut in 2001. Her Master's degree (1998) and M.Phil. dissertations (2000) are respectively dedicated to a study of the performer's codified language and to anthropological research into the Cākyārs. As a fellowship doctorate student, Virginie Johan combined teaching and research assignments in Paris III. She learnt Sanskrit at EPHE. Virgine Johan also developed a method of editing Kūṭiyāṭṭam performances based on frozen images. In 2006, she obtained a doctoral scholarship of the Quai Branly Museum and dedicated herself to the writing of her Ph.D. thesis: *From the person to the persona: an ethnoscenological approach to kutiyattam as epic theatre*. From 2001 until now, she has presented her research at a number of symposia and seminars, at an international and national level. Sixteen of her scientific papers have been published, or are in the process of being published, in academic books and journals. She has disseminated her scientific findings through popular presentations and film projections. She also was the co-author and scientific advisor of a documentary about Rāma Cākyār and Kūṭiyāṭṭam training at the Kēraḷa Kalāmaṇḍalam. *virginie.johan@gmail.com*

HEIKE MOSER (Tübingen): Heike Moser studied Indology and Social Anthropology at Tübingen University, Germany. She completed her Ph.D. at Würzburg University with a work about Kūṭiyāṭṭam (*Naṅṅyār-Kūttu – ein Teilaspekt des Sanskrittheaterkomplexes Kūṭiyāṭṭam*, Harrassowitz 2008). Her dissertation was awarded the *Ernst-Waldschmidt-Preis 2008*. From 1995 to 2001 she studied and performed Kūṭiyāṭṭam and Naṅṅyār-Kūttu with Kalamandalam Girija and Raman Chakyar at Kerala Kalamandalam. She still performs and gives lecture-demonstrations at universities, theatres and schools. Currently she is working as Scientific Coordinator of the Institute of Asian and Oriental Studies at Tübingen University and as Assistant Professor at its Department of Indology. In addition, she is affiliated as Research Fellow to the Cluster of Excellence »Asia and Europe in a Global Context« at Heidelberg University.
heike.moser@uni-tuebingen.de

MARLENE PITKOW (Santa Cruz): Marlene Pitkow received her Master's Degree in Dance from UCLA in 1978 and a Ph.D. in Performance Studies from New York University in 1998. She has published several articles and reviews for *The Drama Review* and *Asian Theatre Journal*. She has lectured on Kathakali at numerous institutions, including serving as part time faculty in the Theatre Arts division at the University of California at Santa Cruz from 1997–2001. She has given lecture-demonstrations on Kathakali in the New York City schools, and on tour with New York's Asian American Dance Theatre. *marsp7@pacbell.net*

VIVEKA RAI (Mangalore and Würzburg): B.A. Viveka Rai (b. 1946) is retired professor of Kannada Literature and Folklore at the University of Mangalore and is presently guest professor at the department of Indology, University of

Würzburg, Germany. He has been Vice-Chancellor of Kannada University Hampi and of Karnataka State Open University Mysore as well as President of the Karnataka Tulu Academy. His major areas of research and publication are classical and modern Kannada literature, modern literary theory, folklore studies with special focus on oral traditions, and Tulu oral literature, especially oral epics. He has been involved in international research collaboration with scholars mainly in Finland and Germany. Major publications include *Tulu Janapada Sahitya (Tulu Folk Literature)* (Bangalore 1985) and *The Siri Epic as performed by Gopala Naika* (co-authored with Lauri Honko, Anneli Honko and Chinnappa Gowda, Helsinki 1998). *bavivekarai@gmail.com*

ELISABETH SCHÖMBUCHER (Würzburg): Elisabeth Schömbucher is Professor of Social Anthropology and teaches at the Universities of Würzburg and Heidelberg. She has conducted extensive fieldwork and published widely on the performative aspects of spirit possession and spirit mediumship in India. Her present research focuses on death and afterlife among the Hindus in the West.
elisabeth.schoembucher@mail.uni-wuerzburg.de

BRIGITTE SCHULZE (Frankfurt): Brigitte Schulze – a sociologist of culture, media, and ›third world‹ participatory pedagogy by profession – is living, researching, learning and teaching since nearly two decades between India and Europe, university and forest, class room and field, between books, films and self made videos and the human body, its diverse other modes of expression like dance, song, or performance. With those who are fragile, sensitive, oppressed and nonetheless energetically resisting the violent and destructive dynamics of capitalist nation states worldwide, she tries to secure, document and enlarge socially, ecologically, spiritually and somatically »healing humane spaces« by means of a self controlled, holistic and peaceful ›good life‹. She is the author of *Humanist and Emotional Beginnings of a Nationalist Indian Cinema in Bombay. With Kracauer in the Footsteps of Phalke* (Berlin: Avinus, 2003).
Brigitte.Schulze@soz.uni-frankfurt.de

SINA SOMMER (Würzburg): Sina Sommer (b. 1985) is a student of Indology and European Ethnology at the Julius-Maximilians University Würzburg, Germany. She studied Hindi and Kannada and attended a Hindi intensive course in Jaipur (2007). In 2008 she participated in an International Workshop on Fieldwork and Archival Training at the MGM College in Udupi / Karnataka, where she came into contact with the Siri cult and Bhuta worship in general. She gave her first public presentation on Bhuta worship at the opening of an exhibition of Bhuta masks at the Rietberg Museum, Zürich / Switzerland. At present (2010) she is preparing to write her Master thesis in Indology. *c-na@hotmail.de*

Index